Hitler's Bounty Hunters

Hitler's Bounty Hunters
The Betrayal of the Jews

Ad van Liempt

**Translated by
S. J. Leinbach**

Oxford • New York

English edition
First published in 2005 by
Berg
Editorial offices:
First Floor, Angel Court, 81 St Clements Street, Oxford OX4 1AW, UK
175 Fifth Avenue, New York, NY 10010, USA

© Ad van Liempt 2005

First published in the Netherlands as "Kopgeld: Nederlandse premiejagers op zoek naar joden, 1943" by Uitgeverij Balans, Amsterdam
© 2002 Ad van Liempt and Uitgeverij Balans

All rights reserved.
No part of this publication may be reproduced in any form
or by any means without the written permission of Berg.

Berg is the imprint of Oxford International Publishers Ltd.

Library of Congress Cataloging-in-Publication Data
Liempt, Ad van.
  [Kopgeld. English]
  Hitler's bounty hunters : the betrayal of the Jews / Ad van Liempt ; translated by Stephen J. Leinbach. — English ed.
    p. cm.
  Includes bibliographical references and index.
  ISBN 1-84520-203-1 (pbk.) — ISBN 1-84520-202-3 (cloth)
  1. World War, 1939-1945 — Collaborationists — Netherlands. 2. World War, 1939-1945 — Netherlands. 3. Holocaust, Jewish (1939-1945) — Netherlands. 4. Netherlands — History — German occupation, 1940-1945. I. Title.
  D802.N4L5413 2005
  940.53'18'09492 — dc22   2005001814

British Library Cataloguing-in-Publication Data
A catalogue record for this book is available from the British Library.

ISBN-13 978 1 84520 202 6 (Cloth)
        978 1 84520 203 3 (Paper)
ISBN-10 1 84520 202 3 (Cloth)
        1 84520 203 1 (Paper)

Typeset by Avocet Typeset, Chilton, Aylesbury, Bucks.
Printed in the United Kingdom by Biddles Ltd, King's Lynn.

www.bergpublishers.com

Contents

Preface		ix
1	An Excursion to Utrecht	1
2	The Deportations	6
3	The Colonne Henneicke	19
4	Betrayal	46
5	The Money	58
6	The Leaders' Style	75
7	The Men from the Card Catalogue	85
8	Herman Bertinga: "Familiar with Stock Control"	93
9	The Men at the Dutch Theater	99
10	Harm Jan van den Heuvel: "An Insignificant Player on the Stage of Life"	108
11	Everyday Arrests	114
12	Eddy Moerberg: "A Gentle Character"	126
13	Chris de Hout and the Hunt for Floortje Citroen	137
14	Tonny Kroon and "the Job He Always Wanted"	145
15	Lawbreakers: Henk van den Heuvel	155
16	What Did the Jew Hunters Know?	166
17	On Trial	173
18	Group Portrait	199
19	The End of the Leaders	214
Notes		220
Bibliography		253
Index		255

Acknowledgments

Publication has been made possible with financial support from the Foundation for the Production and Translation of Dutch Literature.

Prins Bernhard **Cultuurfonds** *geeft cultuur de kans*

The publication was also supported by a grant from the Prins Bernhard Cultuurfonds.

For Charrel Viskoop,
Floortje Citroen,
André Ossendrijver,
Yte and Joke Presser,
Jack Mok,
and all the others, children and adults, who were arrested by
Dutch bounty hunters and murdered in concentration camps

Preface

This is a book about an unfamiliar subject: of the more than 100,000 Jews living in the Netherlands who were murdered in the Second World War, a substantial number were arrested on the basis of an incentive system. There were two distinct groups eligible for a bonus of seven guilders and fifty cents (fl.7.50) – in today's money about US$47.50 – for every Jew brought in: certain members of the Amsterdam police force and some officials working at the *Zentralstelle für jüdische Auswanderung* (Central Bureau for Jewish Emigration). The role of the latter group, the so-called Colonne Henneicke, has never been studied in any depth. Historians who have written about the Holocaust in the Netherlands (Herzberg, De Jong, Presser, Moore) have mentioned it, but their accounts remained superficial.

The fact that it has taken so long for the true nature of the hunt for Jews to be revealed is remarkable to say the least. One obvious explanation for this would be that it is typical of the Dutch character to turn a blind eye to the very blackest pages of our nation's history. But the reason might also be far simpler: this in-depth study of the perpetrators was based largely on information revealed in the course of their trials, and such records remain classified for a long time in the Netherlands. Even serious researchers have always had difficulty obtaining access to them, and this is probably the reason so little is known about this episode.

The dossiers of political delinquents from the Second World War were transferred from the Ministry of Justice to the National Archive (NA) in 2000. For me that was the occasion to apply for permission to study the Colonne Henneicke, a request that was promptly granted. However, my fascination for this chapter in Dutch history began much earlier. In 1989, during preparations for a television program on the German occupation, historian Loe de Jong showed me a receipt that proved that premiums were collected for arrested Jews. That slip of paper has haunted me ever since, and the result was, ultimately, this book.

For many the content will come as shocking, particularly for survivors and victims' relatives: some of them will be learning for the first time how their loved ones were removed from society. I first realized that that knowledge can have a certain value during a very special conversation with Mr Philip Plas, who was in this way able to find another missing piece of the sad puzzle that was his childhood.

The events described in this book will no doubt also make a deep impression on the relatives of the Jew hunters. Because they are innocent of the crimes of their fathers and grandfathers, I have chosen to change the names of virtually all the perpetrators. However, I saw little sense in doing this for the two organizers, Henneicke and Briedé, and two other men. In the other cases I felt that protecting the privacy of relatives was more important than absolute authenticity. The first time a name is mentioned, an asterisk will indicate that the surname has been changed. Occasionally pseudonymous surnames have also been used in other instances, for example for victims, if published details would violate the privacy of those concerned. In the notes all pseudonyms are italicized.[a]

This book would never have been written without the help of many people. First of all, the two eminent researchers Gerard Nijssen and Esmeralda Böhm, who took a lot of work off my hands and turned up a massive amount of additional information in the process. They also functioned as readers, as did Tony van der Meulen and the NIOD (Netherlands Institute for War Documentation) specialist in this area, Johannes Houwink ten Cate. I owe them all a debt of gratitude, particularly Dr Houwink ten Cate, who suggested numerous corrections to the text.

I am very grateful to Professor Sjoerd Faber, Gretha Donker and Professor Peter Romijn for their advice in the complicated field of Special Justice. Bert Jan Flim helped me a great deal with the history of Jewish children who were hidden by the resistance in an effort to save them from deportation, a subject about which Dr Flim has a treasure trove of information.

I am also indebted to all those archivists who lent their knowledge and expertise to this project, in particular Nico van Egmond of the National Archive, who helped me find my way through the labyrinthine Central Archive for Special Justice and for whom no effort was too great. In the final phase Dr Francien van Anrooij did me a number of important favors. I must also mention Sierk Plantinga, the head of the reading room and a constant source of useful advice, and his co-workers. At the Amsterdam Municipal Archive I was aided by Odette Vlessing, Jaap Verseput and Peter Kroesen, and at the NIOD by René Kok and René Kruis.

Finally, and most of all, it is my wife Joke who deserves praise, for her unfailing support and understanding.

Ad van Liempt
Nieuwegein

–1–

An Excursion to Utrecht

It is a summery Tuesday afternoon, June 8, 1943. Around 4:30, a taxi leaves Utrecht Central Station and drives into the River District, via Croeselaan and Rijnlaan. Right turn, Waalstraat, left turn, Schiestraat, another left, Schipbeekstraat. Taxis are a rare sight in this well-kept working class neighborhood, where the houses are small and the families are, on average, rather large. The car stops at number 25, the front doors of which are hidden beneath an elegant arch. Two men get out; they are wearing plain clothes. Before they ring the bell, they take a peek inside.[1]

Actually it is quite unusual for the two of them to be out on a job together. In this hectic period they really cannot afford to be out of the office for more than a moment, the office being a converted secondary school on Adama van Scheltemaplein in South Amsterdam. But today they saw a chance to slip out for a short while. As it happens, they had a great deal to discuss and this was a chance to combine the two things. And besides, the fact that the bosses set a good example by attending to the daily work themselves every now and then always had a stimulating effect on personnel. The two men are "playing captains," Willem Briedé (43) and Wim Henneicke (34), the two central figures in the hunt for Dutch Jews.[2]

Briedé is the higher ranking of the two. He is the head of the *Hausraterfassungsstelle*, the organization responsible for registering and confiscating the furniture from the homes of deported Jews. He has overall responsibility; he manages the staff and also pays the weekly wages personally. That said, it would seem that Henneicke is at least as important. He leads one of the four subdivisions of the *Hausraterfassung*, the investigative division, also known as the Colonne Henneicke. In March his department was given an interesting new task: tracking down Jews in hiding and arresting them. The work is so demanding, and so lucrative (there is a premium for every Jew brought in) that Henneicke can hardly keep pace. Not long before, they agreed that Briedé would lend a hand and send out some of his subordinates to hunt for fugitive Jews. They make use of this excursion to Utrecht to talk shop; in reality Henneicke is showing his boss the ropes. He has been leading his unit of men for about eight months now and has been so successful and gained so much influence that he has begun to eclipse Briedé. The work is piling up, and this comes at the expense of the bookkeeping, which has never been Henneicke's strong suit. Both have agreed that Briedé will take over part of the work, enlisting men from the other "columns" of the *Hausraterfassung*. On their way there they also make some arrangements about coordinating of forces, now that the Colonne is scheduled to move at the end of June. Henneicke and his men are relocating to another building, 244 Noorder Amstellaan (today the Churchilllaan), also in South Amsterdam. But now they had to get to work, on Schipbeekstraat in Utrecht, and pick up two Jewish children.

Briedé and Henneicke both have access to an extensive network of informants, but despite that they are unaware that they have just entered the sphere of activity of a group of Utrecht students who have already found homes for dozens of Jewish children in the River District.[3] Trustworthy families are continually recruiting other trustworthy families who are willing to take in a Jewish child. Schipbeekstraat is presently home to scores of Jewish children in hiding, and neither Briedé nor Henneicke has an inkling of this. At the request of the Utrecht Children's Committee, the home of the Kamperman family at number 25 functions as a sort of temporary refuge. Although the father of the family has already been arrested by the Germans for underground activities, his wife, Dirkje Kamperman-De Vries (50) carries on. She herself has two very young Jewish children staying with her, and through her efforts many more have been placed in other homes in the neighborhood. But now things are starting to unravel. Henneicke and Briedé ring the bell just after 4:30; they have come for Gerrit and Juda Metzelaar, two and almost four, respectively. They know the children's names from their parents. Victor and Bertha Metzelaar had gone into hiding themselves, in Amsterdam, but they had expressly agreed that they would only board the transport with their children. Therefore they told their interrogators at once where Gerrit and Juda could be found. Mrs Kamperman-De Vries is aware of the parents' wishes (which were quite exceptional, incidentally).[4] But there is just one problem: she has placed Gerrit and Juda Metzelaar elsewhere, with a family living on nearby Merwedekade. And she herself has a boy of four and a nine-month-old baby living with her. In the meantime Briedé and Henneicke have come in and sat down. They have seen the twenty-two-year-old daughter of the house, Suze, who happens to have the afternoon off from her job at a bakery, sitting at the organ in the living room. And they have seen the two small children. "So," says Briedé to the boy of four, "you must be Judie Metzelaar." The decidedly Jewish-looking boy denies this: "I'm Flipje Kamperman, and I live at 25 Schipbeekstraat." Briedé does not believe a word of it and presses the matter, but Flipje stands by his answer: "I'm Flipje Kamperman, and I live at 25 Schipbeekstraat." That was what he learned to say when he arrived in Utrecht.

His real name is Flipje Plas, but, as so often happened, his new name has been drilled into him well. In fact he does not even know his real last name. "Come to uncle," says Briedé at a certain point. "How would you like to go for a ride with me?"

Dirkje Kamperman protests the men's actions. She wants them to leave the baby with her. She goes on the offensive and asks Briedé if he has a family of his own. Briedé snarls, "I ask the questions here. You'll do what I say." Mrs Kamperman finds herself in an impossible position. Flipje is going to be taken away, as is the baby, Appie de Leeuwe – that is inevitable. The two "inspectors" (that is how they introduce themselves at any rate) also demand the Metzelaar children, and Mrs Kamperman naturally assumes that she too will be taken and will no longer be able to care for her large family.[5]

What happened next is not exactly unclear. After the war Mrs Kamperman stated that she told Henneicke and Briedé that the two Metzelaar children were visiting another family in the neighborhood. "So go and get them," was the response from the two men. According to her statement, Mrs Kamperman had them brought over. Her daughter Suze, who can still tell the tale, remembers things differently.[6] Her mother had offered to go to Amsterdam herself to look after the baby. "Of course you're coming along," Briedé had barked at her. "You don't think I was going to have that little Jew on my lap, did you? Now if it had been an Aryan child . . ." At that point Suze volunteered to go in her mother's place and take care of the baby. The men agreed. She remembers going to get the two Metzelaar children in a car, from a house on Merwedekade. After that they picked up a fifth child, whom she no longer remembers anything about. And there she sat, with five children in the back of a taxi. In the records kept by Henneicke and Briedé – all arrests were logged in reports, the so-called *Berichte* – one can read that Gerrit and Juda Metzelaar had been living with the Kamperman family. It seems that Mrs Kamperman wanted to abide by the wishes of Gerrit and Juda's parents, without endangering their foster family on Merwedekade and therefore said they lived with her and were visiting another family in the neighborhood.

Suze Kamperman still remembers that the taxi first stopped at the police headquarters, on the Paardenveld. She had to wait in the car, with the children, while Henneicke and Briedé went inside. In accordance with the rules of the time, they notified the local police of the arrest of the Jewish children.

Afterward the car drove on to central station, a few hundred yards away. There Suze had to wait on a bench with the five children on the first platform. She recalls that she momentarily considered fleeing with the baby, but to do so she would have had to leave the other children, including Flipje, her favorite, who had been with them for over six months. "I was scared they might start shooting, so I just stayed put, there on the platform," she says fifty-nine years later. In the interim – it is now nearly six o'clock – the group has been enlarged even further. Henneicke, a specialist in his field, sees a couple with what look to him like Jewish features walking down the main concourse. He accosts the couple and checks their papers. He sees at once that they are false, indicates to Briedé how he was able to tell this and arrests the pair. They are Eliazar Peeper and his wife Estella Peeper-De Swarte. They too will have to come along to Amsterdam. Just before the train departs, the two men see another Jewish-looking couple on the other side of the platform. They exchange glances and look at their watches. "No," says one of the two according to a statement Suze Kamperman made after the war, "we haven't got time."

After the trip to Amsterdam, Suze is given a bit of unexpected good news: she can go home. She is given a ticket for the train to Utrecht and a few sandwiches; after that she hears nothing more from the men. "I couldn't believe my ears," she says, looking back on that day. "I was completely convinced I wouldn't be coming back." From that moment Henneicke and Briedé follow the standard procedure for these sorts of cases. At Amstel Station in Amsterdam they call for a police car. They take their detainees to the Dutch Theater on Plantage Middenlaan, the point of assembly for Jews prior to deportation. Across the street is the nursery, where Jewish children are cared for until they are shipped off to Westerbork, the transit camp in the northeast of the country. By chance, the "transfer receipt" from this operation has survived. A copy can be found in the files of the Ministry of Justice. It is a small sheet of paper with names, addresses and some birth dates on it:[7] the entire Metzelaar family, father Victor, mother Bertha, Grandma Marianne and the children Gerrit and Juda, of Hunzestraat in Amsterdam; Eliazar and Estella Peeper, of Lekstraat, also Amsterdam; Philip Plas, Appie de Leeuwe. There is also a Koosje Troostwijk listed; that must have been the fifth child who was picked up, the one whose name Suze Kamperman could no longer remember. Sure enough, a boy by that name, who was in hiding somewhere in the River District, was arrested during that same period, so this must be right. And then there is another signature on the paper, from the guard at the Dutch Theater, acknowledging a proper transfer. It reads: Preusz.

The dossiers also contain the *Bericht* that was written up following Henneicke and Briedé's excursion, most likely by Briedé, as Henneicke was not much of a writer.[8] On the basis of that *Bericht* (and many hundreds like it have been found) the case could be processed, financially and administratively. "The Jews were taken to the Jewish [i.e. Dutch] Theater," it concludes dryly.

What ultimately happened to the victims of Henneicke and Briedé's well-spent Tuesday afternoon? Eliazar and Estella Peeper were shipped off almost at once and spent a month in Westerbork. Then, on July 13, they were moved to Sobibor, where they were murdered in the gas chamber on July 16.[9] The whole Metzelaar family was sent to Westerbork on June 12, 1943, and a few weeks later, on June 29, to Sobibor. There all five of them were gassed immediately upon arrival on July 2, twenty-four days after Gerrit and Juda had been picked up in the Utrecht River District.

Appie de Leeuwe, the nine-month-old baby, survived the war. His foster mother, Mrs Kamperman-De Vries, was so furious about what had happened that she took a train to Amsterdam the next day, Wednesday June 9, together with a member of the Dutch resistance, also from the River District. They were not able to enter the nursery and went home empty-handed. But a few days later she returned, and this time she succeeded in getting into the nursery. She soon tracked down the baby who had been in her care until a few days earlier and took him away. By way of the garden and the adjacent Reformed Teacher Training College, she managed to smuggle Appie out of the nursery, hidden under her clothes.[10] Appie was then given a new home.

They were unable to find Flipje Plas, the little boy who had maintained that his name was Flipje Kamperman, in the nursery. At that point he had probably already been taken to hospital. The nursing staff, who did their best to save as many children as possible from deportation, had pretended the boy had scarlet fever and was contagious. Under that pretext Flipje was taken to the New Israelite Hospital not long afterward, and from there he was abducted by the resistance. This was almost certainly due to the efforts of Hester van Lennep, one of the leading figures of the so-called Loyalty Group, an organization that hid Jewish children, mainly in the northern province of Friesland.[11] There, at two different safe-houses, Flipje Plas would survive the war. After the liberation he was taken in by an aunt, after spending some time in a children's home. His father and mother were deported in August 1943 and never came back. His sister, who had also gone into hiding, survived the war as well.[12]

After hearing the story of his arrest fifty-nine years after the fact, Plas says he vaguely remembers something about some friendly men who let him ride in their car.[13] In the nursery he had to pretend he was sick; he remembered that too. He later heard that his parents had learned he had been picked up in Utrecht but not that he had been saved: they were deported in the belief that their four-year-old son had gone before them.

And Henneicke and Briedé? Apparently they had more to discuss and Briedé more to learn, because the next day they went out together again, this time to Ammerstol. Up until late September 1943 they continued leading the very successful hunt for the remaining Jews in the Netherlands, and in the process they became the two leading figures in the final chapter of the deportation of the Dutch Jews. We will meet them again.[14]

–2–

The Deportations

When the Germans invaded the Netherlands on May 10, 1940, the over 160,000 people of Jewish descent in the country were more worried than others. Everyone knew about the government-sponsored anti-Semitism that had Germany in its grip. Everyone remembered November 9, 1938, *Kristallnacht*, when the Nazis declared open season on Jews and their property. Thousands of Jews tried to leave the Netherlands before it was too late. Only a few hundred succeeded, most of them via the port of IJmuiden. Five coachloads of Jewish children, most of them refugees from an Amsterdam orphanage, were maneuvered on to a boat just in time, thanks to the efforts of Truus Wijsmuller-Meijer. Just under 200 Dutch Jews committed suicide; the rest anxiously awaited the repercussions of the German invasion.

As early as May 21, 1940 the AVRO, a Dutch broadcasting company, took the precaution of firing all nine of its Jewish employees. But initially the occupying forces took no steps in that direction.[1] After about two months we see the first of an endless series of official measures, designed to isolate and rob the Jews, before ultimately removing them from Dutch society. It started with the Air Raid Defense: by July 15 the corps had to be "purged" of Jews and anti-German Dutchmen.[2] Behind the scenes of the German bureaucracy, officials were busy with the preparations for other, more far-reaching measures. We only know this because by some chance the minutes of the weekly meeting of the senior German officials in the Netherlands, the so-called *Chefsitzung*, survived the war.[3] Every Saturday, Reich Commissioner Arthur Seyss-Inquart would discuss policy with his closest associates. On 24 August 1940 General Commissioner F. Schmidt reported on the progress of the anti-Jewish laws: "Anti-Jewish operations are in preparation and will be expanded in the near future, to the point of aryanization." The last part is a reference to the plan to rob Jews of their businesses. Schmidt told his colleagues that a whole stack of regulations was ready for implementation. The rules mandating the registration of all Jews had already been drawn up, and plans to expel Jews from cultural life were also ready to be put in place. It is clear from the exchange of ideas during the *Chefsitzung* that misleading the public was an essential part of the strategy. These measures would be introduced gradually, and the Jews would be disenfranchised bit by bit.

This can be seen in the way the occupying forces removed the Jews from public service. It all started with a letter sent by the general commissioner for justice and governmental affairs, F. Wimmer, to the secretaries-general of the various ministries, the highest-ranking civil authorities left in the Netherlands: they were not to hire any more Jews, and any Jews who were already there were not to be promoted.[4] The Dutch Press Agency, which was already under German control, reported this news in an eight-line bulletin. The secretaries-general protested, but eventually they bowed under the pressure. In future all applicants would be asked if they were of Jewish descent. The only protest against these policies came from academia: scores of students in Leiden signed a letter of protest. After that, half of all teachers and professors at institutions of higher learning signed the letter. The protest had no effect, and the next German demand soon followed: the secretaries-general had to register all Jewish officials and any Jews employed by publicly subsidized institutions. While their staffs were still gathering this information, the next order had already been issued in October 1940: all Jewish officials were to be discharged.

The secretaries-general hesitated. There were long and in-depth discussions about whether they should resign in protest, but in the end they shrank from the chaos that might ensue. They decided to accede to the demand under protest, particularly after Seyss-Inquart made a kind of concession: the officials would only be "discharged from performing the duties of their office," meaning that for the time being they could continue collecting their pay checks. Meanwhile all officials had to fill in a "Declaration of Aryan Origin"; that is to say, they had to indicate how many Jewish grandparents they had.[5] Anyone who refused to fill in the form was sacked; in the end all but a few complied. Anyone with three or four Jewish grandparents was also suspended from work; there were about 2,500 people in that category.

In the meantime, the first anti-Jewish measures in the commercial sphere had been announced. On October 22 the occupying authority published an ordinance – since May 10, Holland had in fact been ruled by decree – stipulating that all Jewish businesses be registered.[6] This ordinance included a whole series of provisions to ensure that even firms with one Jewish director or companies "under predominantly Jewish influence" would be registered. This ordinance also established the basic guidelines for who was to be considered Jewish. It is a definition which would later be applied quite frequently during the deportations: anyone with three or more Jewish grandparents was a Jew; the same went for anyone with two Jewish grandparents who was also a member of a Jewish congregation, or married to a Jew.

All decrees were coupled with harsh sanctions, and therefore the vast majority complied with the wishes of the occupying forces, including the demand made in Ordinance 6 of January 10, 1941: all Jews, without exception – thus even people who were one-half or one-quarter Jewish – had to be reported to and registered with the Office of Public Records. The *Deutsche Zeitung in den Niederlanden* contained a brief sentence explaining why the registration was necessary: "The Jewish influence on Dutch life as a whole has become intolerable," according to the official state publication.[7]

In his book *Ondergang* (Doom), historian Jacques Presser describes the history of this ordinance: it apparently went through at least ten different versions and had been drafted nearly six months before being issued. The German bureaucracy worked thoroughly, and thoroughness takes time. This ordinance preceded compulsory identification for the entire population, which would be introduced later in 1941. All Jews would have a large "J" stamped on their identify cards, making them instantly recognizable. Meanwhile the Germans were also working on a modern, technologically ingenious identity card in order to thwart would-be forgers. The development of such a document was another important condition for the total isolation of the Jewish segment of the population.

The registration would ultimately be done in writing. Approximately 160,000 registration forms (at the cost of one guilder a piece) were submitted; according to historian Loe de Jong no more than twenty Jews refused to submit one.[8] Every city was given four weeks to carry out this operation. Only Amsterdam, which was home to some 80,000 Jews, was allowed an additional six weeks. The Municipal Bureau of Public Records already had its hands full processing all the forms, but there was more to come. H. Böhmcker, who had been appointed supervisor of the Amsterdam city council by Seyss-Inquart, had a special request.

As it was of crucial importance for his plans that he knew exactly where the Jews were living, Böhmcker sent the city council a letter on 16 January 1941 with seven questions regarding the predominantly Jewish sections of town.[9] How many houses were Jewish and how many were not? How many shops, schools and other institutions were there? And which trolley-car and bus lines ran through these districts?

These data were necessary to make preparations for a ghetto, the plans for which were already under way. Four days later, the city's leading officials under acting city manager J. Franken (the previous city manager, S.J. van Lier, was Jewish and had been suspended from duty in May 1940) met to discuss their response. The head of the Bureau of Public Records, F. Sijdzes, said that with a team of twenty men he would need about six days to complete the task Böhmcker had given them. Sijdzes already had a list of streets that were thought to be more than fifty percent Jewish.

The eagerness with which Sijdzes tackled the assignment is remarkable, particularly when one considers the jobs he had ahead of him: the introduction of identity cards and the registration of Amsterdam's Jews, both of them enormous projects, which would mean a huge amount of work for scores of civil servants.

On Tuesday, January 28, Sijdzes submitted his response. He gave detailed answers to Böhmcker's questions and produced a map showing the 120 streets where there were more Jewish than non-Jewish residents. Together the streets actually form a single extended urban area: from the Nieuwmarkt, past St Antoniebreestraat and Jodenbreestraat, along with their side streets, up to Jonas Daniel Meyerplein. From there it seems the Jews spread out over Amsterdam, to Weesperstraat/Wibautstraat, with its side streets, and in the direction of the Oosterpark Quarter, Transvaal Quarter and Watergraafsmeer, by way of the Plantage. In the end the planned ghetto was never realized. No matter how the officials drew the boundaries, there proved to be too many non-Jewish workers living in the neighborhoods in question to create a ghetto without causing tremendous social upheaval. Later that year, in October, the *Chefsitzung* discussed all the pros and cons of an Amsterdam ghetto modelled on those in a number of Eastern European cities, but in late November Seyss-Inquart personally decided to scrap the project.

In early 1941 tensions were running high in Amsterdam.[10] In addition to the discriminatory measures against the Jews (in the meantime a cinema ban had been issued, and the Aryan declarations had also become mandatory for the professions), there were also regular confrontations between Jewish youths and militant members of the Defense Division (*Weerafdeling*, WA), the uniformed branch of the *Nationaal-Socialistische Beweging* (NSB), the Dutch National Socialist Movement. These clashes began as early as November 1940, when the NSB organized a march through the Jewish section of the city. In December the NSB turned its attention to eating establishments: the WA wanted to force cafés and restaurants to put up signs saying "Jews not welcome." Jewish youths organized themselves into so-called commando groups and battled the WA men. The result was a sort of guerilla war, and there was even a death: the WA man H. Koot died of wounds suffered in a street fight. His funeral was turned into an NSB demonstration on a grand scale. In retaliation for the killing, Böhmcker closed off part of the Jewish quarter. At that point he was still obsessed with the idea of a ghetto, but this latest action caused more trouble than it was worth: there were more non-Jews living in the area than he had thought, and he quietly reopened the neighborhood.

A week later there was another incident between a gang of NSB men and a Jewish commando group, and at that point the highest-ranking German police official in the country, H.A. Rauter, demanded firm action. He proposed the arrest of a large group of Jewish men and was given permission to do so by his superiors: in Germany, Heinrich Himmler, and in the Netherlands, Arthur Seyss-Inquart. On Saturday afternoon, February 22, 1941, and the following Sunday morning, 600 men from the *Ordnungspolizei* staged a major operation in the Jewish section of Amsterdam. They arrested 389 Jewish men between twenty and thirty-five years of age. The detainees were sent, via Schoorl, to German concentration camps like Mauthausen. Virtually none of them would ever return.

In response to this – by Dutch standards – unprecedented display of violence, a strike broke out at the instigation of Willem Kraan and Piet Nak of the Dutch Communist Party. Factory workers, office clerks and civil servants answered the call ("These pogroms are an attack on all working people. Strike, Strike, Strike!!!") and took to the streets. Once Hanns Rauter had gotten over his initial shock (strikes were unheard of in the Third Reich) he sent a battalion of the Waffen SS to Amsterdam to clamp down on the unrest. They were given permission to use live ammunition and did so. Nine people were killed in the streets of Amsterdam and twenty were seriously wounded. The strike spread to neighboring cities, like Hilversum, Zaandam, Haarlem and Utrecht and continued on into the next day. But the violence of the Waffen SS and the threat of even harsher reprisals (mass arrests of Jews) put an end to the demonstrations. The Germans arrested those who were suspected of having a part in organizing the strikes, and at least twenty of these men were executed by firing squad. They replaced the mayors of striking cities with pro-German successors. And they imposed millions of guilders in fines on the city councils, which they held responsible for striking civil servants. The Dutch capital got the message: when the April/May strikes broke out on a much larger scale two years later, Amsterdam did not take part. Even so, the February strike was a significant event as a symbol of action and as a catalyst for resistance; it was in fact the only anti-pogrom strike during the whole of the Second World War.[11]

But the strike had no influence on the expansion of anti-Jewish measures. A short time before, the Jewish Council had been established. The Germans demanded the creation of an organization which they could hold responsible for the implementation of their policy. Two leading members of the Jewish community, the diamond dealer Abraham Asscher and the classics professor David Cohen, volunteered to act as co-chairmen; fifteen other notables joined the Council. This moment marked the start of a process of non-stop blackmail. It was primarily the city commissioner Böhmcker who pressured the Jewish Council to carry out the most degrading measures, with the standing threat that if they refused, he would do it himself, and less mercifully. And thus began a pattern, in which the Jewish Council *itself* had to nip protests in the bud and select the victims of the each successive decree. To this end the Jewish Council was given its own newspaper, the *Joodsch Weekblad*, which would announce the week's bad news to the Jewish community.[12] Jews had to turn in their radios. They were no longer allowed in swimming pools and parks, cafés and restaurants, museums and theaters. Jewish children were forced to attend different schools. Jews had to resign from any clubs of which they were members. By mid-1941 they all had a "J" on their identity cards: all told, there were 160,820 Jews in the Netherlands, including 15,549 half-Jews and 5,719 quarter-Jews. The registration was complete, and the mass plunder could now begin. Underlying all these anti-Jewish measure was a single, steadfast principle: the extermination of the Jews would be financed entirely with Jewish money. It was not to cost the state and its Aryan citizens a penny.

Central to this strategy was the establishment of a *roofbank* (quite literally, a "plunder bank").[13] For this purpose the Germans chose the venerable Jewish bank Lippmann, Rosenthal & Co., which had to undergo a special reorganization. The bank was split into two. The office on Nieuwe Spiegelstraat remained a bank, albeit under German management. But the office at 47–55 Sarphatistraat, which had previously been a branch of the Bank of Amsterdam, became the *roofbank*. In reality it was more like a storage depot/sales office for stolen Jewish property than a regular bank.[14] It became an executive agency under direct supervision of Seyss-Inquart's Reich Commissariat; its primary task was selling off Jewish possessions as they came in. A number of the personnel were regular bank employees. At the urging of the management, approximately twenty-five workers accepted a post at the new branch.

This reorganization was the direct result of the ordinance VO 148/1941 of August 8, 1941, the "ordnance on the handling of Jewish capital." This official resolution has become known as the First LiRo Decree – LiRo being the customary abbreviation of Lippmann, Rosenthal & Co. – and its aim was the seizure of the Jews' private property. The first phase of the operation was characterized by wholesale deception: all Jews were required to report and surrender control over their money and securities to the bank. In return, they were given receipts and proofs of transfer, and they had the option of withdrawing money to cover the basic costs of living. Interest was calculated; costs were declared. In short everybody thought this was a temporary measure, and very few Jews seemed to suspect their money was gone for good.

The German approach worked perfectly. Right after the proclamation of the First LiRo Decree, all hell broke loose. So many packages with securities and money started coming in that the processing soon started to back up.[15]

The Second LiRO Decree dated from May 1942. Once this was issued, the floodgates opened in earnest. Jews were now required to hand in all valuables to the office of Lippmann, Rosenthal & Co. on Sarphatistraat. The valuables had to be enclosed in packages. Once this ordinance went into effect, there was no holding back the tidal wave of goods. Hundreds of thousands of articles were dropped off at LiRo; sometimes the owners' names were not even recorded. LiRo was forced to rent extra facilities to store it all, including two floors of the immense diamond exchange. There was also plenty of junk mixed in with the rest, from Jews who were not willing to part with their possessions without a fight. They sought out other possibilities and, for form's sake, turned in various trinkets.

Part of the LiRo Decree was the provision that money could be kept in a special account, a so-called *Sicherungskonto* (security account), to cover any costs that might arise from the deportations. Needless to say, the language of the regulation was not nearly this explicit, but in this way the entire deportation could be financed with Jewish money. The basic idea behind the LiRo regulations was conceived by H. Fischböck, one of the four general commissioners, who worked directly under Seyss-Inquart. Photos have survived of Fischböck and Böhmcker, the city commissioner, both of them looking quite distinguished, strolling through the Jewish market in Amsterdam and smiling broadly: to all appearances the organizers were quite relaxed on the eve of the big operation.[16]

In the last few months of 1941 the Jews' ability to travel was drastically limited, and changing address became an outright impossibility. And with that the isolation was almost complete. On December 5 the first step in the deportation policy was a fact: all non-Dutch Jews were requested to report to the *Zentralstelle für jüdische Auswanderung*, the Central Bureau for Jewish Emigration, as it was euphemistically known, "for voluntary emigration." Some of them would spend the coming months in Westerbork, a camp measuring 500 by 500 meters, on the heath of the northern province of Drenthe. It was built in 1938 to house German refugees.[17] The Germans would give it a special function, that of transit camp. In the period of the deportations, it assumed the function of a depot: sometimes as many as 15,000 Jews were there at one time. Starting in late 1942, trains would be able to stop at and depart from the camp; at the request of the Germans, Dutch Rail laid a one-track line from the village of Hooghalen to the camp. In ordering the new installation, the official in question added that the new line could be dismantled again after a year: the Nazis apparently thought that was all the time they would need to deport all the Jews.

The operation was simplified by concentrating virtually all Jews from the province of North Holland (and some from South Holland) in Amsterdam: village by village, town by town, the Jews were instructed to leave their homes and find accommodation in the Dutch capital. They were only allowed to take what they could carry. Their houses were sealed. There were exceptions to this rule, but there were also exceptions to the exceptions, but only sometimes: the result of such a system was chaos and panic, and it would seem that this is precisely what the Germans had in mind. At the same time, fear began to take hold of the Jewish community, as men and boys were now being forced to go to special labor camps in the region.[18] And although the Jewish Council swore that these were normal measures aimed at combating unemployment, many sensed the danger: Jewish labor camps offered the possibility for mass arrests of Jewish men.

Meanwhile Seyss-Inquart was creating the organizational structure for the upcoming deportations. Working under Rauter, the police commissioner, was

W. Harster, the commander of the *Sicherheitspolizei*, the Security Police (SP). Within the SP a separate bureau was set up, designated IVB4, just like Eichmann's bureau in Berlin. In the Netherlands Willi Zöpf was appointed to head up IVB4. The *Zentralstelle für jüdische Auswanderung* in Amsterdam was run from The Hague, and the senior official there was Willi Lages, who left Ferdinand Aus der Fünten and his colleague K. Wörlein in charge of day-to-day operations at the *Zentralstelle*. As far as we know, Adolf Eichmann visited the Netherlands only once, to check on the progress of the preparations.[19] That was in April 1942. To meet his quotas, the Netherlands had to ship 15,000 Jews to Poland during the 1942 calendar year. IVB4 in The Hague was confident it would attain this target: it could actually be met simply by deporting Jewish immigrants. Mindful of the possibility of national unrest, Seyss-Inquart had a marked preference for this option. The day after Eichmann's visit, the *Zentralstelle* demanded a list of the names and addresses of all Jews of foreign origin in Amsterdam. The mayor passed the order on to the Municipal Office of Public Records, which ensured its prompt execution.

But early that summer there was a change in plans, when it became known that France, which was supposed to deport 100,000 Jews in 1942, was seriously lagging behind. Holland would have to do more, and the quota for 1942 was raised to 40,000.[20] Thus the names and addresses of Dutch-born Jews had to be made available as well. On June 19, 1942 the *Zentralstelle* demanded this list: another job for the Office of Public Records. At that point Jews could also be recognized by their appearance. Starting on May 2, 1942, they had to wear a yellow star on a visible place on their clothing.[21] For those who refused there was the threat of the infamous concentration camp Mauthausen. Non-Jews who objected to the measure, or who wore a star themselves in protest, were sent to the concentration camp in Amersfoort for several weeks. In the weeks to come, all conceivable restrictive measures that were not already in effect were introduced: bikes had to be turned in; a curfew was imposed, from eight in the evening to six in the morning, with the additional requirement that Jews had to remain in their own homes during that time; there were also severe restrictions on grocery shopping: greengrocer's, butcher's shops and fishmonger's were all off limits.

Exactly one week after the *Zentralstelle* demanded the addresses of the Jewish population of Amsterdam, the leaders of the Jewish Council were summoned to Aus der Fünten's office.[22] His colleague K. Wörlein was also present. Asscher was the only one absent from the Jewish Council delegation; he had taken some time off. It was Friday, June 26, 1942, 10 p.m.: Shabbat, but the Germans consistently chose that day for important meetings. Aus der Fünten informed them that *polizeilicher Arbeitseinsatz* in Germany – that is to say, forced labor under police supervision – was imminent. The Jewish representatives were thunderstruck. David Cohen said that forced labor was a violation of international law. "We'll decide international law," replied Ferdinand Aus der Fünten. Cohen was told that his Jewish Council would play an important role in selecting who was exempt. Simple forms were designed for the transports; the *Zentralstelle* wanted 800 cases processed per day.

The Jewish Council was faced with a diabolical dilemma: refusing meant the Germans would round up the victims themselves in police raids. After much soul-searching and various attempts to secure concessions from the German authorities, the Jewish Council decided to cooperate. The personnel of the Jewish Council were, for the time being, exempt. The organization expanded its staff substantially in order to buy time for as many people as possible. But among those Jews who *did* have to go, the Council did not, understandably, enjoy the best reputation. On July 5 the first summonses started appearing in people's mailboxes. The plan was for 4,000 Jews to report to Amsterdam Central Station on July 15, where they would then be transported to Westerbork. Quite unexpectedly, the Germans picked up 700 Jews in a raid the day before. They were held as hostages. In an special edition the *Joodsch Weekblad* reported that all 700 would be sent to a concentration camp (this meant Mauthausen, and certain death) if the 4,000 designated Jews did not report on time. At that point the Jewish Council was already in such a dependent position that it felt compelled "to point out the seriousness of this warning. Think it over carefully. It means the fate of 700 of your fellow Jews."

The *Zentralstelle* was disappointed by the results: on the day in question 962 Jews turned up at Central Station. They were taken to Hooghalen in two trains because the new line to Camp Westerbork was not yet complete. On that same day the first trainload of Jews departed for Auschwitz. In the days that followed, three more trains would make the trip, carrying a total of 2,030 Jews, slightly less than half of whom had just been brought in from Amsterdam. Starting in mid-July that camp, that patch of ground on the heath of Drenthe, became the gateway to annihilation. Westerbork became a city where life revolved around the weekly departure of the train to the east, "that venomous snake," as Westerbork chronicler Philip Mechanicus called it in his diary, which he kept until he too had to leave the camp.[23]

Another seven transports would leave Amsterdam for Westerbork in July 1942. Nearly 4,000 more Jews were deported from Westerbork to Auschwitz. Holland would meet the targets set by IVB4 in Berlin, where Eichmann called the shots. In the Netherlands the deportations went relatively smoothly because the authorities knew where all the Jews were living and because the Amsterdam police were generally cooperative. Within the Jewish Council, there was an important policy shift when it became clear that staff members were eligible for a dispensation from transport to Westerbork: they were issued a *Sperr*, an exemption.[24] The Jewish Council decided to try its luck and requested 35,000 *Sperren*; the Germans gave them 17,500. In the Jewish community there was a run on the coveted stamps, which gave the bearer the right to remain in Amsterdam. Like so many policies of the Nazi regime, such an exemption was only temporary, provisional, *bis auf weiteres* ("until further notice"). Many years later, Loe de Jong would write about this policy: "Oh, the Germans were crafty! Anyone looking to deport an entire ethnic group shouldn't ever say: everybody out, now! He should say that some can remain, temporarily, and this will spark an internal struggle over who is allowed to stay."[25]

That struggle tended to favor the social elite. Those who were seen as being of great importance to the Jewish community were more likely to be given an exemption than the simple Jewish fruit peddler. And the men who made these decisions were in that position precisely because they themselves were regarded as pillars of the Jewish community. A person with acquaintances within the upper echelons of the Jewish Council had a better chance than someone without connections. Rightly or wrongly, accusations of favoritism and corruption soon began to fly. The debate about the moral conduct of the Jewish Council will never go away, and there is no way of knowing what would have happened if the Jewish Council had flatly refused to cooperate with the deportations.[26]

At this point, the leaders of the *Zentralstelle* decided to refine the system of deportations somewhat. Thus the Dutch Theater on Plantage Middenlaan was turned into a depot for two groups: Jews who had been called up for *Arbeitseinsatz* had to report there, and Jews who had been arrested were held there until they could be taken to Drenthe by train. After that a new police unit, the Amsterdam Police Battalion, was sent into action.[27] The members of the battalion had been trained by the Nazis, so the Germans had no cause to fear sabotage or opposition from them: they could always be deployed in mass round-ups. The ordinary Amsterdam policeman was an unstable factor in such operations. That notwithstanding, within the municipal police force a Bureau of Jewish Affairs was established, consisting mainly of NSB men and led by the fanatical Nazi R. Dahmen von Buchholz. It would be an important factor in the gigantic operation awaiting Amsterdam: the deportation of about ten percent of the population.[28]

At the beginning of August 1942, there was a new raid, which put 1,600 Jews under Aus der Fünten's control. Remarkably, he let 1,000 of them go; the other 600 were soon sent to Auschwitz, via Westerbork. Three days later there was another raid, and the panic among the population mounted rapidly. Because children and the elderly were also being arrested, the story about forced labor soon lost credibility: the official version from the *Zentralstelle* was that the Germans preferred not to break up families. But old people were being dragged out of nursing homes and children out of orphanages, entirely independently of their families. There was only one law that counted: the quota set by Berlin. When a disabled veteran who had lost one of his legs asked to be exempted, his request was denied on the grounds that "a Jew is a Jew, with or without legs."[29]

In late September, Rauter wrote to Berlin to say that by that time he had 7,000 Jewish men in work camps, whom he could easily have deported.[30] And they had 22,000 relatives who could also be shipped off without too much trouble. "*Sehr gut*," the great architect of the Holocaust, Heinrich Himmler, wrote in the margin – these were impressive numbers. On October 2 and 3, 1942 the Germans assembled all available men plus the entire Amsterdam police force for the largest raid up to that point. In the course of a few days, 15,000 Jews were arrested, including those who were already in labor camps. They were taken to Westerbork almost at once, where the crowded conditions in the barracks and the chaos immediately became indescribable.

It was around this time that a new commandant made his appearance: Albert Konrad Gemmeker, a man who differed somewhat from the typical image of a camp commandant.[31] He looked like a gentleman and eschewed violence. He had been a policeman and was previously in charge of the hostage camp Beekvliet in St Michelsgestel. He personally coordinated the drafting of lists of those who were to be sent to the death camps. Every week he led the meeting in which those lists were drawn up, on the advice of his twelve Jewish *Dienstleiter*. Gemmeker settled differences in opinion and made difficult decisions. At the camp he was all-powerful. A single incident is sufficient to illustrate this. As one camp inmate was saying goodbye to another, who was on her way to Auschwitz, the former was heard to say, "Is this what you call the civilized world?" Gemmeker promptly had her deported. "Our previous camp commandant kicked us to Poland," one prisoner remarked. "This one laughs us there."[32]

Gemmeker stimulated recreation in the camp, encouraging sports and games, even cabaret. He organized a social evening at the close of 1942. At the time no one knew the reason: the 40,000th Jew had been deported, and thus Westerbork had met Berlin's demands.

After the war Gemmeker would insist he was unaware of the fate of the deported Jews and for that reason could not be considered guilty of war crimes. Because the prosecution was unable to prove Gemmeker had prior knowledge of the death camps, his punishment was limited to ten years, four of which he did not even have to serve, as he was released early for good behavior.

In early 1943 the deportations carried on apace. In January there was a moral nadir when the Germans under Aus der Fünten and "gentleman" Gemmeker cleared out the Jewish psychiatric centre Apeldoornse Bos in a grisly operation.[33] Perhaps this was done because they had another use in mind for the complex, but, whatever the ultimate reason, they were working under direct orders of Adolf Eichmann in Berlin: he sent a special train with twenty-five cars to transport the nearly 1,000 patients. The scenes that took place there truly beggar description, according to the account in Presser's *Ondergang*. The train did not stop at Westerbork but went straight to Auschwitz, where all the patients were killed upon arrival, without exception.

And thus the operation to make the Netherlands *judenrein* continued according to plan. It entered a new phase with the construction of a new concentration camp in Vught: in the spring of 1943 the Jewish Council was told that there, in the heart of the province of North Brabant, a permanent *Judenlager* was to be built and that it would be a labor camp. All Jews who had not yet been deported and did not live in Amsterdam were notified that they would have to move to Vught, to *Konzentrationslager Herzogenbusch*. But they were walking into a trap. Over the course of that year they were deported to the death camps anyway, either directly or via Westerbork. Yet another instance of Nazi deception, like the lie about the *Arbeitseinsatz*. An entire sham postal service was even set up: tens of thousands of letters, written by the families of deported Jews, were collected by the Jewish Council and then translated, ostensibly for the German censor. After that the letters were sent to the *Zentralstelle*, where they were burned.[34]

There were also letters and postcards from Auschwitz and other camps, all containing reassuring words: the food was good, and there were enough blankets; the work was hard but bearable, and there was a nice shower at the end of the day. All of this was written under duress, by Jews who were about to be gassed. The Jewish Council received thousands of such letters, and by distributing them to families, they helped perpetuate the Great Lie.

In March 1943 these letters and postcards started coming from a new location: Sobibor, a camp near the Polish city of Lublin.[35] Its designation as a "death camp" was certainly well deserved. The survival rate was almost nil: nineteen Dutchmen out of 34,313 deportees. Starting in March 1943, nineteen out of every twenty transports departing from Westerbork went to Sobibor, bypassing Auschwitz, because at the time the murder of the Greek Jews was deemed a higher priority. Eichmann kept the tempo of deportations from the Netherlands high; thanks to the well-functioning municipal administration, the whole process went relatively smoothly there, more smoothly, at any rate, than in Belgium and France.

Not only the deportation of the Jews themselves was going according to plan. By this time the seizure of Jewish possessions was also well under way. A complex structure in which all sorts of organizations competed with and undermined one another nevertheless led to the desired result: the houses left behind by the deported Jews were now vacant, and the contents were soon taken elsewhere, mainly to German cities, where the need for household effects was on the rise with the increase in Allied bombardments. The fact that much of the property was stolen on the way was regrettable of course, but that was to be expected if some 29,000 homes had to be cleaned out in a little over a year's time. It remains a stunning logistical achievement all the same.

In the spring of 1943, there was another point of concern: catching the remaining Jews. The ones with a stamp in their identity cards would not be a problem. Ultimately the Germans would revoke those stamps (they were, after all, only temporarily valid, *bis auf weiteres*). But more worrisome for the Nazi leaders of the Netherlands was the discovery that quite a few Jews had slipped through the net. According to the Germans' figures, tens of thousands of Jews, likely around 25,000, were unaccounted for; they must have gone into hiding somewhere.[36] The philosophy of the *Endlösung der Judenfrage* dictated that all Jews, without exception, had to be exterminated: Himmler would say as much himself to the Nazi top brass at a meeting in the Polish city of Poznan, on October 5, 1943.[37] To convince his colleagues in the leadership of the Third Reich that genocide was the right policy, he said, "Perhaps you will have realized that we were faced with the question, 'What should be done with the women and children?' I have decided that our answer to this question must be just as unequivocal, as it is my opinion that it is not right to eliminate just the men – and that means, gentlemen, murder or orders to that effect – and let the children grow up so that they can later take revenge on our children and grandchildren. We have made the difficult decision to wipe this nation off the face of the earth."

The words of Heinrich Himmler in October 1943. And in that same spirit, a number of key figures behind the murder of the Dutch Jews met some six months earlier, probably in the office of Wilhelm Harster, *Befehlshaber der Sicherheitspolizei*, in The Hague.[38] Also present were Willi Zöpf, the leader of IVB4 in The Hague, and Willi Lages, the head of the *Zentralstelle* in Amsterdam, and perhaps also a few lesser gods. It was there, Lages later confirmed under interrogation, that the decision was made to stimulate the search for the missing Jews with premiums. The amount was set by Harster at fl.7.50 per Jew, to start with. That sum could be doubled if the person in question was a "penal case" – a Jew who had violated one of the ordinances.

The possibility of earning such bonuses was offered to policemen at the Bureau of Jewish Affairs, but also to the civil servants working for the various subdivisions of the *Zentralstelle*. In addition, there was also a sizable budget for informants. And thus in its final phases the hunt for Jews in the Netherlands acquired a new dimension: for a few dozen highly motivated men, it became a money-making enterprise.

—3—

The Colonne Henneicke

The *roofbank* on Sarphatistraat, Lippmann, Rosenthal & Co., played a major role in the despoliation of the Dutch Jews, but there were other official bodies active in that area as well. These included the organization that "inherited" the contents of the deported Jews' vacant homes: the *Einsatzstab Reichsleiter Rosenberg* (ERR), the Special Operations Staff of *Reichsleiter* Rosenberg, named after Alfred Rosenberg, Hitler's representative in the occupied territories of Eastern Europe.[1] He submitted a claim to the Führer for the possessions of Western European Jews in order to meet the enormous demand for goods in the East. The Third Reich had to install a government there, house officials and furnish offices, and to that end Rosenberg established an organization to cart away Jewish goods in France, Belgium and the Netherlands. Hitler's protection was indispensable for this undertaking. In France and Belgium his organization was called the *Dienststelle Westen* (Administrative Office for the West), while in the Netherlands it was the *Einsatzstab Reichsleiter Rosenberg, Hauptarbeitsgruppe Niederlände* (Main Task Force for the Netherlands). Quite a mouthful for a group that actually accomplished very little: in the end the logistical problems were too much for Rosenberg's men. If there were hardly any trains to ship *people* to the East, where were they going to get the railroad capacity to transport furniture?

Moreover, there were powerful competitors: the *Gauleiter* (governors) in the largest cities in the Ruhr Valley also reported to Hitler. Beginning in 1942, they increasingly had to cope with the consequences of large-scale Allied bombardments and wanted to use the excess furniture from the Western countries in order to refurnish houses and offices. Hitler agreed to this proposal too, which was the usual state of affairs within the Nazi leadership. Contradictory instructions from Hitler promoted competition among officials and institutions, thus ensuring their dependence on the Führer.[2] This internal German row assumed major proportions in the Netherlands even before the deportations had well and truly begun. Ultimately, on June 1, 1942, Reich Commissioner Arthur Seyss-Inquart decided, by way of a compromise, that the furniture that would soon become available belonged to Rosenberg in theory, but only on the condition that a reasonable proportion of it be shipped to the cities of western Germany on Rhine barges.

In practice, virtually none of it would end up in Eastern Europe. It is Loe de Jong's conclusion that there was no transportation available, and Rosenberg's organization proved to be far from effective. At least that was the case for the occupied territories in Eastern Europe. In the Netherlands, and particularly in Amsterdam, the process was quite successful. Historian Gerard Aalders speaks of it as a well-oiled "looting machine," which finished the job in a year and two months; during that period the contents of 29,000 houses were hauled away.[3]

To realize this massive undertaking, a number of organizations were linked together. In the Netherlands the chain ended in Amsterdam harbor, where barges were loaded with furniture. In the autumn of 1943 no fewer than 666 canal boats and 100 train cars traveled to the Ruhr Valley, filled with Jewish property – though a small fraction of it was left in the Netherlands, in order to spruce up the *Wehrmachtheime*.[a] Rosenberg's *Einsatzstab* took care of the transportation. In the disputes that arose over areas of responsibility, this organization almost always came out on top. At the slightest provocation the head of the *Einsatzstab* in the Netherlands, A. Schmidt-Stähler, would produce the document showing that all household furnishings were reserved for the disciples of Alfred Rosenberg. They had a signed decree from the Führer on the subject, and this shortened discussions considerably.

Transporting the goods to the harbor was the work of a moving company that would win eternal infamy for its role during the occupation: the firm of A. Puls cleared out vacant Jewish homes and brought the contents to the harbor. During that time a new verb, *pulsen*, came into vogue; the word was more or less synonymous with *roven* ("to rob").

But before the Puls moving vans pulled up to the front door, a number of things had already happened. This part of the procedure was the responsibility of the *Hausraterfassungsstelle* (Office for the Registration of Household Effects). Established in the spring of 1942, this agency was in charge of taking stock of Jewish goods.[4] Although the organization was staffed almost entirely by Dutchmen, the underlying idea was decidedly German, that is to say, decidedly precise. All property belonging to deported Jews – every table, every desk lamp, every teacup, every letter opener – was recorded in lists. For this purpose the *Hausraterfassungsstelle* had a small army of inventory clerks, who compiled lists of the contents of every house left vacant by Jewish families sent to the camps. Copies were made of all the lists, and these were sent to the relevant bodies: one copy to the *Zentralstelle*, one to the *Einsatzstab Rosenberg* and one to the *roofbank* Lippmann, Rosenthal & Co.[5]

The *Hausraterfassungsstelle* was initially a kind of administrative centre, which was responsible for making sure the operation proceeded in an orderly fashion. Even before the deportations began in earnest, a comprehensive inventory system had been set up. There was a central card catalogue, in which each object was individually registered. Every Jew received one or more cards, sorted on the basis of *Hausraterfassungsnummer*, or HR number. There were separate departments (and warehouses) for carpets; paintings; antiques; furniture and bronze; gold, silver and jewels; and bric-a-brac. The warehouse records are lost to history, but the card catalogue survives, full of thousands of index cards on which the goods were recorded.[6]

Such a rigid system demanded a rigid hierarchy. The *Hausraterfassung* had four subdivisions, known as "Colonnes," which were named after their leaders: the Colonne Docter, the Colonne Ragut, the Colonne Stork and the Colonne Harmans. The last of these was not without importance: it was the investigative division, which had the task of tracking down missing (stolen or misappropriated) Jewish goods. After the Second LiRo Decree in the spring of 1942, many Jews gave some of their valuables to acquaintances (or sometimes even strangers) for safekeeping, to prevent them from being confiscated. The investigative division of the *Hausraterfassung* was supposed to recover these items and turn the guilty parties over to the police. It was not trained detectives who did this work; the *Hausraterfassung* got its people wherever it could, mainly from the files of the unemployed at the municipal job centre. As the deportation of Jews and the accompanying administrative machinery required more and more manpower, the prerequisites for new workers were soon relaxed. Membership of the NSB was a plus in this sort of work: virtually all new employees of the *Hausraterfassung* were in the NSB.[7]

In the hectic circumstances of the time, control over the entire process was distinctly lax, and thus it is hardly surprising that in the whole chain, from stocktaking up to and including the loading of the boats, quite a few things disappeared. However rigorous the design of the administrative system might have been, it was not immune to theft and fraud. It happened everywhere: when the Jews were taken from their homes, when the furnishings were catalogued, when the goods were hoisted into the Puls vans, and even when the canal boats were loaded. In many cases the freight carried by the Rhine barges had already been divested of anything of value. "It became a total shambles," writes Loe de Jong.[8] The investigative division of the *Hausraterfassung*, the Colonne Harmans, was given a new job in the summer of 1942. When necessary, the Colonne was to conduct internal investigations into allegations of fraud and theft among colleagues. But this did not seem to help either. The top man at the *Zentralstelle*, Lages, decided to look into the matter. He was the stereotypical Prussian police chief, the consummate professional, and he abhorred these sorts of criminal shenanigans. From time to time he would harangue his subordinates in the hope of putting the fear of God into them. One of the Colonne's members would later recall one of these tirades. "Following a theft Lages called upon all of us to obey the rules and conduct ourselves in a professional and courteous manner. He promised us that there would be severe penalties for anyone who broke the law. He threatened us, 'If you so much as take the dust from underneath the Jews' fingernails, you'll be arrested.'"[9]

The End of Harmans

What happened at the *Hausraterfassung* in early October 1942 must have made Lages' blood boil. The incident was the subject of a painstaking investigation by the Dutch police, even while the war was still going on. The report on the investigation is in the police file of a former member of the Colonne Harmans. It is indicative of the way this civilian investigation division operated.[10]

On September 30 at 11:30 in the morning, a nervous man appeared at the office of prosecutor H.A. Wassenberg. He was accompanied by his wife and introduced himself as Simon van der Maas, contractor and realtor, of Koninginneweg in Amsterdam. It took some time before Van der Maas dared to tell his story. The prosecutor first had to reassure him and swear to him that he was in no danger if he spoke freely: Holland might not have been a free country anymore, but Wassenberg did get Van der Maas to talk. The previous Saturday, Van der Maas told the prosecutor, September 25, two men in civilian attire appeared at his door. Van der Maas was not feeling well and was in bed; his wife Josina answered the door. The two men, who did not identify themselves, said they had reason to believe they were hiding a Jew in their home, namely the former occupant of the vacant house next door, a certain Van Dien. Josina van der Maas was terrified. There was no one in their house, really, she insisted, but the men did not believe her. In the meantime they had been joined by a third man, and together they searched the house. They asked if the Van der Maas family were keeping any things belonging to their Jewish neighbor. They denied it, which was in fact the truth.

But Van der Maas was unlucky: the three men found fifty-three gold coins in a vase. This was against the law, as everyone – including non-Jews – was supposed to have turned in his gold some time ago. The well-to-do contractor/realtor had already turned in hundreds of coins, but he kept these fifty-three for his children. And there was more: the men also discovered large quantities of food in the house, far more than was permitted under the rules of the new economic order. Van der Maas and his wife were in clear violation of these rules. The men – Van der Maas still did not know where they were from, some kind of economic inspection agency, he thought – used Van der Maas's phone to call police headquarters and request that a car be sent over to confiscate the forbidden items. They also called a locksmith, whom they asked to break into the house of the neighbor, Van Dien, so they could have a look around there as well.

Meanwhile Simon and Josina van der Maas were in a state of total panic. From the words of the unknown men, Simon gathered that he would have to go along for further questioning. His wife refused to go through that: if her husband was taken away, she would take her own life, she announced. Simon van der Maas asked, "Isn't there anything I can do?" Perceiving a look of understanding he took the shortest of the three aside for a moment, in the bedroom.

The man asked: What's it worth to you to not have to go?
Van der Maas: You tell me.
The official: No, you have to say it.
Van der Maas: 5,000

The official demanded 10,000 (today that would be about US$65,100). Van der Maas agreed, but said he did not have the money in the house and would pay them on Monday. They accepted this, and the deal was done. The men disappeared and left Mr and Mrs Van der Maas behind in great confusion.

Van der Maas did not dare call the police, but he did talk things over with his lawyer. The latter was hesitant about the best course of action, but Van der Maas knew one thing for certain: he did not want to take any risks and was prepared to pay the money. He did, however, make a note of the serial numbers of the bills he was going to be giving the men. On Monday he handed over the money, at his own office, in an envelope. Prior to that there had been some confusion, a misunderstanding about the time and place of the transfer. The official – once again the short one, the one with whom he had made the deal – warned him to keep quiet about the transaction; otherwise he might be prosecuted anyway.

That was the story a still nervous Van der Maas told prosecutor Wassenberg that same Monday. Wassenberg put inspector J. Posthuma on the case. Posthuma was an experienced investigator and immediately got his teeth into the case. There was detective work to be done: just who were those men?

Posthuma first found out which police officers went to the house to pick up the groceries. That was fairly easy; they were his colleagues, after all. From them he learned that the order originated from the *Zentralstelle*. He then contacted the bureau with the German name and the predominantly Dutch staff and got the head of the *Hausraterfassung* on the line, one Piet Docter. Before the conversation was even over, Docter could see that there was trouble brewing. He knew his boss Lages was strongly opposed to fraud within the corps, and he promised his full cooperation. Posthuma and Docter agreed to hold a full-scale confrontation the following day at the offices of the *Hausraterfassung*, early in the morning.

Then Posthuma tracked down the locksmith who had forced open a door on Koninginneweg. He wanted to know if the men who called him mentioned their names, and it proved to be a good question. The order sheet for the locksmith was signed with the name Harmans.

Early the next morning the detectives arranged for a little spectacle, designed to unmask the guilty parties. The offices of the *Hausraterfassung* were located at a vacant school building on Adama van Scheltemaplein. Halfway below ground level was the gymnasium, where many Jews would be held in the coming year after being taken from their homes. But now the gym was the scene of a confrontation. At quarter past eight, eighty men lined up there in four rows. The complete personnel of the *Hausraterfassungsstelle* had been summoned. Department head Piet Docter entered the room first with inspector Posthuma and his colleague Kaay. He asked the men who had seized a stockpile of food from an address on Koninginneweg to make themselves known. Three hands went up, those of Messrs Harmans, Zilver and Vastmaar, as could be seen from the identity cards they handed the detectives. At this point half the men were sent away; they could go back to work. Then the remaining men regrouped, forming three rows of fifteen men each, with the three suspects distributed randomly over the rows. One by one five witnesses were let in and asked which of the men, if any, they recognized from last Saturday. Officer Pronk (the man who drove to the house to pick up the food) indicated Harmans and Zilver. Officer Lieftink, his colleague, did not recognize anyone. The apprentice locksmith recognized Harmans. Mrs Van der Maas recognized all three: Harmans, Zilver and Vastmaas. Finally her husband, Simon van der Maas, came into the room. He immediately pointed to the same three. The rest were allowed to go; the three culprits were arrested. The case was solved within scarcely twenty hours.

One by one Harmans, Zilver and Vastmaar were interrogated by Docter, his right-hand man Ragut and the detectives. Harmans confessed straightaway. According to his statement, he not only blackmailed Van der Maas but cheated his colleagues as well. He misled them into believing that Van der Maas had only been willing to pay fl.5,000 for his freedom and not 10,000. Then he stole the fl.5,000 and subsequently pocketed a third of the other 5,000. His two co-workers never had an inkling of the deception. Harmans had promised them a share of fl.1,666 each (about $10,600 now), and this was gratefully accepted.

The money, Harmans said in his first interrogation, was at his house in Naarden, as were the gold coins, which he "had planned to give back to Van der Maas." He promptly admitted that there had been other such incidents in the past, one or two. Zilver said the same thing: this inventory clerk had previously been given fl.300 by Harmans, after a similar shakedown. Vastmaar claimed he had already gone through a large part of the money. He allegedly gave fl.1,000 to his wife, but in their final report the detectives concluded that this was a lie. They followed the money and found out that Vastmaar had not told his wife anything about his lucrative little deal. In fact he had given the money to his father for safekeeping, though his wife did tell the police that her husband *had* given her fl.1,000 a short time before, as a little something extra.

It turned out that the now disgraced leader of the investigative division of the *Hausraterfassung* was living in a nice house on Graaf Willem den Oudenlaan in the town of Naarden. During a search of his home the detectives hit the jackpot when they opened up his bedside table: jewels, a Jewish identity card, heaps of gold coins and fl.10,345 ($66,400). The maid, it turned out, knew nothing about the stolen goods. She had been with the family for eight months, but she had only been working at this fine house, which Harman's rapid rise up the social ladder had taken him to a short time before, for the last four weeks.

The next day Posthuma went to Lages, who bore the ultimate responsibility for the *Zentralstelle*, and there he was given orders to investigate the matter thoroughly. Lages ruled that Van der Maas should be given back his fl.10,000 at once, and this was done the very same day. The investigation brought a string of other abuses to light, committed by the same men who had just been exposed, plus a certain Gerrit de Groot, also an inventory clerk. In various configurations the foursome had misappropriated valuables in Arnhem, Hilversum, Leiden and other cities. They seemed to have a marked preference for gold and silver. In anticipation of their trial they were taken into custody. Needless to say, they were fired on the spot: Lages did not want to have criminals working for him. Gerrit de Groot was sacked as well. It couldn't have come as much of a surprise, as he was present for the confrontation in the gymnasium, though his name was not mentioned at the time. He subsequently decided to take a business trip to Maastricht, but was soon summoned back. Detectives Posthuma and Kaay had uncovered his shady sideline too.

A New Leader

The day Harmans was discharged, the investigative division was given a new boss from within its own ranks. Wim Henneicke, a thirty-three-year-old subordinate of Harmans', was appointed to lead the Colonne.[11] From that moment on the group would be known as the Colonne Henneicke. Henneicke did not have a background in police work either. He even had a modest criminal record, for operating an unlicensed taxi service. He was an auto mechanic by trade but maintained contacts in the underworld. A short time before, in April 1942, he had joined the NSB. He would lead his Colonne with an iron fist. His policy was one of divide-and-conquer, and he kept a firm hold on the reins: under Henneicke discipline would prevail.

He was the undisputed ruler of Room 25, where his Colonne had its office. Because of the negative experiences of the recent past, a couple of policemen were posted to the *Hausraterfassung* in order to prevent that kind of massive fraud from ever happening again. The policemen in question were, contrary to what might be expected, anti-German. One of them was detective Elias. He had contacts with the resistance, for which he would be executed later in the war. In reality he was a mole in Henneicke's immediate surroundings. The same was true for his colleagues, A. Japin and K. Weeling. They were also known to be anti-German, but according to the chief of the *Hausraterfassung*, Piet Docter, this was intentional: "If it had been comrades doing the monitoring, there wouldn't have been any monitoring to speak of."[12] They had learned their lesson. There was another former policeman working at the *Hausraterfassung*, a Frisian, Hylke Wierda. He wrote a number of reports on embezzlement and fraud, but by October he had already had enough and resigned from the service. In his view the place was hopeless.[13]

He was one of the few to do so. Beginning in the fall of 1942, the *Hausraterfassung* became a flourishing division of the *Zentralstelle für jüdische Auswanderung*. The size of the staff quickly increased. Their employment contracts, which were officially with Lippmann, Rosenthal & Co., have survived.[14] This was one of the functions of the *roofbank*: acting as the formal employer of the personnel of the *Zentralstelle*. The Jew hunters were paid from the proceeds of stolen Jewish property, and in this way the Dutch Jews financed their own demise. At home the men of the *Hausraterfassung* could say that they were doing administrative work at a bank, and later on many would stick to this story in court. Henneicke signed a similar contract when he was hired by the *Hausraterfassung* in June 1942. He was paid fl.270 a month; nowadays that would be about $1,675.[15] That may seem like a modest salary, but appearances can be deceiving. With their LiRo contracts, the financial situation of the new employees of the *Hausraterfassung* improved dramatically, and Henneicke, who was still on welfare when he signed on, was certainly no exception to this. In signing his contract, he also declared that he was not a Jew and would refrain from any activities which could be construed as anti-German. With his fl.270 he was earning slightly more than average; most signed on for fl.230 a month. Furthermore, the contract was not for an indefinite period. Their employment would terminate when there was no more work. The LiRo personnel department figured that the whole job would take a little over a year.

In 1942 the men of the *Hausraterfassung* traveled around the country in the pursuit of their activities. The "branch offices" of the *Sicherheitsdienst* (Security Service, henceforth SD) in other parts of the country had no inventory specialists on their payroll and therefore had to appeal to "Amsterdam" for help. This made for a little variety in the daily routine. It was not uncommon for the men to spend a week in Groningen or Maastricht, Arnhem or Den Bosch, and during the time they were out of town, they received an attractive expense allowance. The clerks often did their work while the homes' occupants were still there, awaiting deportation. And they always did their work by the book, according to the established rules. In a post-war interrogation Ben Eggink* (an asterisk identifies a pseudonym), one of Henneicke's most active subordinates, said the following about his book of receipts: "I gave one receipt to the Jews whose belongings I had confiscated, while another copy was dropped off at the offices of the *Zentralstelle*. One copy went with the seized property, and another copy stayed in the book, and that one I kept myself until the book was full, at which time it was turned over to the *Zentralstelle*."[16]

The Colonne Henneicke, which expanded considerably between October 1942 and March 1943, worked mainly on the basis of tips. The former auto mechanic built up a vast network of informants, who would pass on information to him by phone and by post. Most of the tips dealt with goods that had not been reported according to the rules of the Second LiRo Decree, but which had instead been diverted to unknown storehouses. Henneicke's informers were paid for their assistance, usually quite generously. For this purpose he was given access to special funds at the *roofbank*. It is no longer possible to trace the money back to its source, but, according to Gerard Aalders, the *Einsatzstab Rosenberg* must have deposited a modest percentage of the estimated value of the goods in a special account, the *Sonderkonto HR II*, in exchange for all the canal boats full of furniture.[17] It is very likely that Henneicke was allowed to dip into this slush fund to pay for his tips.

The Colonne's leader lived well off his earnings: after work he could usually be found enjoying a glass of beer in an Amsterdam pub and waving around wads of bills. His desk drawer burgeoned with slips of paper containing names, addresses and telephone numbers: his working capital.

In those few months Henneicke rose quickly through the ranks of the organization; the same could be said for Willem Briedé, who began as chief of personnel at the *Hausraterfassung*.[18] He was a bookkeeper by profession and his last job had been at the Amsterdam slaughterhouse. He had had a smattering of high school but never graduated, and he had been a member of the NSB since 1934. When he was hired on April 1, 1942, he was promised a salary of fl.290 a month. This was hardly unusual, since his was a position involving a considerable degree of confidentiality. Once a month he would pick up a suitcase full of money at the LiRo branch on Sarphatistraat, from which he paid the salaries of the staff of the *Hausraterfassung*. Eight months after appearing on the scene, he got his big break when he was asked to succeed Piet Docter as head of the *Hausraterfassung*. The leadership of the *Zentralstelle* saw fit to grant him a pay rise of fl.100.

From that moment on Briedé and Henneicke formed a powerful duo within the *Hausraterfassung*. They seemed to get on well together. They both had a marked preference for the direct approach, and neither one had any qualms about using violence to get the job done. Their task was to track down and impound Jewish goods, and they demanded the same fanaticism of their subordinates.

It should almost go without saying that Briedé and Henneicke were in their element when their jobs acquired a new dimension in March 1943. At a meeting Willi Lages, the head of the *Zentralstelle*, announced that a new weapon was to be introduced in the hunt for Jews who had failed to report for *Arbeitseinsatz*: premiums, or *kopgeld* ("head-money") as it was called, that is to say a bonus of fl.7.50 for every Jew brought in.[19]

There are no records of how it came to be decided that the Colonne Henneicke would be given responsibility for this task, but in retrospect it is hardly surprising. Henneicke was extremely well-suited for this sort of work; he was surrounded by a troop of fanatical men and had Briedé's full support. Starting in March, Henneicke was given more and more men. In their respective studies, Jacques Presser and Loe de Jong each proceeded from the assumption that the Colonne Henneicke consisted of some thirty people, but after studying the police records of this group I have come to the conclusion that there were considerably more than that. Under the direct supervision of Henneicke or, later, Briedé no fewer than fifty-four people participated at least once in the hunt for Jews. For most of them this was their main occupation for months. During that time a given individual might have made hundreds of arrests, each one of which would have earned him a bonus. In addition to the "hardcore" members, there were also cases of men who filled in for others temporarily, or who were briefly stationed with the Colonne during a particularly busy period.

That said, the Colonne Henneicke was not the only group with this particular specialty. Within the municipal police force, the Bureau of Jewish Affairs was also engaged in the same sort of work. This organization was first headed by the Nazi Dahmen von Buchholz, but when von Buchholz was caught embezzling, he was replaced by the German Chief Inspector Otto Kempin. The uniformed Jew hunters were highly active and made use of tips from the general public. In reality they were competitors of the Colonne Henneicke, which was perfectly in keeping with the view of the Third Reich that an application of free-market principles would ensure dedicated workers, and thus results. The work of the uniformed Jew hunters has been studied and described, by Guus Meerhoek in his book *Dienaren van het gezag* (Servants to authority).

After the war Willi Lages, as head man at the *Zentralstelle*, was often questioned about his involvement with the Colonne Henneicke. His strategy was to feign ignorance: "I know that among the personnel of the *Hausraterfassung* a group had formed calling itself the Colonne Henneicke," he said to his interrogators, "but this was not established by the Germans or on their orders."[20] And he added that the Colonne Henneicke was not authorized to make arrests either. If they *were* making arrests, they were doing so, according to the transcript of the interrogation, "entirely of their own accord." Lages had played fast and loose with the truth before, but this one was a real whopper. He knew full well that his subordinates had arrested Jews during the war. He must have been particularly pleased that there were Dutchmen willing to do this dirty – albeit relatively well-paid – work. There was only one German in the entire Colonne Henneicke: Hugo Heinrich Berten, a somewhat older man (when the bounty hunt began, he was already fifty-two), in reality a "small fish," who fled the country after the war and went into hiding, thus escaping justice.[21] Everyone else was Dutch. When they first went out in search of Jews, they were sometimes accompanied by police officers who *did* have the authority to make arrests, but these sorts of rules were soon ignored. When they announced themselves at someone's door, they would say they were "from the SD"; sometimes they carried guns, and they could appeal to the local police if they were outside the city and needed to transport detainees back to Amsterdam. This was also an option within Amsterdam in the case of particularly large groups. They often avoided using the term "arrest," preferring to speak of "picking someone up" or "bringing a person in for questioning" or "escorting somebody to the Dutch Theater," but they did like to do the work themselves, since that was the only way of qualifying for the bonus of fl.7.50 per Jew, which was paid by Henneicke personally at the end of each month. That was the basic division of labor: Briedé paid the salaries, Henneicke the premiums.

When Lages testified at the trial of Bob Verlugt* on October 8, 1948, he sounded far less sure of himself: "The policy was that the arrest of Jews was always supposed to be done with the assistance of the police. It was no secret that Henneicke sometimes exceeded his authority, and it is also possible that some of his inferiors knew this."[22] Strictly speaking, Lages was right of course. The members of the Colonne had no official status whatsoever, and thus no right to carry firearms or bring in people "for questioning." At the same trial Lages repeated this: "The members of this Colonne did not have the so-called *Waffenschein* [weapons permit], nor were they armed by the SD. As employees of the *Hausraterfassung* they had a white card, an *Ausweis* [identification card] with a seal on it. This certainly did not give them the authority to make arrests."

This was true, needless to say, but Lages knew as well as anyone that between March and October 1943 there was no power that could stop them.

A Discovery in a Synagogue

During the war only a few people were aware that in the spring and summer of 1943 a group of Dutchmen were scouring the cities and the countryside in order to arrest as many Jews as possible. Thanks to police officer J. Elias, who was placed in the vicinity of the Colonne as a kind of informer, some of the resistance organizations were aware of what was going on. Indeed, in those circles there was a list circulating with names of "Gestapo agents," a somewhat imprecise designation applied to anyone working for the Germans.[23] The lists contained no fewer than thirty-two names of staff members of the *Hausraterfassung* who could be considered part of the Colonne Henneicke. Starting in May 1945, that list would also play a role in the prosecution of collaborators. These trials were conducted on the basis of the Special Justice Act, which the government had drawn up during its exile in London.[24] Tribunals were set up throughout the country; there were also Special Courts for the more serious cases. At the same time, there were a growing number of PRAs, *Politieke Recherche Afdelingen* (Political Investigation Departments),[b] which, under the guidance of the Office of the Public Prosecutor, conducted preliminary investigations into the thousands, indeed hundreds of thousands, of suspects. A total of 450,000 dossiers were compiled, and 200,000 of these were forwarded to the public prosecutor. Not surprisingly, chaos quickly ensued, with overcrowded prisons and penal camps where less serious offenders were mixed in with hardened criminals. In retrospect it was a miracle 50,000 people ultimately appeared before the Tribunals and 16,000 before the Special Courts. And it is no wonder that the investigators and the courts needed some time to separate the wheat from the chaff and ascertain the facts of the crimes committed by Dutchmen working for the Germans or under German orders.

For nearly three years after the liberation there was a total lack of understanding of the role played by the Colonne Henneicke. There were scraps of information here and there, but nothing conclusive. Men suspected of having been involved in serious crimes were held in camps, while the evidence against them gradually mounted; a few of them had even been convicted. But despite all this, the context remained shadowy. The men who updated the card catalogue at the *Zentralstelle* had already received frighteningly harsh sentences. We will meet them again later.[25]

But the real breakthrough for the Amsterdam PRA did not come until February 2, 1948, when investigators W. Prasing and C.J. Verduin received a package from the *Rijksinstituut voor Oorlogsdocumentatie* (RIOD), the National Institute for War Documentation. Inside, for their inspection, was a portion of the records of the *Zentralstelle*.[26] Why they were not destroyed and how they wound up in the basement of the Central Synagogue at 19 Tulpstraat in Amsterdam will probably always remain a mystery. Hans Simon Ottenstein, a RIOD staff member, was unable to give the detectives any explanation. All he knew was that in November 1947 his boss, Loe de Jong, received a call from the secretary of the Jewish Community, which was then based on Tulpstraat. There were a few boxfuls of paper in the basement, which might be of importance for the institute. As the newspaper *Het Vrije Volk* would later write, De Jong "didn't let any grass grow under his feet" and promptly had the boxes brought in.[27] To everyone's surprise, they turned out to contain part of the archive of the *Zentralstelle für jüdische Auswanderung*. At the RIOD the archive was sorted into twenty-nine binders and a few loose folders. After that the police and the public prosecutor were notified. M.H. Gelinck, the prosecutor at the Special Court, soon realized the value of the discovery. Even though it was already the spring of 1948, from that point on he could start putting together a case against the Jew hunters. Prior to that time there had scarcely been any evidence against them, given the lack of survivors. On April 11, 1948 the detectives came forward with this material. All the newspapers wrote about the discovery and about the possibility that the hunters would now become the hunted. From the April 12 issue of *Het Vrije Volk*: "Detectives Prasing and Verduin and their boss, Chief Inspector Haye, know that no one can escape now. They have all the cards, and the SD's henchmen are destined to lose from the very start. In due course judge-advocate Gelinck will lay these cards on the table, the cards of retribution."

At that point Prasing and his colleagues had already been on the job for over two months. The most striking material was a handful of receipts showing that money had been paid to the Colonne Henneicke for bringing in Jews. There was room for five names on such a form, along with their birth dates and addresses. The papers also contained signatures and initials, as well as stamps. There must have been hundreds of them, but for some reason these five, all from April 6, 1943, escaped destruction and were sent to the police. Compelling evidence, highly suited for motivating teams of detectives to do their utmost. There were also a large number of so-called *Berichte*: brief arrest reports, in German. The *Berichte* contained the names of the arrestees, plus some additional information about them: whether they were arrested on the street or at a hiding place, how much money they had on them and whether any possessions were confiscated. And the reports nearly always concluded with: "taken to the Jewish [i.e. Dutch] Theater," followed by the signatures, generally two names, sometimes three, of members of the Colonne Henneicke. This material was also a major find for the investigators. At first count there were 513 of these *Berichte* in the records. Prasing had all of them typed out – at the time a copy machine was not yet standard equipment for the Dutch police. There were also *Berichte* from the autumn of 1942, identical in format, only at that point they did not contain information about people but about impounded property. A very interesting discovery was a stack of paper marked "production lists" – they contained the numbers of Jews arrested during the months of August and September. Finally, the boxes the detectives received also contained some correspondence on the size of the Colonne's personnel roster. All in all it was a highly significant find: extraordinarily important for unravelling the secrets of the Colonne Henneicke, but at the same time a collection of cold numbers, behind which lay an incomprehensible reality.

The team of detectives regularly conferred with M.H. Gelinck, who as judge-advocate, would be leading the prosecution against members of the Colonne Henneicke before the Special Court. The team decided to compile a detailed report, which would form the basis for the charges in all the cases. This relieved them of having to reinvent the wheel for each individual case. "A study of the methods of the Colonne Henneicke of the *Zentralstelle für jüdische Auswanderung*" is the name of the mimeographed document that dominates all the Henneicke dossiers to this very day.

In early April, shortly before the public prosecutor's office came forward with the evidence, the suspects who were not already in prison or who had served short sentences were arrested. In some cases they had already been convicted by the Tribunal for more minor offenses and wisely kept quiet about their activities as bounty hunters. Some of them were arrested at work and would not return home for another ten years.[28]

Over the course of the general investigation Prasing and Verduin would hear dozens of witnesses, beginning with the Germans Lages and Aus der Fünten. Even at this early stage it was clear that the two wanted to distance themselves from what they called "the Dutch department." Lages and Aus der Fünten both signed off on the payroll, and thus they could not very well deny knowing about its existence. But Aus der Fünten said, "I never ordered the creation of this group and once it existed, it was tacitly accepted as such. I do not know how many Jewish persons were brought in by the Colonne Henneicke, but I do know that it was quite a few. I knew this; this was what I was told."[29]

The general investigation focused a great deal on the numbers, yet these very numbers were the source of misunderstandings which have persisted to this very day. Prasing and Verduin made neatly organized lists of all the information they had at their disposal, endless lists of arrested Jews. They included the date, the ages, the addresses, and wherever possible the names of those who had carried out the arrest and the guard at the gate of the Dutch Theater who signed for receipt of the prisoners. On the basis of all this they came to a total of 2,915 arrests for the period covered by the documents, and this number has assumed a life of its own. For example De Jong writes: "The exact number of arrests made by the Colonne Henneicke in the period from 5 April to 8 July 1943 is known to be 2,915. In the months of August and September 1943 an additional 513 arrests were made."[30] And thus he arrived at a total of over 3,400 – but this is inaccurate. Later on Prasing wrote a second, supplemental report, after the discovery of a number of *Wachezettel*, slips of paper concerning the transfer of detainees, signed by guards. In that later report Prasing came to the conclusion that his data were far from complete. Entire weeks were missing from the surviving part of the Colonne's records. Furthermore, the whole month of March was absent, and there were indications that this had been the Colonne Henneicke's most productive month. Thus the figure of 3,400 is much too low.

Some time later, when the investigation was well under way, a document was found written in Henneicke's own hand.[31] The chief of the Colonne was not much of a writer; he was more of a numbers man, and it is mainly numbers that the document contains, numbers of Jews arrested during the first ten weeks after the introduction of the premiums. These are the figures:

March 4–10	425
March 11–17	990
March 18–24	1,034
March 25–31	741
April 1–7	808
April 8–14	577
April 15–19	380
April 27–May 5	699
May 6–12	423

Altogether that makes 6,077 arrested Jews. According to an overview written by Henneicke on June 9, another 757 arrests were made during the period of May 13 to June 8. After the first three months, the counter had reached 6,834. Then there was also a detailed overview of the months of August and September: during that time "production" fell off somewhat, as most Jews were already gone and those that were left had found better hiding places. The combined total for these two months was 723. This brings the number to 7,557, and the only figures we lack are those for the period from June 9 to August 1, for which there are no reliable data. It is likely that the number of Jews arrested during that time was somewhere between 500 and 1,500. In that case 8,500 would be a reasonable estimate of the total number of victims of the Colonne Henneicke. It is highly probable that it was Wim Henneicke himself who neglected the paperwork in June and July – he was, after all, quite busy that summer. This theory becomes all the more plausible after perusing the file on Eddy Moerberg.[32] This employee of the *Hausraterfassung*, who had a background in office management, was transferred to the Colonne in late July at the insistence of his boss Willem Briedé. "The bookkeeping there was a mess, and I had to put things right," Moerberg said to his interrogators. "I cleared the backlog, which dated from before August 1943. Then I immediately shifted my focus to the current business, which I updated on a daily basis; this included processing arrests as they occurred."

From that moment on the Colonne's books were in order again. Detective Wijnand Prasing apparently came to the same conclusion. In the countless times he was called upon to testify against suspects from the Colonne Henneicke, he was only seldom asked for an estimate of the total number of victims. March 18, 1949 was one of those rare occasions. After working on the case against Henk Saaldijk* for nearly eighteen months, Prasing knew the material backward and forward. In Saaldijk's trial, he stated that in his opinion the Colonne made "between 8,000 and 9,000" arrests, a number "which can be inferred from the payroll slips."[33]

However, it should be noted that this does not necessarily mean that 8,000 to 9,000 Jews were also deported through the efforts of Henneicke and Briedé's men. Hundreds are known to have escaped from the Dutch Theater, mostly with the help of the Jewish staff there, sometimes by bribing guards. Hundreds of children also found their way out of the nursery across the street, and even the headquarters of the *Zentralstelle* was not escape-proof. There is a story of a Jewish man who was arrested four times by a member of the Colonne and managed to get away every time.[34] Moreover, countless Jews were brought in only to be let go again, because they turned out to have a *Sperr* or for some other reason.

All things considered, it is very likely that Prasing's testimony in Saaldijk's trial was near to the truth, though at the time the papers made no mention of it. By then the interest in the trials of war criminals had faded considerably, and it was thanks to this lack of coverage that it escaped the attention of historians like Presser and De Jong. And thus, until now, the productivity of Henneicke's band of bounty hunters has been badly underestimated.

Daily Routine

It is unlikely that the day-to-day routine at the Colonne's headquarters, first in the school on Adama van Scheltemaplein, later in the building at 244 Noorder Amstellaan, was marked by ideological or political discussions. Not that such discussions would have been necessary, given the considerable degree of consensus among the staff. Practically all the members of the Colonne were also in the NSB, and there was no reason to expect any protests from the few who were not. Wim Henneicke was the only one to ever say anything about the background of the work they were doing. In the morning, when he would give instructions for the day's work, he occasionally took some time to say a few words, particularly if there were newcomers present. "The Germans are planning to establish a Jewish state in Poland," he told his men, according to subordinate Sjef Sweeger*. "We are helping to implement this plan."[35]

Henneicke received his ideological training when he joined the organization a year earlier, from the then-head of the *Hausraterfassung*, Piet Docter. According to Aaldert Dassen*, who had been with the Colonne since day one, Docter had given a speech in which he said: "The Jewish presence in ... the Netherlands is unsustainable; they are the enemies of Germany. Therefore they are being put to work in factories in Germany and Poland, prior to being resettled in a country outside Europe – Palestine, for example. They cannot take their furniture to the camps where they will be housed, hence the need for an inventory system. The German state will transfer the estimated value of their assets to an account at Lippmann, Rosenthal. We all believed that."[36]

But, as has already been said, little time was wasted on ideology or background. Henneicke sent his men out to work bright and early each morning. One of the most active of his followers, Jan Rudolfs*, spoke about this in a police interrogation: "Every morning during roll call Henneicke would give us various tasks to do, locating Jewish property or visiting addresses where Jews were thought to be hiding. We were always assigned these tasks in pairs. If Henneicke suspected there were a lot of Jews or a lot of Jewish goods at a particular address, the investigation was often conducted under his immediate supervision."[37]

Additional information was provided by an eyewitness, Abraham Pach, an Amsterdam butcher of Jewish descent, who worked for the Jewish Council from June 1942 to October 1943 and for that reason had permission to be out on the street late at night: "They would go out every day, even in the evenings or at night, with the express purpose of picking up Jews. I often spoke to Henneicke's subordinates while they were out on such missions." And his colleague on the Jewish Council, Maurits Allegro, told detective Prasing: "I had to go collect the luggage of Jewish people who had been picked up by members of the Colonne Henneicke. They picked up the Jews without any outside help. On several occasions I even saw them bring handicapped Jews to the Theater. Often they would first gather them together at various addresses in the city, like police stations or houses where other Jewish people had been arrested before."[38] Allegro also claimed to have witnessed assaults. That is certainly credible, as there were widely divergent reports on the arrests. In some cases brute force was used, but in most cases the Jews simply went along once they had been discovered.

The members of the Colonne Henneicke frequently worked in set teams of two. That can be seen from the signatures on the *Berichte*, the short reports that were filled out following an arrest; very often the same two names were at the bottom of the form. The aforementioned Jan Rudolfs made at least 225 arrests with Martin Hintink*, whose personal total was even higher. It was an unusual duo: the two men were brothers-in-law. Hintink was married to Jannetje Rudolfs. Jan Rudolfs was a simple soul, not too quick on the uptake, but Hintink was a fanatic. After the war it did not take long for the police to get wind of his activities, but because there was not enough evidence they placed an appeal for information in the newspapers.[39] That did the trick: because Hintink was an enthusiastic athlete (he had played professional football for thirteen years with one of the smaller Amsterdam clubs, eventually leaving "because everyone there is anti[-German]"), the tips started pouring in. But there were also those who came to his defense, including his wife: "I froze when I saw the ad in the paper, not just from fear but also outrage. After all I'm his wife, and I should know better than anyone what he did and didn't do." Jannetje Hintink-Rudolfs added: "Under command of the armed forces he had to go along to organize the Jewish transports, but he didn't arrest anyone himself. He wasn't authorized to do so and didn't like the idea either."[40]

It seems that Hintink and Rudolfs were highly selective about what they chose to say about their work at home, because the PRA had more evidence against these two brothers-in-law than against anybody else. For some reason they seemed to be especially susceptible to Henneicke's methods. Henneicke did not use sophisticated motivational techniques; he was a hardliner. If his men came back after a day out with nothing to show for it, he would let them have it. Rudolfs, in a police interrogation, said: "If we came back without any Jews, Henneicke would say, 'So I guess you two spent the day at the movies.'"[41]

Henneicke's system was based on threats. Subordinates who were no longer willing to arrest Jews on the street or in their homes had no reason to expect any sympathy from the boss. Jan Casteels* considered resigning, but was pressured into changing his mind. "This pressure consisted of the threat that we would end up in a camp ourselves if we didn't do our jobs. We at the *Zentralstelle* were told this by Henneicke. At the time I didn't consider going into hiding because I also had to provide for my wife," Casteels said to the detectives questioning him.[42] The same went for Sjef Sweeger. He claimed that when he tried to quit, he was told it was out of the question. He was only allowed to leave the Colonne if he went to work for another Nazi organization. He applied for a job with the National Labour Front, but without success – Sweeger continued arresting Jews for another six months, eventually ending up as one of the top five most productive bounty hunters.[43]

A similar story was told by Henk van den Heuvel*, who claimed to have been afraid of his boss, Willem Briedé, the big man at the *Hausraterfassung*. When he attempted to resign, Briedé not only refused but promptly transferred Van den Heuvel to the Colonne Henneicke. In his interrogation Van den Heuvel said: "This was the worst thing that could have happened. Henneicke threatened me, saying that if I didn't get results, he wouldn't be as patient with me as Briedé. He was a monster, and I was scared of him too. During the conversation he toyed very nonchalantly with his gun."[44]

Every now and again co-worker Alex Hoogers* dared to defy the wishes of Messrs Briedé and Henneicke. He was an outsider in the Colonne; his specialty was appraising paintings, a field in which he appeared to have genuine expertise. But, like all the others, over the course of time he too was ordered to arrest Jews, and he evidently had a certain talent for that as well, as the Special Court would later hold him responsible for the deaths of thirty-three people. In an interrogation Hoogers said, "I repeatedly told Briedé that I refused to arrest or detain Jewish people, but Briedé said, 'You're not arresting or detaining anyone; you're just picking them up for me. If you don't do it, I'll have you thrown into the House of Detention on Amstelveenseweg.'" Hoogers told the detectives that he once spent an entire day locked in a tiny room at the *Zentralstelle* on Briedé's orders, supposedly in an effort to make him change his mind.⁴⁵

Nevertheless, for those who really did not want to keep working, there *were* ways to get out of arresting Jews, as evidenced by the experiences of those involved. Nico Evertsen* for example, a thirty-two-year-old taxi driver, did not want to arrest Jews. He was asked to do so after returning from a stint with the *Einsatzstab Rosenberg*.⁴⁶ He called in sick, and according to him this soon led to a "discharge on the grounds of ill-health." That said, Evertsen was hardly a model citizen. To make ends meet, he applied for a job with the *Wehrmacht* as a driver. After the war he would spend two years in an internment camp.

Evertsen managed to get out of work by feigning illness, but we do know of one instance of someone who simply refused, Cornelis Rietveld*.⁴⁷ According to the Colonne's records, he went out to make arrests on two occasions, once with Dassen and once with the boss himself, Henneicke. But in early March he had had enough, "because I didn't agree with the work they were slowly but surely trying to impose on us." Head of Personnel Briedé, who handled the case, would not accept his resignation and said, "If you leave, you're going to Germany." Many other members of the Colonne must have heard that same threat, but Rietveld was the only one to call Briedé's bluff. His attitude was evidently: if that's the way it is, I suppose I'll just have to go to Germany. He ignored the first few summonses, but when the fourth one came, he complied and boarded the train to the east. He worked at the Fieseler airplane factory in Kassel until April 1945. He was not arrested until November 1948, and he expected to be let off. But because his name appeared in the records of the Colonne Henneicke, he was put on trial. Since he had turned Jews over to the Germans, the court sentenced him to four years in prison, even though the prosecution had only demanded two and a half. His refusal to continue arresting Jews was certainly a mitigating factor, but despite that he ended up serving three years. The Queen granted him partial clemency, reducing his sentence by a year.

Three years in prison for the only man who chose forced labor in Germany over arresting Jews – the Special Court showed little mercy to those who were affiliated with the Colonne Henneicke in 1943.

The Hunt Intensifies

As the summer of 1943 wore on, the Colonne turned up the heat on fugitive Jews. There are any number of reasons for this. Inurement certainly played a role. Those who were uncomfortable early on and unhappy with their additional job duties gradually grew accustomed to the new routine and consequently became more productive. But it cannot be denied that Henneicke also began to make more demands on his men, mercilessly spurring his personnel on to greater productivity. At a certain point he decided to try a new tack: the Colonne would no longer work on the basis of tips alone. Anyone with extra time on his hands would now be expected to patrol the streets, on the look-out for people with Jewish features. The brothers-in-law Hintink and Rudolfs both testified in court, at the session of September 25, 1948, that Henneicke ordered them to patrol certain neighborhoods and accost people on the street to check their papers.[48] A former neighbor of another particularly active employee, the ex-radio salesman Elmink, also made a statement to that effect. In 1943 the woman moved to another part of the city and saw him by chance when he knocked on her door, together with another man. They had lists in their hands and asked "if there [were] any Jews present in the house." When she answered in the negative, he nodded and left, but afterward, the woman saw the duo "going from door to door, looking for Jews." Perhaps it is worth noting that this variant does not appear in any of the other dossiers.[49]

But another method does. One lovely summery Sunday evening Colonne member Cool* was walking down Weteringschans, near Vijzelgracht, when he saw a woman he suspected was Jewish. In a communicative mood he later said to an employee of the Jewish Council (Machiel Gobets, a bookkeeper), "I thought: if I pick up a Jew today, that's a quick fifteen guilders for me. So I asked her for her ID." It had been a good decision, Cool went on to say; her papers were fake. At the office (which was also open on Sundays) it was determined that she was Jewish, and Cool could look forward to a fl.15 bonus, double the usual fl.7.50. This was possible because the detainee was clearly a "penal case," a Jew who had broken a National Socialist law. Later Gobets would testify in court that Cool had told him this story at the Dutch Theater, while the woman in question stood by. "The woman was later deported," according to Gobets. In court Cool swore that this was not true.[50]

No stone was left unturned in the crusade to capture as many Jews as possible. A leading Jewish journalist, Mozes Vaz Dias, experienced this personally. Vaz Dias had been the head of his own press agency. He was in fact exempt from arrest; he had a *Sperr*, a stamp in his identity card. Nonetheless on March 28 he received a visit from two members of the Colonne, De Hout* and Saaldijk. They marched straight to his desk and inspected the lockbox. They asked Vaz Dias to leave the room for a moment. He refused. After some sleight of hand Saaldijk suddenly produced a false identity card, which he supposedly found in the desk. He called out in surprise, "So I guess that tip was good." Vaz Dias, who realized what the men were up to, could only say: "How can a person do a thing like that?" Vaz Dias and his wife had to go along with the men. At the Colonne's office on Adama van Scheltemaplein they protested vehemently. After a week they were released, without ever being charged with anything. It was an absurd case, really, since anyone with a *Sperr* was, at least for the time being, safe and had no need for false papers. As was typical in such situations, when the family returned home they found that a number of things had been stolen. De Hout admitted under interrogation that it must have been a set-up: his colleague Saaldijk had wanted to bring these people in, whatever the cost. Saaldijk himself no longer remembered anything about the incident. In the end he was willing to concede that *if* it had happened that way, they must have been working under orders from Henneicke. He must have been the one to give them the false papers, and he probably had some special reason for wanting these people brought in.[51]

Saaldijk was actually one of Henneicke's specialists. This relatively well-educated ex-salesman (high school plus evening classes at a business school) had a unique position in the Colonne: he would pick up sick Jews from their homes. Not at first though; initially the practice of arresting the sick was highly contentious.[52] Because the members of the Colonne wanted to follow their orders to the letter, they dragged the elderly, the handicapped and the sick out of their chairs or beds and took them to the Dutch Theater. But there were protests, from relatives, occasionally from bystanders. Therefore they adopted a new method. Anyone who came across a sick – or at any rate non-ambulatory – Jew during a raid would announce that the patient would be picked up the next day by ambulance. The men then made a note of it, and the staff member responsible for this, Henk Saaldijk, went out on his route the following day. He had a simple solution for this. In the morning Saaldijk called the Amsterdam Health Authority and ordered an ambulance, which first drove to his house to pick him up, before starting off on the day's rounds. At the end of the day, when all the Jews on his list had been picked up, Saaldijk appreciated being dropped off at his front door by the ambulance.

It is no wonder that there were soon protests within the ranks of the Health Authority. But the directors of the Authority argued that their hands were tied; they had orders from the Germans to cooperate. If they refused, the management was told, the SD would carry the Jews off in a handcart or load them into the back of a delivery van.

Detective Prasing conducted a special investigation into this matter in 1948. He invited C.J. Broeksma, who was a paramedic during the war, to come and explain how the system worked. Broeksma stated: "Saaldijk had information, mostly ID cards, and, with the driver's assistance, I would treat the sick Jews who were arrested by Saaldijk and brought to the Jewish Theater. In most cases a gurney had to be used." Broeksma was present for approximately thirty-five such arrests by ambulance. His colleagues had similar experiences, so by Broeksma's estimation hundreds of such arrests must have been made. A fellow nurse, Jan van Zon, confirmed that Saaldijk was taken home by the ambulance at the end of the day. He too put the number of arrests in the hundreds. Most of the time the trip ended at the infirmary at the Dutch Theater, though sometimes they stopped at the office of the *Zentralstelle*. According to another nurse, Herman Vieyra, countless children, often with contagious diseases, were picked up by ambulance using this same method. The children were then brought to the nursery across the street from the Dutch Theater.

All this should come as no surprise to anyone familiar with the case files of the members of the Colonne Henneicke. A Jew is a Jew – this was the basic operating principle in these circles. Age was irrelevant. Arguments that the infirm, the elderly and children were not suited for work in the East were brushed aside; an official decision had been made that families would be deported as a whole, and this meant children too. At the end of the day, they were worth just as much to the bounty hunters as Jews who *could* work.

This same Saaldijk, who was so active in the health care sector, was also responsible for the deportation of three-year-old Jewish twins, both boys.[53] One day he paid a visit to the home of a paramedic he regularly worked with, Herman Vieyra, who lived on Plantage Franschelaan. He was following up a tip that the Vieyras were hiding Jews, and with the help of two colleagues he searched this non-Jewish family's home. The men found nothing. Afterward they sat down for a cup of coffee, and Saaldijk said to Mrs Vieyra-Pek, "What lovely children you have." He was referring to the two blond boys, Yte and Joke, who were scampering about the house. It must have been an unbearably tense visit for the Vieyras. Even though Yte and Joke did not look it, they were both Jews. Their mother was Herman Vieyra's sister, who was married to a certain Mr Presser. By the standards of the German racial laws, they were Jews. The Vieyra family took them in to save the boys from deportation. Herman Vierya and his wife wanted to raise them as their own children, after having lost their older son.

Two days later Saaldijk returned to arrest the children; he was positive they were Jewish. When Mrs Vieyra denied it and claimed the two children regularly attended services at the Reformed Church with them, one of Saaldijk's companions snapped back at her: "Are you trying to tell us these aren't Jews? If you deny it, I'll just pull down their pants and check."

Mrs Vieyra-Pek was held for a short time and then released. Later on she figured out who had betrayed the children, and after the war she pointed out the guilty party to the police. Yte and Joke Presser, two little boys who were taken away by three grown men, were sent to Sobibor shortly after their arrest. There they were gassed. At that moment Saaldijk's own child, also a boy, was not yet three.

The Presser brothers were just two of the hundreds of toddlers tracked down by the Colonne Henneicke. Even when it meant traveling outside the city, the bounty hunters were utterly dedicated to the pursuit of their quarry. On August 31, 1943 Johan Keuling* and Lambert Schipper* went to Zuilen, then a small town just north of Utrecht, to arrest a certain André Ossendrijver at 11 Van Edmondkade.[54] André was two and a half. He had been with his new family for a year and a half. In early 1942 Nel Schoonderwoerd-Alkelijen and her husband had taken the boy in.

After he and Keuling had been let in, Lambert Schipper did most of the talking. He asked how many people there were in the house. Mrs Schoonderwoerd answered: "Husband, wife, child." Schipper: "You mean that little Jew, I suppose." Mrs Schoonderwoerd did not deny it. Little André was circumcised and had a Jewish appearance; denial seemed pointless. The child had just come into the room, awakened by the noise. Schipper's reaction: "Are you trying to tell me this isn't a Jew?" The child's foster mother did not answer. Schipper said that the boy would have to come along to Amsterdam. Mrs Schoonderwoerd replied that that was out of the question and refused to hand over the child. The discussion continued as follows:

Schipper: I guess you'd prefer to have a police van outside your door.
Mrs Schoonderwoerd: It's no disgrace.
Schipper: It breaks my heart too, to have to do this.
Mrs Schoonderwoerd: No, it doesn't, otherwise you wouldn't be doing it.
Schipper: It's still a baby Jew yet, but a baby Jew turns into a Jew boy and then a full-grown Jew.

At that point Nel Schoonderwoerd called her husband, who had been in another part of the house. Later he would testify in court that, like his wife, he refused to let them take the boy: "We were very attached to the child because we didn't have any children of our own." But their protests were in vain; Mr and Mrs Schoonderwoerd had no choice but to take the child to the nearest police station, in Zuilen. Schipper and Keuling went along with them. Mrs Schoonderwoerd told the court in November 1948: "There we were attended to by the policeman N., whom we both knew. N. is still in the force and has even been promoted. He put the child on the lap of a Jewish woman, who was already there at the station."

That was Rebecca van Bergen, who had been picked up by the same duo a short time before, along with her husband Meijer van Bergen, in a house on Amsterdamsestraatweg, also in Zuilen. Meijer had tried to flee, but Schipper caught up with him and punched him in the face. "No hitting in my house," cried Mrs Post, 78, who had been hiding the Van Bergens, but to no avail. "You have a Jew in your home. That's a criminal offense," Schipper snarled at her. Mrs Post and the Van Bergens then kissed each other goodbye. The 54-year-old Lambert Schipper, who came from Limburg and had had a strict Catholic upbringing (he had been an acolyte for many years), then said, "Oh, just look at how devoted they are to one another."

And thus little André Ossendrijver was thrust into Rebecca's arms at the police station in Zuilen. "Please take good care of him," Mrs Schoonderwoerd begged her. Then the policeman N. arranged for the transportation personally. The choice of vehicle was most unusual: motorcycle and sidecar. Meijer van Bergen sat in the back, Rebecca in the side car with André Ossendrijver on her lap. N. rode up front. André Ossendrijver, two and a half years old, was never seen again. He was killed in Poland, as were Meijer and Rebecca van Bergen.

In short, age was of no importance when Henneicke's disciples were out on the job. Another example: Max Vogel, who was staying with the Van der Meulen family at 63 Linnaeusparkweg, Amsterdam.[55] Max was almost two and had infectious TB. He was very weak and had to lie in front of an open window as much as possible. His mother was also in hiding and could not see him. His father had already been taken away. Only his grandmother, Vogeltje Emmerik, could come visit him on September 7, Max's second birthday. She stayed the night at the Van der Meulen's, a reckless move in those circumstances. The next morning at nine o'clock two men rang the bell, Elmink and Van der Kraal*. They were there to arrest little Max and his grandma. Later Mrs Van der Meulen would explain the tragic course of events. In the presence of the two Colonne members the grandmother began sobbing loudly, begging them to spare her grandson. "But they hadn't discovered the child yet, and if she hadn't mentioned him, he might never have been found," Mrs Van der Meulen said to the detective investigating the case.

Vogeltje Emmerink was taken to the Dutch Theater straightaway, while Max would be brought there some time later by Mrs Van der Meulen's housekeeper. Max was sent to the nursery on Plantage Middenlaan, across the street from the theater where his grandma was being held. He did not stay there long. After a fortnight a friend of his mother's was able to spirit him away, that is to say kidnap him. Through this woman's actions Max Vogel survived the war, in hiding, as did his mother. But his grandma, Vogeltje Emmerik, who came to visit him on his second birthday, was murdered at Auschwitz.

Max Vogel, André Ossendrijver, Yte and Joke Presser – these were just a few of the thousands of victims of the Colonne Henneicke. The group had an unprecedented degree of autonomy and freedom of action. To be sure, Henneicke and Briedé would regularly confer with their German superiors at the *Zentralstelle*, but there was little evidence of this in the day-to-day operations. It was Dutchmen who ran the Colonne and Dutchmen who carried out the policy. In late June, when Henneicke and his team moved to a new office on Noorder Amstellaan, there was a redivision of labor. The Colonne Henneicke went on working as before, but now, under Briedé, other employees of the *Hausraterfassung* started pursuing tips as well. They formed a Department for Tracking Jewish Goods. They made arrests on their own initiative, and they also collected premiums. In fact, it would not be inaccurate to characterize the group as a Colonne Briedé. During the Special Court trials, all this remained somewhat vague: the prosecution estimated that approximately fifty men served under Henneicke. But Jacob Gist* mentioned this reorganization in a police interrogation. He was an inventory clerk with the

Hausraterfassung and admitted that at a certain point in time he too was ordered to make arrests: "Around June 1943 I was finished with stocktaking. I was then transferred against my will to the Department for Tracking Jewish Goods, and the work there sometimes involved arresting Jews. This was not the Colonne Henneicke, but a special department led by Briedé."[56] The same was true for some of Gist's co-workers, who admitted under interrogation that they had taken part in arrests but had nothing to do with Henneicke and in some cases did not even know him.

In the period from March to October 1943 there were only a few instances when the Colonne was forced to relinquish some of its authority, those times when the Germans would stage large-scale raids. The Colonne Henneicke participated in such roundups, albeit in a subordinate role.

At the end of May the Germans began to roll up the Jewish Council. Of the over 12,000 exempt staff members, 6,000 were called up for *Arbeitseinsatz*. Naturally, the need to decide who would stay and who would go led to enormous tensions within the Council. In the end, 1,200 Jews reported to Polderweg, near the Muiderpoort train station, on May 25, not nearly enough for the Germans' taste. Countless photographs were taken of those who did show up, for *Storm*, the weekly publication of the Germanic SS.[57] A number of Colonne members tried to make a little fast money out of the operation, according to statements made by Alexander Jacobs after the war.[58] In 1943 Jacobs was the doorkeeper at the Dutch Theater. He claimed that on the way there a group of Colonne members intercepted a large number of Jews who were going to the meeting place on foot and informed them that from now on they would be brought there by car. But first they would have to walk to the Dutch Theater. The idea, according to Jacobs, was that in this way the Colonne members could get hold of transfer receipts with the names of dozens, even hundreds, of Jews, which they could later redeem for bonuses. In the view of the avaricious Colonne members, such raids were a blatant case of unfair competition: the Germans were stealing their business. Jacobs later heard from colleagues that the scheme hadn't worked. The *Zentralstelle* started making trouble, and the Colonne members in question had to kiss their bonuses goodbye.

Since the turnout was a disappointment, the next day the Germans organized a raid in which 3,000 Jews were arrested and deported. According to Presser, the operation went smoothly; it was as if the victims had prepared themselves for it.[59] Despite reassuring words from Lages that there were no new operations on the horizon, a little less than four weeks later there was an even bigger raid.

The whole Colonne Henneicke took part. The entire staff of the *Zentralstelle*, including the members of the Colonne, were required to attend a film screening at the Roxy Theater on Kalverstraat on the eve of the big razzia – a sort of staff outing.[60] Afterward Willy Lages climbed up on stage and invited everyone to the building on Euterpestraat.[61] There the men were given a bowl of soup. After that the big raid began in the eastern and southern sections of the city, in collaboration with the German *Grüne Polizei*. The raid lasted two full days, Sunday and Monday, June 20 and 21, and a total of 5,500 Jews were deported. No bonuses were paid during this operation; detective Prasing looked into this after the war, just to be sure. However in the course of his investigation he did come across various witnesses who had seen members of the Colonne in action. One was described as "driving [the Jews] along with his fists"; another was said to be "going at it with dozens of detainees." The man in question, Martin Hintink, remembered nothing about it, but, as he said in 1948 to detective Slob in a police interview: "The reason I remember so few particulars is because I *arrested so many Jewish people*, and it was such a long time ago" (italics mine).[62]

Following the raid at the end of May, a German official wrote in an enthusiastic report that great progress was being made. The tone of the document was festive: he calculated that in this last operation the 100,000th Jew had been deported.[63] It is clear that the number of Jews left in Amsterdam was decreasing rapidly, due to the raids and the activities of the Colonne Henneicke. And let us not forget the work of the specialized Jew hunters of the Amsterdam police, who were now under the direct control of the *Sicherheitsdienst*. At the end of September there was one final raid, during which both chairmen of the Jewish Council, Cohen and Asscher, were sent to Westerbork. The Dutch Theater was emptied out, and the nursery across the street was closed. And the Colonne Henneicke was dissolved. Eighteen members of the Colonne received a short letter, informing them that their employment with Lippmann, Rosenthal & Co. (the *roofbank* that paid their salaries) had been terminated as operations were now finished. Briedé and Henneicke were not among this number, but key players like Hintink, De Hout and Kroon were. (We will meet these three again later.) Several members of the Colonne Henneicke got a job with another branch of the *Hausraterfassung*, namely the fur department. The need for fur on the Eastern Front was on the rise, and the Germans were willing to pay to have it collected. Some members of the Colonne were asked to go on doing the same work, this time within the ranks of the *Sicherheitsdienst*. There was also the possibility of working exclusively on the basis of premiums, as an informant, and some decided to do this. Others chose a job with the police, where they essentially continued doing the same sort of work as before.

But most of Henneicke's disciples opted for other work. A small group went into business, but the majority chose a career in other Nazi organizations, like the *Landwacht*. In tracking down resistance fighters and people trying to shirk the *Arbeitseinsatz*, they could put the methods they had learned from Henneicke into practice in other parts of the country.

One such person was Jan Takkert*, who wound up with the Germanic SS and was also the leader of the South Holland Labour Front. Not such a bad career for a former distiller. And no doubt he would long remember his time with the Colonne Henneicke after being released from prison in June 1950. He went back to his home at 244 Churchilllaan, the wide road in South Amsterdam which was called Noorder Amstellaan during the war. Takkert, who had always got on well with Henneicke, was given permission to live in the offices of the Colonne as of October 1, 1943. It took some time before all the filing cabinets were removed and the place was cleaned, but on October 15, Takkert could move into his nice new house, a house with a history.

—4—

Betrayal

Two stories, both from the spring of 1943. One is from Alida van Amerongen.[1] A Jew in hiding, she was arrested by Colonne members Elmink and Van der Kraal. She was taken to Henneicke's office on Adama van Scheltemaplein. In Room 25 she was brought before Wim Henneicke himself and subjected to an interrogation. "If I gave him the names of twenty Jews in hiding, I'd be set free and I wouldn't have to wear my star anymore," she stated during Elmink's trial in January 1949. She refused and was sent to the Dutch Theater. She survived the war and was later able to testify.

The other story took place in March 1943. The new system, in which arresting Jews was the most important task and bonuses the most important weapon, had just been introduced. Wim Henneicke arrested a Jewish woman on Eemsstraat in South Amsterdam.[2] The woman was a certain Mrs V. Henneicke took care of the job himself. He saw she was not wearing a Star of David at home and took her along to Adama van Scheltemaplein. While questioning her, he was struck by how many addresses of Jews in hiding Mrs V. seemed to know. He was apparently somewhat unsure about how to proceed, because he picked up the phone and called *Untersturmführer* E. Hassel, his most important contact at the *Sicherheitspolizei*. Hassel advised him to let Mrs V. go and try to get as many addresses out of her as possible. This proved to be, from a German standpoint, excellent advice: Henneicke put Mrs V. under massive pressure, and the results were better than he could have expected. Between March 11 and 28, Mrs V. supplied him with the addresses of eighty non-exempt and fugitive Jews. After every tip Henneicke sent one of his teams to the address, and every one of Mrs V.'s tips turned out to be accurate. According to a note on a *Bericht* about this case, all eighty Jews were taken into custody, and thus Mrs V. made a substantial contribution to the Colonne's unprecedented productivity in the month of March, when they tracked down more than 3,100 Jews.

But despite that, Mrs V. was unable to save herself. On April 1 in South Amsterdam she walked straight into the arms of Henneicke's colleague Aaldert

Dassen, who, on the basis of her appearance, decided to check her papers. He could see they were false and wanted to arrest her. She was not wearing a Star of David and was thus guilty of multiple infractions. Mrs V. tried to escape arrest by explaining to Dassen that she was one of Henneicke's contacts and regularly provided him with tips. Dassen was hesitant and called the office on Adama van Scheltemaplein, and got Henneicke on the line. There is no way of knowing exactly what Henneicke said, but the essence of his response can be found in a *Bericht* that bears his signature: "I then replied that it was a shame that she had to be taken in because she was a good V-woman [*V-Frau* = *Vertrauensfrau*, i.e. informer]. Dassen then brought the Jewess to the *Zentralstelle*." That same month Mrs V. would be gassed at Sobibor. Her sacrifice, eighty useful tips, was not enough to save her life.

These are just two examples of many. The Colonne Henneicke owed a great deal of its effectiveness to treachery and anonymous tips. All suspects who were questioned about this after the war made similar statements: Wim Henneicke and Willem Briedé took charge of gathering and processing information. The men were never particularly forthcoming about their tactics, but they plainly had access to substantial funds, which they could use to reward informants. As "business" began to pick up, Henneicke's recordkeeping became sloppier, and at a certain point he had a folder full of scraps of paper in his desk drawer, some of them containing names and addresses of Jews and some of them containing names and phone numbers of informants.[3] Some of his subordinates also maintained private networks, but in the end most of the tips came from the two bosses. It is difficult to get an idea of how many tips reached the Colonne, particularly when one considers that the police received quite a few tips themselves. Indeed, the Bureau of Jewish Affairs was responsible for the arrest of a few thousand Jews.[4] In 1943 Amsterdam was crawling with squealers and snitches, and much of the time bonuses were not even necessary. A Dutch Jew had no one he could trust; you could be betrayed by anyone.

By your sister-in-law, for example, as happened to a Jewish woman on Vrolikstraat.[5] She lived in a second-floor flat with her non-Jewish husband, Brouwer. Living one floor below them was her sister-in-law, who loathed her and had threatened her on multiple occasions. At a certain point the woman was arrested: her sister-in-law had filed charges against her over an alleged dispute over a radio. Mrs Brouwer was released after a short time. There was no proof, nor could she be held on the basis of her race. She was married to a non-Jew and thus exempt from deportation.

But her sister-in-law, Mrs Van der W., refused to let the matter rest. She dreamt up a diabolical ruse: she went to the *Sicherheitsdienst* with the story that her brother, Brouwer, actually had a Jewish father. She claimed their mother had had an affair with a Jewish man after her divorce and that her brother was the product of that relationship. He was therefore, according to German racial laws, a Jew. Consequently, this meant their marriage was not mixed at all; her sister-in-law was married to a Jew, and thus had to be deported. In this way Mrs Van der W. could have gotten both her brother and her sister-in-law sent to Poland in one fell swoop.

But she didn't get her way. Brouwer was held for some time at the offices of the Colonne Henneicke but was eventually released, as there was no evidence to support his sister's story. He returned home to find a substantial portion of his furniture missing; it had been seized ahead of time. But in the end he and his wife survived this sister's machinations and thus the war.

You could also be betrayed by the concierge. That was what happened to the Houthakker family, who were hiding out at an address on Oosteinde in Amsterdam.[6] The Federation of Playground Associations had their offices in the same building, and sometimes, at the end of the workday, Mr Houthakker would go there to use the phone. There was a lot to discuss and many arrangements to be made. He had given all his belongings to acquaintances for safekeeping. His possessions were spread out over a variety of different addresses, in various cities, and the people he had chosen to look after them did not know each other. Nevertheless, in a relatively short span of time, members of the Colonne Henneicke searched all these people's homes and confiscated his belongings. They knew exactly where to go and what to look for. The elderly Mr and Mrs Houthakker were taken from their hiding place by one of the most fanatical members of the Colonne, Henk Klingeberg*. The couple's son-in-law, Professor I. Kisch, refused to take this lying down. He found out that the concierge of the building in question, Ben van W., worked for the Colonne Henneicke as an informant. Kisch was even brash enough to call up Klingeberg, who confirmed it: "Yeah, Ben van W., he works for us." The concierge quickly converted his earnings into liquor, according to Klingeberg's dossier. "On the evening of our arrest," Mr Houthakker wrote in a post-war deposition, "he bragged in a pub that that day he had rid Oosteinde of another Jew." Houthakker's son-in-law, Professor Kisch, himself a survivor of Theresienstadt, reported the betrayal to the police after the war, and wrote to the prosecutors: "As a reward for their betrayal, the Van W. family made off with our food, our clothes, our shoes and so on. Now that we have returned, penniless and ragged, after over two and a half years in various camps, it is infuriating to see people who have enriched themselves through criminal acts walking around with impunity. I'm certain a search of their house would turn up a great deal." After the war the concierge was tried for treason.

It could be your sister-in-law or the concierge or even someone you barely knew. The Van den Berg family, who were hiding out at a place on Amstelveenseweg, were betrayed by a sixteen-year-old girl who happened to know the address. Beppie A. was a maid in the house of Colonne member Frans van Tol. Van Tol was forty-two when he entered into an affair with his sixteen-year-old servant. That led to all kinds of complications and subterfuge, but also to betrayal: Beppie was present one time when her lover was talking with German acquaintances about fugitive Jews, and she spontaneously mentioned the address where the Van den Berg family – and an interesting amount of gold objects – could be found. After the war Beppie admitted to the betrayal herself.[7]

Betrayed by Supposed Saviours

The criminal records of the members of the Colonne Henneicke are teeming with examples of betrayal. They are often unclear, impossible to prove or based on gossip and insinuations. It will always remain one of the most shadowy aspects of the Second World War.

There are a number of cases in which Jews were clearly betrayed by the people on whom they had pinned all their hopes: the men and women who were hiding them. This can be found in black and white in a number of the Colonne's *Berichte*: "*Der Arier hat die Juden selbst gemeldet.*" (The Aryan turned in the Jews himself.) Take the case of the Wegloop family, father Salomon, mother Heintje and children Heyman, 18, Klara, 16, and Abraham, 14.[8] They were taken in by a sailor in Haarlem, not far from Smit's Second-hand Clothing Shop on Lange Raamstraat, where Salomon had worked for many years. On Whit Saturday, June 12, the ragman Smit was picked up at his home. The active Jew hunter Sjef Sweeger took him back to headquarters, his pistol drawn, saying: "Across the street from here are the Jews you've been looking after, and that's why you're going to have to come with me." Sweeger was all the more fanatical since his partner that day was the boss, Wim Henneicke, who was obviously not averse to picking up a little extra money so close to the spring holidays. He immediately confiscated a portion of Smit's money, on the grounds that he had been holding it for the Wegloops, in violation of the LiRo decrees. After that they crossed the street and went to the home of the sailor Van der M., whose wife had turned in the Jews. After the war she would explain that "the Jews were making her life so difficult that she just couldn't take it anymore." Sweeger and Henneicke took the Wegloop family to the Dutch Theater. The *Bericht* subtly indicated how Van der M. managed to get off scot-free: "*Der Arier hat die Juden selbst gemeldet.*"

In the last days of the Colonne Henneicke, on Wednesday, September 22, Sjef Sweeger was party to a similar case of betrayal.[9] On that occasion six people were arrested at once, on Valeriusstraat in Amsterdam, at the home of a certain Mrs M., with whom they had been staying for no less than seven months. One of the six was a boy of fifteen, Lodewijk Gompertz, a student, whose parents and sister had already been sent to Westerbork. No action was taken against Mrs M., it says in the *Bericht*, as she had turned in Lodewijk herself. And not just Lodewijk. She also reported 64-year-old Saliena Vos, Nico Prins (32), his wife Suze Prins-Goel (34), and the Kassel-born Heinz Schulenklapper (20), a student whose parents had already been "*abtransportiert*," according to the *Bericht*. And finally there was 80-year-old Kaatje Gompertz, née Goudsmit, Lodewijk's grandmother. She told her interrogators, Sweeger, Rudolfs and Hintink, that her husband was dead and her two sons (including Lodewijk's father) had already been taken away. Some fl.97.50 was found on her person. Sweeger would later tell the detectives interrogating him that he did not know if they were betrayed: "Those kinds of reports went straight to Henneicke, and he didn't tell us where he got his information from." But a glance at the Colonne's records soon clears things up: "*Die Arierin hat die Juden selbst gemeldet.*"

The "Jew Trap"

It is unclear in such cases whether these were calculated acts, motivated by greed, or whether the methods of the Colonne Henneicke prompted the betrayals. The latter appears to be the case in an unusual incident involving Colonne member Frederik Cool, a fanatical anti-Semite.[10] He was violent, hitting even female detainees in the face, and once, while transporting a number of arrestees, he lifted a Jewish boy into a trolley by his collar. Cool was the central figure in the story of Elfriede Heinemann. In 1945 she wrote a letter detailing her wartime experiences to the public prosecutor in Amsterdam. She was writing from New York, where she had emigrated after surviving the war in hiding. In her letter she made mention of an Amsterdam family who ran a boarding house on Weteringschans, where they offered Jews accommodation with the express intention of turning them over to the Colonne Henneicke, but only after they had paid a substantial amount in advance. According to Elfriede, this happened at least five times at that particular boarding house.

The misfortunes began for Elfriede and her family (her parents and her brother) when they were taken in by a family on Tweede Helmersstraat. They lived in different rooms, on different floors, under new names. They were especially worried because the woman who ran the household turned out to be a rabid anti-Semite. They had nowhere to go, and all they could do was wait for the inevitable. The inevitable came on Thursday, July 22, at 12:30, in the person of Colonne member Frederik Cool. He began to check their papers. The parents' and the brother's identify cards checked out, but Elfriede's did not. She would have to come along "for questioning." Cool showed himself to be a fanatical Nazi; in her letter Elfriede called him a "virulent NSB man and anti-Semite." The next day, Cool came back to the address, examined the papers again and once again they checked out. He freely shared his views with Mr Heinemann: "The Jews should all be exterminated."

At the *Zentralstelle* Elfriede was subject to interrogations and mistreatment, but in the end she escaped from her enemies – for the time being. Along with twenty others she managed to squeeze through a window in the gym on Adama van Scheltemaplein. Sixty detainees were left behind. The next day Elfriede showed up at the home of some friends, who made arrangements for a new hiding place for her and her family: a boarding house at 155 Weteringschans run by the P. family. Immediately after arriving, Mr Heinemann built several hiding places, "which Mr P. was quite pleased with." They were happy to have escaped the danger of an anti-Semitic "safe house." But this sense of relief did not last long.

On August 15, around 1:30 in the afternoon, Elfriede was doing some ironing when she had a terrible fright. Somewhere in the house she heard a voice she knew all too well: Cool's voice. She immediately dropped her ironing and dashed out the door, and once again she was able to escape. This time the situation was reversed. Elfriede got away, while her parents and brother were picked up by Cool, who was accompanied by his colleague Gist. They all went to the Dutch Theater. There they were able to write a note to Elfriede about the circumstances of their arrest, in guarded language. Elfriede read that "there is apparently an extremely lucrative business relationship between the P. family and the SD." Less than a week later Elfriede's mother smuggled out another note to her daughter. She reported that another family, six people in total, had been brought in after staying at the boarding house on Weteringschans. The letter was written in code, so as not to endanger the bearer. "After the people had paid two weeks in advance, the same nice men came the following day and invited them out for a drive."

Elfriede Heinemann would never see her parents again. From New York she explained to the prosecutors in Amsterdam that her father (65) and mother (64) were sent to Westerbork as "penal cases." They arrived at Auschwitz on September 17 and were immediately murdered. She wrote: "If these savage murderers – Cool and P. – had not sold my parents' lives for a pittance, they could have experienced peace, freedom and the wonderful world here in America."

One could hardly disagree with Heinemann's viewpoint. But an examination of Frederik Cool's dossier reveals that the case is a bit more complicated than it might appear on the face of it. Detective Willem Slob tracked down and interrogated P. after the war. P. explained that he actually worked at a warehouse and ran the boarding house on the side. He said he did not charge extortionate rates, just the standard price of five or six guilders a day, and he did not give the names of Jews to the police. P. claimed he was not at home for the first arrest. At midnight he got a visit from a man from the SD. He did not know who it was and did not recognize any of the photographs he was later shown. He thought he was going to be arrested, but instead the stranger proposed that he continue renting rooms to Jews. The man, who claimed to be from the SD (it turned out to be Frederick Cool), gave him his phone number, which he was to call if he had any new guests staying at the boarding house. During interrogation P. said to detective Slob: "I accepted this offer. A few days later four Jewish people came to the boarding house, a young couple and a mother and child, to be exact. I then called the phone number the detective had given me and said I had Jews staying at the house again. That same day detectives from the SD took the aforementioned Jews out of my house. I didn't see them because I wasn't at home at the time. I reported these Jews to the SD because otherwise I would have been arrested myself."

It seems quite likely that P. was not entirely forthcoming about all the cases that took place and was trying to limit his punishment by saying he was not present for the arrests. P. also denied receiving money for his phone calls; fear of arrest was his sole motive. "I feel awful about having to inform on Jews to save myself," he said during the interrogation. Eventually he would find himself before the Special Court on charges of treason. He was sentenced to three years in prison. In her testimony his wife, who gave the guests food and cleaned their rooms, confirmed Cool's role. After his first visit, at night, the bounty hunter had gone into the bedroom, where Mrs P. was already in bed. He had his own way of making it clear to her that a deal had been made: "Now look here, lady, you're just going to go right on renting out your rooms to those Jews." Mrs P. had burst into tears (she said to the court) and cried out, "Never again." But then Cool threatened to send her to a concentration camp, and so the P. family betrayed several more Jewish families to Cool. Their boarding house, said the judge-advocate in the case against P., was a "Jew trap."

The P. affair is particularly useful for our purposes as it sheds light on the Colonne's methods. In theory anyone sheltering a fugitive Jew was liable to punishment, but it was relatively rare for such people to be actually arrested. One way they could save themselves was by cooperating with the Colonne, by providing information, as P. did. Often the *Berichte* report that the people sheltering the Jews were unaware their lodgers were in fact Jewish. That could indicate that they were given an offer to cooperate. But often this sentence was included in the reports to cut down on paperwork: the members of the Colonne seemed to have little interest in arresting the Jews' protectors. In their trials they often tried to use this to their advantage, as proof of their human side. But it is more likely they let the Aryans go because there was no price on their heads and thus nothing to be earned from them. This was against Henneicke's wishes however: the boss wanted anyone found to be harboring Jews arrested and turned over to the SD. Except, of course, if the person was prepared to inform on more Jews; in that case Henneicke was always willing to talk.

We have already seen examples of Jews who broke under pressure. Henneicke extracted eighty names and addresses from Mrs V., who was seen out without a star, and when she was caught again later, she was sent to a concentration camp herself. An even more disturbing example comes from the Colonne's counterpart within the municipal police force, the Bureau of Jewish Affairs. The thirty-seven-year-old Jewish shop assistant Ans van Dijk was able to escape deportation in 1943 by informing on other Jews.[11] She found herself trapped in a vicious circle of fear and treachery and would become the most "successful" *V-Frau* in the whole history of the war. She betrayed at least 100 Jews, maybe more. She was ultimately sentenced to death; her request for clemency was denied. On January 14, 1948 she was executed, the only woman to receive the ultimate punishment. In the view of L. de Jong, the treatment of Ans van Dijk stands in stark contrast to that of a large number of Jew hunters who managed to escape with their lives.[12]

In the files of the members of the Colonne, one can find other cases in this category, but they are few in number and extremely complex. Henneicke himself left behind papers from which it can be gathered that he enlisted various Jews to work as informants. In an interrogation, leading Colonne member Bob Verlugt claimed that one Jew would turn in another in order to get rid of a competitor for a certain job. This seems rather unlikely. And Henk van den Heuvel, a member of the Colonne who also worked at the Dutch Theater, shed crocodile tears in his interrogation, outraged at such wickedness: "The [degree of] betrayal among the Jews was appalling, both inside and outside the theater. Dozens of addresses . . . were disclosed to me. I never made use of them, because squealing is horrible and degrading."[13] The words of Henk van den Heuvel, the same man, it would later transpire over the course of his trial, who bought his house on Nicolaas Maesstraat for a song after its Jewish owner had been deported.

His colleague Van der Kraal made quite a few arrests in September 1943 thanks to his regular informant, Mrs D.[14] It is a sad story. She herself was not Jewish, but her husband was. He was arrested in Rhenen, in the province of Utrecht. Since he was married to a non-Jew, he was not subject to deportation, but he was also sheltering his mother and had procured false papers for her. That was a criminal offense, and it was for that reason that he was taken to the Dutch Theater on August 31. His wife was willing to do anything to get him released, and she contacted Van der Kraal, who lived two houses away, on Waalstraat in South Amsterdam. Van der Kraal had a proposal for her: if Mrs D. supplied him with the addresses of fugitive Jews, he would try to do something for her husband. Among the *Berichte* are five cases of forced betrayal by Mrs D. On one occasion Mrs D. even turned in a Jewish family who had been staying with her; she had had them pay fl.125 in advance. But none of this helped in the end. Van der Kraal left her hanging, and despite her useful tips she would never see her husband again. Before the Special Court, Van der Kraal vociferously denied ever having received any tips from his neighbor. But this former policeman, who was briefly a member of the Social Democratic Party before joining the NSB, should not be taken at his word. He had previously been fired from the police department for buying a bag of coal without a ration card. He was going to ticket the seller for violating the pricing regulations, but he was prepared to look the other way if he could have the coal for fl.2.50. The coal seller consented but then reported him to the commissioner, and

Van der Kraal was given the sack. The only place he could find work was the *Hausraterfassung*, where he would soon grow into a dedicated subordinate of Henneicke's. And his police experience came in handy, as Van der Kraal had a growing network of informers, mostly people who were themselves under threat of deportation. It was with good reason that prosecutor N. Bakhoven would say the following about him to the Court of Appeals: "In my view one of the worst things about this defendant is that he repeatedly tried to exploit arrested Jews' fear to compel them to reveal the hiding places of other Jews so he could arrest still more Jews."[15]

Every conceivable method was used to extract information from the arrestees. Sometimes the threat of deportation was sufficient. But if that didn't work, the members of the Colonne used violence. There are not many statements about this in the dossiers, because in virtually every case the people who were assaulted did not survive the war. It seems they were given priority when it came time to be deported. In some instances there is testimony from third parties. Poul Keizer, for example, a Jewish furniture maker who worked for the Jewish Council and could often be found at the Colonne's offices, once saw Hintink and Henneicke roughing up a Jewish prisoner together. Blood was pouring out of the man's nose and mouth. He later heard Henneicke say that "they had shown the Jew his place."[16]

Another story concerns Adolf Smit*, a fifty-three-year-old former welfare inspector, who had just celebrated his silver wedding anniversary when he joined the Colonne in 1942.[17] He arrested a Mr Sealtiel and his son in early June 1943. The son's name was Rafael; he was fifteen. When he asked to go to the toilet, Smit snapped at him, "Don't run away or you'll get shot." Smit took the father to a separate room on Adama van Scheltemaplein, known among the Jewish detainees as "the torture chamber." Smit was looking for Rafael's brother, who had been able to escape arrest. They would "beat [his hiding place] out of his father," they told the son. And they meant this quite literally; Rafael could hear his father's screams. The next day father and son were taken to Plantage Middenlaan, the father to the Dutch Theater, the son to the nursery across the street. He was allowed to visit his father for two hours every day. One day the fifteen-year-old succeeded in escaping while crossing the street. He survived the war, but he never saw his father again.

Even more violence: this time it was the handiwork of Engelbert Koops*, a forty-seven-year old former waiter, who began working for the *Hausraterfassung* in October 1942 and had been a prominent member of the Colonne since March 1943. One of his cronies said during questioning that Koops's specialty was "so-called street cases" – that is, arresting people with a more or less Jewish appearance on the street.[18] Mr and Mrs Sanders must have been just such a case. At the time of his arrest, David was forty-one, as was his wife, Clara Sanders-Keizer. They were staying on Eerste Helmersstraat, with a certain widow Esser. They were arrested in late August 1943 when David was in a restaurant, waiting for his wife, who suffered from asthma and was with a physiotherapist. They had to come along to Henneicke's office on Noorder Amstellaan, where Koops demanded to know where their children were. They had three, and they were hiding out at various addresses. Marie (8) and Elbert (4) were somewhere in Sliedrecht in South Holland, while the ten-year-old Eline was staying with a farmer in the village of Barchem, in the province of Gelderland. Koops wanted to know the addresses, but David Sanders refused to reveal them. It must have been a hellish situation: first to have to decide to send your three children into hiding and then to endure an interrogation in which you were forced to divulge their location. Sanders' determination was put to the ultimate test. Eventually Koops turned violent, and when that failed to get him the information he wanted, he became downright brutal. He literally knocked all the teeth out of Sanders' mouth. This had the desired effect: David Sanders gave him the addresses of his three children.

The next day Koops went off to find the two youngest, Marie and Elbert. At that point he did not know he was on his way to a rather special hiding place: 70 Hugo de Grootstraat, Sliedrecht, the home of Johan Hollebrands, a detective with the state police.[19] It is thanks to him that we now know the exact course of events. Hollebrands began taking statements from witnesses immediately after the war and used this information to write a crystal-clear report on the incident. From this we know that Koops went to the police station in Sliedrecht, where he picked up a certain officer Verhoeven to assist him. Verhoeven was not told what they were going to do, so he could not take steps to warn his colleague Hollebrands' family.

It was Friday, August 27, 1943, 2:30 in the afternoon. Hollebrands himself was not at home when the two rang the bell. But his niece, Sietske Schuyt, who *was* at home, looked out the window and saw there was trouble afoot. Mrs Hollebrands quickly lay down on the divan under a flannel blanket and pretended to be sick. Koops and Verhoeven had already accosted the two small children playing outside and they brought them in with them. "These are Jewish children," said Koops, "and you know it." Mrs Hollebrands denied this ("They are guests, children of friends") but was unable to keep up this fiction for long. Koops had the parents' identity cards in his hand: "These are their parents, aren't they?" Mrs Hollebrands no longer dared to deny it, because the children would never be able to keep that to themselves. Koops said the parents had been arrested and lied that the mother had revealed where their children were staying.

All four of them would have to come along. Mrs Hollebrands continued to feign illness, and after some time she managed to talk her way out of having to go. The niece did have to go, at least as far as Sliedrecht Station. Mrs Hollebrands had to pack a suitcase full of clothes, and she would later remember that she did this "with a heavy heart. We had had the little ones with us for over a year, and I was very attached to them. With big, frightened eyes Marie stood by as I packed the suitcase, and she asked me if the man was from the NSB and if it was true that she and her brother would have to go with them. I reassured her and said she would be taken to her parents. The pity of it all just broke my heart because I understood what the children were in for."

She waved good-bye to them. The niece, Sietske Schuyt, had to carry the suitcase and buy the train tickets at the station. After that she was let go. They departed on the 15:13 train (right on time), Engelbert Koops and his two young charges, Marie and Elbert Sanders, like a father on a day out with his children. We will meet Koops again, in the context of Colonne members who were never punished for their crimes. In late 1943 he settled in Germany and hid out there after the war, first just over the border in Meppen, later in Wuppertal, where he died in 1956, without ever having spent a single day in prison.

This was certainly through no fault of detective Hollebrands. Right after the children were taken, he started investigating the matter personally. He spent Saturday, August 28, through Tuesday, August 31, looking for the children – it *was* his job, after all. With the help of a "German Jewess working in Amsterdam" (as he put it in his report), he succeeded in getting through "the electric doors" of the Dutch Theater. There he met David and Clara Sanders, the parents of the children he had been looking after. He heard the whole story, their arrest, the interrogation, David's beating by Koops. He wrote: "According to his statement Sanders was badly assaulted, in an effort to make him reveal the addresses where his children were staying. In addition to other injuries he suffered, he had all his teeth knocked out of his mouth, which I was able to see for myself. In the end he gave in and told them what they wanted to hear."

Hollebrands also found the children, in the Jewish nursery across the street, which he also managed to enter. Eight-year-old Marie and four-year-old Elbert had been reunited with ten-year-old Eline. Hollebrands learned how Eline was arrested. It was also the work of members of the Colonne: Johan Keuling and Lambert Schipper, the former acolyte from Limburg. They made a regular field trip out of it. They first took the train to Lochem, and after that it was a two-hour walk to the hamlet of Barchem where little Eline had been taken in by farmer Johan Eggink and his family. When Schipper and Keuling got there, they started carrying on like savages, threatening the family with everything in the book. Eggink said they were mistaken and the girl was actually Dutch Reformed, but they weren't buying that. "You have a Jewish girl staying here, and that's a capital offense," they told Mrs Eggink. She had to tell the girl that she would be taken to Amsterdam, to her mother.

Gradually Schipper and Keuling calmed down a bit. There was evidently a strategic reason for this. The two actually had the nerve to ask the Egginks if they could spend the night at the farm, in view of the long journey. The Egginks let them stay, and not just that: the following day Schipper and Keuling were spared the long walk back to Lochem station. Mrs Eggink brought the two men and little Eline there in a horse and buggy.

Thus Hollebrands found the three Sanders children together when he visited the nursery. In his report he noted: "The suitcase with Marie and Elbert's clothing had already been stolen, while Elbert, who was in poor health, was delirious with fever." Hollebrands did his best to save the Sanders family from their fate, even enlisting the help of the Low German Reformed Church – the family were so-called "Christian Jews" – but because they had already been classified as "penal cases," there was nothing to be done. The detective from Sliedrecht tried to get some money together to buy the family's freedom, but in vain.

On Sunday, September 5, there was a glimmer of hope: David Sanders, his wife Clara and two of the three children escaped from the Dutch Theater, but they were caught again a few hours later. There was no saving them now. Hollebrands concluded his report with an official-sounding sentence, behind which he could conceal his anger: "One can reasonably assume that the whole Sanders family was killed through the actions of the occupier." Information from the Red Cross would later confirm that this was indeed the case.

–5–

The Money

In addition to the bonus of fl.7.50 per Jew (and even more later on), the Colonne Henneicke offered its employees an especially attractive salary. All the employment contracts with Lippmann, Rosenthal & Co. have survived, and they show monthly salaries ranging from fl.200 to fl.270. Employees with families also received a children's allowance. When you factor in inflation, an average monthly salary of fl.230 was not a bad living. Of course, the standard of living in 1943 was on a completely different level from today. Luxury goods, if they even existed, were rare, and that meant the members of the Colonne could manage reasonably well on their basic salaries. In the autumn of 1943, when Gerrit Mijnsma* went to work for the National Labour Front after his stint with Henneicke, he was paid fl.140 a month – a forty percent decrease.[1] For most of the men, working for the Colonne was a downright financial boon. Henk Hopman* first worked for the National Post Office Savings and Loans for fl.22.50 a week, then at a pawnbroker's shop for fl.45 a week. Following that, he found work as an job counsellor with the Employment Office for fl.28 a week, and after that he was hired by a firm in IJmuiden, once again for fl.45 a week. Then the Employment Office drew his attention to an opening at the *Hausraterfassung* for fl.65. It is no wonder Hopman jumped at the chance.[2] And there are even more dramatic increases. During the war Chris van den Borch*, a fairly well-educated insurance broker, worked for the Haarlem Air Raid Defense for fl.24 a week. This was still considerably more than he was getting when he was unemployed, having been fired by his former employer, an insurance company, on account of his fanatical National Socialist views. At that point he was receiving fl.16 a week in welfare.[3] But even that was more than what bankrupt taxi driver Nico Evertsen received in public assistance: fl.13 a week.

During this period Jacob Gist barely had enough to eat. His girlfriend, with whom he was living, could sometimes eat at her mother's, but the latter refused to let Gist in her home. Consequently, he would sometimes go for weeks without a warm meal. We know this from a letter from Gist's mother to the Special Court.[4]

For men like Evertsen and Gist, the Colonne Henneicke was a goldmine. Their lifestyle changed practically overnight. After six years of unemployment Pieter van Amersfoort* found himself earning fl.250 a month as a member of the Colonne. When questioned, his downstairs neighbor said: "They seemed to be doing all right. They never had to go without, and they ate well too."[5] And the employees of the Jewish Council, who often ran into members of the Colonne, particularly at the Dutch Theater, also noticed their growing prosperity. Maurits Allegro was able to observe a couple of Jew hunters from close by. "Every day I saw them smoking expensive cigarettes," he told detectives Prasing and Verduin after the war, "and everything about their lifestyle suggested they were rolling in money."[6]

Was this attributable to their salaries or the bonuses? On the basis of the trials of dozens of suspected Colonne members in 1948 and 1949, one could easily conclude that bonuses were never part of the equation. Every member of the Colonne, without exception, denied ever collecting a bonus. Nothing but lies and gossip – that was their unanimous verdict. As a result, the prosecution ultimately ceased pursuing the matter. Strangely enough, the issue of bonuses almost never came up in the trials. The suspects disavowed any knowledge of bonuses, and the evidence in individual cases was exceptionally scarce. For that reason the prosecution elected not to delay the trials by attempting to prove the existence of an incentive system.[7]

There was an additional reason for this, which was connected to the events of March 24, 1946.[8] That Thursday, in the Special Courthouse on Herengracht in Amsterdam, three men were tried on charges of arresting helpless Jews and turning them over to the Germans. The three men were friends, who worked together in the card catalogue at the *Zentralstelle für jüdische Auswanderung* in the summer of 1943, where the records of the deportations were updated with meticulous care. But they found themselves with a lot of free time on their hands, and so they asked the heads of the *Zentralstelle* for permission to go out and arrest Jews as overtime work, just like their colleagues in the Colonne Henneicke. They also asked their superiors if there was any chance of receiving compensation for such work. Eventually they were given the green light: they could look forward to a bonus of fl.5 per Jew (now about $32). Over the course of the trial, it became clear they had brought between 200 and 300 Jews to the Dutch Theater. For the prosecution it was an open and shut case. The three men were not only in the courtroom as defendants but also as sworn witnesses for the state. Their statements were thus legal evidence. For that reason judge-advocate Gelinck demanded the death penalty at the close of the session. Two weeks later the President of the Court, E. van Schaeck Mathon, complied with Gelinck's demand and handed down three death sentences. On appeal, the youngest of the three, a former barber who was known to have helped some Jews, had his sentence commuted to life imprisonment. The other two were executed in March 1947.

In the thin newspapers of the post-war years the case was given a significant amount of coverage. "Vile overtime" read a headline in *De Volkskrant*. And *Trouw* quoted the president of the court as saying he "felt physically ill" when he examined the facts of the case.[9] It is safe to assume that a number of people in the country's penal camps and prisons had a similar feeling when they learned of the verdicts. From that moment on, the dozens of men who had hunted Jews for profit, and who were then awaiting their trials, knew that they were facing a possible death sentence for their crimes. The Netherlands of 1946, which was gradually beginning to realize that eighty percent of the Jewish population had been exterminated, would have no pity for those who earned money from this monstrous enterprise. The media hype worked well. From then on not a single suspect admitted to receiving bonuses for arresting Jews. The question came up time and again in hundreds of interrogations, but it was always met with a denial – the files on the members of the Colonne Henneicke are full of them.

It was to the suspects' advantage that there was no persuasive evidence on paper. When a portion of the records of the *Hausraterfassung* turned up in late 1947 in the Main Synagogue on Tulpstraat, it was evident that premiums had been paid. There were receipts showing this, but the name on the receipts was that of Wim Henneicke, who signed for delivery. There is no longer any way of proving that he paid out the money, in whole or in part, to his subordinates, though this does not make the receipts any less shocking. A few of them have survived. There is, for example, one for the sum of fl.37.50, five times fl.7.50.[10] On March 17, the date on the receipt, five Jews were brought in. It is not easy to decipher the florid handwriting on the form, which was evidently filled in with great care, in German, but the five people in question were members of the Roos family: father (47), mother (45) and three children (17, 14 and 11). *SS-Hauptsturmführer* Ferdinand Aus der Fünten put his initials under the words "*richtig übernommen*" – indicating that the five were "duly received." There is also the word *festgestellt* ("confirmed"), followed by the signature of a certain Frank, *Polizeisekretär*, apparently a sort of official overseer, and a stamp, "*Sachlich richtig*" ("factually correct"), in case a future visitor to the archives had any doubts as to its authenticity. At the bottom of the form is an *Empfangsbescheinigung* (notice of receipt), which reads: "From the cashier of the chief of the *Sicherheitspolizei*, Amsterdam precinct, I have received 37.50 guilders. This amount has been paid from Jewish capital as an advance." And finally, below that, the practically indecipherable signature of the man who received the money: W. Henneicke.

This is clear-cut evidence that money *was* paid, but then the trail runs cold. There is no trace of the money Henneicke paid his subordinates. The only time anyone brought up the prosecution's shaky position on this issue was in the trial of Bob Verlugt. Verlugt's attorney B. Perridon put the blame squarely on the shoulders of Colonne commander Henneicke and advanced the theory that he did not let his inferiors share in the takings but kept everything for himself, after deducting the costs of tips and paying off a number of high-ranking Germans. Perridon contended: "Personally I believe he was in league with a senior German official, which would explain why so many people were arrested by the Colonne. I also believe he paid a certain amount [of the money] to informants, as he could not do without those people. However there was no reason whatsoever for him to give his subordinates, people like this defendant, additional remuneration. They only had to do what they were told."[11]

Indeed it is nearly impossible for the prosecution to find evidence of cash payments from Henneicke to his subordinates. The one side, the dozens of suspects, categorically denied this ever happened; the other side, Wim Henneicke himself, could no longer tell his side of the story. He had been eliminated by the Amsterdam resistance on December 8, 1944.

In 1948 the prosecutor's office soon had a good reason to let the matter of bonuses drop. Even without evidence of bonuses, defendants were being given the death sentence.[12] Turning over large numbers of defenseless Jews to their mortal enemies, as the charge read in many cases, was sufficient justification for the ultimate punishment in the eyes of the Special Court.

But the question remains: is there enough evidence outside the courtroom to prove that the members of Colonne Henneicke received money for every Jew they brought to the Dutch Theater? In their summary report "Investigation into the methods of the Colonne Henneicke of the *Zentralstelle für jüdische Auswanderung*," detectives Prasing and Verduin included statements on the subject from a whole series of witnesses. Employees of the Jewish Council, who were often in close proximity to members of the Colonne in their capacity as guards, firemen or couriers, were particularly definite in their views. A random sample follows, starting with Jacob Brand: "Among the personnel of the Jewish Council it was common knowledge that the staff of the Colonne Henneicke received a premium for every Jewish person they took into custody. I even heard it said that higher premiums were paid for sick and handicapped Jewish refugees."[13] Brand went on to say that he saw members of the Colonne settling up with one another in the cafeteria of the Dutch Theater on numerous occasions.

Salomon van Thijn often heard them talking about it as well: "I also heard them say that when there were fewer Jewish people coming in, the bonuses were higher." Butcher Abraham Pach also heard about it a number of times; according to him the premiums varied from fl.5 to fl.15. Samson Koopman heard the same thing, second hand, from a guard called Veldhuijsen. The latter was tracked down by detectives, and he told them about a fight he once had with an official from the *Zentralstelle*. In his anger he reproached him for earning money from arrests, and that outburst almost cost Veldhuijsen dearly. Briedé bawled him out, and Veldhuijsen only narrowly escaped arrest himself.

Then there was Machiel Gobets, an accountant who worked for the Jewish Council. He too had heard that the rate was fl.7.50, and twice that for a so-called "penal case." Gobets said in a police interview: "They would create these penal cases themselves, by going through the garbage of Jewish people they had arrested, to see if they could find any fruit peels. Jews were forbidden to eat fruit, you see. They would also check the bookshelves for banned books. They talked about all this amongst themselves, and that was how I came to hear about it."

In 1943 Mozes Jacobs, another employee of the Jewish Council, worked as a doorkeeper at the Dutch Theater. It was obvious that money was being earned from the arrests, he said. Why else would the members of the Colonne always have the German officer on duty sign a paper with names on it? Jacobs once overheard four members of the Colonne talking about the fl.60 they had earned that night, fl.15 per man. Jacobs repeated this statement later in his testimony at the trial of Hintink and Rudolfs (the two brothers-in-law): "They said that after earning sixty guilders they could spare five cents for a cup of coffee."[14] And what is more, his colleague Jacques van der Kar, who also worked for the Jewish Council, happened to catch a glimpse of the payroll, which showed that some members of the Colonne were being paid as much as fl.200 a week.

These statements are certainly persuasive, in part due to the sheer number of them. But there is also room for doubt. Without exception these were people who must have been deeply scarred by the consequences of things that had gone on under their very noses. But there is other, more crucial testimony on the subject, from the pro-German side. Henk Klijn for example, the office manager at the *Einsatzstab Rosenberg*, was near the heart of the action during the war. Henneicke would give him the addresses of houses that had been vacated by their Jewish occupants, and Klijn would then send his men there to take away the furniture. He knew about the bonuses "because I heard members of Henneicke's staff speak about them amongst themselves on several occasions. It was common knowledge." And even the Colonne's major competitor said something similar on the subject. On March 11, 1948 Prasing and Verduin found themselves sitting across the table from Abraham Kaper, the station sergeant at the Bureau of Jewish Affairs. He had done his share of Jew hunting, just like Henneicke, and could thus be considered an insider: "I was aware that an incentive scheme had been set up for this Colonne, by which I mean they were given a bonus for every Jewish person they arrested. Initially this bonus was approximately seven guilders fifty, but it was later increased to forty guilders per person. I know this not only from Kempin but from Henneicke himself." Kempin was Kaper's German boss at the Bureau of Jewish Affairs.

Kaper became a bit more exact when he testified in the trial of the brothers-in-law Hintink and Rudolfs. Under oath Kaper, who would himself later be executed, stated: "The head of this group, Henneicke, told me there was an incentive scheme, whereby a certain amount was paid out for every Jew, whether arrested by a member of his Colonne or on the basis of a tip provided by one of his men. I personally saw Henneicke pick up the money at the cashier's desk." Kaper added that Henneicke used the same receipt forms for his bookkeeping as the ones that were in circulation in his own office. "At the Bureau of Jewish Affairs the rule was that the person who provided the tip or made the arrest received part of the premium. I surmise that Henneicke employed a similar system for his Colonne."[15]

And then there is also a statement from a police officer who was on the inside: Karel Weeling, one of the "good" policemen who had been assigned to the *Zentralstelle* in 1943 as monitor/spy. In 1948 he told his colleagues Prasing and Verduin what he knew about the premiums: "It was common knowledge that the staff of the Colonne Henneicke received a bonus for every Jewish person they brought to the *Zentralstelle*." Weeling was "present several times when Henneicke paid his personnel. This was always at the end of the month. I saw that the personnel then had to sign a number of receipts. I believe there were three in total. In any case there were more than one. At that same time I also saw Henneicke paying out sums varying from 300 to 450 guilders per person. In my opinion these sums were much higher than their salaries."[16]

If Weeling is right – and in theory any policeman making a sworn statement can be relied on to tell the truth – the men were receiving between $1,850 and $2,790 in today's money. It might be an explanation for the unremitting zeal of the leading members of the Colonne, some of whom were accustomed to receiving only fl.15 a week in welfare when they first went to work for the *Hausraterfassung*.

We are now getting closer and closer to the heart of the matter, the suspects themselves. As has already been said, all of them denied the existence of an incentive scheme, but every so often cracks would show up in their stories. Take Joop Bouman*, for example. In his police interrogation he said he knew that the Germans paid fl.2.50 for every Jew turned in.[17] That seems like an extraordinary confession, but Bouman hastened to add, as if he was shocked by his own words, that he never received any of that money himself and could not speak for his colleagues. Yet a remarkable clue about the payment of premiums came out in his trial, in the testimony of Bouman's ex-wife, Riki. She divorced him after the liberation. Perhaps that makes her somewhat less trustworthy, all the more so as there are indications that the break-up was anything but amicable. Even so, her statements seem credible, and she *was* speaking under oath: "When I got married to him, he wasn't earning enough to provide for us. He then got a job with the *Hausraterfassung*, where he earned sixty guilders instead of nineteen, which had previously been the case. At a certain point he started arresting Jews, and all of a sudden he went from making 60 guilders a week to making 150. I told him to stop doing that work, but I couldn't talk him out of it. He said he was forced to arrest

Jews, but he said a lot of things. He was very pro-German, and he told me terrible stories about the Jews who were picked up."[18]

Riki Bouman had said similar things before, in a police interrogation. The amounts she mentioned to the detectives were slightly different. According to her then, his weekly income had jumped from fl.65 to fl.165: "My husband had a lot of money at the time, but I don't know how much he was paid in total."

The tension between the two of them peaked in 1943 when Joop, in Riki's presence, offered another couple fl.5 for any tip that led to the arrest of a Jew. For Riki this was the last straw. She wanted out of the marriage and took her things to her parents for safekeeping, she told the detectives questioning her. The investigators tried to find out whether Riki was telling the truth or making up stories out of spite. They tracked down the acquaintances who had been offered fl.5 per tip. The woman in question was one Beppie Nouwen-Van Hommert. It turned out she had been witness to an unadulterated marital row. According to Mrs Nouwen, Riki Bouman called her husband "a traitor and a filthy pig." And she confirmed the offer made by Joop Bouman: "We've got to get rid of those Jewish scum. I'll give you five guilders for every Jew you can bring me."[19] All of which strongly suggests that even though emotions were running high, Riki Bouman was being honest with the police and the court.

Anyone who needs more proof that premiums were being paid need look no further than the trial of Martin Hintink, on September 24, 1948. One of the witnesses for the prosecution was Mozes Jacobs, a businessman who worked for the Jewish Council as a doorkeeper at the Dutch Theater in 1942–3. Jacobs ultimately ended up in Westerbork, but he was never deported. He was among the few who were there to witness the liberation of the camp by the Canadians in April 1945. Because Amsterdam had not yet been liberated, he had to remain at Camp Westerbork for some time, along with many others. As early as the beginning of May, the first political delinquents – people who were suspected of helping the Germans during the occupation – began arriving at the camp. Mozes Jacobs told the court about how he had run into Martin Hintink at Camp Westerbork; in the chaos of 1945 perpetrators and victims wound up behind the same barbed wire. The meeting took place on May 7, Jacobs remembered. "I saw that he was standing apart from the others, and I saw and heard four Jews yelling and gesticulating at the defendant. I then called out to the defendant, 'You got seven guilders fifty in bonus money for every Jew you brought in.'"[20] Hintink, Jacobs recalled, admitted it. The furious victims around him accused Hintink of having worked for the SD. Jacobs to the court: "The defendant denied this and said he had been with the Colonne Henneicke. After the defendant admitted receiving seven guilders fifty for turning in Jews, I saw the military police strike the defendant with a truncheon about twenty times, after which the Jews also laid into the defendant."

It is a surreal tableau: the victims forcing the perpetrator to confess and venting their rage on him with the support of the military police – the same MPs, incidentally, who had served as guards at Westerbork when it was still a concentration camp. Jacobs' testimony was corroborated by a number of other witnesses. There on the heath of Westerbork, on May 7, 1945, Roosje Schrijver had also run over to see what all the commotion was about. She recognized Hintink as the man who had arrested her neighbors, the Kleins. And there was another witness: Jacob Barend, a businessman. Hintink arrested his mother-in-law, even though she had just been discharged from the hospital and was recovering from an operation. "She had to go along, despite my appeals and my wife's pleas," Barend wrote in his deposition. "We saw and recognized each other here at Westerbork."[21]

Finally, the businessman L. Benninga was also present for the confrontation at Westerbork. This was not his first run-in with Hintink. On August 24, 1943 Benninga and his wife Catharina Nopol heard that Catharina's younger sister, Sophie Nopol, had been arrested on Amstelveenseweg in Amsterdam. Fearing they would be next, they left the city and went to stay with acquaintances in Tilburg, but two days later, August 26, 1943, they were arrested there by Hintink and his inseparable partner and brother-in-law Rudolfs. Everything was confiscated, even a nail file. At the time Hintink said, "I'm sure you're a nice Jew, but a person can do funny things with a nail file." When Hintink heard the name Nopol, he boasted to Catharina Nopol, "Two days ago I arrested your little sister." The girl had torn up a letter and thrown it away, but Hintink had picked up the scraps of paper and glued them together and was thus able to reconstruct the address 145 Oosterwijksebaan, Tilburg. He then went to Tilburg, to the home of the Wesselius family, to arrest the Benningas. Hintink had glowed with self-satisfaction.

They got to talking, and in the course of the conversation Hintink offered his thoughts on his own position: "If Germany loses, we've already got one foot in the grave." They drove back to Amsterdam together. Benninga's wife Catharina never came back, but Benninga did. He was actually never deported from Westerbork. There on the heath, after the liberation, he came face to face with Hintink, the man he held responsible for the death of his wife. Benninga said in his testimony: "Hintink then said, in the presence of myself and Jacobs, that he received seven guilders fifty for every Jew he arrested. After this statement the defendant was beaten up. Hintink also needed a couple of good punches to come round again."[22]

That same day, May 7, 1945, Benninga wrote an official statement in English for the benefit of the Canadian authorities, who were in charge of tracking down war criminals. The letter is in Hintink's dossier. Benninga wrote: "It was here (Westerbork) I recognized Hintink and when he told me that for every jew he did arrest and deliver to the Jewish Theater he collected zeven gulden vijftig (seven guilders and a half) from the *Zentralstelle fur Judische Auswanderung*."[23] There was thus evidence on the table as early as May 7, 1945.

And not just from victims: Hintink himself wrote a statement at Westerbork on May 7. The paper is included in his criminal record. In the document he described his less than heroic exploits during the war. It is unmistakably his handwriting; there are other letters in the dossier in that same careful, elegant script. Hintink, who had been a traveling salesmen in shaving supplies (for Gillette) before the war, noted: "In addition, from March 1943 through September 1943, I received a bonus based on the number of people brought in by me and my colleagues. After a few months I realized I was doing this work for the *Sicherheitsdienst*."[24] He emphasized in this statement that he did the work against his will and that resigning was not a possibility, nor was stopping. "I hereby declare that I did not join [the Colonne] for the purpose of arresting Jews but rather because I was forced to do this work." There, at Camp Westerbork, he also added: "I declare that this report is true and that I have written it and read it over."

There was a certain consistency to Hintink's behavior, at least initially. Thus on July 23, during an interrogation by detective Schouten of the POD, he confessed to having hunted Jews: "I participated in the arrest of Jews, for which a bonus was paid of seven guilders fifty per Jew. It was only later I discovered that I was doing work for the *Sicherheitsdienst*."[25]

Six months later Hintink repeated his confession once again, this time in the city where he had arrested hundreds of Jews, Amsterdam. Police Sergeant Evert Jan Mensink (55) testified about this in court: "I interrogated the suspect Hintink on January 28, 1946. During this interrogation the suspect stated that he received a bonus of seven guilders fifty on top of his salary for every Jew he brought in."

The original transcript of this interrogation can also be found in Hintink's police record, typed on the back of an arrest report. Hintink made his confession more or less in passing, among a number of other factual statements. His exact words were: "I earned 220 or 230 guilders a month there. I also got a bonus of seven guilders fifty a month for every Jew brought in. This was introduced in 1943."[26]

But by the time of the trial (September 24, 1948) things had changed. In the two years leading up to that time, Hintink had sworn that he had never received any bonuses for arresting Jews. His former mates from the Colonne – they sometimes bumped into one another in the camps – must have demanded that he retract his statement; there is scarcely any other explanation. Hintink's words could mean the firing squad for all of them. So Hintink had to find a way to worm his way out of this predicament. In court he said, "I stated to Mensink that a bonus of seven guilders fifty was given for every Jew brought in. I said this because the witness was in possession of a transcript of a statement I had made in Westerbork under or after intense physical pressure. When [Mensink] interviewed me, I was in a deplorable state." Mensink categorically denied this in court: "The defendant made a statement to me in complete freedom, without any pressure. I don't remember Hintink being in a deplorable state, though the guards did tell me that he was aggressive."[27]

After disavowing his earlier confessions, Hintink explained to the court that while he did occasionally receive overtime, it was never anywhere near fl.200 a month. He tried to tell a detective that "the statement in Westerbork was dictated to me by an English soldier, who interrogated me with the help of the Jews who were still in the camp."

His previous confession may have lacked evidentiary value for the Special Court – though this didn't stop them from giving him the death sentence – but for anyone genuinely interested in knowing whether Hintink collected bonuses, the matter should be quite clear by now, even without a statement Hintink's wife made at Camp Westerbork. She was interned in the women's barracks as a former member of the NSB. Jannetje Hintink-Rudolfs said quite openly to the detectives questioning her: "In the time he was with Lippmann-Rosenthal, he would be called up for work in the evening and sent out to arrest Jews. In addition to his salary of 230 guilders a month, he received a bonus of seven guilders fifty for every Jew he brought in. He was responsible for checking [the papers of] Jews during the day as well."[28]

And thus, in Westerbork of all places, Mr and Mrs Hintink provided more than enough evidence that the members of the Colonne received a premium of fl.7.50 per Jew, equivalent to $48 in today's money, a fact that went largely unmentioned in the men's trials.

It is on the basis of this chain of clues and evidence that at a certain point detective Wijnand Prasing ventured to make an unambiguous pronouncement on the subject of the bonuses, under oath. He had been called to testify before the Court of Appeals in the case of Ben Eggink, a musician who was among the most active of the Jew hunters. By now we are well into 1950, and this session would be one of the very last devoted to the Colonne Henneicke.[29] When asked, Prasing answered plainly, "There were also bonuses paid for turning in Jews. However it was no longer possible to determine what amounts were paid to each individual." At which point the president of the Special Court of Appeals asked the defendant how much he received in bonuses. Eggink answered, "The bonus system didn't apply to me." To which detective Prasing said, under oath: "The defendant did receive bonuses. The rule was seven guilders fifty per Jew."

Additional Earnings

There were other ways of making money for the members of Briedé and Henneicke's club; this is clear from various other fragments in the dossiers. To stay within the same family, in one of his interrogations Jan Rudolfs made much of the Colonne's overtime payments. There were others who mentioned the possibility of earning a little extra by working overtime, but Rudolfs was the clearest about this. He denied ever having received premiums – Hintink's none-too-bright brother-in-law had obviously had that drummed into him. When questioned, he said: "We did not get money for every Jew we picked up, though Henneicke did pay us for any overtime we worked. He paid us overtime once a month. Sometimes we would get 100 guilders, sometimes 200, depending on how much overtime we had worked. Normally we worked an eight hour day."[30]

Overtime of fl.200 a month: in 1943 that was more than an average monthly income, much more for most. The overtime mounted up quickly, as the arrests were usually made after office hours, in the evenings, when the curfew was in effect and Jewish citizens had to stay at home. But it is uncertain if there is any truth to this. Rudolfs was one of the few to mention such a large amount. It might simply have been his way of explaining his large income while simultaneously glossing over the issue of the bonuses. Members of the Colonne did receive a substantial expense allowance when they had to do inventory work outside the city. They were given fl.10 a day, and anyone who watched his pennies could pocket more than half of that. As Colonne member Henk Hopman said in a police interrogation: "Practically from the start of my employment there, I received an expense allowance of ten guilders a day in addition to my salary. I was also paid overtime on top of that."[31] Some of the men also reported receiving an additional allowance for working on Sundays.

Just as complex as the issue of who received exactly which premium is the matter of the bonuses Colonne members received for seized goods. No attention was paid to that aspect of the job in the Special Court trials, nor did it form part of the body of evidence against the suspects. But it did happen. Why else would Joop den Ouden* have gotten the nickname "ten percent man"? Den Ouden was a central figure in the Colonne. He knew the criminal underworld like the back of his hand, and he also had a police record as a result of a number of minor offenses. He was a genuine hustler. He tried to earn money any way he could, and he hunted down Jewish property with grim determination. It is unclear whether his special talents in this area enabled him to claim a percentage of the spoils. There is testimony from a witness about another commercially minded colleague which seemed to suggest this. The colleague in question is Tonny Kroon, perhaps the shrewdest Jew hunter of them all. His sister-in-law Anna Kroon said the following about him: "Tonny was earning a lot of money then. He received ten percent of the capital and jewelry of the Jews he had arrested. In addition he received five or ten guilders in bonuses for every Jew he had picked up. I am quite sure about this, as he told me about it himself on a number of occasions."[32] She is yet another relative with incriminating testimony which comes across as quite persuasive. Kroon was one of the Colonne's big earners and proved to be a big spender too, as we shall see.

And then there is a statement by Chris van den Borch, who appeared to have a bad memory and pled not guilty to most of the charges against him, though he did confirm that he once received fl.100 (now $630), that is to say, ten percent of the value of goods he had confiscated.³³ His colleague Sjef Sweeger made a similar admission. He apparently once said during an interrogation that he and his coworkers received ten percent of the value of the items they seized.

The evidence is scant, but that is to be expected. No records have been found showing that bonuses were paid, and it was not in the interest of the Colonne's members to confess to this under questioning, whether by detectives or judges. But all in all it is obvious that a percentage of the confiscated goods found its way into the pockets of the members of the Colonne Henneicke, in any case the most prominent members and the most daring. After all, Wim Henneicke handled the payment of premiums and bonuses himself, and you could count on him to keep his most important Jew hunters on their toes with financial incentives.

There is also every reason to assume that the bounty hunters regularly took bribes. We have already seen this with Henneicke's predecessor Harmans, when he tried to enrich himself at the expense of the contractor/realtor Van der Maas, a lapse that would cost him his job. Henk van den Heuvel was known to be open to favors from Jews who wanted to flee the Dutch Theater. ("I would call him a good lad. He always behaved decently," witness Jacob Barend would later say about him.) Many people took advantage of that opportunity; the number of escapes was exceptionally high. Once when he was on guard duty, Van den Heuvel let five people go at once. They had asked in advance what they could give him in return, and it turned out the thing he wanted most was a record player, a prized luxury item in 1943. Barend remembered contributing fl.50 (about $320 today). The phonograph was bought, and sure enough the five prisoners did escape.³⁴ Van den Heuvel also tore up a citation for a Jewish detainee, so he would no longer be considered a penal case, though to do so Van den Heuvel did have to bribe a German guard with a bottle of gin.

There must have been many more cases of bribery, but these too were difficult to document, as it was not in the interest of either party that such deals came to light.

There is, however, a strange story Colonne member Henk Hopman told the detectives who interrogated him. He said that while working as an inventory clerk in Jewish homes, he would often receive money from the owners of the houses, who were glad to be able to rent out their properties again after the previous occupants had been forced out. According to Hopman, the procedure went as follows. The goods that were to be inventoried were stored in one room. The room was then sealed, and the rest of the building could then be rented out. And the owner was so pleased that he was willing to pay the clerk for his cooperation.³⁵

Hopman was the only one to report this particular sort of income. He did that in the form of an explanatory note on his tax return for 1943. That year he declared fl.6,000 in earnings, an astronomical income for the time. Whether this can be attributed to this special maneuver, to expense allowances or to premiums, it was yet another piece of evidence that in 1943 the Colonne Henneicke was on its way to becoming a club of *nouveaux riches*.

Another member in this category was Frans van Tol, who was able to support his substantial drinking habit thanks to his various side jobs. Frans was the son of a garbage man and was one of seventeen children, twelve (!) of whom died young. In 1942 and 1943 Frans shuttled back and forth between the *Hausraterfassung*, the Colonne Henneicke and the *Einsatzstab Rosenberg*. He became concierge for the latter organization, in the building at 39–41 Vondelstraat, the former (and current) headquarters of the Freemasons. His bosses were apparently so pleased with his work that in 1943 he became *Lagerchef*, storeroom manager, a position which afforded him a considerable amount of freedom. In the evenings he picked up some extra money by going out with his friends from the Colonne Henneicke. Afterward they would invariably wind up in a café, where they were known to consume as much as a liter of gin apiece. In July, together with a policeman who had been assigned to work with him, Van Tol confiscated a large amount of jewelry which had supposedly belonged to Jews in hiding. The injured party engaged a lawyer but to no avail. A short time after that, according to a statement he made to the police, he saw "the suspect's wife, decked out in jewels, in the building on Vondelstraat." In 1948, when Van Tol had to account for his actions in court, he came up with an unusual explanation: "During the Occupation I bought a lottery ticket and won a hundred thousand on it. I spent part of that money on jewelry for my wife."[36]

But it turned out that Van Tol had another source of extra income. After the war Meyer Wurms, an employee of the Jewish Council who had worked at the building on Vondelstraat, stated that Van Tol had a network of informants and received countless letters from his legion of snitches. "I saw them there myself," said Wurms, "and then Van Tol would go out on his own and play Gestapo." In essence Van Tol's headquarters on Vondelstraat functioned as a branch office of the *Zentralstelle*. Wurms: "The Jews who were taken into custody were sometimes sent on and sometimes let go. I assume that those who were let go had to pay for their freedom."[37]

The picture is clear. Van Tol was effectively running his own "column" on the side, relieving wealthy detainees of their money and then (temporarily) letting them go, while sending the less well-to-do to the Dutch Theater via the normal channels and collecting bonuses for them. Van Tol's cronies – we have already met his sixteen-year-old lover/maid Beppie – were Cool and Hopman, but Klingeberg and Henneicke himself were also seen in his company. A certain Pieter Pijtak, a pub owner whose establishment the men frequented, told the PRA: "He could really put it away, that Van Tol." And if a bartender says that, it must be true.

It should almost go without saying that Colonne members would occasionally help themselves to some of the items they confiscated, especially money. It is really a miracle that such cases surfaced at all, as most of the victims did not live to tell the tale. But Rosetta de Leeuw was one of the lucky ones. She was arrested by Mijnsma and a colleague on June 28, 1943 on the roof of 70 Uilenburgerstraat, while attempting to escape. She survived the war, and when she was asked by the PRA to make a deposition, Rosetta learned that Mijnsma and his companion told the *Sicherheitsdienst* that they had confiscated fl.520. But Rosetta swore it was actually fl.775. And she could explain the discrepancy too: "This is absolutely untrue; the two men from the SD took 775 guilders from me. This was the first thing they did after my arrest. When we were on the way to the Theater, the two men first divided 250 amongst themselves and then turned over the rest. I saw this with my own eyes, and the German who took the money gave them a receipt. Of course, I didn't dare say anything about the 250 they kept for themselves."[38] Mind you, regardless of the exact amount, Rosetta had lost £4,750 in today's money.

And this was by no means an isolated occurrence. Because the Jews were afraid to say anything at the time, and afterward there was almost no one left *to* say anything, this is special testimony indeed. Rosetta was able to see firsthand how the thieves operated.

Sometimes Mijnsma would claim an even higher percentage. He was involved in the arrest of Jozef van der Hal, a doctor from The Hague. They confiscated fl.800 from him. At the *Zentralstelle* Van der Hal had to sign for just fl.49. This time Mijnsma had taken a ninety-four per cent margin.[39]

In 1943 the members of the Colonne Henneicke had good luck in finding new housing. A substantial number of them moved that year, and for more than half of them their new place of residence was a house that had just been vacated by a Jewish family. We have already seen how Henk van den Heuvel suddenly became the owner of a house on Nicolaas Maesstraat in Amsterdam. When the detectives picked him up for questioning, he had a bout of amnesia: "I don't know what the sum was, and I don't know how I got the money to pay for it." He was forced to leave the house, and at that point he could no longer pay his lawyer either. Lambert Schipper was known to have moved into a house that had belonged to deported Jews on the same street he had been living on before, Kerkstraat. After the war his neighbor reported that Schipper had also appropriated the family's furniture; for an inventory clerk at the *Hausraterfassung* this must have been child's play.[40] And for fl.8,000 Mattijs van de Wert* was suddenly the proud owner of a magnificent house in Zandvoort, coincidentally the very first city he was sent to after being hired by the *Hausraterfassung*. Needless to say, he bought it from its Jewish owner.[41]

And it is almost endearing to read how Henk Saaldijk – the man who specialized in picking up sick Jews, sometimes as many as ten a day – confessed a minor instance of corruption to the authorities. In 1943 Saaldijk had seized some Jewish property from an importer of raincoats, and he had asked the man if there might be a new coat in it for him. His had got torn while biking. The importer readily agreed and gave him the raincoat for nothing. Saaldijk wrote a favorable report, which ensured that there would be no consequences for the importer for withholding Jewish property.

But in some strange way Saaldijk was still a man of rules. Thus, his police record contains a note in which he thanked the importer and, for the sake of completeness, sent him the ration cards which were required for purchasing a coat. The text reads: "Enclosed please find twenty-five textile points. Thank you once again for you helpfulness, Sincerely yours, H.C. Saaldijk."[42] Henk Saaldijk, such a decent man.

But these sorts of nickel and dime jobs were the exception. There are numerous instances of much more serious corruption, for example the case of Klaas Westerhoff, a fur dealer who lived along the Amstel. He had been betrayed to the SD by a female spy, and on suspicion of possessing Jewish goods he had to go to Noorder Amstellaan, to Wim Henneicke's office. The latter repeatedly threatened him with the death penalty if he refused to cooperate with the investigation. During an interrogation by Henneicke's colleagues Van den Borch and Den Ouden, Westerhoff noticed the two were "receptive to favors," that is to say, corrupt. Westerhoff then proposed a deal, he told detectives from the Political Investigation Service (POD) after the war.[43] In return for immunity, he was prepared to auction off his stock of furs and turn over the money to the two men. The deal was accepted. According to Westerhoff, the sale brought in fl.40,000 (nowadays about $253,000!), which he gave to Van den Borch and Den Ouden, fl.20,000 each. Westerhoff's wife confirmed this story to investigators in 1948, adding that at the time (1943) she had been forbidden to tell anyone.

Astonished that the bounty hunters had been party to such a lucrative deal, the detectives questioned Joop den Ouden, who told a very different story. According to Den Ouden, the matter of the Jewish goods, which Westerhoff had allegedly been storing at his home, had been settled long before that time. Westerhoff was afraid of being arrested and wanted to buy Van den Borch and Den Ouden's protection. He was willing to let them share in a consignment of furs which belonged to him. Initially Den Ouden and Van den Borch had wanted to decline the offer. But Westerhoff was afraid his fur would be confiscated, since no one would ever believe it had not belonged to Jews. And so he insisted the two share in the proceeds of the sale in exchange for protection. After a long hesitation, again according to Den Ouden, they finally agreed. Westerhoff collected fl.30,000 for the merchandise, and Van den Borch and Den Ouden each received 10,000, as did Westerhoff himself. "And not a penny more," claimed Den Ouden. But either way these were astronomical amounts, which instantly made Den Ouden and Van den Borch rich men, and the two barely had to lift a finger for it. According to Den Ouden, after that Westerhoff was nearly arrested several times. Van den Borch and he were always able to rescue him though. On one occasion Van den Borch took him from the police station in Huizen, on the pretext that he was an important informant for the SD.

The detectives who took Den Ouden's statement brought in Westerhoff again. This time his story was closer to that of the other two men. He no longer remembered the details and the exact amounts, though he did recall that the consignment in question consisted of 120 dozen rabbit skins and 125 goat skins, which fetched a total of fl.40,000. Westerhoff maintained that he turned over fl.10,000 to Van den Borch and fl.22,000 to Den Ouden, keeping fl.8,000 for himself. If this was true, Den Ouden would have made $139,500 in today's money from this transaction. It is suddenly utterly incomprehensible that Den Ouden and his colleagues went on dragging Jews out of their beds for fl.7.50 per person.

We know that Van den Borch was unable to find work after being laid off from the Colonne Henneicke. But he was in no hurry, he confirmed to the detectives who questioned him in 1948. The money he earned from the deal with Westerhoff was easily enough to take him through to the end of the war.

It is hardly worth mentioning that the money the men acquired through theft, extortion, bribery, robbery and other crimes was almost never paid back. In most cases the victims did not return. There were occasional attempts to win legal compensation, and from time to time a returning deportee did get his things back, but these were the exceptions.

Throughout the dossiers on the members of the Colonne there are examples of people who tried to recover their possessions after the war. One such person was Celine den Hartoch*, the widow of Abraham Cohen.[44] The couple was taken, along with three others, from a hiding place at 70 Willem Barentszstraat, a street in East Utrecht lined with stately old homes. The Colonne team, under the leadership of former policeman Henk van der Kraal, also took gold jewelry worth some fl.20,000. Was it seized? Stolen? Mrs Den Hartoch was convinced of the latter. She would never get her husband back, but she was determined to find her jewels again. Her dogged search for the gold jewelry led to countless addresses, but she never found a trace of it anywhere. Eventually she learned that it was Henk van der Kraal who had arrested her and her family. She induced the PRA to search the home of Van der Kraal's wife, who was at the time living without a husband (he was being held in an internment camp) and without any income, trying to get by on fl.15 a week in welfare. Christina van der Kraal, who claimed to know nothing about the work her husband did in 1943, did not look forward to this sort of visit. She received the victim of her husband's activities coolly. When Mrs Den Hartoch started to get involved in the search for valuables herself, she became hysterical, shouting abuse at the other woman.

It was a tragic but not unusual scene: two bitter, desperate women, one whose husband had been gassed, the other whose husband was facing the possibility of life in prison. "I suppose this wedding ring is yours too?" Mrs Van der Kraal shrieked at one point. The search turned up nothing.

Mrs Den Hartoch never saw her husband or her jewelry again. Mrs Van der Kraal's husband never came home either. In 1955 he died at the prison hospital in Vught.

–6–

The Leaders' Style

There is precious little personal information about the two undisputed leaders of the hunt for Dutch Jews in their respective police files. The reason for this is that the Political Investigation Department was unable to interrogate either one of them about their crimes. Henneicke did not live to see the end of the war, having been assassinated by the resistance in late 1944. Briedé managed to elude justice and hid out in Germany until his death. He was tried in absentia, but there was never an opportunity to ask him about his methods, his organizational skills and his motivations. In the case of Willem Christiaan Heinrich Henneicke, we have other ways of finding out what he did before being appointed to run the Colonne that bore his name. As the son of a German immigrant, there was a file on him with the aliens' police, and as a regular client of the Amsterdam social services there are stacks of paperwork chronicling his time on the dole.

The first thing one notices about his alien identification card is that he apparently never became a Dutch citizen.[1] He was born in the Netherlands in March 1909 in Amsterdam, but his father was a German, who came to the Netherlands at the beginning of the century. Eventually his father became a naturalized citizen in 1939. The younger Henneicke never did; according to his aliens' ID card, he was stateless. His status remained unclear until the war, but in September 1941 a certain Herr Michel from a certain German governmental agency issued a definitive ruling, rendering him stateless. This made Henneicke something of an exception in his own organization: of the fifty-four men who could be classified as civilian Jew hunters, only Heinrich Berten was German. Everyone else was Dutch.

From his file with Amsterdam Social Services, which was then called the Municipal Welfare Bureau, we learn that Henneicke was married three times.[2] In 1930, at twenty-one years of age, he married Maria Johanna Arnold, who was one year his senior. The couple were registered in the municipal welfare rolls in February 1931. At the time they were living on Van Rappardstraat. Henneicke's wife, who, like her husband, was a member of the Evangelical Lutheran Church, suffered from struma, a disorder of the thyroid gland. Henneicke's initial application for welfare benefits was rejected because he had failed to turn up for an appointment that had been made with him. According to a form filled out during this same time, the Henneicke household had a total income of fl.20 a month, namely fl.5 from "woman's earnings" and fl.15 in the form of "board wages" from Henneicke's father-in-law, who lived with him and his wife. The marriage ended in divorce, and Henneicke got married again in 1933, to the twenty-three-year-old Catharina Johanna Kroet. He divorced her as well, in the summer of 1939. Henneicke had been living with his mother for some time before he moved in with one of her neighbors on Van Ostadestraat in the autumn of 1939. This was Maria Carolina Trilling, who was the same age as Henneicke but had three children to care for. This was her third marriage too, after being widowed twice before.

The three children – Elly (1928), Fritz (1930) and Maria (1932) – were all from her first marriage. Her child from her second marriage was being raised by the grandparents. When Henneicke moved in with her (on forms he described the union as a "common-law marriage"), he suddenly became father to three children. In the spring of 1930 she became pregnant again, and at that point they decided to get married, on May 15, 1940. They could not have known that that would be the day the Netherlands would capitulate to Germany. Their son, Willem Christiaan, was born on November 4, 1940. Money was tight in a family of six, and Henneicke repeatedly attempted to secure "special allowances" for the registered unemployed. Thus in July 1940 he was given a suit and a pair of shoes, and in September "underwear for wife and expected child," as it says on the application.

Willem Henneicke's social career was hardly impressive.[3] After finishing school he went to work as an apprentice shipwright for two different firms for a period of just over three years. After that he got a job at the warehouse of the Amstel Brewery, where he would remain for another three years. He spent a year looking for work before becoming a taxi driver. After nine weeks at the wheel of a car for Economy Taxi, he started out on his own, with a garage and a bicycle shed. According to his version of events, he got out of the business because he was being swindled by a partner. He emerged from the venture flat broke. In 1935 he went back to work again, this time as manager of a cooperative taxi company. He kept that up for two years, for the very respectable salary of fl.40 a week, until the business went bankrupt. At that point he switched from taxis to vacuum cleaners and became a salesman for the Nilfisk Company. He was paid fl.20 to peddle vacuum cleaners door-to-door; the rest he had to earn in commission. After three months he resigned and went to work for the competition, Excelsior Vacuums. He was there for two years, but then sales declined so much that Henneicke was let go, in September 1939. After that he worked for a time at the headquarters of Dordrecht Gas Works, an ominous position for a future Jew hunter. He was laid off from this job as well, this time as a result of a reorganization. He applied for unemployment compensation but was a few days late in doing so and was punished for this with a reduction in benefits. Another factor in determining how much money he would receive was the fact that his new wife had a widow's pension and her children an orphans' allowance. When two of the children were given permission to go to Egmond for some social project or other, Henneicke requested (and received) shorts, shirts and underwear for them, at a value of fl.4.95. In the spring of 1940 Henneicke found work with another vacuum cleaner firm. This lasted just two months. May 10, the start of the war in the Netherlands, also marked the end of that particular position: five days before his third marriage Henneicke was fired again.

In the first year of the war, poverty was rampant. Henneicke tried his best to get out of the back-breaking excavation work that was part and parcel of the so-called *werkverruiming* – that is to say, government-sponsored work creation projects. He was issued with a shovel and a pair of work shoes (at a total value of fl.10.50, a sum he did not pay back until 1944), but he rarely showed up at the Moorland Reclamation Society. In the end he procured himself a certificate from a medical examiner exempting him from work on the grounds of an illness we never hear anything more about. In 1941 he rejoined the ranks of the employed, this time as a salesman for the MijDa pharmaceutical firm. He worked on a fifteen percent commission, but in the end this was not enough to live on, as sales were dropping off visibly. He quit this job when his wife became seriously ill and was admitted to hospital. He had to care for the children himself and was forced to go back on the dole. To relieve the worst financial distress he sold some tools and a table to a junkman. It was in that period that he started doing odd jobs for the *Sicherheitsdienst*. We know this because one of his neighbors wrote to the authorities about this in 1942.[4]

A certain K. wrote that Mr Henneicke, who was receiving welfare from the General Federation of Commercial Employees and Clerks, was also working for the *Sicherheitsdienst* on Euterpestraat. "Just ask Mr Olij who works there." Moreover, the author of the letter continued, Henneicke was also employed as "a traveling salesman for a firm in Hilversum in pharmaceutical articles or medicine." K.'s conclusion: Henneicke was committing massive welfare fraud. But that was not all. "Furthermore he is attempting to obtain WHN benefits." WHN, that is *Winterhulp Nederland* (Netherlands Winter Aid), was an organization that collected for the downtrodden in society, with a marked preference for those with National Socialist leanings. And indeed, it was also during that period that Willem Henneicke suddenly applied for NSB membership.

The Municipal Welfare Bureau evidently felt that these allegations warranted a serious investigation, since the dossiers contain a statement from SD duty officer Olij, who said, "Henneicke tracks down black market goods, which are then confiscated. I don't know if he ever received money for this work, though he was promised it. None of these people have ever received anything, as far as I know."

The investigation was part of the effort to stamp out benefit fraud. Henneicke was summoned to the welfare office to account for himself. He told them that he no longer had the job in Hilversum but maintained contact with a black marketeer there, by order of the SD. This organization also paid him the sum of fl.150, in three instalments of fl.50, during the final months of 1941. Henneicke also explained that the clothes he bought for his children were financed with a fl.20 loan from his mother-in-law and "by pawning a suit for twelve guilders." In Henneicke's file there are no indications that any action was taken, even though benefit fraud was generally dealt with quite severely at that time. The officials at the Welfare Bureau wisely turned a blind eye to his extra income from the *Sicherheitsdienst*.

All things considered, Henneicke was a small-timer. But this would change in June 1942, when Henneicke began his meteoric rise up the income ladder. In the beginning he was still living at 171 Van Ostadestraat, a long, gray street in a lower middle class neighborhood. Shortly after being given a permanent position at the *Hausraterfassung*, Henneicke and his family moved into a downstairs flat on Linnaeusparkweg, in a quiet, upscale neighborhood in the Watergraafsmeer part of town. It was undoubtedly one of the thousands of such flats and houses to become vacant during this period because the occupants had been sent to Poland.

From the various files, we know that Henneicke was five foot nine inches tall, with reddish-blond hair, gray eyes, an oval face, a healthy color and good posture. In the police records of his subordinates, one occasionally finds a description of the big boss. "Henneicke was a young-looking and well-built man with curly hair," said Eddy Moerberg, one of his confidants, in 1943.[5] "A tall blond chap with a round face," said one of his arrestees who survived the confrontation.[6] Another arrestee recalled that Henneicke spoke with a German accent.[7] But by and large it remains unclear what Henneicke's motivations were and how he managed to work his way up to such a powerful position. Apparently he was exceptionally well-suited for special assignments. The number of *Berichte* for confiscated goods with his name at the bottom is extraordinarily high. In one of his more bizarre assignments, Henneicke was ordered by the head of the *Hausraterfassung*, P. Docter, to go to the home of Rosa Spier to impound her harp.[8] At that time Rosa Spier was already something of a celebrity, as a soloist with the Royal Concertgebouw Orchestra. On the basis of her fame she was a member of the so-called Barneveld group, a group of privileged Jews who were temporarily held in a castle in Barneveld. Henneicke took her harp from her home on Milletstraat to the headquarters of the *Zentralstelle*. After the war the harp was recovered from the bottom of a houseboat and returned to Rosa Spier, who had survived the camps.

B. Perridon, the defense attorney for leading Colonne member Bob Verlugt, said to the Court of Appeals in the spring of 1949: "What sort of person was this Henneicke? Prior to becoming unemployed, Henneicke had run an illegal taxi service. He was a man from the underworld who exploited his contacts with that world to the utmost during his so-called 'regime.'"[9] The picture painted by Perridon is consistent with what can be gathered from other witnesses and dossiers. He was a hard man, suspicious, ruthless; no one had a nice word to say about him. His authority must have been based on threats, on power politics. Henneicke could not stand indecisiveness. Anyone who hesitated was "soft" – and such men were no longer eligible for the most lucrative jobs.

Henneicke's dossier also contains an employment contract with Lippmann, Rosenthal & Co. He was hired at a monthly salary of fl.270, a spectacular increase from the fl.15 a week in welfare he had been receiving the year before. The starting date on the contract was June 22, 1942. It was typical of his underhandedness that he continued collecting welfare for another month after that. He endorsed the contract (thereby confirming that he was not a Jew) with an elegant signature: a graceful W flowing seamlessly into the H, underlined with a modest flourish. His registration form for the NSB has also survived.[10] He did not become a member until April 23, 1942, shortly before going to work for the *Hausraterfassung*. He gave his occupation as driver/mechanic. He had never served in the armed forces and had four children. The contribution to the Movement amounted to seventy-five cents a month, and he indicated his willingness to deliver NSB information pamphlets door-to-door.

And thus Henneicke became a member of the team run by kindred spirit Willem Hendrik Benjamin Briedé. Briedé was six years older than Henneicke and had been a member of the NSB for much longer, having become one of Anton Mussert's disciples on July 12, 1934.[11] From his registration form we learn that he attended high school but did not graduate, though he did state that he was "familiar with bookkeeping and modern languages." Briedé worked for quite some time as a bookkeeper at a slaughterhouse. There is no information about how he came to work for the *Hausraterfassung*. His contract went into effect April 1, 1942, as the organization was being set up for the mass plunder that was to come. Briedé lived on Zacharias Jansestraat in East Amsterdam, not far from where Henneicke would later wind up. His starting salary was fl.270 a month, slightly more than what the others received. In the beginning he was the leader of an eponymous Colonne but soon moved up to the position of head of personnel. His superior Piet Docter dropped out of the picture, and other potential competitors for the leadership of the *Hausraterfassung* also stepped aside. Thus "Briedé [was] given the opportunity to assume control of the *Hausraterfassung*," Colonne member Elmink would later say in an interrogation.[12] According to the report that detective Wijnand Prasing wrote on him, Briedé was a powerful man.[13] He could hire and fire employees at will (his German boss K. Wörlein had given him carte blanche in this area), and he could also refuse to accept an employee's resignation. The latter occurred fairly often, if we are to believe the claims made by numerous members of the Colonne in their interrogations. According to Henk Saaldijk, "Briedé was in charge of day-to-day operations; on the basis of orders, tips and letters he received from the Germans, he gave the inventory clerks their assignments." Briedé was, as it were, the link between the Germans in the upper echelons of the *Zentralstelle*, the *roofbank* Lippmann Rosenthal, which supplied the money, and the personnel, who carried out the orders. Saaldijk had little to say about his personal relationship with Henneicke, though he did know that "Briedé gave Henneicke cases to work on, and Henneicke accepted them." Thus Briedé ranked above Henneicke in the hierarchy, but Elmink's testimony offers us a striking insight into this aspect of the organization. The latter was a reliable source for these sorts of questions; he had been the owner of a number of thriving radio shops and must have had a certain amount of experience with staff relations. "Henneicke would often ask Briedé for employees to help out with all the work," Elmink told detective Prasing. "Briedé then decided which employees would be transferred to Henneicke's investigative unit." And on the subject of the relationship between the two men, he said: "My impression was that Briedé was afraid to defy Henneicke. The men he sent to work for Henneicke were subordinate to him and received their orders from him. Although Briedé ranked above Henneicke, Henneicke has acquired a certain degree of autonomy, which Briedé didn't dare question."

It seems clear that possible disputes between the two undisputed leaders about spheres of authority were solved when the organization was split sometime around July 1, 1943. Henneicke and his group left the school on Adama van Scheltemaplein, right across the street from the SD, and moved to 244 Noorder Amstellaan. From that moment Briedé started having other members of the *Hausraterfassung* follow up on tips and pick up Jews in return for bonuses. He gradually went from bookkeeper and chief of personnel to coordinator of the entire operation, the same position Henneicke had held for several months. Briedé also made arrests himself. On August 16, he was present for a raid at a house on Westeinde, at eight o'clock in the evening, which netted nine Jews in one go. The authorities must have been tipped off, because Briedé walked straight to the place where the money and securities were hidden.

Briedé was quite aggressive that Monday evening. He said to fifty-three-year-old businessman Jacob Rubens, who lived to tell the tale: "If you say another word, you dirty Jew, I'll fill you full of lead." And that's not all. According to Rubens, as far back as August 16, 1943, Briedé intimated that he was aware of what would happen to his arrestees. During police questioning Rubens stated categorically that Briedé had said during the arrest: "I'll be straight with you, since you're going to be gassed anyway. You're going right to Germany, and you won't be coming back." In the trial in absentia Rubens expanded upon his original statement. He had asked Briedé who had betrayed him, and Briedé had replied: "You're going to be gassed, and dead men tell no tales. I can tell you it was Mrs X. She works for us."[14]

After that the whole group was loaded into a paddy wagon and taken to the Dutch Theater, where Rubens succeeded in bribing a German involved in organizing the transports. Together the two went back to the address where Rubens had been hiding. There Rubens gave the guard some of his remaining valuables. On August 26 the group captured on Westeinde were driven away in a truck covered with a tarpaulin, which was loose on one side, as per their agreement. Rubens and his wife Eva were to escape through the opening and jump out of the vehicle. Their children had already been shepherded out of the Jewish nursery across the street from the Theater.

Briedé and Henneicke went out on assignment together a few times. We already know the story of their excursion to Utrecht, on Tuesday June 8, when they went out to pick up two children and came back with five children and two adults. The next day they went out together again – apparently to continue the on-the-job training Henneicke had been giving his boss Briedé. This time their destination was Ammerstol, where their mission was to arrest fugitive Jews staying at the home of the fifty-five-year-old minister B.T. Hugenholtz. But first they paid a visit to the mayor of Ammerstol, J.H. Winkler.[15] Two men, who introduced themselves as representatives of the Amsterdam *Sicherheitsdienst*, stormed into his office at city hall. They forced him to accompany them to the minister's house. Winkler reluctantly complied. Later on he would remember the names of the two men perfectly: Briedé and Henneicke.

Reverend Hugenholtz was not at home when his house was raided. When he arrived a short time later, two men from the SD and Mayor Winkler were waiting for him. Mr and Mrs Dukker, a Jewish couple, had just been arrested, along with Simone Mogendorf. The fourth person who had been staying with him, a certain Mr Denneboom, got away. The whole company was taken to Amsterdam, the Jews to the Dutch Theater and Hugenholtz to Euterpestraat. The minister was imprisoned for two months in Amsterdam; after that he would spend seven months in Vught. He was released in March 1944.

The arrestees were never heard from again. All that remains is the paperwork. According to a report, written in German and signed by Briedé and Henneicke, Hugenholtz stated that "he knew from the very first day that the people were Jews. He considered it his duty as a Christian to hide the Jews, seeing that he was a minister." In their report Henneicke and Briedé added that it was their impression that both the mayor and the local police were "very anti-German. It is likely that they are aware of many other addresses where Jews are being harbored."

All that remained was to wrap up the financial side of things. There is a declaration from Henneicke and Briedé stating that the three prisoners were brought to the Dutch Theater. They had found fl.669.50 on Dukker; nowadays that would be more than $4,180. "That money was given to the *Sicherheitspolizei, Aussenstelle Amsterdam, Abteilung IV-B*." Signed by the *Recherchegruppe Henneicke*, W. Briedé and W. Henneicke.[16]

No doubt they turned over every last cent of the money, as required. Neither man could afford to undermine his position vis-à-vis the other by proposing a deal. Nonetheless even Henneicke and Briedé were not averse to a lucrative transaction on the side from time to time, however closely they were being monitored and however daunting the example of Henneicke's predecessor Harmans must have been. After the war Mr H. Boersma, who owned a housing complex in the Amsterdam River District, filed a complaint against Briedé.[17] Boersma was suspected of hiding the furniture of deported Jewish tenants. On Saturday, May 22, Boersma was interrogated by three men, Oudinga*, Gist and Briedé. Since Boersma initially refused to admit that he had been concealing Jewish belongings, he was subjected to a barrage of threats for six hours, chief among them the threat of being turned over to the Germans. Ultimately Boersma buckled: he admitted to selling some of the Jewish goods, mainly carpets. He then proposed a deal. Oudinga, a former policeman and a minor figure in the *Hausraterfassung*, would soon find himself fl.2,000 richer, and on May 24 Briedé was given fl.1,520. In Briedé's trial in absentia, Boersma would admit: "Briedé had said that maybe we could work something out. Then, in the presence of Gist and Oudinga, I arranged with Briedé to pay 520 guilders to cover the carpets I had sold and 1,000 guilders as a sort of fine. I paid Briedé the sum of 1,520 guilders on May 24 at the *Zentralstelle*." For the sake of completeness, that would be some $9,670 today.

Henneicke was not known to have been involved in such flagrant corruption and extortion, though that does not necessarily mean much. As I remarked earlier, most victims of such practices did not survive the war, and generally there were no other witnesses. However, we do know of a small, more characteristic incident involving Henneicke. A certain Jozeph Leijden van Amstel was arrested with false papers by Moerberg and Henneicke. He later succeeded in escaping from the Dutch Theater and testified in court after the war. He was positive that he had been robbed of fl.230, even though Moerberg and Henneicke wrote in their *Bericht* that the arrestee had had no money with him. On the evening of September 24, the two men divided the fl.230 between them. After the war Leijden van Amstel told the judges that Moerberg had threatened him with a gun. Because the man refused to reveal where his wife and child were hiding, Moerberg brought him along to Noorder Amstellaan and snarled at him, "Take off your glasses, Jew, so I can beat [it] out of you."[18]

In any case, Henneicke kept a tight hold on the Colonne's purse strings. The surviving receipts showing the payment of bonuses were all signed by him. It is impossible to say whether he divided the bonuses equally among his troops or gave each man his share, nor does it really matter. He was able to use financial incentives to stimulate, to pressure or, if he so wished, to punish his subordinates. There is no way of finding out how much of the money, if any, he kept for himself. There were several witnesses from his Colonne who regularly saw him at pubs. There was also a lawyer who claimed Henneicke would promise generous rewards for tips that led to the arrest of Jews.[19] After the war his house was found to be modestly furnished, and his wife even had to go on the dole. If he did enrich himself during the heyday of the Jew hunt, he assiduously erased any trace of his wrongdoing.

In reading over Henneicke's dossier, one is struck most by the sheer ruthlessness of the man. In January 1943 – thus before he was able to offer or collect bonuses – he reported the arrest of two Jewish couples at 83 II Linnaeusparkweg.[20] That was two houses down the street from his own; only the true diehards in the Colonne were capable of that. The series of *Berichte* with the name Henneicke at the bottom is practically endless. And time and again, one arrest would lead to another. Henneicke was always on the lookout for clues, for new addresses, for places where Jewish property might be stored. Together with Elmink he went to the New Israelite Hospital to arrest a sixty-three-year-old woman. On June 17, apparently without assistance, he raided the ground floor flat at 212 Willemsparkweg and arrested twelve people. Eleven Jews and the woman who had been hiding them, Mrs Lentink-De Boer. Eleven of the arrestees were taken to the Dutch Theater, while their protector went to the *Sicherheitspolizei*.[21] Henneicke never let them go.

On July 12, Henneicke went to Utrecht again, once more on the basis of a tip. On Schröder van der Kolkstraat, a chic street near the University Hospital, he surprised Markus Emmanuel, a Jewish man who was hiding out there with his wife Martha and their eight children: Hermann, Leo, Jona, Sam, Berud, Bella, Felix and Beatrice. Ten Jews in total. Wim Henneicke was the only one to sign the *Bericht* for this operation, so in addition to his travel allowance he also collected a fl.75 bonus.[22]

The only hint that Henneicke also had a compassionate side came from Herman van Eiken*, his neighbor on Linnaeusparkweg and colleague at the *Hausraterfassung* from day one. They made quite a few arrests together. In such cases Van Eiken would always write the reports, since Henneicke tended to avoid writing whenever possible, claiming that Van Eiken was more suited to that kind of work. In his interrogation Van Eiken stated that once in a while he was able to persuade Henneicke to let someone go. "But that was only possible if no one else was around."[23] Thus, at a certain point Van Eiken was on good terms with his boss. But there would later be a falling out. In a kind of review of his life, he wrote that he had submitted his resignation following an argument: Van Eiken refused to arrest a Jewish woman with a baby (a two-day-old baby, Van Eiken noted). Henneicke then allegedly said he was "too soft" and forced him out of the Colonne, Van Eiken explained to the Special Court in December 1948.[24]

Van Eiken lived at 80 Linnaeusparkweg, across the street from Henneicke, and after his resignation he and his wife were constantly harassed by Henneicke's children. In his personal history he wrote that on one occasion this degenerated into a shouting match in the street. After that incident he moved to Naarden. The name Henneicke is like a leitmotiv in Van Eiken's tale. He called him the fatal factor in his life, the evil spirit.[25]

Of course all this is relative. Van Eiken joined the *Hausraterfassung* for financial reasons; he was on the skids after taking on his father's debt and being fired by the Gouda police department. The financial benefits of the Jew hunt got him back on his feet and enabled him to afford a beautiful house on posh Linnaeusparkweg. But in 1949, before the Special Court, the obvious strategy was naturally to put all the blame on Wim Henneicke, the heartless, stateless man who could hardly write but who was a dab hand with figures, and who, perhaps most importantly, could no longer respond to the accusations.

–7–

The Men from the Card Catalogue

Some time in late March 1943 Ferdinand Aus der Fünten, one of the heads of the *Zentralstelle für jüdische Auswanderung* in Amsterdam, was approached with a strange request. Five staff members from the card catalogue came to ask his permission to earn some extra money, in addition to their regular work. More specifically, they wanted to know if they could hunt down and arrest Jews in hiding, preferably under the same system as their colleagues in the Colonne Henneicke, who worked elsewhere in the former school on Adama van Scheltemaplein.

Aus der Fünten promptly rejected the request, but less than a week later he changed his mind. He told the men from the card catalogue that they would also be eligible for a premium but that it would be less than the fl.7.50 received by the *Gruppe Henneicke*. They could earn money for every Jew they arrested, on the condition that they hunted their prey on their own, that is without the help of tips – that would remain Henneicke's domain. Furthermore they would be expected to do this outside regular business hours. This work was to be considered overtime.[1]

The card catalogue of the *Zentralstelle* was the place where the records of the deportation were kept. There was a personal identity card for every Jew living in Amsterdam. A copy of every list of deported Jews was sent to this department and then processed. In this way the drawers containing the names of remaining Jews emptied out rapidly in 1942 and 1943, while the number of cards for deported Jews increased at an equal rate. Five men worked at this department. The German Reinig was formally the boss, but he was rarely there. Of the permanent staff, Herman Bertinga*, an experienced bookkeeper in his sixties, was the oldest. Fred Meiloo* (41) was officially a clerk but spent most of his time unemployed. And then there were two 30-year-olds, Pieter Huisman* and Hubert Tomson*, a former taxi driver and a barber, respectively. The fifth position was temporarily occupied by two men, a Mr van den Oort and a Mr van het Lam. Little is known about them, since their whereabouts proved untraceable after the war: the former was reportedly in Germany, and the latter apparently died in Austria.

It is not entirely clear who first came up with the idea of asking Aus der Fünten's permission to take part in the hunt for Jews. In his first interrogation, shortly after his arrest in 1945, Meiloo told a detective from the Political Investigation Service that Henneicke had bragged to him about all the money his men were earning from arresting Jews.[2] According to him, his colleagues went to Aus der Fünten as a group to ask if they could do the same. But according to another version, one of the five was given the task; it makes little difference in the end. The three who were questioned after the liberation about the exact chain of events all readily admitted to taking the initiative together. Moreover, they confirmed that they had made a deal early on to divide up the money equally. Each man would receive a guilder for every Jew turned in, regardless of who actually did the work. This arrangement was particularly advantageous for Bertinga. As the oldest, he went out the least, but he still got his share of the spoils: one guilder per Jew per man.

The most remarkable thing about the case of the men from the card catalogue is that their activities were already known in the autumn of 1945. In their interrogations they freely discussed the course of events at their department. The men were honest but naïve, since in doing so they could be used as witnesses in one another's trials, and that made things especially easy for the prosecution. Sworn testimony generally leads straight to convictions, and thus in March 1946 the Fifth Division of the Amsterdam Special Court was able to set aside a day to try the three available defendants. This was a full year and a half before the records of the *Zentralstelle* turned up on Tulpstraat, a year and a half before it became clear that there was an organization called the Colonne Henneicke which hunted down Jews for six months on an incentive scheme, and two and a half years before the long series of trials of the rest of the Jew hunters of Adama van Scheltemaplein would begin.

The life stories of the clerks at the card catalogue were not happy ones. Fred Meiloo, for example, was the quintessential victim of the economic crisis of the 1930s. But perhaps the crisis was also an excuse, a legitimization. Meiloo didn't much care for work. Amsterdam Social Services has a voluminous file on him. From 1926 he was almost permanently unemployed and dependent on welfare. When the POD tried to learn more about him by making inquiries in his neighborhood, one of his neighbors reported that "Meiloo was always on the dole."[3] In addition, he was portrayed as an ardent Nazi. This cannot be inferred simply from the fact that he was a member of the NSB, since he only joined the movement in November 1940. In most cases that indicated an attempt to attain a better social position through the NSB. "He was in the WA," one of his neighbors mentioned, "and always went out of his way to show favor to the Germans." He was apparently just as pro-German as his wife Anna, who was German by birth and evidently quite fanatical herself. In the course of the investigation detectives found one neighbor who claimed that upon returning from her homeland in 1945, Mrs Meiloo had stated "that it was a crying shame that Germany (*Deutschland über alles*) had lost." They had four children; the two youngest were twins, born in 1932.

The Provincial Employment Office played a crucial role for Meiloo, as it had for dozens of his colleagues. Although there is no written evidence to substantiate this, it seems quite plausible that this organization gave the NSB members on its rolls preferential treatment for jobs at the *Zentralstelle*. From the dossiers we know that a certain Rövecamp from the Employment Office was in direct contact with the German authorities, for the purpose of supplying personnel who could assist with the deportations. More than half of the future Jew hunters came directly from the official employment agency.[4] It was an obvious choice really: the most motivated workers for this job could be found among the ranks of the NSB, and thus unemployed NSB members were given priority when positions opened up at the *Zentralstelle*. For the work that had to be done – registering household furnishings at first – no special training was required, and so any unemployed person, even a ne'er-do-well like Meiloo, was welcome. And naturally, the success of this project in reducing unemployment was largely attributable to the attractive salary. On the basis of the contract he signed with Lippmann, Rosenthal & Co., Meiloo would earn far more than he had been making on welfare, nearly five times as much.[5] He took in fl.280 a month, even more than his older colleague Bertinga.

During the war Meiloo gradually became ever more fanatical. He enrolled all four of his children in the *Nationale Jeugdstorm* (the NSB's answer to the Hitler Youth). But after the war he was less than satisfied with their conduct: "After six months they quit, because they were too lazy to take part in the drills" – this from a man whom even social services considered to be an incorrigible layabout.[6] On June 1, 1942 he began working for the *Zentralstelle*, and after a short time he was transferred to the card catalogue, where he met the colleagues who would become his partners in the hunt for Jews in 1943. In his police interrogation in July 1945, he estimated that they picked up between 250 and 300 Jews altogether. Thus each man would have made over fl.250, according to Meiloo's own calculations. Most of the time they would go out in pairs, he said, armed with an employee card from the *Zentralstelle*, with a German stamp on it. The Jews were first brought to the *Zentralstelle*, then to the Dutch Theater. There were no hard and fast teams; he had gone out with all his co-workers at least once. After the war he no longer remembered the names and addresses of the people he had arrested. "Later, when there weren't that many Jews left, we weren't allowed to arrest Jews anymore, and Henneicke took care of it on his own," Fred Meiloo said, speaking of the summer of 1943. When they ran out of work in 1944, and the tides of war began to turn, he followed the *Zentralstelle* to the town of Velp. Not long afterward he went to Germany along with the rest of his family and moved in with his in-laws. He found a job there, in a factory in Bremen, where he was responsible for cleaning batteries for U-boats. In early July 1945 he returned to the Netherlands and was arrested at the border. According to the arrest report he had dark gray hair, blue-gray eyes and was missing his two front teeth. He was taken to Amsterdam, where he told detective Henk van den Broek about his period at the card catalogue. His candor was striking: "It's true that I volunteered to go out and arrest Jews. I only did that to earn a little extra money. I now realize that it was a very shabby thing to do. I never knew that the Jews would be treated so badly. I've since learned in Germany that those Jews were killed."[7] And the transcript of his interrogation ends with: "I now realize that I let my country down. But what's done is done, and I will have to pay the price."

It is doubtful that Meiloo realized how high that price would be. He saw himself as a little man in a big organization, which was exactly what he was. But along with his co-workers he formed the first group to be tried in the Netherlands for participating in the hunt for Jews.

Meiloo appeared before the Special Court on March 4, 1946. It was an open and shut case. Bertinga and Tomson were there too, as witnesses against Meiloo and against each other, and also as defendants. There were thus two identical sworn statements that could be used against each of the three defendants. The prosecution's case was airtight. The President of the Court, E. van Schaeck Mathon, even declined to hear Bertinga's testimony – by that point he already had a good idea of how the situation at the card catalogue had developed. Finally, Meiloo also told the president of the court *why* he did what he did. The answer was as simple as the rest of the case: "We got five guilders for every Jew, which was divided amongst the five of us. *I really needed the money, and that's why I took part in arresting Jews*" (italics mine).[8]

In the person of judge-advocate M.H. Gelinck, the prosecution demanded that Meiloo be sentenced to death. "A guilder for a Jew" was the headline in the next morning's *Volkskrant*.[9] Gelinck delivered a fiery closing statement, expressing his repugnance at the defendants' crimes. Two weeks later, the three justices of the court proved to be in agreement with him. In their judgment they stated that it was "common knowledge" that "the enemy strove . . . to deport the Jews from the Netherlands and exterminate them." And on that basis the court's conclusion was logical: "Anyone who voluntarily hands over 250 to 300 people to an enemy with this ambition is guilty of acts so reprehensible that the ultimate penalty must be imposed."[10] Meiloo was sentenced to death. It was suddenly clear how seriously the special courts would take the bounty hunters' actions.

The prosecution demanded the same punishment for Meiloo's younger colleague Tomson, who was born in Venlo in 1912. But this former barber was considerably less reconciled to his fate than Meiloo and used all possible means to escape the firing squad.[11] For him the shock might have been even greater than for Meiloo. Less than a year before it looked like he was home free. It was his own stupidity that alerted the authorities and brought about his arrest. In July 1944

Tomson had moved to the seaside town of Scheveningen, and after the liberation he found himself a job as a barber in the city's prison. In June 1945 Tomson wrote a lengthy letter to the police in Amsterdam, requesting that his furniture be returned to him.[12] It had been impounded, and he objected to this. Tomson explained in great detail how exemplary his conduct had been during the war. He *did* work for the *Zentralstelle*, that much was true, but the way he tells it, he performed one act of heroism after another during his time there. "After a few weeks, various acquaintances, mainly Jews, had found out that I was working there and came to my home a number of times to ask for help, which I was more than happy to give them. Things steadily got worse; the tasks became more involved and the danger to my own safety increased."

The letter gives the impression that we are dealing with a humanitarian of the first order. Tomson wrote that once he had the confidence of his superiors, he did not hesitate to destroy hundreds of identity cards, deliberately misplace various documents and warn people if a raid was imminent. There is no end to the lifesaving activities mentioned in Tomson's letter: entering false names into the system and issuing travel permits, moving permits, night-time permits and bicycle permits – the list goes on and on.

No wonder he was arrested by the Germans on March 24, 1944, by G. Nagel, an SS-*Oberscharführer* working for the SD, to be precise. On June 6, 1944 he was sent to Vught concentration camp, on suspicion of *jodenbegunstiging* (favoritism toward Jews), which in those days was a serious offense that could cause major problems for anyone accused of it. He was released from Vught on July 14, and of course, he writes, he did not inform on anyone during that period. He then moved to Scheveningen, while his wife and two small children (both sons, four and two years old) stayed behind in Amsterdam. And that was why he was now asking for his old furniture back, in this remarkable letter.

But things did not turn out as expected. There are strong indications that Hubert Tomson actually engineered his own downfall; the letter wound up at the same department of the POD that had already questioned Tomson's colleague Herman Bertinga about the course of events at the card catalogue. They were already familiar with the name Tomson, as one of the men who picked up Jews for fl.5 a head. Tomson's arrest was only a matter of time, this time not by the Germans but by the Dutch authorities, and not for *jodenbegunstiging* but for his role in the deportations. On July 19, 1945 the POD decided to pick him up at his home. He was interned at Camp Duinoord in Scheveningen, and there he was visited by a detective, Henk van den Broek, who knew the ins and outs of the case, as he had already interviewed a few of Tomson's co-workers.

Tomson soon confessed the rest of his story, which was considerably less heroic than his letter of a month before had suggested.[13] According to Tomson, beginning in March 1943 the daily routine at the card catalogue was as follows: "We had to pick up Jews in our free time, that meant in the evenings, after the workday was done. We looked up the addresses of the Jews who were missing and couldn't be located by the regular staff. We often came back empty-handed. We just had to hope that the Jews were home. We had no informants."

Tomson estimated he earned an extra fl.300 in total, or in other words he believed he and his colleagues picked up 300 Jews. Like Meiloo, he regretted what he had done, detective Van den Broek noted: "It was a rotten thing to do, volunteering for that kind of work. For the sole purpose of earning a little extra money, I offered to go out and round up Jews."

Tomson stated that he generally went out with Huisman, who also ended up being imprisoned by the Germans for *jodenbegunstiging*. And he stressed that neither he nor his wife, Wilhelmina Kleiman, had ever been a member of the NSB. He could not understand what had possessed him: "I had absolutely no reason to help deport the Jews," he lamented.

Meanwhile his wife had no idea of what was going on. Seven weeks after his arrest she still didn't have her furniture back – it was still being held by the authorities. The tone of her letter to the POD is slightly indignant: they didn't hurt anyone; they never got involved in politics, her husband had always helped so many Jews, and now this. Wasn't there any justice in the world? It is clear from the letter that Tomson, like so many other former bounty hunters, was not entirely honest at home about how he earned his money.[14] Meanwhile Mrs Tomson had to try to get by on fl.11 a week in post-war Holland with two children. "It's not easy with two mouths to feed," she wrote to investigators not long afterward. "I hope my husband will be home soon." Her hope was not justified. Little by little she too would realize that even if her husband was able to escape the death penalty, he would be away from home for many years, as the Special Court had categorized him as one of the most serious offenders.

The judges spent most of that March 4 session considering Tomson's case. Bertinga and Meiloo were dealt with quickly. They called no witnesses to speak in their defense. Tomson, however, called several. One Gerrit Vermeulen (67), an engineer, came to say that Tomson always warned him if round-ups of Jews were imminent. He stated: "I also gave him false papers when he needed to help a Jew in hiding."[15] These were likely for the husband of Marie van der Haaf, who testified that Tomson helped out Mr van der Haaf on several occasions. With false papers, but also by warning them about raids. A lunchroom manager, Max Gallasch, was prepared to say that he "didn't think [Tomson] was a Nazi," but that was as far as he was willing to go. Tomson had worked for the *Zentralstelle*, after all. One Norbert Loeb said that he owed his life to Tomson and wanted to testify on his behalf. Later, when all this was over, he even wanted to offer him a job – at least once he had rebuilt his ruined business.

The court also had a statement to consider from the priest of the Scheveningen parish that included Tomson.[16] Father Verhoeckx wrote: "Though his actions might have been weak and very foolish, he did what he did to stay with his wife and children, as his is a very happy marriage. This is a man who now clearly realizes the wrong he has done; he seems quite intelligent, and he will again become a valuable member of society after his release." In his own testimony Tomson emphasized his many good works. He even claimed he only went along to pick up Jews as a sort of cover, to avoid arousing any suspicion. "I often let Jews I had picked up escape along the way."

This claim was apparently too much for his former colleague Herman Bertinga to stomach, since he testified, "I never noticed the defendant letting any Jews escape." And detective Van den Broek, who conducted the interrogation in preparation for this case, also questioned this assertion: "Tomson never said anything about saving Jews during the interrogation, even though he had ample opportunity to do so." Van den Broek also added that in the very first interrogation Tomson even tried to deny ever having worked for the *Zentralstelle*, even though he was known to the resistance as a *Gestapo* agent – Tomson's name was on the long list of suspected agents that circulated during the war.

Unlike Bertinga and Meiloo, the barber from Scheveningen was not sentenced to death. The witnesses who came to testify on his behalf succeeded in tipping the scales of justice in favor of a life sentence. Tomson would be out of commission for a long time, which prompted his wife to write a letter to the court the very next day, March 19, to ask "if you would send my husband back home to me. Since I'm his wife and 26 years old with two small children. My husband has always been good to us. I don't know what will become of me and my children, because we can't live without him. Your honors, I hope you can make our young lives happy again." Signed: "Your humble servant, W. Tomson-Kleiman."[17]

The letter was the start of a long series of attempts to get his sentence reduced. An appeal of the sentence was unsuccessful, as were repeated requests for clemency. After upholding the death sentence for his two workmates, the Court of Appeals actually considered giving Tomson the same punishment. But because he was able to show that he had helped Jews from time to time, the Special Court substituted the most serious punishment with the second most serious – and the Court of Appeals supported this decision.[18] At that same time they issued a judgment on the case of Fred Meiloo. He was not as lucky as his co-worker. The ruling on Meiloo's appeal reads as follows: "By his own admission, for the purpose of augmenting their income, he and his associates asked the enemy to be given the task of arresting Jews, for which they earned one guilder per man per Jew and for which he received a total of 250 to 300 guilders. In the absence of any mitigating circumstances, such heinous crimes can only be punished with the ultimate penalty."[19] The sentence was carried out on March 28, 1947.

At that point one of the five, Peter Huisman, had already been dead for over two years. He was thirty when he signed a contract with Lippmann, Rosenthal & Co. and joined the bureaucracy of the mass deportations.[20] He had originally been a taxi driver. He was from a respectable middle class family and was a member of the Reformed Apostolic Church in Amsterdam. During the war, when virtually all taxi services ground to a halt, he found himself out of work. He then switched to a pedicab, as did many of his colleagues, but the Germans put an end to that particular line of work on the grounds that it was "contrary to human dignity." Huisman eventually became a barber on Ferdinand Bolstraat. Like Tomson, he feared being dispatched to Germany and thought he could get out of it by applying for a job with the *Zentralstelle für jüdische Auswanderung*. After the war his widow said she thought he was working for "some office at the *Wehrmacht*." When a detective asked her for information about her husband, she was not much help. "I know for a fact that he never arrested Jews but, on the contrary, tried to help them."

There is no way of checking the accuracy of that assertion. There can be no doubt that he picked up Jews, given the testimony of his colleagues Bertinga, Meiloo and Tomson. There was no indication that Huisman's role was any different from that of the others. It is quite possible that he was arrested by the SD for *jodenbegunstiging*, but it is no longer possible to unearth the facts that led up to the arrest. According to his wife, he helped Jews but, according to his colleague Bertinga in a police interrogation: "Huisman had been arrested by the Germans for taking bribes from Jews."[21] That is also plausible. Under the German system, accepting bribes was just as abhorrent as helping Jews out of altruism.

All we know is that Huisman was held for four weeks on Amstelveenseweg, before being interned at Camp Vught. After that he ended up in Neuengamme, by way of Haren. And it was there he died, on February 19, 1945. Five weeks later, on March 26, a German came to deliver the news to his widow, Mrs Francisca Noteboom. Later, when the POD conducted a detailed investigation into the course of events at the card catalogue, Mrs Noteboom would passionately take up her husband's case. He had never been a member of the NSB; he had never been pro-German; he had only helped Jews, and he had only taken the job because he needed the work.[22]

Nevertheless, it would mean his death. Chance played a bizarre role in the life of the Jew hunters. This is also clear from the story of Herman Bertinga, who deserves a chapter of his own.

—8—

Herman Bertinga
"Familiar with Stock Control"

On Monday, June 15, 1942, the classified section of the NSB newspaper *Het Nationale Dagblad* contained an inconspicuous advertisement of unknown origin. It took up two columns on page six, the back page of this thin paper, the size of which was dictated by the paper shortage. "Wanted: Female or male office worker" is the bold-faced line meant to catch the eye. The text continued: "Must have wide experience and be familiar with card indices and stock control."[1]

There were no indications of who placed the ad. "Send detailed application to 2557, PO Box 58, Utrecht," it said. It was thus an advertisement from a business that preferred to remain anonymous. The text also mentioned a number of other prerequisites: "Preferably someone who has worked in an office setting before. Good prospects for advancement. NSB membership."

The person who answered this ad and was ultimately hired was Herman Bertinga*. This can be gathered from his police record, which contains the letter of introduction Bertinga wrote to the unknown firm, on June 16, 1942.[2] The letter was written with a fountain pen, in an elegant hand and in impeccable style. The names of all the companies he cited as former employers are neatly underlined, without a single spot of ink, and at the top left corner of the sheet of paper there is a name stamp. It is obvious that Bertinga did not know where he would end up, as he indicated his willingness to move, should the firm be located outside Amsterdam. Morever, it is an exceedingly polite letter, in which Bertinga refers to himself in the third person. "The applicant is married, has no children under his care and is, along with his wife, a member of the NSB, registration number 77101." Bertinga reports that from 1920 to 1923 he worked "to his complete satisfaction" at a new branch of the Albert Heijn grocery store in Zaandam. Between 1924 and 1936 he lent his talents to Van Berkel Patent (as head of sales), and spent a short time with Rietschoten, Inc. in Rotterdam. During the period 1937–9 he was "executive bookkeeper for the Bosch Technical Trade Company in Amsterdam," but the firm went bankrupt. Despite all his excellent qualities, we read later, Bertinga found himself out of work. In 1941 he got a job as a truck driver with the NSKK (the Nazi's transport organization in Germany), and he was sent to France, Poland and Russia (including the Eastern Front). "He has outstanding references from each one of his employers," the letter goes on to say. Bertinga describes himself as a good, diligent and very accurate worker. He is also healthy and has a "robust constitution." And moreover, the letter says, he met another one of the requirements mentioned in the advertisement; he had experience "with designing and maintaining card catalogues and all the things that are necessary for good stock control."

On the basis of this letter, Hermanus Petrus Maria Bertinga, born in 1881 and thus at that moment sixty years old, was hired to work at the card catalogue of the *Zentralstelle für jüdische Auswanderung*, for it was they who proved to be behind the mysterious advertisement. The office was still under construction. In mid-June 1942 the deportations had not yet begun, and thus the *Zentralstelle* could not very well advertise openly. The fact that the position was evidently open only to members of the NSB was yet another sign that the German occupiers preferred to recruit their workers from this particular segment of the Dutch population. And the bit about being familiar with card indices and stock control is just an example of the macabre humor you sometimes come across among the architects of the Holocaust. In any case, Bertinga would not have to move; the office was on Adama van Scheltemaplein, not far from his home on Amazonestraat. And the *Zentralstelle* did not discriminate on the basis of age, so a sixty-year-old like Bertinga had just as much chance as anybody else. Naturally, the authorities knew the position was temporary and would only last until the job had been completed and all the cards could go into the same drawer. Bertinga signed his contract with Lippmann, Rosenthal & Co. for fl.230 a month – a lavish salary in comparison to what he had been receiving in welfare benefits over the last few months, but still less than some of his younger colleagues.[3]

Bertinga was definitely not work-shy. In March he applied (unsuccessfully) for a position with the municipal rationing service in The Hague. It is clear from his dossier why he was not hired. His potential employer went behind his back and made some inquiries with the NSB chapter of which Bertinga was a member; this was not uncommon. In that way the individual NSB chapter heads had a considerable amount of informal power. In this case the rationing service in The Hague was told that Bertinga had not done anything for the Movement recently, and with a negative report like that Bertinga could forget about the job.[4]

This was not the first time that the short, almost white-haired Bertinga had been hampered by the very party he joined with such great conviction in 1937. The NSB looked into his past and concluded that he was not terribly trustworthy. In 1918, at the age of thirty-six, he was convicted of embezzlement. According to an NSB report, "as an official of a public transport agency [he] misappropriated a letter containing money." At that time the Dutch judiciary gave no quarter for such offenses, and he was sentenced to eight months in prison. He also earned a black mark on his NSB record, as a result of another financial impropriety. He was a so-called "warden" at Chapter 39 for a time, and when he left there was a shortfall of fl.65.96, which was never paid back. This was plainly the work of a small-time crook.

No wonder the leadership of his NSB chapter attempted to thwart him. According to an internal report, he had a "bad reputation." He did nothing for the Movement; his attitude as a National Socialist was very poor, and he was considered unsuitable for any position within the party. He did finish high school, making him more educated than many of his NSB associates, but he could not be accused of possessing any particular talents. A later NSB report suggested that his reputation had improved somewhat over time but that he was still not trustworthy enough for a position with financial responsibility. This certainly had nothing to do with his family situation. His wife was also a member of the NSB, as well as the movement's women's organization, NSVO, and his daughter and son-in-law were National Socialists as well.[5]

Thanks to his well-written application, Herman Bertinga ended up at the card catalogue of the *Zentralstelle*, alongside Tomson, Huisman and Meiloo. He was the oldest one there – the others were rather protective of him – but he shared equally in the takings of their after-hours activities. This period of extra income did not last long, however. His dossier contains a notice that he was discharged on August 15, 1943. The personnel department of Lippmann, Rosenthal & Co. had their own special jargon for this as well: "We hereby inform you that the work for which you were temporarily engaged, by order of the *Beauftragte für die Stadt Amsterdam*, should be considered complete."

There was another job waiting for Bertinga, with Omnia Treuhand, a firm that took over a number of Jewish businesses. There was no opportunity here for him to pad his income by picking up Jews, but the starting salary of fl.250 a month was good. He stayed at that job until August 1, 1944. Then Bertinga returned to the private sector for a time, to a joinery works on Duivendrechtsekade, to be precise.

He was arrested on May 12, 1945. Two weeks later he found himself sitting across from detective Henk van den Broek, to whom he told his life story.[6] He spoke about his conviction for embezzlement in 1918, about his membership of the NSB, starting in 1937, and about his time with the *National-Sozialistische Kraftfahrer Korps (Brigade Luftwaffe)*, from April 1941 to February 1942. And, undoubtedly to the astonishment of detective Van den Broek, who was hearing the story for the first time, he spoke openly about the overtime earned by the staff of the card catalogue: "For every Jew I picked up, I got five or ten guilders on top of my salary. The addresses of Jews who were to be picked up were given to me." He told Van den Broek he was given his share even when he stayed at the office; he estimated that he was personally involved in the arrest of fourteen Jews. He admitted to being an anti-Semite. "In principle I wasn't against the deportation of the Jews, but I did object to how they were treated." And he told Van den Broek that the five of them had begun rounding up Jews "after asking to help out. We did it for financial reasons. Looking back on things, it was a rotten thing to do, earning money in that way. I helped to deport Jews just to earn a little extra. I now regret what I did."

Hermanus Petrus Maria Bertinga was a Roman Catholic and, according to the description in his file, he had a big crooked nose, a full set of false teeth and a bent back. He was severely bowlegged and deaf in his right ear. He looked seventy, in the opinion of the detective. He concluded his interrogation with: "I would like to apologize for what I did. If I knew then what I know now, I never would have gotten involved in it, and I wouldn't have joined the NSB either. I'm 63 now, and my life is ruined."

It is unclear if Bertinga actually realized just how true his words were. Perhaps he had got his hopes up a bit during his internment: on October 15, after being locked up for just five months, he already wanted to go home. He wrote a very polished letter to the "Head of the Bureau for National Security, Political Crimes Div."[7] He "politely requested [his] kind attention." He would be turning sixty-five soon; his wife was already sixty-eight, and she was paralyzed on the left side, suffered from hardening of the arteries and was being treated by a nerve specialist. She was alone all the time now but urgently needed daily care and assistance. Bertinga politely asked "to be released from prison, under whatever conditions you deem appropriate." Once again he used the third person, this time in the plural, when speaking about himself and his wife: "So they can spend the little time they have left together."

The request was denied. There was no cause to complain about the speediness of special justice in the case of the men from the card catalogue. We already know the outcome of the trial, which took place on March 4, 1946. The picture Bertinga painted in his interrogation was confirmed. Even though he was often given a break by his younger colleagues and did not always have to go out Jew hunting with them, he still received his share. And Bertinga himself suddenly remembered that it was his colleague Pieter Huisman who originally took the initiative and asked if they could participate in the bounty hunt.[8]

There was not a single witness present who had anything positive to say about Bertinga. The case was over before he knew what hit him. Two weeks later, the president of the court, E. van Schaeck Mathon, read out the verdict.[9] The crucial sentence was the following: "By handing over his Jewish countrymen to the Germans – who, as was generally known, intended to deport and exterminate the Jews by all possible means – [Bertinga] is guilty of crimes so reprehensible that, in the view of this Court, the ultimate punishment must be imposed."

Bertinga's attorney, A. Dunselman, filed an appeal, attempting to portray Bertinga as a simple soul, a stupid, insignificant, pitiful little man.[10] In the process he tried to forestall the impending execution. His written defense is full of the florid language that was typical of lawyers of his day. Here's an excerpt:

> His repeated attempts to support his family ended in failure; a litany of misfortunes left him an embittered man; in 1937 he joined the NSB, out of despair. This uncultured, petty man was driven to this most base of crimes, the full implications of which lie beyond his comprehension.
>
> Like so many German officials who were upstanding citizens during peacetime, he does not think his actions especially strange.
>
> Mentally speaking, he was completely in the grasp of the occupier, into whose service he fell one ill-fated day.
>
> The elderly defendant feels his execution would be shameful and injurious for his children.
>
> His life has been destroyed; this is beyond dispute, whatever your verdict may be.
>
> It is not in the interest of the Dutch state that short-sighted helpers of the enemy, among whom B. unfortunately must be numbered, be put to death.
>
> This short-sighted man, whose actions were those of an automaton, does not meet the standards for the death penalty, a punishment which should, as a rule, be regarded as reprehensible, despite the distaste the work in which he took part rightly elicits.

Dunselman's impressive plea sowed doubt in the minds of the justices of the Special Court of Appeals. The prosecutor, G.E. Langemeijer, seemed to have no such misgivings. He advised the court to uphold the punishment and said, quite plainly: "It is hardly possible to speak of this man's behavior in human terms. If the ultimate punishment was ever appropriate, it is [in this case]." But the Court of Appeals asked for extra time to consider Bertinga's case. On July 2, 1946, two weeks after Meiloo was condemned and Tomson's life sentence was upheld, the justices issued a ruling on the elderly bookkeeper who so wanted to spend his final years in the company of his wife. The result of the deliberations, in which all eleven members of the Court of Appeals took part, was that five of the eleven moved for the sentence to be commuted to life in prison.[11] "They base their decision," according to the minority opinion, "on the fact that [the defendant] was an insignificant man or on the fact that the defendant was at an age when his emotions and reason might not have reacted completely normally." Bertinga received one vote too few. Six members of the Court of Appeals concurred with the Special Court. "They consider the arrest of Jews in return for a bonus of one guilder a piece so repugnant that they can find no reason to give Your Majesty a favorable decision to consider."

Following that, Bertinga appealed for clemency, but that request was also denied. This was due to the fact that his application was received in the spring of

1947, at a time when all requests for clemency were judged on their merits. Later the government would drastically limit the number of executions to "a few dozen," according to the official, but classified policy. Ultimately, that would save the lives of all the other members of the Colonne Henneicke who had been condemned to death.

For Meiloo and Bertinga the change in policy came too late. On March 6 an item of just a few lines appeared in the newspaper *De Maasbode*. It read: "The Ministry of Justice has announced that the death sentence of H.P.M. Bertinga, whose petition for clemency was denied by H.M. the Queen, was carried out this morning."[12]

–9–

The Men at the Dutch Theater

In 1942 and 1943 the Dutch Theater on Plantage Middenlaan, near the Amsterdam zoo, was a special place for Jews and Jew hunters alike. Approximately 15,000 Jews passed through the doors of the Theater; it was a way station on the road that led to Westerbork (or sometimes Vught) and, ultimately, to the death camps. Jew hunters turned in their prey there and were given a valuable slip of paper by the guard on duty. You can see they did their best to write as legibly as possible. On April 24, for example, the names of Hartog Groenman, Hester Groenman-Polak, Sara Polak and Sofie Büchenbacher were copied down in meticulous block letters. Also included on the paper were their birth dates and the addresses where they were last living, plus the signature of the SS officer who took down the information.[1] The men who arrested the Jews could turn in these notes back at the office, where the information they contained was incorporated into reports, the so-called *Berichte*. After that all that remained was for the men to collect their bonuses.

Sometimes the members of the Colonne would hang around afterward in the Theater canteen. They would enjoy a cup of coffee, and now and then, as we know from eye witnesses, they would divide up the money. Their additional income was a popular topic of conversation – various employees of the Jewish Council who were regulars at the Theater overheard bits and pieces of these conversations, according to statements they later gave to the authorities.

A handful of members of the Colonne Henneicke were in the Theater quite frequently. They worked there as security guards and effectively had the run of the place, even though they were not officially guards. One of those involved, Henk van den Heuvel, explained after the war that the real guards came from the ranks of the SS and that a small group of Briedé and Henneicke's personnel were occasionally asked to fill in and "maintain order, by enforcing the ban on smoking, answering the phone and distributing food."[2] But it is clear from the files on the Colonne Henneicke that their duties often went beyond that.

In the early days of the deportations, the *Zentralstelle* building on Adama van Scheltemaplein served as the point of assembly; when Jews began receiving summonses in the summer of 1942, they were told to report there. For a short time they were required to report directly to Central Station, but in the third week of July the Dutch Theater became the hub of the deportations. Initially, Aus der Fünten had had his eye on the Portuguese-Israelite Synagogue on Jonas Daniel Meyerplein, but after an inspection it proved to be less suitable than he had thought. It was too dark inside, and if they installed lighting, the place would be too difficult to black out again. At that point the Jewish Council was ordered to negotiate a rental contract with the corporation that administered the Theater.[3] The contract stipulated a monthly rent of fl.300.

In the beginning the Jews spent just a few hours there, or a day at most. Then, in the evening, or at night, they were forced to walk to Central Station, from where the train to Westerbork would depart. Later the city trolley-cars were used to transport the deportees to the station. The trolleys generally rode at night. Presser mentions that a single phone call was enough to summon as many night trolleys as the Germans desired: "Those trolleys were ready on time every night."[4] The occupying forces had no cause for complaint about cooperation from the city's department of public transportation.

During the period from the final months of 1942 through September 1943, the Jews had to spend days, and sometimes as much as two weeks, in the Theater. At times the place would get unbelievably crowded, and conditions there were often intolerable, due to the heat, the stench, the thirst and the lice. There are few statements about the Theater from survivors, as most never came back and those who did survive the war would later experience conditions that were so much worse that their memory of the Theater faded. The freelance journalist S. Santcroos wrote a detailed, cynical account of his time there as an employee of the Jewish Council. His journal was hidden in a tube and buried in a garden on Plantage Muidergracht, where it remained until it was discovered after the war.[5] In his account Santcroos tells of a woman who cried out: "This place is unbearable! I'm practically choking. Can you smell the stench whenever someone opens the door to the toilet? We're not animals, are we? They just toss the mattresses on to the carpet. The children are covered with fleas from the rugs. Doesn't any man have the guts to set fire to the curtains? If there's a fire, they'll have to let us out. We're not animals!'

According to Loe de Jong, there was in fact an attempt to set the building on fire. In April 1943, when the Theater was temporarily vacant for cleaning, a resistance group smuggled some materials inside, but the conflagration they had hoped for never materialized.[6]

The above fragment from Santcroos's account is similar to the description provided by Benno Stokvis, a lawyer whose business occasionally took him to the Dutch Theater during the occupation. In his memoirs he wrote: "My throat closed up the first time I entered this inferno. It was like being in a giant mousetrap, teeming with questioning, searching, shouting women, men and children, who had no way out."[7]

According to the most reliable estimates, some 15,000 Jews were interned at the Dutch Theater.[8] The number of people being held there at any given time could vary dramatically. On occasion there were as many as 1,600 people, according to Santcroos, but there were also times when the building was empty, just after a train had departed, for example, or when the German staff was on leave. These changes can be observed in the sharp fluctuations in the costs of food in the accounts kept by the Jewish Council. From these records we can see that the busiest period was during March and April 1943 and that the figures for June and July were significantly lower; in fact, the curve follows the numbers of Jews arrested by the Colonne Henneicke perfectly.

The atmosphere at the Theater changed gradually as well. This can be gathered from the account of a local resident who experienced the war as a young girl in the Plantage quarter.[9] She wrote: "The Theater here behind our house was the gateway to Auschwitz, but the people didn't realize that. In the beginning there were even comical scenes in the courtyard of the Theater. At first the people were allowed to walk around freely, and relatives would come through the [adjacent] gardens, and they would have conversations over the fence. I had an old portable phonograph sitting on the windowsill, and I would play records, and the people loved that. That was in the beginning; at that point the people had no idea they would be killed. They thought they were going to work camps; they were light-hearted, even happy. When the SS started posting guards in the dressing rooms, behind the courtyard, the socializing ceased, and escape was no longer a possibility."

Her story seems to be quite an apt description of the situation, up until the last few words. At the Dutch Theater escapes were in fact the order of the day, though they almost always required the support of a third party. Anyone who wanted to get away needed help, in some form or another, and one possible source was the members of the Jewish Council who worked at the Theater. They had a wide variety of tasks: they distributed food and helped with luggage; they assisted people in all sorts of ways, including advising the detainees about the possibilities of an exemption. The office of the *Expositur* (a subdivision of the Jewish Council) at the Theater was charged not only with registering the detainees but also with familiarizing the candidates for deportation with the labyrinth of rules governing the issuance of a *Sperr*. Anyone employed by a business that supplied the *Wehrmacht* had a chance of an exemption, as did those in mixed marriages, employees of the Jewish Council, Jews who had been baptized Protestants, Jewish ex-front soldiers, Jews with dual citizenship and so on. The vagueness of these sorts of rules left a certain latitude for negotiation, the outcome of which was largely dependent on chance. In a report on the state of affairs in the Theater on the eve of a transport, one of those involved said: "The number of exemptions was dependent on the size of the haul. After the arrestees were counted, the list was produced, and after much haggling an agreement was reached. Most of the time the number of those released on a given evening was between fifty and eighty, about ten percent of the total, though this was also dependent on the mood of Messrs Aus der Fünten and Streich and the amount of alcohol they had consumed."[10] The employees of the Jewish Council did all they could to increase a person's chances of an exemption.

And sometimes they even helped people to escape. Often they would bribe the guards to look the other way. Walter Suskind was the head of the Jewish Council staff at the Theater and was responsible for helping countless Jews to escape. He had so much freedom of movement that he was sometimes able to walk out of the Theater with someone and come back alone. He made sure that captive Jews were given false Jewish Council identity cards, which they could use to escape. If it turned out that a group of Jews was exempt from deportation because they had the appropriate *Sperr*, non-exempt Jews were often surreptitiously added to their number, so they could leave the building unnoticed. Former Jewish Council staff member Jacques van der Kar wrote in his memoirs *Joods Verzet* (Jewish resistance): "There was an *Unterscharführer* [SS sergeant] who did business with a few employees of the Jewish Council. They would get him drunk, and on the nights that he was on duty he would allow them to let a few people out."[11]

After the war Hijman van der Kar, the son of a milkman who delivered milk to the Theater, told of another way of getting people out of the Theater: "Anyone who wanted to get somebody out of the Theater would give the name to the head of the Theater, Suskind. In the course of the day seven or eight people would be released, with the guards' consent. These guards had naturally been 'compensated' beforehand ... Without their cooperation such releases would never have been possible."[12]

Van der Kar added that those who were looking to bribe guards had to focus their attention on the Dutchmen – the Germans were implacable. But the testimony of scores of other witnesses suggests that this characterization did not always correspond to reality. A familiar face at the Theater was the Colonne member Rinus Schutten* – and he was known to all to be incorruptible. According to witnesses, he was so scared of the Germans that escape was impossible whenever he was around. This former office clerk, who was one of the few in the Colonne to have completed high school, attracted attention by regularly parading around the Theater in his black *Weerafdeling* (WA) uniform.[13] Later, when he was interrogated by investigators, he would deny it ("Maybe I had it on once when I was coming back from a meeting"). But the eyewitnesses who worked in the Theater remembered it well. "He was a hardliner, a real NSB man," Raphael Polak recalled after the war. "He never overlooked anything. If someone had a child in his arms, he would go right up to the person to make sure the child was registered separately." Another notorious Dutch guard was Anton Veldhuijsen*. Jacques van der

Kar remembered him as a "rabid anti-Semite," and described him in his testimony before the court in 1949 as follows: "He boasted of being able to tell if an identity card was a forgery with one look and claimed he could see straightaway whether someone was a Jew."[14] After the war Veldhuijsen denied arresting Jews; he claimed he had only been there to carry blankets and other belongings for the arrestees, and take care of their pets. But the memories of the survivors painted a different picture. As a child Veldhuijsen had trouble keeping up in school, and at the age of eight he often had to take over his alcoholic father's paper route. As a guard in the Dutch Theater, the former plumber Veldhuijsen, then thirty-nine years old, distinguished himself through his brutality. He assaulted a number of Jewish detainees; one woman was so badly beaten that she could no longer walk. Veldhuijsen, who had joined the NSB way back in 1933, was at his worst when escorting Jews to the train that would take them to Westerbork. "He acted like a beast, especially if there were Germans around," remembered Raphael Polak, a former employee of the Jewish Council, after the war. And his colleague Samson Koopman testified: "His main hobby was kicking and beating Jews who were about to be deported." Anton Veldhuijsen, Koopman explained to the court, "literally beat the Jews into the trains." Veldhuijsen had been posted to the Dutch Theater by the *Hausraterfassung*, together with a few colleagues. During his trial he denied being a member of the Colonne Henneicke, but evidence to the contrary was found in the group's official records. He had signed some of the *Berichte* as a staff member of the *Recherchegruppe Henneicke*, and once he even went out with the big boss in search of Jews. The Special Court showed him little mercy: considering that "he did his degrading work with enthusiasm and pleasure," he was sentenced to death in 1949, though the High Court of Appeals later commuted the sentence to life in prison.

But there were other guards who *were* prepared to look the other way, provided there was something in it for them. "As far as I know," said Hijman van der Kar, "those guards only received goods in kind for their cooperation, like gin, butter, cheese and eggs, etc. I never heard anything about any money changing hands."[15]

Today the best known of the German guards at the Theater is Alfons Zündler. He helped so many Jews that a German court ultimately convicted him of *jodenbegunstiging*.[16] In their books on the deportation of the Dutch Jews, Jacques Presser and Loe de Jong called him "a member of the conspiracy" to allow Jews to escape.[17] In doing so, they set a chain of events in motion. On the basis of a journalistic investigation and his own statements, Zündler was awarded the Yad Vashem medal. But shortly thereafter a committee was formed that cast doubt on Zündler's merits. The National Institute for War Documentation opened an investigation. After six months of laborious research – there was precious little information about the rather shadowy Zündler – J. Houwink ten Cate concluded that Zündler had not been brought before a German court for helping Jews, as he himself maintained, but rather for *Rassenschande*: sexual relations with Jewish women.[18] Although no hard evidence was ever found, Zündler was stripped of his Yad Vashem medal a short time later.

Houwink ten Cate's research also showed that an atmosphere had developed in the Theater "in which a relatively large number of guards were 'open to favors.'" Among them were three members of the Colonne, which was not surprising. These were men who were accustomed to making money from Jewish deportees, and thus it was obvious that they would leap at the chance to let Jews escape, provided it meant a financial reward for them. Henk van den Heuvel was the most active in this regard. He was also known to have arrested dozens of Jews, with his Henneicke cap on, but in court he produced a list of twenty-four names: all Jews he allowed to escape, "together with Suskind," he added. And he wrote at the end of his deposition: "I am proud I let these people escape, especially since they were completely innocent."[19]

And sure enough, this helped Van den Heuvel. Though judge-advocate Gelinck demanded the death penalty for him in February 1949, the court would eventually hand down a life sentence, based on the consideration that "his assistance to some Jews can be deemed a mitigating circumstance."[20]

Relatively speaking, there were even more escapes from the building on the other side of Plantage Middenlaan, the Jewish nursery.[21] This well-functioning institution had been located in this building (number 31) since 1942; prior to that time it had been a Jewish school. The director was Henriëtte Pimentel, and in addition to running the nursery she was also in charge of giving in-service training to childcare workers, this being the other main task of the institution. Starting in October 1942 the nursery effectively became an annex to the Theater across the street. All children younger than thirteen were kept separate from their parents, right up until the moment they were shipped to Westerbork. The number of children increased rapidly, and at a certain point they had to spend the night there as well. On the first floor large dormitories were set up, which were supervised by three childcare workers. Downstairs there was a special nursery, which Pimentel would keep an eye on at night. During the day the mothers were allowed to come and feed their babies. The nursery workers accompanied them back and forth; they wore a special armband for that purpose. The personnel of the Jewish Council frequently went there on all sorts of errands, and medical workers also came to the nursery on a regular basis. In the autumn of 1942 the leadership of the nursery struggled to handle the huge influx of children; from 1943 onward they could devote themselves to organizing escapes.[22]

In the beginning the most obvious way out was through the front door. There were no German guards at the door; the German standing guard in front of the Theater was supposed to monitor the nursery as well. That created the possibility of slipping out unnoticed with a child, when a trolley-car was passing by, for example. Often a member of one of the children's organizations would dash out the door under cover of a trolley, sprint alongside the vehicle and hop in at the next stop, with the abducted child. "The whole trolley started to laugh," remembered a woman who once pulled off this stunt. "They had all seen where we came from, but no one told on us."[23] One of her colleagues also praised the trolley drivers "as great chaps, or at least nine out of ten of them." In his book *Omdat hun hart sprak* (Because their heart spoke) on the efforts to rescue Jewish children, Bert Jan Flim also recorded stories about brave men who dared to don SS uniforms in order to "claim" Jewish children. One day a group even pretended to be Germans and took away an entire carload of children. And babies were regularly liberated from captivity in backpacks and wash baskets.

Most escapes had to be smoothed over in the official records. Walter Suskind was generally the one to do this, with the assistance of specialists. He saw to it that only children whose parents had given permission for such actions were taken from the nursery. He wanted to do all he could to prevent parents from discovering their children had disappeared just before they themselves were to be loaded onto the trains; that could lead to dramatic scenes, which would impede the rescue efforts.[24] In addition, children who were picked up from safe houses were given priority in such operations: they were "penal cases" and were thus at greater risk. Moreover, the parents of such children were almost always in hiding as well. In the nursery they were called orphans. If there were too few Jews on a given transport, these orphans were generally used to make up the difference. Suskind and his people, particularly his right-hand man Felix Halverstad, were organizational geniuses, who used every conceivable trick to cover up disappearances in the books and the card catalogue (the Theater maintained its own records of incoming and outgoing Jews). According to Flim, Suskind once succeeded in misleading a tipsy German guard by skipping from eighty-seven to ninety-eight when counting – if this went unnoticed, it meant that eleven children were temporarily saved from deportation.[25]

From May 1943 there was a sharp increase in the number of escapes from the nursery, in part because the groups responsible for finding hiding places were functioning more smoothly and also because more and more Dutch families were willing to take children into their homes; after the April/May strike of 1943 the mood in the country had become distinctly anti-German. A new escape route had also been opened up: the adjoining properties. Two houses away from the nursery was the Dutch Reformed Teacher Training College, run by director Johan W. van Hulst; from the yard, children could be lifted over the hedges to safety. In May 1943 a room in the college was added to the nursery. There toddlers could take their afternoon naps. The Amsterdam organization that found hiding places for Jewish children in the Dutch countryside now began to concentrate on abducting children by way of the college.[26] The director kept his eyes peeled for trouble, and almost every day the elderly concierge would open the door to guests who would later disappear with a small child. Later on, when oral exams were being held at the college, one of the external examiners happened to be Gesina van der Molen. As a prominent member of the Loyalty Group, which also coordinated hiding places for Jewish children, she had a chance to see first hand what the possibilities were, and from that moment on, the organization started smuggling children out of the nursery as well.[27] The Loyalty Group purchased alcohol, which Suskind could use to bribe German guards on the other side of the street.

During this same period another smuggling method came into vogue: the walk. Aus der Fünten was persuaded that the children in the nursery needed fresh air at regular intervals. Bert Jan Flim calculated that a few hundred Jewish children were abducted during these walks. Representatives of four different organizations made arrangements with the personnel of the nursery about the way the transfers would take place. The German guard who had to count the children when they left and when they returned was bamboozled time and time again. Sometimes an extra child would be smuggled along (under a cape); sometimes a toddler would be passed through a window during the walk. And later on, children from the annex or the teachers' college were put into line just before the end of the walk to take the place of the children who had been spirited away.[28]

In the last few weeks the nursery was open, the "kidnappers" began taking greater and greater risks. During a walk in mid-September eight children were pulled from the line. On one occasion, members of the resistance took fourteen children at once, by way of the teachers' college. Another time childcare worker Virrie Cohen, the daughter of the chairman of the Jewish Council, took fifteen children to a nearby office used by the Jewish community. On September 29 the nursery was closed, and the remaining children had to await deportation on the other side of the street. This took place on October 8; on that day two busses rode back and forth between Middenlaan and Panamakade (where the train was waiting) for four hours. This was the final transport from the Dutch Theater.

In *Omdat hun hart sprak*, Bert Jan Flim concluded that a total of 600 Jewish children were abducted from the nursery, almost 400 of them by the four organizations that were specifically devoted to helping Jewish children.[29]

The building that housed the nursery was demolished long ago. An apartment complex now stands on the site. Today the Dutch Theater is a memorial to the murder of the Dutch Jews. The auditorium was torn down some time ago; a monument now marks the spot. The front section of the complex is home to a permanent exhibit, with photographs of the Holocaust, along with documents and video images.

But there is no reminder of the bizarre struggle that took place on that spot between, on one side, those Dutch men and women who risked their lives to save a few hundred Jewish countrymen from the gas chambers and, on the other, the dozens of Dutchmen who earned a little extra money by dropping off as many of their Jewish countrymen as possible at the front door of the Theater and picking up a receipt.

–10–

Harm Jan van den Heuvel
"An Insignificant Player on the Stage of Life"

Of all the guards who worked at the Dutch Theater, Harm Jan van den Heuvel was the most infamous. He was known as "the blond Van den Heuvel," to distinguish him from his colleague Henk van den Heuvel, who had black hair. He was also called "the short Van den Heuvel," as was he a mere five foot four. But this thirty-seven-year-old NSB man was feared like no other. He would lash out at the slightest provocation and threw more than his share of punches, according to the testimony of various witnesses. "I saw him hit Jewish people several times. Before doing so, he would sometimes put on gloves," said Harry Wijnschenk, an ex-prisoner at the Dutch Theater.[1] In this respect Harm Jan was an exception; assaults were a rare occurrence at this *Umschlagplatz* (transit center) on Plantage Middenlaan. In a summary review of the Colonne Henneicke, the prosecutor in his trial, M.H. Gelinck, needed just a few words to characterize Van den Heuvel: "A brute who let his fists do all the talking."

Van den Heuvel was a part-time guard. Half the time he was one of Wim Henneicke's more active subordinates, but if an extra guard was needed at the Theater, Van den Heuvel was always prepared to fill in. He was described as fanatical, quick-tempered and unpredictable. When he appeared before the Special Court in March 1949, a veritable throng of people came to testify about the crimes he had committed six years before. And in his dossier the judges found the customary stack of *Berichte*, brief accounts of Van den Heuvel's forays through Amsterdam in search of Jews. Here's one example, chosen at random. On August 11, 1943 Bertje Moscou (52), widow of Simon de Haan, was walking down Stadionkade. She was arrested by Van den Heuvel and one of his mates from the Colonne. She had false papers and was carrying fl.170 in cash. The money went to the *Zentralstelle* and Mrs Moscou was taken to the Dutch Theater. From a note made by the detective who wrote up the arrest report on Van den Heuvel, we know the Jewish woman was sent to Westerbork on August 26, shipped off to Auschwitz on August 31 and gassed there on September 3, just after arriving.[2] And her story was by no means unique.

The testimony came from those who lived to tell about their experiences. Philip Keizer was one such person. He was arrested by Van den Heuvel on Nieuwe Herengracht, even though he had an English passport and, according to the rules, did not have to wear a star. He lost the battle against the Nazi bureaucracy, and after a fortnight in the Dutch Theater he was moved to a variety of concentration camps, which he ultimately survived.

Emanuel Davids was another victim who lived to testify. He and his wife were arrested in a building on Keizersgracht. At first Davids was able to get away by punching Johan Keuling, one of the four men who had come to arrest him, but the others caught him and exacted a bloody revenge. The four of them beat him badly, not just with their fists, but with truncheons as well. The men in question were, apart from Van den Heuvel and Keuling, Lambert Schipper, the ex-policeman from Limburg, and Hugo Berten, the only German in the Colonne. Davids was not able to tell the Special Court exactly who hit him and how. Berten apparently did not join in. Two of the men used truncheons, and Davids was left with a shattered jaw – in 1949 he still had a metal device in his mouth. Davids suspected he was betrayed by Van den Heuvel's brother, who worked as an accountant in his diamond business. Van den Heuvel denied beating Davids. On the contrary, he claimed in court, he actually helped Davids in the Theater. First he got blankets for him, before the departure to Poland, and later he helped him escape. Davids refuted this in no uncertain terms: the part about the blankets was true, "but he did not help me escape." And Davids concluded his testimony with the following sentence: "I have forgiven him for beating me, but not for arresting me as a Jew."[3]

Machiel Gobets, who worked for the Jewish Council at the Dutch Theater, subsequently confirmed that Van den Heuvel brought in a great many arrestees. "As a guard he was quite rough. I saw him hit a Jewish girl, who had been hiding. He hit others as well, though I never saw him seriously assault any Jewish people." Gobets remembered Van den Heuvel mainly for his fanaticism: "He once asked me for my *Ausweis* when I was talking with a non-Jewish girl. He said it was *Rassenschande*."[4]

Gobets' colleague Samson Koopman, another Jewish Council staff member at the Theater, estimated the total number of people brought in by Van den Heuvel to be somewhere around 100. "He was one of the most feared guards at the Dutch Theater. I saw him hit Jewish people on several occasions. Once, when a Jewish girl wouldn't say where her family were hiding, the defendant and other guards refused to give her anything to eat or drink for 24 hours." Witness Louis van der Kar, who was himself incarcerated in the Theater, added yet another accusation to the list: "As a guard he was quite rough. I once saw him kick a Jewish woman." Van der Kar had to look on as Van den Heuvel brought in his wife's parents, Mr and Mrs De Hoop, and his sister-in-law Lena. They said they had been arrested by Van den Heuvel. A short time after that they were deported. Van der Kar never saw them again.

Jacob Barend, who also worked at the Theater, had the following to say about the blond guard: "He yelled and he hit, and that made him worse than the other guards. He gave many Jews black eyes." Raphael Polak, who worked at the Theater as a twenty year old, had an even more negative memory: "In a word he was a monster. I saw the blond Van den Heuvel arrest Jewish people on the street. I also saw him assault defenseless people. He did it to demonstrate his power. I saw him lock up Mr Soep, of Amsterdam, in a special closet, where he beat him. I seem to remember that he was also involved in a sex crime that took place at the Dutch Theater, but I didn't witness it myself."

But nonetheless the court was given a fairly clear account of the incident. Harry Wijnschenk told the judges about a certain Tiny van den Brink. Van den Brink had told Wijnschenk that she might be let free but first had to submit to an examination in the Theater. Wijnschenk: "Around eight o'clock in the evening she was led away by the blond Van den Heuvel. She came back about 1:30, sick and queasy, clutching her underpants in her hand. She then told me she had been assaulted by the defendant and two others. She was later deported anyway."

In his testimony Machiel Gobets added: "Tiny van den Brink was a cousin of mine. She told me that Van den Heuvel had told her she would be released. But first, she said, she had to sleep with him. Based on what she later told me, I gathered that he had indeed had intercourse with her." The court transcript contains the defendant's response: "I categorically deny having anything to do with the girl in question."

With the story of Judith Hofman, the litany of disasters caused by Van den Heuvel is complete.[5] In late June 1943 Van den Heuvel paid her a visit at her home on Reitzstraat. He had a list in his hand, a list of names. He was there to take her and her husband into custody. Judith replied that this was out of the question. She was pregnant and, as such, entitled to a deferment of deportation until four weeks after the birth. In court Judith Hofman said that Van den Heuvel came by regularly over the next several weeks, apparently to check on the situation: "My child was born on July 8. Three weeks later Van den Heuvel said to me, 'Yeah, I know, you've got a four week deferment.' But the next morning he came back, in the company of another man." Van den Heuvel had come to arrest her, along with her child and her husband, S. Delden. While he was there, Van den Heuvel decided to pick up their Jewish neighbors as well, Mr M. Roet and his wife Mrs Roet-Scheffer. Mrs Hofman and her husband were sent to Vught and then Auschwitz; her husband never returned.

Like her neighbor, Mrs Roet-Scheffer survived Auschwitz and lost her husband. In court she testified that she had a medical certificate which exempted her from arrest. Van den Heuvel had come by a few days earlier with a small group, read the certificate and left Mrs Roet in peace. But a few days later he arrested her anyway, without explanation, along with her neighbors, in an ambulance.

This endless list of misdeeds caused the Special Court to take an unusual step during Van den Heuvel's trial in December 1948: it requested an expert evaluation of the defendant's mental state. In those days the psychiatrist was hardly a common sight in the courtroom. In the records of Special Justice one comes across the insanity defense only sporadically. As far as I could determine, of the whole series of suspects who could be considered members of the Colonne Henneicke, only three were given psychological examinations. Van den Heuvel was one of them, and he was examined by Dr S. Tammenoms Bakker of Amsterdam.[6] The two men were not strangers; during the war Van den Heuvel had gone to see the doctor before, for stomach problems that were ascribed to nerves.

In the psychiatrist's report we can read that Van den Heuvel was a latecomer – nine years younger than his youngest brother. His father and mother had four children. His father ran a pub for many years and earned a good living, but unfortunately he was one of his own best customers. Nowadays we would say he had an alcohol problem. Van den Heuvel's mother did not have an easy life. She and her husband fought constantly; she suffered from epilepsy and once attempted suicide by slitting her wrists. Even as a boy Van den Heuvel was not in the best of health: he had bronchial asthma and stomach problems. On top of that he stuttered as a child. He did not receive much attention; his parents were too busy. He had trouble at school as well, having had to repeat a year twice in primary school; at fourteen he was only in the seventh grade. After that he went to work, first as a busboy in a cafeteria, later as a bellboy in a hotel. Following that he attempted a career as an apprentice plumber, but he was not very successful at that either. His father got out of the pub business and opened a greengrocer's, where Van den Heuvel also worked. When he was twenty-three he started seeing a girl. She got pregnant, and the two were forced to get married. Van den Heuvel then became a taxi driver but lost his job during the Depression. The family grew quickly; they soon had five children, and their only source of income was Van den Heuvel's welfare checks. He underwent various stomach operations and did not rejoin the ranks of the employed until after the German invasion. He got a job at Schiphol Airport, as a groundskeeper at the tennis courts used by the German occupying forces. He was fired from that job too.

The Labor Exchange sent him to Lippmann, Rosenthal & Co., where he signed a contract for fl.270 a month in July 1942.[7] The money started rolling in, and Van den Heuvel's financial troubles vanished overnight, even though he started out working in the kitchen and cleaning the offices of the *Hausraterfassung*; initially they did not trust him to do much else. But in time he was promoted to inventory clerk – even Harm Jan van den Heuvel should have been able to learn how to update lists of confiscated goods. The *Hausraterfassung* sent him to Groningen for about five months, where he did the same sort of work. After returning to Amsterdam, he divided his time between picking up Jews for the Colonne Henneicke and working as a guard at the Dutch Theater. "This is where the trouble began," psychiatrist Tammenoms Bakker noted in his report. "He had to go along to make arrests and he became sick." Here it is clear that the psychiatrist gave a great deal of credence to his patient's story, especially considering that his work for the Colonne hardly suffered under this supposed illness. Van den Heuvel went on arresting Jews until September 1943. His name was on the list of Colonne members who were let go on October 1 because the work had dried up. Van den Heuvel was first granted a few months of sick leave. After that he moved to Haarlem, where he became a messenger at the offices of the provincial government. Later his job would include guarding the city park: he was expected to act as a kind of forest ranger and prevent people from illegally cutting down trees during the "hunger winter" of 1944.

In 1948 the psychiatrist concluded that while Van den Heuvel's health was not genuinely poor, he wasn't exactly in top physical condition either. "He speaks with a broken voice," the psychiatrist noted, "and exhibits nervous tics." His reactions were "functionally hysterical," and he blamed others for his misfortune: "There is little evidence of any deep, inner stirrings due to feelings of guilt." Tammenoms Bakker did not believe he was mentally deficient or demented to any serious extent: "At most he could be classified as mentally limited." His personality was not fully developed, and he exhibited signs of "puerile-hysterical forms of expression." The psychiatrist summarized his assessment neatly: "He is an insignificant player on the stage of life." But Tammenoms Bakker did not believe that all these limitations rendered Van den Heuvel incompetent to stand trial. "He is certainly not so pathologically disturbed or so deficiently developed that he would be unable to foresee the consequences of his actions."

Thus the court could focus on the seriousness of his crimes. The judges must surely have scratched their heads when Van den Heuvel made his final statement to the court, a rather confused summary of his ideological views: "Before the war I was opposed to fascism. When I became a member of the NSB, I did so to build anti-National Socialist cells. Later on I was blinded by the fact that Jews, who I had always considered to be the most fierce opponents of National Socialism, were making large deliveries to the Germans, and that the Jewish Council was always willing to help out the Germans, etc. This left me completely bewildered. Despite that I was not an anti-Semite during the occupation. I even made a hiding place for Jews at my parents' house. I deeply regret my actions during the occupation."[8]

This was not the first time the judges came across such convoluted reasoning in his dossier. In 1942 Van den Heuvel told the NSB he had a high school diploma and that he had previously been a member of the NSNAP, the Dutch Nazi Party, which was even more radical than the NSB. In the period after his arrest in 1945 he persistently denied ever having anything to do with the hunt for Dutch Jews. In an interrogation by the Bureau of National Security, in October 1945, Van den Heuvel's lies were so audacious that the detective on duty granted him a temporary release. Van den Heuvel told the detective he had been in charge of procuring travel clothes for Jews who had been arrested, and that all he had done was help Jews. When evidence later surfaced showing that he had been a member of the Colonne Henneicke, he claimed his temporary release had been a permanent one, and the state had a hard time re-arresting him.

The court did not impose the death sentence recommended by Prosecutor Gelinck; Van den Heuvel was given life in prison.[9] On the basis of the psychiatrist's report, the court concluded that he had not been entirely responsible for his actions, even though the document gives little cause for such an inference. The most important passages from the verdict are the following:

> The defendant aided the enemy of the Netherlands in carrying out its criminal measures, principal among them the deportation of the Jewish segment of the Dutch population.
>
> The defendant turned over countless Jewish people to their mortal enemies. He did not shrink from turning over a sick Jewish woman, a Jewish couple and their newborn child – the latter prior to the expiration of their deferment – to the Germans.
>
> At the Dutch Theater he went so far as to mistreat defenseless Jewish prisoners and to sexually abuse a young Jewish girl who was being held there.
>
> For such a heinous series of crimes he should be removed from society permanently.

For Van den Heuvel, "permanently" would mean until 1959. An appeal by his lawyer was once again rejected. In 1958 his sentence was reduced to twenty years, and six months later he was granted temporary release. At that point he was nearly fifty-three years old.

Van den Heuvel's dossier contains a letter from a certain Gerard van der Heide, a psychologist who returned from Auschwitz too weak to testify in the trial three years later. He still clearly recalled the day he was arrested by Van den Heuvel; he remembered his features down to the last detail, even better than those of his own mother, who died in the camp, he wrote. Van der Heide concluded his letter to the court as follows: "I only hope that this person, whose conscience remained mute in the midst of the most horrible work one could imagine, surrendering human lives for a few guilders per person, will not escape his just punishment."[10]

Released in 1959 – it is debatable whether Van den Heuvel could be said to have received a "just punishment."

−11−

Everyday Arrests

"I got sucked into doing it. It started with taking inventory of Jewish property; then every so often Henneicke would order me to go out and arrest a Jewish person, and in the end I was doing this on an almost daily basis. I'd estimate that I arrested about fifty people in total and brought them to the Dutch Theater or the *Zentralstelle*."[1]

This quote is taken from an interrogation of Colonne member Sjef Sweeger, and he should not be taken at his word. According to detective Prasing's records he was not responsible for fifty, but rather 210 arrests – and those records were far from complete. Sweeger was thus concealing numerous arrests. But the first part of his statement might very well have been true. Almost all the bounty hunters began their grisly new jobs with great reluctance. Anyone who has read the hundreds of interrogations of the over fifty participants in the hunt for Jews will see the same pattern over and over. It all started with registering Jewish goods, and from February 1942 to March 1943 that was the main task of the *Hausraterfassungsstelle*. Even that could sometimes be a shock. Mattijs van de Wert, for example, maintained under interrogation that he initially thought that he was working for a furniture dealer.[2] On his first day of work he was sent to Zandvoort, to take inventories of summer cottages belonging to Jews. This assignment lasted a week, and at that point he already wanted to quit, but his boss, Ragut, refused to accept his resignation. And so he stayed.

Henk Hopman told a similar story.[3] On his first day he had to report to Amsterdam Central Station. There he met up with Briedé, who took him and a few others to the ritzy town of Wassenaar to register and appraise the contents of a vacant villa. That was on June 22, 1942: his very first day of work, and he was already being sent to a posh villa in Wassenaar, with the big boss. And thus Henk Hopman gradually became accustomed to his new job as well.

In early March 1943 the emphasis shifted from tracking down Jewish goods to tracking down Jewish *people* in return for premiums, and not everyone found this transition so easy to make. At least seven of Wim Henneicke's subordinates told the detectives who interrogated them after the war that they considered resigning, or did actually resign. However, most of these claims should not be taken seriously. There were numerous discrepancies and inconsistencies in the suspects' statements, which is to be expected, as they all realized they were facing a possible death sentence. Among those who said they wanted to quit were seasoned Jew hunters like Hintink, Sweeger and Saaldijk, each of whom was responsible for the deaths of hundreds of individuals. Nevertheless, it is not inconceivable that they were telling the truth and that they were initially quite hesitant about doing such work. The attorney for the highly productive Colonne member Bob Verlugt contended that his client did in fact quit, but his letter of resignation was ripped up in front of him and he was told that from then on he would be under suspicion of sabotage and monitored closely.[4]

Henneicke and Briedé knew exactly what to do with their grumbling subordinates. The newcomers and ditherers were sent out with men who had no scruples about taking Jews from their homes. In this way they would become accustomed to the daily routine and gain the necessary mental toughness. Peer pressure undoubtedly played a major role. There was no room for ethics in this harsh world of NSB men who had suddenly got a chance to earn large sums of money, following years of poverty and public assistance. Anyone who didn't take part was, to use Henneicke's word, "soft." The leaders constantly made threats about forced labor in Germany. Some members of the Colonne soothed their consciences by letting arrestees go free; others released a Jew every once in a while, particularly if there was money in it for them or if they knew the person in question. There seemed to be a sliding scale. Those who had reservations and considered quitting in March or April were well past that stage by July and August and arrested every Jew they could get their hands on.

One man whose conduct was utterly shameless from the very beginning was Egbert Elmink, who was co-owner of a number of flourishing radio shops before he started arresting Jews. After the war he denied any involvement, but there was a mountain of evidence against him. In one of the interrogations he said, at least according to the official transcript: "In principle I was an anti-Semite, but even so some of my best friends were Jewish."[5] On April 27 Elmink had an address on Wodanstraat on his list. This was the home of the Scharlach family: father, mother and fourteen-year-old daughter Erika. He dropped by that afternoon and told them to get ready to leave. He announced that Erika's grandparents, Mr and Mrs Sachs, would also have to come along, but in view of their age they were given a day's reprieve – he would be back for them tomorrow. The Scharlach family did not have to hurry either; they lived near Elmink's house on Jasonstraat, and he decided to go home for a cup of tea in the meantime. An hour later he returned to arrest them; these people saw no sense in trying to flee. On the way to the Dutch Theater, Elmink took a long detour down Vrolikstraat, where he picked up Werner Salomon and the widow Cohen-Godhelp. He temporarily parked the Scharlach family *by a tree*, according to the testimony of one witness. Then he leisurely drove his five captives to the Dutch Theater. The neighbors of the families in question were astounded by such a display of arrogance. The Scharlach family was gassed at Sobibor and the Sachs family at Auschwitz.

Yet one time even Elmink was left at a loss for words, the day he and regular partner Gerrit Mijnsma went to arrest two families on Argonautenstraat. The neighbors who lived at number 21, a man of sixty-three, A.J. van Zoelen, and his wife of the same age, were standing outside and could not control themselves when they saw their Jewish neighbors being hauled away. Mr Van Zoelen started making denigrating remarks to Mijnsma and Elmink and subsequently got into an altercation with Mijnsma. Mrs Van Zoelen later confirmed this to investigators: her husband had got into an argument with a man from the SD.[6] Van Zoelen had wondered aloud what sort of person could "stoop to do such work." His wife had added, "What a lousy job you two have." Elmink said nothing (out of shame?), but his colleague Mijnsma answered, "We have to eat too." To which Mrs Van Zoelen replied, "So starve then." Someone who dared to put a Jew hunter in his place: it is a rare, and therefore almost heroic, example.

Far more numerous were the arrests we know nothing about, because there were no survivors. After the war investigators could do nothing more than mention the case in the dossier. One such arrest was made by Richard Kopper*, a thirty-three-year-old insurance agent, who was a good family man, according to his lawyer in 1948. But in spite of this, five years before, he and his partner Jan Casteels took a family of six from their ground floor apartment at 18 Iepenplein. We know that this was on June 29, a Tuesday, and the transfer receipt has survived: the names are in block letters, in beautifully balanced handwriting, the handwriting of Jan Casteels. SS officer P. Sukale signed off on the form at the gate to the Theater, thereby confirming the delivery.[7] Before the war Casteels had been at sea, in the long haul trade. With a great deal of effort he had obtained his diploma as a machinist, fourth class. In 1942 he had enlisted in the Dutch Volunteer Legion, a paramilitary group affiliated with the SS. His rank was *Oberschütze* (private first class), and he was awarded the *Ost Medaille, mit Verwundetenabzeichten* (the Eastern Front Medal, with a "wound badge"). He received five months of training in East Prussia and fought in a battle near Lake Ilmen. It was there that he was wounded, and after returning to the Netherlands he had trouble finding work. In 1942 he joined the *Hausraterfassung*; in that job his stiff right hand was no drawback. His handwriting was certainly no worse for it; the names of his victims of June 29 are still perfectly legible: Salomon Ferares (1902), his wife Frieda Ferares-Hertz (1905), and the children Janny (1928), Josefine (1935), Mozes (1937) and Herman (1939). The Red Cross was able to determine that they did not arrive at Westerbork until July 24. Six weeks later, on September 7, they were moved to Auschwitz. The mother and her four children, aged four to fifteen, were gassed upon arrival (September 10). Father Salomon later succumbed in the camp.

Richard Kopper did not recall this arrest; he was just an insignificant member of the organization, or so he emphasized in all his interrogations.[8] But detective Prasing discovered that Kopper made eighty-nine arrests; seventy-nine of his victims never came back.

Another everyday arrest: Gerrit Mijnsma was out on a job together with Henk Hopman, on Thursday, August 19, 1943.[9] Hopman started out as a clerk and later worked as a tax consultant but spent the majority of his adult life on the dole. Briedé sent the two men to 61 Amstel, as there were indications that Jews were hiding there. Hopman called his boss a short time later to say that he could not find anyone. Briedé looked through his papers for a moment and confirmed the tip: there *had* to be Jews at 61 Amstel. Hopman and Mijnsma went back and searched the house again, and this time they were successful. In the basement they found eight Jews. Hopman – not exactly the model of a take-charge employee – called Briedé again to ask for advice, and the latter sent over a car to pick up the prisoners. Gerrit Van Dien (53), Rachel Van Dien-Kokernoot (50), Abraham Rubens (60), Elisabeth Rubens-Aap (52), Samson Koopman (45), Alida Koopman-Hijman (44), Emanuel Koopman (23) and Theresia Kroonenburg (17) were first taken to the *Zentralstelle* and then followed the by-now familiar route: Dutch Theater, Westerbork, Auschwitz. According to the Red Cross none of them ever came back.

After the war neither Hopman nor Mijnsma could remember this arrest.

There was one thing Mijnsma did remember quite vividly: an attempted arrest on Vrolikstraat.[10] He was supposed to go there with his regular partner Elmink to pick up a Mr Van Gelder. When he rang the bell at the aforementioned address Maria Busnach opened the door and got the shock of her life, for she had two young Jews hiding in her home, Bernard Beugeltas and Barend Roe. When the two visitors asked for Van Gelder, Mrs Busnach said she did not know anyone by that name. But in reality she was worried sick that Van Gelder might come at any minute – she was expecting him with new identity cards for Beugeltas and Roe.

Mijnsma, a paperhanger in a previous life, slapped Maria Busnach in the face, but she still maintained that she did not know any Van Gelder. At that point Elmink left, announcing that he was going to fetch a German policeman (one of the notorious *Grüne Polizei*). He would get her to talk. Mijnsma was left alone with Mrs Busnach. The doorbell rang; it was Van Gelder. Mijnsma welcomed him with: "Come on in, Jew." When Mijnsma slapped Busnach again, Van Gelder flew into a rage. "So you want to hit Marie, do you?" A brawl broke out between the two men, which Maria Busnach described to detectives after the war: "When Van Gelder had the short one underneath him, I kicked him between his legs, which put him out of commission." Mijnsma was left moaning on the floor, and Van Gelder and Maria Busnach bolted, after a loud scream meant for Beugeltas and Roe. According to Mrs Busnach the two were later arrested, but she did not know the particulars. Barend Roe was shot while trying to escape and later died of his injuries, and Beugeltas never came back. Busnach herself went into hiding and survived the war. And the kick to Mijnsma's private parts – that was a unique event in the history of the Colonne Henneicke.

It was almost equally exceptional when someone managed to elude his or her pursuers, by chance, quick-thinking or bravery. In August 1943 things got quite tense for a time on Waalstraal in South Amsterdam, at number 57 II.[11] Christina Herbschleb-Hooyer had seven Jews staying with her at this address. One morning when she was out shopping, two men, one of whom she later positively identified as Colonne member Adolf Smit*, raided the building. They found a Jewish woman, Esther van Amerongen-Polak, in the kitchen. She kept the men talking long enough to give the others a chance to escape, which they did. They were one floor up, and Mrs Herbschleb's foster daughter, Elizabeth Schoneveld, saw her chance to let them out of the house unnoticed. The Jew hunters, who had been tipped off that there were seven Jews hiding at the address, subsequently discovered seven toothbrushes in the house, so they decided to stay put. They stood guard at the house until ten o'clock that night, and managed to catch another person: Mrs Wagener (this was an alias – she never told Mrs Herbschleb her real name), who was seventy-two, had come by the house to pick something up, a fatal mistake. She would later be deported. Esther van Amerongen, who stalled the two Colonne members long enough to allow the others to escape, would suffer the same fate. Her actions saved five lives, but on August 24 she herself was shipped off to Auschwitz, where she was gassed.

Of all the members of the Colonne Henneicke of whom a photograph exists, Adolf Smit, who was recognized by survivors as one of the men at the house that day, is the scariest. He looks angry, aggressive, with a fat, almost bald head. But during his trial, which resulted in Smit's receiving a life sentence, his lawyer portrayed him as a follower, a minor figure who took no initiative himself: "Unfortunately, most of the time he was assigned to a fanatic as a helper," according to B. Perridon.[12] But in his address to the court the attorney failed to mention that the raid at Mrs Herbschleb's took place just forty-eight house numbers away from Smit's own home. Smit also lived on Waalstraat. It was only the most brazen bounty hunters who would arrest Jews on their own street.

A few streets away, on Waverstraat, a young Jewish boy escaped arrest by the skin of his teeth in August.[13] Robby Aak's exact age is unknown: he might have been four, or perhaps six. Though he was actually living with the Van Blankenzees on Van Ostadestraat, he would regularly stay with a son-in-law of the family, the tailor Boomgaard, of Waverstraat. At some point someone must have betrayed Robby Aak. Two men came to take him away; one of them was Pieter van

Amersfoort*, a forty-seven-year-old (mostly unemployed) transport worker, who was posted to the Colonne Henneicke in the summer of 1943.

Van Blankenzee, the boy's unofficial foster father, spoke to the men. Under threat of arrest he eventually admitted that the child was at his daughter's and gave them the address. He immediately sent his son to the address, to warn his brother-in-law and save the child. He arrived there in the nick of time. Boomgaard was about to flee with the child in his arms, but just then he noticed that there were two men at his front door. He dashed back up the stairs and gave the child to his brother-in-law, W. van Blankenzee, who hid with Robby. The two Jew hunters (Van Amersfoort and Frans Takkert*, a thirty-six-year-old distiller) were kept talking inside, and in the meantime brother-in-law Van Blankenzee was able to slip out of the house with the child. In desperation Boomgaard, under severe pressure, gave the men the name and address of another relative where, according to him, the child might be. Van Amersfoort and Takkert continued their search. They ended up at the house of another brother-in-law, and who should be standing there chatting at the front door but Mr Van Blankenzee, at whose home the hunt for Robby Aak had begun. At that point Van Amersfoort and Takkert decided to arrest the entire family, but the interrogations were fruitless. After half a day the family was released. They were given a week to divulge the location of the child, but they refused. Robby Aak's whereabouts remained unknown; he had been placed with another family.

Van Amersfoort later returned to Boomgaard's, but in the end he let the matter drop. Apparently he was not as tenacious as some of his colleagues. After the war he was given seven years, a relatively light sentence for a member of the Colonne. Who knows, perhaps the court took his personal situation into account. Van Amersfoort was a sad example of a dedicated NSB man, who gave up his two sixteen-year-old sons to the SS. At the end of the war he received news that both had perished on the Eastern Front.

In the files on the Colonne Henneicke one can also find the key to the betrayal of the only Jews in the whole of the Second World War whose illegal existence was recorded on film.[14] The people in question lived for some time above the famous Alcazar cabaret on Thorbeckeplein. Their protector there was the owner of the business, Dirk Vreeswijk. Around 1982 a few rolls of 8 mm film were uncovered during renovations, hidden behind a roof beam. The film showed the Jews in their secret hiding place, while one of them operated the movie camera on special occasions. On the one hand, these images were of an unprecedented authenticity, showing people going about their daily life as they awaited their fate. But on the other hand there is also a stagy quality to them. The group listened to the English radio and followed the progress of the Allies, with a map close at hand. You see them celebrating Christmas and New Year in 1943. Two men wash each other's backs in the tub. And then there is an emergency drill. Everybody goes into his or her hiding place, some between double walls, others in the cabinet under the sink, and two people under the stairs.

On May 28, 1943 these emergency measures were to no avail when four men stormed up the stairs at Alcazar. They had been tipped off, and they knew where to find the Jews, though they did miss a few of them in all the commotion. It was not members of the Colonne Hennecke who carried out the raid, but their competitors: policemen from the former Bureau of Jewish Affairs, who were now working for the *Sicherheitsdienst* under the German Otto Kempin. Nevertheless, among their number was a member of the Colonne, Henk Saaldijk, whom we already know as the man who picked up sick Jews in an ambulance and brought them to the Dutch Theater.[15] After the operation, on the morning of May 28, Saaldijk ran into his dentist, Frans Tijhuis. After the war the latter told the detectives who interviewed him: "I was talking to someone on Herengracht, right by my house. Saaldijk, whom I knew, came by with a few boxes of cigarettes under his arm. He stopped next to us and said, 'We just made a big haul. We picked up fourteen Jews at Vreeswijk's on Thorbeckeplein and confiscated gold and cigarettes.'"

Saaldijk had been sent there by his boss Briedé to seize whatever goods were found, this still being the primary task of the *Hausraterfassung*. It was, however, an unusual occurrence. In general, Kempin's police officers and Hennecke and Briedé's civilian Jew hunters worked at cross purposes. For the latter the arrest of fourteen Jews by the competition was a painful financial setback.

Another notable arrest was that of A. Smit, the Jewish vice president of the Amstel Hotel, who had been the boss of Colonne member Aaldert Dassen when the latter worked there as a waiter.[16] One day in April 1943 he saw Smit in a trolley-car; Dassen himself was on the front platform of line 5. He loathed Smit because the latter never made any secret of his feelings about the NSB, as Dassen put it in a post-war interrogation. Dassen often felt he had been unfairly treated and longed to get even with his old boss. Dassen later explained to investigators that "all Jews had to work in Germany, but this Smit had a lot of money so they left him alone." The former KLM steward, who was just thirty-three in 1943, saw that Smit was accompanied by his wife and followed the two to Central Station. He observed them buying tickets and boarding the train to Alkmaar. Dassen did not know what to do, so he called Briedé from the platform. His boss said: "Ask them to come with you to have their papers checked." He did so, and the two went with him to Adama van Scheltemaplein, where they were handed over to "detectives" from the Colonne Hennecke. The next day Dassen heard that Smit and his wife had taken poison. Dassen apparently made an effort to have them transported to hospital, which they were. But Mrs Smit was beyond help; she succumbed to the effects of the poison. Her husband recovered and was sent to the Dutch Theater and then to a concentration camp, where he too died.

Aaldert Dassen was only with the Colonne Henneicke for a short time. He applied for a job with the *Landwacht*, the NSB militia, and started work there in May 1943. He served out the rest of the war in a black uniform. In 1949 his lawyer called him an idealist; at eighteen Dassen was already a member of the NSB. In court he claimed he did not know the fate of the Jews, and thus that of his former boss at the Amstel Hotel. He maintained that he did not hear about it until after the war, in the internment camp: "I suffered a serious mental breakdown, but I managed to recover from this breakdown thanks to my reborn faith in Jesus."[17] In 1949 Dassen was sentenced to life in prison, mainly for his dastardly actions against his former boss and his wife.

One quality typified by the men in Henneicke's service was cunning, particularly after they had gained some experience in tracking down Jews. Without a doubt two of the most cunning of all were Chris van den Borch and Joop den Ouden, who generally worked as a team and were together responsible for hundreds of arrests. They were quite adept at working their way from one address to another; by means of threats, detective work and all manner of trickery they formed a sort of private intelligence agency. At one point Van den Borch and Den Ouden arrested a man, a Mr D., who initially denied being Jewish.[18] Den Ouden "perform[ed] a physical examination to determine whether the suspect [was] a Jew," according to the report, and extracted a number of other names from him, like that of Willem Lodeizen, a member of the resistance who specialized in making false identity cards, ration cards and stamps. When they raided Lodeizen's house, he was not at home. They did find his wife, who was pregnant. They asked when the baby was due, and came back regularly in the weeks leading up to the birth, in the hope of catching the father at home with his family. Lodeizen, however, did not turn up, although during their first visit the men did find a note, ready to be delivered. The note was addressed to a certain widow Sipsma, and informed her that, as per her request, a radio repairman would be sent to fix her wireless. Van den Borch and Den Ouden pursued every lead and decided on a plan. Den Ouden would wait nearby, while Van den Borch took the note to Mrs Sipsma's home, where he only expected to find an illegal radio set. But when a Jewish-looking man opened the door, he understood that there was more to be had. The man obviously trusted him completely and inquired about the state of things. Van den Borch replied that things were looking up and then told the man that he was going to get the radio repairman. He met Den Ouden at the appointed place, not far from the house, and informed him that there was a Jew staying with Mrs Sipsma. Then Den Ouden went to the house, rang the bell and unscrewed the radio. After a seemingly expert look, he said he had to go and fetch some spare parts. Shortly after that Van den Borch and Den Ouden burst through the door. They were now armed, and the haul was even bigger than they had expected: no fewer than six Jews were hiding out at Mrs Sipsma's house, and one of them lived to tell about it. Judith de Leeuw-Cardozo, of Utrecht, remembered after the war how rough and abusive the men had been. "Anyone who moves is going to get shot," Joop den Ouden had said several times. Every sentence uttered by Den Ouden and Van den Borch ended with the word "Jew." When a cheesemonger rang the bell to drop off two cheeses, Van den Borch snarled at him, "Are you telling me you *feed* these Jews too?" Van den Borch and Den Ouden cut themselves some of the cheese, which they ate then and there. They took the rest back to the office, where Henneicke could decide what should be done with it.

They confiscated a large sum of money from the detainees (more than fl.2,000 – today that would be $12,650) and some gold objects, while the Jews and Mrs Sipsma were taken away in a police van. The next day the latter was allowed to return home; her daughter Clazina, a forty-two-year-old civil servant, had to report back to Scheltemaplein every day for the next two weeks. When she ran into the duo Van den Borch and Den Ouden a few weeks later on Oosterparkstraat, she greeted them, she would later say, with a nod of the head. A few hours later she was summoned to Noorder Amstellaan by Henneicke. "He accused me of not having greeted two of his officials, even though I knew them quite well," Clazina Sipsma later explained to the police. "According to Henneicke that was tantamount to insulting an official on duty. After a lot of threats and some very profane language I was locked in a room for four hours." After that she was allowed to go, with a warning from Henneicke "never to have anything to do with Jews again." Afterward it turned out that it was Joop den Ouden who had taken offense at Clazina Sipsma's "arrogant behavior." She had not greeted the men who had dragged six Jews from her mother's house enthusiastically enough. Den Ouden had complained about this to Henneicke and, as a boss who stands up for his employees, he had set things right.

Of the six Jews, Judith de Leeuw was the only one to survive Auschwitz. The other five perished there; they were so-called penal cases and, as such, were given priority for deportation. Judith and her sister Liena ended up in the experimental barracks (Block X) of Dr Glauberg from Berlin. Liena was sent to the gas chambers. Judith told detectives after the war that "her reproductive abilities had been taken away" from her, but not her life. Eventually she was transferred from Auschwitz to Ravensbrück. After enduring yet another camp, she was ultimately liberated by the Russians.

The line between getting caught and not getting caught was sometimes extremely thin. That one note waiting to be delivered was fatal to five people. On June 16 it was a small, sudden movement that spelled the end for twelve Jews in hiding, or at least the end of their very limited freedom.[19] This happened at 212 Willemsparkweg, where Eelkje de Boer (51), a dressmaker by trade, had three legal boarders in her house and twelve Jews. On Wednesday, June 16, she received a visit from the two brothers-in-law in the Colonne, Martin Hintink and Jan

Rudolfs. Mrs De Boer was outside repairing the doorbell when the two approached. They asked her for the papers of the people living in the house. Mrs De Boer was busy getting together the papers of her legal boarders, when one of the illegal occupants made a careless mistake, sticking her head over the landing of the basement stairs. One of the two men spotted her. The two highly experienced Jew hunters (they were among the most productive of the group) marched down to the basement. There they found twelve Jews: two men, eight women and two children, eleven and six years old. According to information from the Red Cross the two children were saved, though there is no way of finding out exactly how. The other ten were taken from Westerbork to Sobibor on June 26, and most likely murdered there on June 29.

Displaying great presence of mind, Mrs De Boer prevented an even greater catastrophe. When Hintink and Rudolfs found a note in the basement containing seven addresses where Jewish children were being housed, she immediately tore it up and gave each of the two men a fl.100 note, as compensation. With that action she probably saved seven young Jewish lives, although we do not know who they were and what ultimately happened to them. Hintink and Rudolfs let the matter rest, apparently because they figured they were much better off with fl.100 each than they would have been sharing a bonus of fl.52.50. After the war Mrs De Boer said to detectives: "Those two men behaved professionally, but they said I was to blame [for what had happened] and they had to arrest me as well." On Noorder Amstellaan, the morning after she had been arrested, she saw Hintink at his desk and heard him "telling [his co-workers] with obvious pleasure about the big haul he had just made, namely ten Jews and two Jewish children."

Eelkje de Boer was imprisoned and sent to Vught concentration camp. When that camp was evacuated as the Allied liberators were approaching, in September 1944, she was transported to Ravensbrück. She survived and was the only one who could testify about this mass arrest, which occurred because someone had stuck her head over the basement stairs at the wrong moment.

Some Jews spent part of the war in very unusual hiding places. The revolving bookcase leading to the Frank family's secret annex is, of course, a world-famous example, but there were other creative solutions. At an address on Rafaelplein in South Amsterdam, a few blocks from Euterpestraat and Adama van Scheltemaplein, where the SD and the *Hausraterfassung* had their headquarters, a hiding place was constructed that was as good as undetectable.[20] Two properties, numbers 34 and 36, formed a boarding house with three entrances and exits. Mrs Asman-Del Valle ran the boarding house. She was married to a gentile, but they had her Jewish parents and brother staying with them. If there was trouble, they could hide in a room no one would be able to find. The only problem was that trouble was the order of the day. One of the lodgers there must have been working for Henneicke as an informant some time in early August 1943, because the number of targeted searches steadily increased during that time. Former policeman Van der Kraal was involved in most of these searches and many was the time that he would walk around the top floor of the building, shaking his head, unable to find the Jews he knew were hiding there. On August 6 it was Henk Hopman's turn. This rather dim-witted, almost permanently unemployed bookkeeper showed up bright and early one morning to conduct a search of Mrs Asman-Del Valle's boarding house, but he was unable to find anything either. He had been ordered to monitor the house closely, and he announced that he would spend the entire day there, if necessary, to solve the mystery of the missing Jews. Hopman was not above eating the two meals that the hospitable landlady offered him. Apart from that, he did nothing that whole Friday. At the end of the day reinforcements came: all the leading Jew hunters took part in the search. Henk van der Kraal, Willem Briedé and Wim Henneicke went over both houses with a fine-tooth comb, knocking on every single wall. Ultimately it was Henneicke – naturally – who found the hiding place. Mrs Asman-Del Valle explained to investigators after the war: "By connecting the two properties, we were able to block off part of the attic completely. The entrance to this hidden room consisted of the bottom section of a door, against which we had built a full washstand, with running water. The top part of the door remained where it was, flush with the wall. If you wanted to go into the room when there were people inside, they had to unlock the lock from the inside, after which the entire washstand, which was affixed to the bottom half of the door, would turn inward. You then had to crouch down to get into the room."

At the house on Rafaelplein it is still possible to get an idea of how the whole thing must have worked.[21] The attic level consists of fairly large, open-plan rooms with a sort of alcove on the side, about a meter in width. At one time it had contained a kitchenette; one section of it is now used for storage, and elsewhere there is a shower stall, which was put in later. It is there that the wall with the revolving washstand must have been in 1943. This clever setup made the hidden room almost impossible to detect, except for a zealous Jew hunter like Henneicke. According to the *Bericht* on the case, three Jews were taken away from the boarding house on Rafaelplein that day. Mr and Mrs Del Valle would never return; their son jumped from a moving train and managed to find a new hiding place.

One of the members of the Colonne later returned to the house on Rafaelplein. It was Henk van der Kraal, who appeared at the door a few weeks after the raid. He had come to talk to Mrs Asman-Del Valle. He had a question for her: if the tides of war should turn and he should find that his own life was in danger, could he possibly make use of that fantastic hiding place upstairs? According to the trial transcript, Mrs Asman "naturally promised him [the use of the room] straightaway."

Things never got to that point though. Henk van der Kraal, who joined the club of Jew hunters in the Amsterdam police force after his time with the Colonne

Henneicke, was picked up early on, in May 1945, and as one of the most serious offenders he was sentenced to death in November 1948.[22] He was ultimately pardoned. In his file there is a sort of testimonial from the German Wörlein, one of the three *Hauptsturmführer* (captains) of the *Zentralstelle für jüdische Auswanderung*, which reads, in part: "Van der Kraal is currently working for the group that tracks down Jews in hiding; in his work there he has shown once again that he is utterly dedicated to the German cause."

–12–

Eddy Moerberg
"A Gentle Character"

In going through the files on the members of the Colonne Henneicke, one regularly comes across facts or circumstances which, at the very least, can elicit a certain understanding for the crimes these men would later commit. Neglect as a child, for example, or a speech impediment that led to bullying. Or a sexual relationship between an adolescent and an older woman, or intense pressure from one's family to bring home more money. Although these things were certainly no excuse for hunting Jews in exchange for bonuses, a judge might decide that such factors constituted mitigating circumstances.

In the case of Eddy Moerberg*, born in 1902 and thus forty-one when he joined the Colonne, none of the above applies. He had an exemplary childhood, with loving parents, in a harmonious environment. In fact his file contains a letter to the Special Court from a relative, who wrote: "No member of our family has ever been in trouble with the law. The older ones among us hang our heads in shame."[1]

A cousin of Moerberg's, Mrs De Gans, had already written a letter to the court in which she spoke of Moerberg's character and upbringing: "I can also say that, as a boy, and later as a man, he had a very sweet, gentle character. It simply was not in his nature to hurt others."[2] And then, the cousin continued, there was Mother Moerberg: "And what is more, it was his great privilege to have a sweet, strict, God-fearing mother, who would say to him every day: now don't let me catch you getting into any mischief." Mrs De Gans ("He was very docile, even at school") expressed her shock at the charges against Moerberg, who was accused of arresting large numbers of Jews and turning them over to the Germans: "It is a mystery to me and the entire family how our cousin could do such things. [The news] left us dumbfounded. A man who would never even hurt a fly. The only real trouble he ever had was a marriage he was forced into. But even then he did the right thing by the woman in question."

She was referring to his marriage to a New Zealander, Edna Mohan, whom he had met in 1936 during one of the voyages he made as a radio operator in the merchant marines. Moerberg and his wife had four children. The oldest, John Edward, was born in 1927 in Wellington. The others came into the world after Edna had settled in the Netherlands: Edward in 1935, Leo in 1941 and Ruby in 1943. Moerboerg's cousin, Mrs De Gans, wrote: "He was a model husband and father to his wife and children." And his own father and mother, who both died in 1939, never had any complaints about him either, according to his cousin: "He was always exceptionally considerate toward his parents and until their death he always treated them the way a man should treat parents like his. A very modest person."

So what went wrong with Eduard Gijsbertus Moerberg? What led attorney general Bakhoven to characterize him later as "one of the worst of the Jew hunters"?[3] His dossier offers no definitive answer to these questions. A psychological examination was never deemed necessary in Moerberg's case, so there is little we can say about the structure of his personality. He was, to say the least, a bundle of contradictions. He was also an adept liar, who tried to escape justice by manipulating the truth whenever possible. In 1946 he was interrogated by a staff member of the Bureau of National Security.[4] He had been brought in under suspicion of having been a Gestapo agent. He stated that he broke his arm in March 1943 and was given six months' (!) sick leave. In this way he was attempting to cover up his time with the Colonne Henneicke. We find another flagrant lie in a letter he wrote to the NSB.[5] Moerberg had been a member from 1936 to 1938. Then he stopped paying his dues and was struck from the membership rolls. When he re-registered in 1942, he had a curious explanation for having terminated his membership three years before: terror. Jewish terror, he noted on his form. "My father owned several houses, most of which were occupied by Jews, and as soon as these people got wind of the fact that the landlord's son was a member of the Movement, my father asked me to cancel my membership to spare him any hassles, since it was a fact that, if they had known for sure, they would have all moved out. After conferring with the group leader, I resigned from the organization."

He denied virtually any involvement in the arrest of Jews, both to police and later before the Special Court. He admitted to having been present, by chance, for just four arrests. Despite a veritable cartload of evidence, he pled not guilty to the other charges.

On two occasions, he admitted, he was cycling home from work with his boss Wim Henneicke when they happened to see people with Jewish features. One time it was two young Jews on Pijnackerstraat, the other time a couple on Ringdijk. On both occasions they brought the arrestees to Noorder Amstellaan, just before dinnertime.

Moerberg denied being involved in an arrest on the street where Wim Henneicke lived, Linnaeusparkweg, in a building used by a Catholic youth group.[6]

In this one raid, no fewer than eleven Jews were taken into custody, on Thursday, August 26, 1943, at eleven o'clock at night. The occupant, G.A. Schröder, had taken these eleven people in; they had a hiding place in the basement. Three men came to call that evening: Moerberg, Henneicke and Andries Riphagen, a well-known figure in the Amsterdam underworld. After Schröder had called down from the balcony to ask why they were there, they said they were from the Air Raid Defense. When Schröder opened the door, the three made straight for the cellar, where they found eleven people hiding. A twelfth, a Mr De Bont, managed to get away. The arrestees were rounded up, the men with their hands up, and driven off a short time later. The next day Mrs Schröder went to warn an acquaintance who was also hiding Jews, a widow Steenman. But the men had been there the night before and had taken the three people away. The three Jews had been living in an ingenious hiding place, concealed in closets. Mrs Steenman was told that she could avoid arrest herself if she could give them two addresses where Jews were being harbored, but she refused. In the end they let her stay at home anyway.

After the war, Moerberg's claim that he was definitely not present on that occasion collapsed under the weight of the evidence. He was positively identified by one of the survivors, but even then he continued to maintain his innocence. At that point the authorities arranged a face-to-face confrontation with Mr and Mrs Schröder, in which the former claimed, with great certainty, to recognize him. But Moerberg stuck to his story that he was not there.

In the beginning things had looked so promising for Eddy Moerberg. After finishing high school, he went to work for a notary in Amsterdam. After that he got himself an office job with the Rotterdam Bank. In his free time he studied to be a radio operator – he wanted to go to sea. He spent his period of national service with the Engineering Corps in Utrecht, and after that his dream came true. He was hired by Radio Holland as a telegrapher and sailed the seven seas, in freighters as well as passenger ships. He did this for twenty years, from 1922 to 1942. By that time employment opportunities in Holland had dried up, and he went to work for the *Hausraterfassung*. He worked there as an inventory clerk and spent much of his time out of the main office, in the provinces of North Brabant, Limburg and Groningen. Beginning in March 1943, he worked regularly with Henneicke's team, where he did a lot of the typing. In contrast to virtually all his colleagues, he had a solid command of German and therefore ended up typing up many of the *Berichte* in German, on the basis of the rough versions dropped off by his co-workers. In August he began organizing the Colonne's records; Henneicke had been neglecting the bookkeeping, and the records were in a terrible state. When detective Wijnand Prasing subjected him to a in-depth interrogation after the war, Moerberg tried to explain why his name appeared at the bottom of so many *Berichte*. The reason, he claimed, was that many arrests were made by people who were not in the Colonne. "Henneicke didn't like that, so we would use names of people who happened to be present at the time, like myself."[7] He never admitted that bonuses were paid based on the number of arrests made by each member of the Colonne. Moerberg, like all his colleagues, denied having received bonuses during this period. Based on the evidence, it is clear that he had a close professional relationship with Henneicke and was privy to confidential information.

The fact that he did his job with dedication and conviction is evident from his decision to continue doing the same work after the Colonne was dismantled on October 1, 1943. At first he joined the fur department of the *Hausraterfassung*, which confiscated all the fur it could find for the benefit of German soldiers on the cold Eastern Front. In January 1944 Moerberg was hired by the former Bureau of Jewish Affairs, which was run directly by the *Sicherheitspolizei* under Station Sergeant Abraham Kaper. At that point Moerberg was on the payroll of the Amsterdam police, but his policeman's salary was not his only source of income. After the war he explained that under Kaper he received a fl.15 premium for every person he arrested. "As always . . . I deposited the money I received in the Red Cross collection box near Kaper's office," Moerberg said in an interrogation. More than likely, this was just another one of his lies. His colleague within the force, Krikke, painted a very different picture: Moerberg was always the one to take the initiative, and all the tips came from him.[8] He had to spend a lot of money on cigarettes for his informants, Moerberg used to claim, according to Krikke, and that was what he used his bonus money for. In a police interview Kaper, his boss, said of Moerberg: "After Schaap and his partners, he was the man who brought in the most Jews. Moerberg was paid many a bonus for arresting Jews. And I should know, since I was the one paying them." The German chief of police Kempin was also questioned about Moerberg, once again about the period *after* January 1944, that is, after his time with the Colonne: "I have no complaints about his work and activities during the time he worked for me. I have to say that he was one of my more productive men, when it came to arresting Jews and cracking cases."

During his time under Kaper, Moerberg proved to be an accomplished Jew hunter who knew all the tricks of the trade. One informant, a certain Beppie, was particularly useful. He had complete control over her and squeezed a great deal of information out of her. One time she gave Moerberg a name in Haarlem, which led to an arrest. And one Sunday she walked down Van Eeghenstraat, picking out Jews; Moerberg was convinced that illegal Jews could be found there, just walking the streets. In one case she followed a Jewish-looking man to his front door and gave Moerberg the address. These arrests often led to new addresses and thus to new arrests. "Beppie" also went out of town with Moerberg for a few days, to go cycling and occasionally arrest someone. She once checked up on a tip in a village in North Holland by asking at the door if "so-and-so" lived there; she had come to bring the person in question the sad news of the death of a relative. When it turned out that the person did in fact live there, Moerberg returned the next day to make the arrest. In reality, she was a *V-Frau*; Moerberg supplied her with new papers and a different identity and Kempin gave her an official letter stating that, as an employee of the SD, she could not be arrested. Beppie did everything Moerberg asked in order to protect her fiancé, a young man who lived in Rotterdam and was threatened with deportation to Poland unless Beppie cooperated with the SD.[9]

Beppie also played an indirect role in one of Moerberg's greatest "successes": the arrest of fifteen Jews at a villa in the town of Huizen.[10] Beppie had been living at the home of a certain Mrs H. Jews had been arrested there before, and Moerberg came by frequently to ask Mrs H. for tips about addresses where Jews might be hiding. If she refused to cooperate, she would be sent to a concentration camp. Mrs H. became increasingly alarmed, because she had no information and could not help Moerberg. When he again threatened to deport her on July 9, 1944, she had just one possibility left. She gave Moerberg a note she had once received from a member of the resistance, in case she ever had to "unload" Jews in an emergency. On the note was written the name Bos, followed by the address of a villa in Huizen.

The next morning the SD, led by Moerberg, raided the house, which was located in a secluded wooded area. At that house the German anti-Nazi Eberhard Rebling ruled the roost. Born in 1922, Rebling was a musician by trade who had left Germany in 1938 and met a Jewish woman in the Netherlands. When he was called up for service in the *Wehrmacht*, he decided to go into hiding and rented a villa in Huizen. He began using the name Bos, and his wife, Rebecca Brillenslijper, started calling herself Van der Horst. From July 1942 they had about fifteen people staying at the house at any given time. At the time of the raid twelve of them were at home: Mrs P. van den Berg-Walvis, Jacob Brillenslijper (Rebling's brother-in-law), S.J. Kreefeld, Mrs J. Drijf, Mr A. Teixeira de Mattos, his wife L. Teixeira de Mattos-Comperz, J. Brillenslijper (his father-in-law), his wife T. Brillenslijper-Gerritsen, G. Jäger, his wife G. Jäger-Teixeira de Mattos and two small children, Kathinka (2), the daughter of Rebling and Rebecca Brillenslijper, and a little girl of three, Lea Brandes. Three others had gone out that morning, C. Brandes, the father of the girl Lea (a gentile, incidentally, and Rebling's brother-in-law), his wife Marianne (the sister of Rebling's wife) and their four-year-old son. There was no way of warning Marianne and her son, and the two were promptly arrested when they returned home that afternoon. During an interrogation right after her arrest, Moerberg slapped her in the face a few times.

The SD operation lasted the whole day, July 10, 1944. During the operation Paulina van den Berg-Walvis did what she always did: she cleaned the house, cooked porridge for the children, etc. Initially the SD was unable to find two groups of people. They were in well-concealed hiding places in the villa but were discovered in the end. At first the SD loudly threatened to shoot through all the doors and walls if they did not come out. Later they yelled out that they were leaving and slammed the doors, but even in their hiding places the people could hear the sound of quiet footsteps. The final group was not found until ten o'clock that night.

As they were being driven away, Rebecca Brillenslijper, Rebling's wife, succeeded in persuading one of the SD men to drop off the three children at the home of a local doctor, Dr Van den Berg. The SD explained to him that there was every indication that the children were not "full-blooded Jews" and for that reason would not have to come with them just then. But if it later turned out that they *were* Jews, they had to be available, so the doctor was told to take good care of them. However Van den Berg was not equipped to handle three children, so he called up his colleague Schaaberg to ask if he would take in two of them, which he did. That same night they picked up cots and clothes from the villa. All three children were brought to safety in time, that is to say, before the investigation into their ethnic origins had been completed.

During a police interview after the war, Rebecca Brillenslijper said the SD apparently had not been aware that there were so many Jews staying there. They had no transportation with them, and they had no luck renting a truck or bus in the area. Eventually they had a bus drive out from Amsterdam.

In Amsterdam there was apparently some confusion about where the prisoners should be taken and the arrestees were driven back and forth around the city. In the commotion Rebling's sister-in-law Brandes attacked one of the SD men at a stop on Spaarndammerstraat. They both fell, rolling around the floor of the bus, which gave Eberhard Rebling the chance to escape. The SD gave chase, but without success. Rebling went into hiding again and survived the war.

Some time later, when he contacted his physician, Dr Van den Berg, he was told that his own child had been abducted by an unknown person. Rebling was not especially concerned about this. The other two children were sent to stay with their grandparents in The Hague; they were not in fact "full-blooded Jews." Six months later Rebling was reunited with his daughter (who by law should have been deported); Kathinka had been taken to a safe house in the nearby town of Naarden.

Of the twelve arrestees, five came back from the camps: Rebling's wife Rebecca, his sister-in-law Marianne Brandes-Brillenslijper, Mrs Van den Berg-Walvis, Mr Jäger and his wife, Mrs Jäger-Teixeira de Mattos. The other seven were murdered.

And this was not even Moerberg's biggest haul. That took place on August 4, 1944, exactly the same day that the Frank family were picked up at 263 Prinsengracht in Amsterdam. Moerberg had to go all the way to Oss, in the southern province of North Brabant. By order of Otto Kempin, the chief of police, he was to pick up a group of Jews there, who were not only staying at private homes but also at a sort of "secret rest home."[11]

Kempin must have been tipped off about the rest home in Oss by Bernard Joseph, a "half-Jewish" young man, who worked for the Amsterdam SD as a *V-Mann* (informant). Joseph had a friend in Oss, a certain Günter Blanken, who spent a lot of time with a Jewish woman, Bertha Zilverberg (30). Bertha worked as a nurse at the rest home and would sometimes tell Joseph, whom she trusted completely, about her work there. Blanken and Joseph were Germans by birth, but Bertha was not the least bit suspicious.

On August 4, 1944, two men from the SD turned up at Bertha's door in Oss, Eddy Moerberg and his partner Krikke. Bertha was placed under arrest and forced to accompany them to the rest home. The people there were arrested immediately, but they had to wait for transportation. Bertha was allowed to go out and get food for the patients, for the trip. Seventeen people were registered as living at the rest home, twelve adults and five children. Some of them spent most of their time at home, but their addresses were known, so it was not difficult to find them. The only reason we know so much about the course of events that day was because, by some miracle, Bertha Zilverberg managed to survive the war. In a post-war interrogation she said: "The SD knew about everything." Moerberg – that's right, the same man who had such a sweet, gentle character according to his cousin – asked her there in Oss to become a *V-Frau*. "Come work for the SD. Otherwise you're going to Poland, and you'll never come back," Moerberg had said, according to Bertha in her testimony before the Special Court. Moerberg had it all worked out: she would live together with Bernard Joseph and the two would work as a team. Joseph was also present for this operation, as Bertha learned when she came back from the shop. "Then I understood it was Bernard Joseph who sold us out. I grabbed him by the throat and called him every name I could think of." He also proposed working together, "since otherwise I'd never come back from Poland," Bertha said to the judges in Moerberg's trial.

In the meantime a truck had been chartered from the *Wehrmacht*, and all the people who were on the list had been rounded up. The procession departed for Amsterdam. Bertha went to Amsterdam by train with two guards, a man from the SD and a number of children. She continued to reject any offers to cooperate; she chose to care for her patients, first in Amsterdam prison and later at Auschwitz. In 1945 she was the only one of the whole group to return. She could only assume that the others were gassed, as most of them were elderly and sick. She was herself liberated by the Russians. During her interview with the police, she gave investigators a list with the names of the seventeen dead. For the rest of her life (she died in 1997) she would have to bear the burden of this unimaginable experience, which had never been recorded anywhere, save in the transcript of Eddy Moerberg's trial.

In that transcript we also read that Bernard Joseph tried to minimize his share in the betrayal by pointing out that the SD had already heard everything from his friend Günter Blanken. Moerberg himself denied being in charge of this operation.

If that seemed to be the case, he told detectives, it was because his colleague Krikke, who was the actual leader, had difficulty expressing himself. You almost feel sorry for Moerberg: it seemed that everybody had it in for him.

On the list of victim we come across the names of two eighty-year-olds who were shipped to Poland, supposedly to work in labor camps. And we see a family with seven children – the Hes-Parfumeurs, and their children Mia (born 1931), Rosina (1933), Hijman (1934), Henriette (1936), Dia (1938), Jehudah (1940), Samuel (1942) – ranging in age from two to fourteen, all arrested the same day as Anne Frank and all gassed at Auschwitz.

Eddy Moerberg was arrested in August 1945. Initially, he tried to convince his interrogators from the Bureau of National Security that he had played no part in the persecution of Jews because he had had good relations with Jews for many years. He had been a good friend to his Jewish neighbor on Archimedesweg in Amsterdam, Levie Kool, who even gave him some of his valuables for safekeeping. Moerberg as *Bewariër*[a] – it doesn't sound credible to anyone familiar with his history, but after the war Kool's son confirmed it. His father left him a list of the items and the names of the people looking after them.[12] All of them had returned Kool's belongings by the end of 1945, except Moerberg. But the younger Kool eventually got his things back with the help of the Stewardship Institute, the official body that "inherited" the property of political delinquents. Moerberg should have surrendered the goods upon being arrested.

Thus the police record of one of the craftiest Jew hunters also contains the correspondence between his Jewish neighbor and his sons, at the moment the former began to fear for his life. One of Kool's sons, Sam, was at sea; he was a radio-telegrapher, just like Moerberg. The war caught him unawares and he was unable to return to the Netherlands. As a precaution, father Kool wrote him a letter on July 15, 1942, when the deportations were just beginning:

Dear Son,

I am forced to write this letter, as a precaution, by the position in which all us Jews in the Netherlands find ourselves. Up till now, the situation has been unbearable for us. Little by little we are quietly being transported to Germany, perhaps with the knowledge that we will never return. Dear son, don't think we are down-hearted, your mother, grandma and I. What happens after today is a mystery to us all. I have brought Lou [the youngest son] to safety as best as I could.

It was Kool's wish that the son at sea, Sam, and the youngest son, Lou, divide up their parents' possessions amongst themselves. In total, the estate was worth at least fl.16,000 ($100,450 today). Kool hoped the Dutchmen he had taken into confidence would prove to be worthy of his trust: "Nonetheless, in spite of all the dangers, I will try to save Mother and myself and Grandma and the rest of the family too, if possible. I'm almost tempted to say that I'm certain I will survive this situation. If that is not the case, be strong and remember us always."

Father Kool asked his sons to donate ten percent of the money to poor Christians, for everything the Christians had done "to comfort us. They were there for us like never before." He also requested that Sam and Lou each wear a special ring, in remembrance. "So once again, be strong and honest, don't try to seek solace in alcohol, but find comfort in your work."

The letter is signed: "Your father Elie." Kool, like his wife and his mother, never returned from the concentration camp. And thus he never found out that he had entrusted a portion of his possessions to a man who turned over hundreds of Jews to the Germans, despite his gentle character and excellent upbringing.

From the attachment to Kool's letter to his son, we know exactly what was left in Moerberg's care in a steel money-box: fl.1,075 in coins; a gold ring engraved with the initials EK; a gold ring engraved with the words "Klara July 1917"; seven diamonds at a value of fl.6,200 (gold value); two diamond stick pins; a few diamond earrings (gold value: fl.500); and a few other pieces of gold and silver jewelry.

Kool Sr. wrote that the total value should come to around fl.8,000, and he anticipated that in the interim the value might have risen to ten times this amount due to currency devaluation.

Moerberg buried the things in his garden on Archimedesweg. In September 1944 he took them with him when he fled to Groningen. For what purpose, we shall never know. But thanks to the intervention of the Stewardship Institute, the valuables were eventually returned to their rightful owner.

When he was arrested, Moerberg was carrying fl.7,000 (now $44,100). His wife claimed that this was money he had saved up during his time as a radio operator. Edna Moerberg-Mohan did not receive the money; it was confiscated. In March 1947 she decided to leave the Netherland, with her four children, to spare them, she later wrote, the shame of a convict father. She went back to New Zealand. And evidently Eddy Moerberg wanted to follow her. In June 1947 two pieces of an iron hacksaw were found in his cell in the Amsterdam House of Detention.[13] An investigation revealed that the chaplain on duty had smuggled them in inside a Bible, or at any rate in a "religious book." Books normally had to be inspected first, but that had not been done in this case. Moerberg was disciplined, and the chaplain, who had apparently been taken in by Moerberg, was banned from further visits. In future the padre himself would attend to the prisoner's spiritual needs.

In November 1948 Moerberg was sentenced to death. The prosecution considered him to be a liar and regarded him as one of the most serious offenders, all the more so because he was one of the few members of the Colonne Henneicke who went on hunting Jews after the autumn of 1943. In the trial his boss Kaper clearly stated once again that he had paid Moerberg bonuses on a number of occasions.[14]

The court did not buy Moerberg's story that he promptly deposited the money in the collection boxes for the Red Cross or Winter Aid. Moerberg appealed the sentence, and at that point he started taking an active role in his own defense. He composed a written defense himself, in his own exquisite handwriting, underscoring parts of the text with beautiful, straight lines, made with a thin fountain pen. He wrote ten pages to the Court of Appeals, in a formal style: "It is quite understandable that the esteemed Court has concluded that, as an employee of LiRo, one must have been an anti-Semite. However it can be demonstrated that I have always had many intimate Jewish acquaintances, so it is scarcely possible that I was harboring anti-Semitic sentiments."

He did express sincere remorse at having cooperated in the deportation of Jews, an "insult to my Jewish acquaintances."

Moerberg quoted from a letter from a minister friend, who wrote: "It is a psychological mystery to me why you chose the wrong path." Moerberg requested leniency, particularly in consideration of his family, who were anxiously awaiting the outcome of the appeal in New Zealand.

The Court of Appeals was advised by attorney general Bakhoven, who uncovered a number of plainly anti-Semitic comments Moerberg had made. Bakhoven also believed Moerberg knew quite well what would happen to the deported Jews.[15] He pointed out a remark Moerberg had made to a man he was trying to recruit as an informer: "If you give me addresses where Jews are staying, you can go home, otherwise you're going to Poland too, and you know you won't be coming back."

"In my opinion," Bakhoven wrote, "Moerberg is one of the worst of the Jew hunters . . . [He] did his very best to capture as many Jews as possible and as evidenced by various comments, he understood perfectly well that a dire fate awaited the Jews he had arrested."

Moerberg's attorney, Blom, conceded during the appeals phase of the trial that "this man has done disgraceful things and exhibited conduct that is beneath contempt. But the punishment he has been given is too severe."[16] He continued: "There are always classes and degrees in any crime, and that is certainly true in this case as well. There are far more serious offenders than this man. He is an insignificant figure, who did not plan all those horrors but, through petty-minded weakness and mindless diligence, did things, the ghastly consequences of which he did not fully comprehend."

The Court of Appeals also received mail from Wellington, New Zealand.[17] Edna Moerberg-Mohan begged the court to be merciful. "We have been married fifteen years and have four children which [sic] he is dearly fond of and has always been a good father to." The fact that he had not seen them for four years and might never see them again was punishment enough for him. She swore he was not the man that his work would make him out to be. Not vicious, not sadistic. His political ideas were totally wrong, but he only realized that after it was too late. He had never wanted to work there, but he was offered a job because he could speak and write German well. She had warned him, but there was no turning back – they would have sent him to a German concentration camp "because he knew too much about their business."

"Please hear me and give him a fair trial, not the Nazi-way," Mrs Moerberg wrote.

She also wrote an emotional letter to the Queen. The appeal was denied, and the death sentence upheld. In keeping with the policy of her government, which tried to limit the number of executions, Queen Juliana pardoned him, as she did many members of the Colonne Henneicke. On November 12, 1949 his sentence was commuted to life in prison. In May 1959 he was granted clemency once again, and the punishment was reduced to twenty-three years, still more jail time than any of his colleagues had received. The Supreme Court refused to go any further; a new request for clemency submitted by his wife from New Zealand was denied. The explanation for this decision had the same sharp tone as the original judgment: "His work was accompanied by assaults and base threats, and from the things he said to his Jewish victims one can infer that he knew their ultimate fate," the Supreme Court wrote about the man, who, according to his family, had such a gentle character and who, according to his lawyer, had been such a diligent and reliable worker. Looking back on the trial, prosecutor Gelinck called him "a two-faced scoundrel." In 1961, after serving two-thirds of his sentence, he was released.

−13−

Chris de Hout and the Hunt for Floortje Citroen

"He is a fierce champion of National Socialist principles. He has worked for the Movement in all areas, including canvassing and distribution, and he has been a group leader for the last two years. Comrade De Hout* is highly respected by all." This exceedingly positive endorsement can be found in a 1941 report on one Christoffel de Hout. Born in 1906, De Hout was a former employee of the tobacco processing firm Lokin and Weisz and already active in the NSB in 1934.[1]

The report led to De Hout's being considered for a position as an "ATL observer" within the party. ATL (*Algemeen Toezicht Leden*) was a secret network of NSB cadre members, who monitored how the rank and file conducted themselves, how active they were and whether they were loyal to supreme leader Anton Mussert. A year later, De Hout resigned from this prestigious position after a murky conflict with a higher-ranking colleague. "I will have to pay for my mistake," he wrote humbly to the head office – Chris de Hout was loyal through thick and thin.[2]

The war had a disastrous effect on the tobacco industry. De Hout had a wife and four young children to provide for, so he applied for a job with the NSKK, the Nazi's corps of lorry drivers. He drove trucks in East Prussia and in the vicinity of Warsaw. When he returned to the Netherlands, he worked for a time as a guard for the Germans. This period was followed by a few months of unemployment, which came to an end when he applied for a job with the *roofbank* Lippmann, Rosenthal & Co. Initially he was not placed with the *Hausraterfassung*, but with the "branch office" at Westerbork. LiRo maintained a department there that checked all Jews upon arrival for money and valuables, which they had been allowed to keep up until that point. De Hout was one of the six to eight staff members there; later only four would be needed. Together they succeeded, in the words of historian Gerard Aalders, "of stealing 825,000 guilders in cash at this gateway to annihilation."[3] In today's money, that would be more than $5 million.

De Hout's experience at Westerbork made him an ideal candidate for a job with the Colonne Henneicke, which he joined in March 1943 at a monthly salary of

137

fl.270.⁴ An astonishing number of *Berichte* from this period have survived, brief reports of operations in which De Hout actively tracked down Jews. He himself admitted after the war that he "arrested at least a few hundred Jews and brought them to the Dutch Theater." This admission is both striking and exceptional, as candour was a rare quality amongst his fellow bounty hunters. These reports are also noteworthy for recording the relatively large sums of money he confiscated and turned over to the officials back at the office (mainly Henneicke and Briedé). He regularly brought in sums ranging from fl.1,000 to fl.3,000. If he did in fact receive ten percent of that – which cannot be proven but is nevertheless quite plausible – Chris de Hout must have lived very comfortably in 1943.

Throughout this time De Hout remained an inveterate supporter of Nazi doctrines. When the Colonne Henneicke was dissolved in October 1943, he reported for training in Schalkhaar, the infamous police academy, modeled after those in Germany, where the occupier drilled and moulded its willing servants. De Hout was given a position in the *Landwacht*, and in that capacity he was placed in command of a troop of men charged with guarding railway installations and hunting for men and women who had gone into hiding. We know little of his exploits during this time, apart from his looting of a house belonging to a fugitive railwayman.

De Hout was not raised to admire Hitler and his teachings. On the contrary, his father was strongly opposed to the Nazis, a fact that must have led to heated arguments within the family. Evidence of this can be found in De Hout's police record, including an angry letter he wrote to his parents on December 5, 1944. De Hout had decided that his wife Leny and their four children should not remain in the Netherlands any longer. In the letter he quoted the leader of the NSB, Anton Mussert, who had said not long before that "the hatred that inspires our enemies is such that the lives of our women and children are no longer safe." De Hout's wife and children were sent to Germany, an arduous journey: "I know this will sadden Mother in particular." And as for himself? "I am a soldier, of course, and will fight with weapons in hand, as befits a good National Socialist." And then the generational conflict within the De Hout family surfaced for a moment: "Yes father, you will be pleased with the turn of events more than anyone, and yet I hope you will never regret your attitude, for these hateful feelings often hurt me, even though I never let it show." De Hout ended his dramatic letter to his father and mother on an optimistic note, despite the impending collapse of the Third Reich and his ideals: "I still look to the future with good spirits and confidence. Our struggle was an honest one and it will remain so."⁵ The letter was signed: Leny, Chris, Annie, Rietje, Eldert and Onno. At that time, the children were between four and ten years of age.

De Hout was a fervent Nazi, but was he also an anti-Semite? The question is not as simple as it may seem. In the records of the police interrogations, one can see that detectives did not pursue that particular angle in their questioning. Speaking of his period with LiRo at Camp Westerbork, for example, he said: "I thought the Jews' life in this camp was tolerable, though I did see them being shipped off in trains." In a later interrogation he stated that he was unaware of the fate that awaited the Jews. This is nothing special; every suspect said that, even if it was only to save his own skin. But in De Hout's case, it is particularly implausible that he was ignorant of what was going on. As a lorry driver for the NSKK on the Eastern Front, he must surely have heard about the fate of the Jews there. Moreover, he worked at Westerbork for some time, and, according to recent research, camp workers were well aware of the death camps, thanks to the reports that came back from the train escorts.[6] We have no way of knowing if this was true for De Hout. "I only thought the Jews were being relocated, and I didn't think that was such a bad thing," he said to a detective. But at a certain point, he hinted at his true feelings about Jews to the president of the Special Court, albeit in very oblique terms. "In my conduct toward Jews I was guided by my racial consciousness."[7] But De Hout's anti-Semitism is most apparent in his actions as a member of the Colonne Henneicke.

For example, there was the excursion he took to Wageningen on Thursday, June 24, 1943. De Hout's destination was the home of Mrs Hovestad-Iprenburg, who was sheltering three Jews: Jacob van de Wieken, his wife Grietje Wijnschenk and her sister Belia. De Hout entered the house, according to Mrs Hovestad, with a revolver in his hand. She claimed the people in her house were not Jews but Dutch evacuees. De Hout checked their papers and concluded that they were in fact Jews, hiding out to evade deportation. He bawled Van de Wieken out, reproaching him for "causing a poor peasant woman so much trouble." He also struck him a few times. De Hout confiscated fl.610 and some jewelry. In court he would say that he did so under orders from Henneicke and Briedé, "because people were earning so much money from Jews."

As a trial witness, Mrs Hovestad recalled that De Hout shouted "all sorts of idiotic profanities" at the women as they were getting dressed to go. Hovestad: "When I said something about it, he answered, 'There'll be more to come.'"[8]

De Hout arrested the Amersfoort city councilman Joseph Koopman on two separate occasions. Koopman was Jewish and active in the resistance. De Hout picked him up in a phone booth, saying, "The game's up." De Hout had been stalking his prey for a long time. Both men actually knew each other, having served together in the military. But a shared history was no help to Koopman; De Hout made no exceptions, not even for an old acquaintance. Koopman managed to stay at the Dutch Theater for an exceptionally long time, and eventually succeeded in escaping by bribing someone on the outside. But a year later, on July 1, 1944, he was arrested a second time, again by De Hout, who happened to run into him on the street. Koopman tried to get away, but De Hout, who was then a commandant in the *Landwacht* – though not on duty at the time – threatened him with a gun and turned him over to the *Sicherheitsdienst*. Koopman was then shipped to Auschwitz, via Westerbork, and lived to see the liberation of the camp. Right after the war Koopman filed an official complaint against De Hout, which would be dealt with in the latter's trial.[9]

There are other charges against this former tobacco plant worker. The court was most impressed by the testimony of Marcus Citroen.[10] In the summer of 1943 he was hiding out in Barneveld, with his wife Louise Citroen-Sluys. The two made the difficult decision to give up their three-year-old daughter Florence Rosette, nicknamed Floortje, and entrust her to the care of relatives in Eindhoven. The Citroen family were not happy about the situation. They learned that the house in which they were staying had been bought by a member of the NSB. As a result, Louise Citroen went out to find a new hiding place for herself and her husband. It was a decision with fatal consequences: she was arrested at Ede train station, by De Hout and his regular partner Bob Verlugt, himself a notorious Jew hunter. Louise succeeded in smuggling out a note, probably from the Dutch Theater, in which she asked her husband to bring Floortje to safety. A search of Louise's person turned up a note in her jacket pocket, containing the address where Floortje was staying. Marcus managed to warn the people who were looking after Floortje just in time. When De Hout and Verlugt arrived at the door, on Pasteurlaan in Eindhoven, Floortje was already gone.

But De Hout and Verlugt were not to be deterred so easily. Two grown men, thirty-six and twenty-seven years old, a former tobacco worker and a former bookkeeper/correspondent, traveled across half the country to track down a three-year-old Jewish girl – the bounty hunters were nothing if not persistent. Mrs Demmink-Oostinga, with whom Floortje had been staying until an hour before their arrival, was given the third degree. "Where's the little Jew?" De Hout and Verlugt demanded to know. The two men were experienced bounty hunters with a whole arsenal of intimidating tricks in reserve. Mrs Demmink had no choice but to give them the name of her friend, whose house Floortje had been rushed to shortly before. De Hout then stayed with Mrs Demmink, while Verlugt went off to the address of the friend in question, Mrs Witmond-Visser. Verlugt was accompanied by V., an SD man from Eindhoven, who had been called in to assist them. When they rang the bell around one o'clock, Floortje had only been in the house for an hour. This was only meant to be a temporary solution; someone was expected at any moment to pick up Floortje and take her to a more permanent address. But things did not go according to plan. When Verlugt and V. crossed the threshold, the three-year-old Floortje was in the hall, curious to see who the new people were. There was no opportunity to hide her, and she was forced to go with the two men. Then someone else rang the doorbell. It was Mr de Wit, a member of the resistance, who had been given the job of picking up the girl and bringing her to a safe house. He quickly assessed the situation and immediately dashed out the door, with V. in hot pursuit. The latter had little trouble overpowering De Wit: he had taken the trouble to lock up his bike and could not just hop on and pedal away.

The catastrophe was now complete: De Wit's house was raided. There V. and his German colleague Seidenstucher found nine Jews, seven of whom would never return from the death camps. But before he set out on this successful operation, he kindly brought De Hout, Verlugt and Floortje to the station.

In court Floortje's father Marcus told of the sad denouement: "I received word that my daughter was with my wife at Westerbork. I never heard anything more from my wife or daughter." The Red Cross determined that mother Louise and daughter Floortje were moved from Westerbork to Sobibor on July 13. They were gassed there on July 16.

In mid-June 1943 De Hout came very close to ending the glorious career of Leo Horn, who would later become the best football referee the Netherlands ever had.[11] Horn, who was staying at a house on the Eerste Helmersstraat in Amsterdam, was going to visit his sister Sophie. They had arranged to meet at a shop belonging to an acquaintance on Constantijn Huygensstraat. Horn had the key, but just as he was about to open the door, a woman walked by and said emphatically that the shop was closed. He took the hint and kept on walking, and in doing so escaped arrest. Inside, Chris de Hout and his colleague Henk van der Kraal were waiting for him. The two members of the Colonne had already made a big haul. It began with the arrest of Sophie Horn, Leo's sister. She had gone to the shop to hand over a young Jewish girl, Selma Egger. They walked right into the arms of the Jew hunters, who had apparently been tipped off. De Hout and Van der Kraal then began to question the ten-year-old girl about where her parents could be found. Sophie Horn twice heard the brave Selma give them the wrong address, but in the end their threats were so extreme that she broke down and told them where her parents were hiding. Sophie Horn heard De Hout call for transportation and announce the arrest of an Egger family in a building on Elandsgracht. The same day De Hout and Van der Kraal went to pay a visit to the address where Selma Egger herself had been hiding out, 119 Tweede Helmersstraat. There they found another Jewish couple, the Van de Ziels.

From the transcript of De Hout's trial we know that Selma was murdered in Auschwitz, along with her parents. The Van de Ziel family met the same fate. Sophie Horn survived the camps, and Leo Horn himself was always able to stay one step ahead of his pursuers. The address where he was hiding was raided several times, but he was always out. All his possessions were stolen. After the war he determined that he had lost, among other things, five suits, a hundred books, an expensive phonograph and numerous records. Horn was not the kind of man to take this sort of thing lying down. In the war he had been active in the armed resistance. In 1945, on that basis, he was entrusted with supervising political prisoners at the camp on Levantkade in Amsterdam. One day he heard that Chris de Hout had been brought in, the same man who had arrested his sister and from whom he himself had barely managed to escape. Horn went to see him, asked if he still remembered Sophie Koster-Horn, and when De Hout said he did, Horn punched him in the face.[12]

Leo Horn subsequently went in search of the things that had been stolen from him, sometimes with a detective, sometimes on his own. He wound up at the house of one of De Hout's brothers, where he found his clothing. He discovered his phonograph at the house of a sister of De Hout's. At De Hout's own home, on Hugo de Grootstraat, he found his records.

At first De Hout steadfastly maintained his innocence to investigators, but in a later interrogation he admitted to certain misdeeds, namely the misappropriation of the phonograph, the records and a suit. During a later interrogation, with detective Verduin in January 1948, he retracted his previous statement. His new story was that he had turned over the phonograph to the *Zentralstelle* and that it got broken there. At that point De Hout asked Henneicke for permission to take it home with him. In De Hout's trial Sophie Horn testified that the defendant had been so kind as to have the bag of clothes she kept in the hallway in case she ever had to leave brought to her at the Dutch Theater. She had appreciated that very much. It was only a shame that the fl.2,500 (now $15,800) it had contained was missing by the time it got to her.

On May 16, 1945, Chris de Hout was arrested. Not long before, he had been forced to go into hiding himself, at the home of his parents, to whom he had written such a bitter letter a year before. Apparently they lovingly took him back. On the day in question they received a visit from V.S. Ohmstede, an officer in the Domestic Forces, an umbrella organization formed in September 1944 by various resistance groups.[13] He had a bone to pick with De Hout. The two men lived on the same street. There, on Hugo de Grootstraat, De Hout was able to move into the house of a family, the Courants, whom he himself had arrested, according to an explanatory note Ohmstede wrote on the arrest report. He also mentioned another one of his neighbor's "accomplishments": "He was so zealous that he even visited people who had been granted exemptions by a German doctor; he then made a note in his pocket diary of the exact moment when the *Sperre* in question would expire, so that he could return promptly on that fatal day."

The aforementioned incident, we learn from Ohmstede's courtroom testimony, concerned the Heller family. One of the children had scarlet fever, and therefore the entire family had been granted a temporary exemption. In his diary he wrote down the date when the child was supposed to be better and the *Sperre* was scheduled to expire, and that very day the family was taken into custody. Because De

Hout also took a fair amount of Jewish property home with him, a fact that was common knowledge in the neighborhood, Ohmstede decided to make the arrest personally.

Remarkably De Hout chose to come clean on the very day of his arrest, during an interrogation by an Amsterdam police sergeant. He admitted to arresting hundreds of Jews, and he did not withhold any significant details about his wartime career. That makes him an exception, but despite that, his trial was not given priority. He was not subpoenaed until after a portion of the Colonne's records had been found and there was also written evidence that he was involved in the hunt for Jews. It was quite some time before he was able to get in touch with his wife and children, who spent the final year of the war in Germany. It was not until January 11, 1946 that he received news from his wife Leny, who told him that a fifth child, Elisabeth, had been born in October 1945. De Hout requested and received permission to see the child.[14]

In the final interrogation before his trial, conducted by detective Tump, Chris de Hout – by then forty-two – expressed something resembling regret for the first time. "At the time I didn't know," he said, "that the Jewish people I had arrested were going to their deaths. I think it's awful to know that I played a part in that, however unwittingly." On October 22 the court sentenced him to death, together with his partner Bob Verlugt. "For several months they tracked down and turned over a great many Jewish people to the enemy, thereby exposing them to appalling treatment, of which the defendants cannot have been unaware."[15]

The sentence was upheld on appeal. A deeply disappointed Leny de Hout wrote to the Ministry of Justice to say that the court had misjudged her husband. "Everyone thinks he's so cynical and calm," she wrote. "He may seem that way on the outside, but he is really a sensitive man. He has trouble expressing himself, but inside it bothers him deeply." She herself felt remorse too: "I always stopped him from going to the Eastern Front; then he might have been given eight years. Now I feel guilty too and feel it is partly my fault that our five children have no father."

The letter ended in an entreaty: "Give my husband twenty years; give the children their father back."[16] It took some time before this request was honored. First Queen Juliana commuted his sentence to life in prison, in 1949, as she did for all members of the Colonne who had been sentenced to death. And in 1958 his punishment was reduced to twenty years and eight months. De Hout himself felt he had been punished for life. In 1949 he suddenly asked for reading material about the events in the concentration camps. After that he wrote to the president of the Court of Appeals, and in that letter he made reference to a lengthy missive to his wife and children in which he admitted to sinning against the concept of humanity. He went on to say: "It was not until quite recently that I was able to become fully acquainted with the indescribable scenes that took place in the German concentration camps. The things I read horrified me. The insane butchering of the people

I had arrested is a heavy burden I will have to bear my whole life long."[17] Could De Hout have had three-year-old Floortje Citroen in mind when he wrote these lines?

—14—

Tonny Kroon and "the Job He Always Wanted"

What made Tonny Kroon* (1916) into the most abusive and brutal member of the Colonne Henneicke, a man who was described by judge-advocate Gelinck as a "great scoundrel"?[1] Was it his childhood, as the youngest of sixteen children, most of whom died young and only four of whom were still alive in 1949? Was it his father, an alcoholic who beat his mother? Was it the accident in 1941, when part of a machine smashed into his leg, leaving him with a permanent limp?

In the late 1940s, Special Justice made little effort to answer these kinds of questions. No psychological examination was deemed necessary for Tonny Kroon. "What kind of person is this?" Kroon's lawyer C.J. Colijn wondered aloud before the Court of Appeals.[2] "It always strikes one that these are really just ordinary people with ordinary problems," he said in response to his own question. But this characterization does not do his client justice; Kroon was far from ordinary. After the dissolution of the Colonne in 1943, Kroon was the only member to hunt down resistance fighters and other fugitives in the Eastern Netherlands, using the same means and with the same fanaticism he had displayed as a Jew hunter in Amsterdam. He seemed to be in his element in this milieu. He was undeniably good at his job, better than most of the others. It even brought him a certain renown within his own circle. During his Amsterdam period he enriched himself extravagantly, according to witnesses from his own family, and in this way he was able to attain a lifestyle that would otherwise have been out of his reach. The pursuit of social standing and wealth caused this man, who came from a family that would nowadays be called "underprivileged," to commit extreme acts. This would seem to be the most likely explanation, although regrettably there is no report from a competent psychologist on Tonny Kroon.

Kroon was one of the youngest men in the Colonne. He was born in 1916, making him twenty-seven when he came under Henneicke's wing. He had a troubled home life. In 1910 his father caught meningitis; he eventually recovered, but would never be the same. "After that," Kroon wrote in prison in 1949, in a personal history, "life had lost any pleasure for my mother. Things got even worse when my oldest brother committed suicide after a minor row with my father. Following that, my father developed a very serious drinking problem; at home there were scenes I would prefer not to describe, to spare my mother's feelings."[3]

Tonny Kroon went to work at a young age, after leaving primary school. At seventeen he was a shop assistant on Nassaukade in Amsterdam. His boss advised him to join the NSB; this was in 1933, and thus he got into the organization quite early on. In 1935 he was struck from the membership rolls for failing to pay his dues, but in 1939 he returned to the Movement, in his words, "because I thought the party would improve the social situation in the Netherlands." It seems he wanted to use the NSB to further his own ambitions, since he asked if he could get his old membership number back.[4] A low number conferred status within the party, so he wrote on the registration form that he was "willing to pay the dues for the years I missed, if necessary." In 1941 he was working at a vacuum cleaner factory, EFA Produka, in Amsterdam. There he suffered a serious industrial accident and was forced to go on disability leave for the next six months. When he left the vacuum cleaner factory for good, he was given a positive letter of reference: his conduct, diligence and honesty were all exemplary. In June 1942 he signed a contract with LiRo and went to work for the *Hausraterfassung*, where he registered the contents of Jewish households. He was actually involved in arresting Jews even *before* his time with the Colonne Henneicke. He could still remember that first time very well, he wrote in his personal history. It was in the presence of an infamous police officer from the Bureau of Jewish Affairs, a certain N., who, for reasons that are not entirely clear, had the nickname "cup and saucer" within the force. "That first arrest left me pretty shook up," wrote Kroon, "so much so that I asked the policeman to let the people go, but he didn't dare." A short time later, according to his story, he put his dilemma to his colleagues: "Later that day I discussed the case with various comrades. They laughed at me and said that if I was a revolutionary, I would have to be a bit harder."[5]

Their prodding evidently worked, since the degree of abusiveness documented in Kroon's dossier is unsurpassed. A Mrs Sterman stated that a woman who was staying at her house with her twelve-year-old daughter denied being Jewish to Kroon. He responded: "Just confess; if you don't we're going to ship you and your kid to Poland, and your things will be confiscated or burned."[6] Several months later Kroon returned to Mrs Sterman's. This time he behaved himself. He came by for a chat, he said. He had a three-month-old baby and wanted to know if he could have her baby scale. Mrs Sterman refused and Kroon left. And sure enough, his only daughter Conny was born in 1943.

That means that his own child was just a few months old when, one Monday afternoon in December 1943, Kroon appeared at the door of the home of Mrs Liscaljet, with a number of policemen in his wake, to pick up a ten-month-old baby, Charrel Viskoop.[7] The child's father and mother had already been arrested, and the mother had entrusted her son to Mrs Liscaljet shortly before being taken into custody. Kroon asked who the child was. There was a registration card for the child. Kroon determined the baby was Jewish but had not been circumcised. Kroon was not interested in listening to Mrs Liscaljet's protests: "Shut your big mouth. Or else I'll revoke your *Sperr* and you can go to Poland with him." Kroon wanted to take the baby with him, but one of the detectives there said, "What are you going to do with a child?" After that they left, but Mrs Liscaljet had not heard the last of it.

Three days later the two detectives from the SD came to demand the child anyway. Mrs Liscaljet had to bring him to the *Sicherheitsdienst* herself. She was followed by two other detectives, who prevented her from escaping. After the war she told investigators: "It is thanks solely to Kroon's overzealousness that the child was deported. It is through his actions that Charrel Viskoop was gassed."

One can gather from the testimony of another witness that, as far back as 1943, Kroon had a very good idea of what was going to happen to the Jews.[8] A certain Mrs Teunisse, herself married to an NSB man, was visited by Kroon. He questioned her about her Jewish neighbors. She told him she was opposed to the persecution of the Jews. "It just breaks my heart whenever I think about those Jewish children being taken away from their mothers." Kroon responded, at least according to this witness, by saying "that all Jews should be gassed. He asked if I felt pity for them." Mrs Teunisse would repeat her story to detectives on several other occasions.

Another case, September 1943. Kroon had gone to confiscate some items from the storeroom of a shipping firm, which was run by a certain Mr Van Ekeren.[9] His widow, Geertruida Schneijer stated to detectives after the war that he had been very abusive toward her. "While he searched the house, the witness repeatedly threatened to send me to the concentration camp in Vught and told me I would lose my child because it would be sent to an institution." She asked for a swatch of fabric back which had belonged to her and had mistakenly been confiscated. Kroon then said, "You must really want to go to Vught. We had another one like you on Euterpestraat who wanted something back and we sent [her] straight to Vught."

Seven truckloads of goods were taken away, including a number of valuables. Mrs Schneijer: "After the defendant had gone, I found I was missing a gold ring my husband had worn. The defendant's conduct toward me was so vicious that, after he left, I had problems with my nerves for months afterward. Before then I had been perfectly healthy."

Businessman Klaas Hidde ter Horst lost his whole inventory as well, thanks to a devious ruse Kroon had employed.[10] While conducting a search for Jewish property, Kroon closely examined all the second-hand goods in Ter Horst's warehouse.

At one point he picked up a magnifying glass, looked at the stitching on a jacket and said, "Men, I see the outline of a Star of David. We're confiscating everything." After being arrested and then released, Ter Horst haughtily demanded his things back, but without success. He explained to detectives that he "fortunately was able to threaten [Kroon] a number of times." Detective Voordenhout, who led the postwar investigation into Tonny Kroon, wrote in a report that Ter Horst and his son were "on edge and [had] plans to murder the suspect."

In his testimony, Daniel Blom* (28) spoke of visiting his sister, who was hiding at 43 Johannes Verhulststraat, in March 1943.[11] When he rang the bell, it was Kroon who answered the door; he had been too quick for him and had already raided the house. Blom tried to flee but he was caught. When he was led inside, Kroon picked up a blackjack and struck Blom on the back with it several times, yelling out: "You dirty son of a bitch, you've had TB for thirteen years and I can still see the TB on your face." Later Blom realized that Kroon must have heard that from his wife, Jenny Kroon-Klumper, who had lived in Blom's neighborhood and knew he had been treated for tuberculosis for six months. Blom recalled that the blackjack actually broke during the course of the beating; the spring popped out and the insides flew into the air. With a belt around his neck, Blom was led by Kroon into a waiting car. He, his sister Judith and her husband were not the only ones to be arrested. Mr and Mrs Van Leer-Keyl were also discovered and picked up in the same raid, along with the twenty-four-year-old Mrs Andriesse-Keyl. And to make matters worse, Blom had been foolish enough to put a letter in his pocket that contained the address of the Mozer family, where he himself had been hiding along with five other Jews. Kroon went straight there and arrested all five. It was a successful outing for Kroon and his partner, Chris de Hout: eleven arrests. Blom and his sister Judith were subjected to every conceivable sort of pressure to reveal where Judith's two children were hiding, but they refused to talk. Blom was the only one who lived to tell about it; the ten other arrestees did not return from Auschwitz. "Kroon was the cause of it all," Blom testified after the war.

Blom's fiancée, the twenty-four-year-old, non-Jewish manicurist E.M. de Roo, also came by on the day in question, to meet her boyfriend and his family. By that time everybody had already been hauled off, but Kroon was still there. She was questioned and threatened and robbed of fl.450, plus a number of other things. She pretended to faint and was eventually let go. She was later allowed to visit her fiancé at the Dutch Theater. At that time he showed clear signs of having been assaulted. De Roo later received a visit from Kroon and De Hout, who were still trying to find out the addresses of Judith Blom's two children; once more the men left empty-handed. She described Kroon as abusive, menacing. He was the more aggressive of the two and plainly the leader.

There was more incriminating testimony against Tonny Kroon than anyone else. This might have been due to the actions of the Amsterdam PRA: in May 1947 they placed an appeal in the newspapers, asking for anyone with information about Kroon to come forward.[12] *Het Vrije Volk* even included a photograph; the "Amsterdam Journal" in *Het Parool* did not, though it did describe him as a "handsome young man with dark eyes and a thin moustache, an oval face and a part in the middle of his hair." Respondents to the appeal included not only survivors of the concentration camps and aggrieved merchants, but also two of the feared Jew hunter's sisters-in-law. And in their candor they provided detective Voordenhout with some very valuable evidence.[13] Mrs C.S. Kroon-Wolfrat drew the detectives' attention to the house Kroon had been living in during the last years of the war. The building in question was located at 173 Verhulststraat, which was even then one of the most expensive streets in South Amsterdam. It is a large, stately home, with huge, high-ceilinged rooms. After he was arrested, Kroon said that he "rented a room there" from the J. family. This was a decidedly disingenuous representation of reality. J. was Kroon's close friend and drinking buddy, an auctioneer and all-around wheeler-dealer, with whom he often did business.

A Jewish family had been forced out of the mansion on Verhulststraat and deported, after which Kroon took up residence on the second story and J. moved in on the first. The inside of the house was just as opulent as the exterior. Kroon and his wife did not bring along much more than a few sticks of second-hand furniture. According to his sister-in-law Kroon-Wolfrat, things changed in 1943: "They moved into a luxurious Jewish house, which was furnished very elegantly. How they managed to get a place like that, I don't know, but I think he profited from what was happening to the Jews. He had a suite of Gothic furniture, with chairs that were emblazoned with a coat of arms. He also had some other lovely pieces, as well as silvery cutlery and Persian rugs." When Kroon was confronted with this statement, he denied the insinuations that these were stolen goods, claiming he had bought everything himself.

But there was another sister-in-law, Anna Kroon-Van der Meer, who also spoke quite openly about her brother and his sudden wealth. Like her sister-in-law Jenny, she spent a long time alone after the war; her husband had been in the Waffen SS and was given an eight year prison sentence. She also lived on Verhulststraat, fifteen houses away from the Kroons, undoubtedly in a house that had been left behind by Jews. She regularly visited Tonny and Jenny; now and again she would even baby-sit little Connie for them. She told investigators: "Tonny was earning a lot of money then. He received ten percent of the capital and jewelry of the Jews he had arrested. In addition, he received five or ten guilders in bonuses for every Jew he had picked up. I am quite sure about this, as he told me about it himself on a number of occasions."

During the war Kroon was apparently quite open about the origins of his new-found wealth. He often spoke about it with acquaintances and relatives who had come over to visit. Anna once heard from his mother about one of Tonny's particularly good weeks. "He earned at least a thousand guilders extra this week," mother Kroon had said. Anna: "They'd often throw huge parties at the house, sometimes spending hundreds of guilders in a single night."

One evening four of them – De Hout, downstairs neighbor J. and his wife, and Tonny – went out together. After the taxi had brought them home, the bill for the evening had to be divided up: the total was between fl.300 and fl.400. On top of that J. and Kroon's wives were each given fl.100 ($630) to buy new hats. "They had hardly been married a year, and they barely owned a bed when they got married," sneered sister-in-law Anna Kroon-Van der Meer in a police interview. She continued: "In the meantime the house had been done up in grand style. In the living room there was a Persian rug that supposedly cost three thousand guilders." The conscientious detective Voordenhout was able to trace the origins of the carpet. It had belonged to the Jewish arrestee Samuel Jessurun de Mesquita, of 24 Linnaeuskade, and had been brought to Kroon's house by a friend with a delivery cycle.

Anna spoke at length about all the luxury items, like a movie projector, that could be found in the Kroon home, and about the parties they would have. The regularly recurring highpoint of the festivities was the moment Tonny and his wife stretched out a sheet on the wall, took out the movie projector and showed a film. That was something special; in 1943 a camera and a projector were reserved only for the very wealthy. They always showed the same film, the only one they had: scenes of a Jewish family enjoying a seaside vacation in the south of France.

The front of the flat on Verhulststraat, sister-in-law Anna continued, was furnished as a bedroom with a suite of white oak furniture, including a well-stocked linen cabinet. Anna herself was also given some fabric from time to time; she made a rug out of the same material that Jenny, Tonny's wife, had lying on the stairs. Jenny owned a fur coat, which had allegedly cost fl.3,500. Tonny had bought it for her, said Jenny, but her sister-in-law had her own ideas about the matter. When she first saw it, the jacket was much too big; it was later taken in.

After the war, detective Voordenhout discovered that the downstairs neighbor J. would regularly auction off Jewish property that Kroon had seized. Sometimes he would do that under his own name, sometimes under Kroon's, sometimes under the name of a third party. Furthermore, he discovered that Jenny Kroon had continued to auction off goods even after the war, after her husband had gone into hiding in Belgium. He even found evidence of it: auction slips for everything from fl.1 salad servers to a fl.250 pendulum. These slips are now part of Kroon's police dossier. After the war Jenny Kroon was able to live comfortably off the proceeds for another year. After that she had to go back to work, as a beautician, at a salary of fl.30 a week. At that point she also had to fire the household help.

Jenny Kroon was forced to get along without her husband for quite a while. After the Colonne Henneicke was disbanded, he stayed on in Amsterdam until January 1944 as a kind of freelancer for the *Sicherheitsdienst*. But because there was not much work left to do, he went to the police academy in Schalkhaar for additional training; he remained there until April. He then joined the State Police in Arnhem, later transferring to the *Arbeitskontrolldienst* (Labor Supervisory Agency). His job involved tracking down people who were trying to evade forced labor in Germany. After the war he stated that he only focused on "antisocial elements," but a colleague from the service knew better.[14] In a short span of time Kroon arrested at least 300 people, according to A. Wiebe. He scrupulously checked people's papers at stations, in trains and in cafés. After his period in Arnhem, Kroon was assigned to the *Polizei Freiwilligen Battalion Niederlände* (Dutch Volunteer Police Battalion) in Schalkhaar. He was stationed with a *Sonderkommando*, which was led by Captain Bakker. His own rank was *Zugwachtmeister* (railroad constable). This *Sonderkommando* hunted down Jews, members of the resistance and other outlaws; in short, Tonny Kroon went on doing the same work at which he had so excelled in Amsterdam. His commando unit was put into action in out-of-the-way places like Almelo, Vriezenveen, Wierden, Nijverdal, Ommen and Oldenzaal. In 1949 a witness, J.H. Kulle, a German barber who lived in the Netherlands and had served with a German guard unit, testified in court: "In Almelo, Kroon walked around with a sten gun on his back when he was in command of the troops. Operations generally took place in the evening. The commando would steal anything that wasn't nailed down. For this reason a large number of the troops were replaced. Kroon himself rode around on a stolen bicycle, and he always had plenty of cigarettes." Kroon himself would later admit in court that during that time he "arrested a large number of hostages and took them to the house of detention in Almelo."

Of all his misdeeds, the one that would come back to haunt him most was his conduct in the so-called Nijverdal affair. Acting on a tip, Kroon went to a silver wedding anniversary along with two other men, his boss Captain Bakker and his pal Arie van Leeuwen. They walked right into the middle of the party, posing as refugees from Germany. The guests held a spontaneous whip round and gave the three men the money that had been collected. After that Kroon mingled a bit with some of the wedding guests, particularly a certain Betsie van Weezep, whom he seemed to get along very well with. It turned out that she had contacts within the resistance and could obtain false papers. Tonny Kroon was then calling himself Tonny de Hout, borrowing the name of his former partner from the Colonne Henneicke.

Tonny met more and more people from Betsie van Weezep's social circle. He flirted with her, and he got an increasingly clear picture of the resistance activities of this group. At that point Captain Bakker intervened. Acting on the information

Kroon had provided, he arrested the group and turned the arrestees over to the SD. One of them was Herman Kampman, Betsie van Weezep's fiancé. He would later be executed by an SD firing squad.

But first there was a staged confrontation, in which Tonny Kroon was led in, in handcuffs, as if he had also been arrested by the SD. But later, after the war, Betsie van Weezep read a newspaper article about the crimes of someone who went by the name of Tonny de Hout, and it was then that everything fell into place. She would later testify in Tonny Kroon's trial about the way she lost her fiancé.

Detective Voordenhout also tracked down a number of members of Kroon's commando unit, who described the way he operated in the east of the country. Van Muijen, a subordinate: "Kroon stopped at nothing to reach his goal." He interrogated people in a special way, "the *Sonderkommando* way," but Van Muijen refused to go into any detail about what that was. He confined himself to this hint: "He had a sadistic complex, which everybody [at the *Sonderkommando* and police battalion] knew about." And also: "He often talked about how successful he had been at the Jewish department in Amsterdam. He claimed that he took fur coats from the homes of Jews on several occasions and appropriated them for his own use."

Van Muijen said that sometimes he made too few arrests for Kroon's liking. "Then Kroon would give me a terrific dressing down." But after a few drinks, he could be friendly, even generous: "He once treated us to gin, cigarettes and pre-war cigars. Kroon was pretty soused at that point, and he said that the stuff had come from a search he had done earlier that week, at a house in Nijverdal."

A. van Leeuwen, the man who ranked directly below Kroon in the *Sonderkommando* hierarchy, confirmed the whole picture of threats, theft and generally abusive behavior: "He was always the leader of a group and was much too active. He spared no one. He was a monster, had sadistic tendencies and was extremely pro-German." The one thing that is abundantly clear from all these statements is that Kroon was despised by his inferiors. If an investigation turned up little or nothing, that was because *he* hadn't been involved. Then he would go out himself, use his own methods and get results. Van Leeuwen: "His unmatched audacity may have had something to do with it, although once again I have to admit that he was very good at what he did."

Over the course of the trial it became clear that Kroon was guilty of gross misconduct toward three arrestees, who were turned over to the SD after being subjected to severe beatings. He was also indirectly responsible for their deaths, because the three were among the 117 hostages shot by a firing squad in revenge for the attack on Waffen SS commandant Hanns Albin Rauter. One of the men was called De Bruin. After the war his widow reported Kroon to the police. Under police questioning she said: "Kroon was a bastard; he swore a blue streak in my house." The second man was named Dommerholt. One witness remembered Dommerholt collapsing like a sack of flour after being interrogated by Kroon. The third victim of this operation was the photographer J. Zandvoort, whose widow also reported Kroon to the police. When Mrs Zandvoort was allowed to visit her husband, two days after the arrest, his right eye was swollen shut and the right side of his face was red and puffy. He whispered to her that he had endured a horrendous beating at the hands of Kroon.

It is no wonder Tonny Kroon tried to run from justice after the war. He met his wife Jenny in Ter Apel, in the province of Groningen. Like many NSB wives, she fled to Germany on Mad Tuesday,[a] along with her young daughter. The three set off from there on bicycles, according to a letter from that time, "Tonny in the uniform of the *Zugwachtmeister*, Connie in a pink and red cape. The child has big brown eyes and blond curls."

In May 1945 they went their separate ways. Jenny and little Connie returned to Amsterdam – she was not a member of the NSB and had no reason to fear arrest. Tonny emigrated to Belgium, where he was taken in by his wife's family. He probably spent a little less than two years there, since he was not arrested until March 1947. We know little about this time; the only thing in the dossier is a rather sad note that he wrote to Jenny in October 1945.[15] He heard that Jenny had found another man, a member of the Domestic Forces no less. He could not bear it. "I can't believe you would leave me now."

He felt sick, he wrote in pencil on a small gray sheet of paper. He didn't think he could go on much longer like this; he was lonely and unhappy: "When I'm back in Holland, let me see Connie just one more time. You don't have to come yourself, you can send your mother or mine." The loneliness, the homesickness – the hard-hearted Tonny Kroon, the fiercest Jew hunter and most ruthless pursuer of resistance fighters had gone soft: "Darling, if I never hear anything from you again, I hope your life is a happy one. Take good care of Connie and always be a good mother to her. Don't ever tell her what happened to me. I'm ashamed to be here."

He was arrested in March 1947, at home with Jenny and Connie on Bilderdijkkade in Amsterdam; naturally the family had had to leave the palatial house on Johannes Verhulststraat. In his first interrogation he said that he "only now realizes the terrible things I helped to bring about." He said that at the time he knew nothing about the fate of the Jews, even though there were plenty of signs that point to the contrary. "I can state in good conscience that the information we were given at that time was completely different from what the facts now show to have been the case."

Kroon's trial in the spring of 1949 lasted two days. Twenty-three witnesses were called. The fact that he was given the death sentence was no surprise to anyone. "[Kroon was] a constant source of misery to his fellow man," judge-advocate Gelinck said in his closing arguments.[16] He made special mention of the betrayal of Betsie van Weezep, a girl he had initially courted. "The crowning moment of caddishness," according to the prosecutor. The court's sentence reads much like the others we have seen, but here and there the court added modifiers like "extremely intensively." In the view of the judges, Kroon personally unleashed a wave of terror upon the population, and they imposed the severest conceivable penalty without a trace of doubt.

On appeal there was little that even an eloquent lawyer like Colijn could do. He admitted that Kroon's conduct was appalling, though he did not think the defendant was an incorrigible criminal. "He deserves another chance." The Court of Appeals disagreed. During the appeals phase of the case a number of letters Tonny Kroon had written to his wife in 1944 were examined.[17] From Almelo he cheerfully wrote to her about his new job, with the *Sonderkommando* Bakker, where he would soon be starting work. Not without a certain pride, he informed his wife that he would be in charge of no fewer than thirty men and that he had been recommended for the *Kriegsverdienstkreuz* (war merit cross). He would tell her how he got it some other time; it would take too long to write down. He had another piece of news: "Wim Henneicke, you know, the man I worked with in the SD, was shot." He was afraid the same thing might have happened to him if he had stayed in Amsterdam.

At the end of this letter he wrote that he was looking forward to his new job with the *Sonderkommando*. "Jenny, it's the same work I did before; it's freer. I can't tell you exactly what it is, darling. But I'm thrilled to have joined them; it's what I always wanted to do."

In view of this letter the Court of Appeals saw little reason to spare Tonny Kroon's life. The crown, however, did. On January 4, 1950, with the approval of the government, Queen Juliana pardoned the man who liked nothing better than hunting his fellow man.

–15–

Lawbreakers
Henk van den Heuvel

Of the men who arrested Jews under Henneicke and Briedé, five (almost ten percent of the total) were themselves arrested because, in the eyes of the Germans, they had broken the law. One of them, Hendrik van den Heuvel, was fired on the spot when it was discovered that he had a criminal record that he had managed to keep secret upto that point. The exact course of events can be found in his police file; he fell victim to the righteous indignation of an Amsterdam policeman, G. Clement.

In 1943 Clement was working for the National Bureau of Investigation, where he was responsible for tailing criminals.[1] In September 1943 Clement's attention was piqued by the actions of two men on Van Woustraat: Henk van den Heuvel and his colleague in the Colonne, Paul Rooskens*, a forty-seven-year-old former foreign exchange broker. He recognized one of the two from the criminal underworld. Clement saw that they were stopping everyone with Jewish features and asking to see their papers. He went up to them and demanded to see *their* identification. Van den Heuvel and Rooskens were furious at the intrusion. They immediately shouted at him that they were from the SD. "With a great deal of effort," Clement wrote in a 1946 report for the Political Investigation Department, "I was able to get them to show me their papers." According to his ID card, one of the men worked for the *Hausraterfassung*; the other was apparently authorized to check automobiles. Detective Clement realized they were from the Colonne Henneicke; he was familiar with the organization and knew what they did. Nevertheless he persisted, ordering Rooskens and Van den Heuvel to come with him to the police precinct on Stadhouderskade. They refused and threatened to turn him in to the SD, where he would certainly be locked up. Clement was not impressed, let alone afraid. In his 1946 report he wrote, "But I stood my ground and drew my gun." Van den Heuvel and Rooskens said that, if it was absolutely necessary, they would be willing to go to the station on Pieter Aertszstraat; at least at that station there was an NSB inspector they both knew well. But Clement would not take no for an answer and, with his pistol at the ready, he brought the duo to Stadhouderskade. Once there, he checked out his two detainees. He searched through the police records and found what he was looking for: Van den Heuvel had quite a few convictions under his belt. Clement then sent the two men on their way, telling them that he would write up a report. They had not heard the last of this.

But neither had Clement. That same afternoon a written notice was delivered to the policeman's home address, ordering him to report to the offices of the Colonne Henneicke on Noorder Amstellaan the following morning. If he failed to appear, the summons said, he would be jailed. It was clear: a power struggle had broken out between the various authorities, and the outcome was anybody's guess.

Clement read the menacing language and decided to call the station sergeant at the Stadhouderskade precinct to find out what had happened. He was told that four men from the Colonne Henneicke had been to the precinct and had made a scene. They carried on for so long that two high-ranking police officials, Commissioner M. van der Heul and Inspector H. Bonenkamp, eventually gave them his home address. By this point Clement was more than a little agitated himself. He said that he could only be called to account by the police or the SD and "not some little agency working on commission." Police Commissioner Van Heul, the man who had been in charge of maintaining order in South Amsterdam since early 1943, did not want to make waves with the German authorities and responded: "Just go there and take your lumps."

But Clement refused. Furious at the cowardice of his superiors in the force, he decided to raise the stakes. He went to police headquarters, removed Van den Heuvel's file and mug shots and headed off to see Willi Lages, the chief of the *Aussenstelle* of the *SiPo*-SD. And sure enough, Lages agreed to see him, obviously because Clement had himself announced with the message that he was there to discuss a very serious matter. At Lages' office he explained the situation: he had discovered that a member of the Colonne Henneicke had a criminal record, but despite that the man in question was conducting random ID checks on the street, which he had no authority to do. And now they expected Clement, a detective with the National Bureau of Investigation, to report to the Colonne? Clement had judged the situation well; Lages agreed with him. In 1946 Clement noted: "He said I did not have to account for myself to the Colonne and that he was unaware that the Colonne was hiring criminals to help catch Jews."

This came as a great relief for Clement, who later heard, much to his pleasure, that Henk van den Heuvel was summarily dismissed from the Colonne. It is difficult to determine exactly how this occurred. We have Van den Heuvel's own version of events, set down in a written defense he composed for his trial. According to this document, he was summoned to Lages' office one day. "Probably because of a complaint that I wasn't doing my job properly. When I said this to

Henneicke, he grinned at me. I was sure the fear in my face was visible. The visit to Mr W. Lages was very brief. I was discharged on the spot, on the grounds that I was unsuitable for the position."

It is hardly surprising that Van den Heuvel chose to gloss over a number of important details. In his position most of his colleagues from the Colonne did the same thing. Much more remarkable was the attitude of Willi Lages, the head of the *Aussenstelle*. This very proper police officer, under whose leadership tens of thousands of Jews were sent to their deaths, could not live with the thought that one of the men doing this dirty job had a criminal record, and promptly sacked him.

Henk Klingeberg

No less remarkable is the story of Henk Klingeberg, who was fifty-one when he joined the Colonne Henneicke.[2] He had had various other occupations before that time; the two jobs he held longest were office clerk and manager at a firm that dealt in chocolate and cocoa butter. Shortly before the war broke out he was earning a good living (between fl.200 and fl.300 a month) in the gasoline industry, but the war dealt a severe blow to that particular sector of the economy; there was virtually no gasoline to be had. After eight months without work, he wound up at the *Hausraterfassung*, ultimately finding his way into the Colonne Henneicke, where he became one of the more active Jew hunters. On September 2, 1943 Klingeberg himself was arrested by the Germans. According to his own story, which he told in 1949, there were two possible reasons: he had been passing himself off as an SD agent (which was officially illegal, even though almost everyone in the Colonne did it) or he had refused to follow an order. Neither of these possibilities bore much resemblance to the truth. It is almost certain that the real reason Klingeberg was dismissed was that he could not keep his hands off the female arrestees. In the subpoena issued by the Special Court, one can read that he "repeatedly attempted to force female victims into having sexual relations with him."[3] After the war a number of people reported him to the authorities, including one woman who did so on behalf of her Jewish maid, whom Klingeberg had allegedly assaulted. During the trial, in March 1949, witness Maria de Vos complained that Klingeberg came over to her house every night for a week to ask for a statement about a Jewish girl she had supposedly been hiding. He repeatedly threatened to have her deported to Mauthausen, which was synonymous with death even then. Mrs de Vos: "I couldn't bear it, particularly since the defendant was so aggressive." On the advice of a friend, she told Klingeberg off and then mustered up her courage and went to the *Sicherheitsdienst* on Euterpestraat. There she filed an official complaint with a certain Maibaum. She did not know what happened after that, but she never heard from Klingeberg again.

A number of the charges against Klingeberg were doubtless the result of the appeal which appeared in the June 7, 1946 edition of the newspaper *Het Parool*, under the heading "Who knows Klingeberg?" Underneath was a request for all women who had been harassed or molested by him to make themselves known to the authorities.[4]

This appeal led to a deposition from a woman who had sheltered two Jewish women during the war, both of whom were arrested. She stated that she "had to give the defendant a kiss and make a date to go out with him." She never showed up for the date. During the trial Klingeberg denied the allegation, and not without a certain bravado: "If I had gotten a kiss from her, I would have remembered it for the rest of my life."[5]

Another witness who responded to the appeal was Betje Pouw-Van der Horst, who was picked up by Klingeberg in February 1943. She attempted to run away, but this underling of Henneicke's beat her and kicked her and threatened her with a gun. He took three gold bracelets from her, and then he brought her to a café on Stadhouderskade and bought her something to eat. While there, he referred to her consistently as "that Jewess." Then a customer came into the café, the man Betje Pouw believed had betrayed her to Klingeberg. He was in the company of Klingeberg's wife. Klingeberg then presented her Mrs Pouw's bracelets, but she refused to take them, saying: "What am I supposed to do with that junk; the house is already jam-packed with it." Mrs Pouw, in her testimony in Klingeberg's trial: "After that the suspect took me to the phone booth in the café. He made me kiss him and he molested me. The defendant also asked me to go home with him to, in his words, make whoopee. I flatly refused and then he let me go." As always, Klingeberg denied everything.

Many more statements poured in, in response to the appeal in *Het Parool*, and the tenor was always the same. He asked every woman who crossed his path, even Jews, to be his girlfriend and invited them all out on dates. He preferred to conduct his interrogations in the bathroom – in short, Klingeberg constantly tried to exploit his superior position in order to gain sexual favors. Ultimately this would lead to his arrest. During the trial it transpired that someone had filed a complaint against him with the *Sicherheitsdienst* before the war was even over. And the response was much more severe than Klingeberg could have imagined: the SD sent him to Camp Amersfoort, where the Germans detained their own political prisoners, generally treating them quite badly. In that camp Klingeberg had to appear before a German court. It was an extremely bizarre trial; we know this from the statements of one of the women called to give evidence – a Mrs Hansen, who ran a boarding house where Klingeberg assaulted and then arrested a Jewish maid.[6]

She recalled that a certain Westerveld functioned as judge at the *Kriegsgericht* (court martial) at Camp Amersfoort. The commandant of the camp, the infamous Karl Peter Berg, served as the counsel for the defense. Years later Mrs Hansen could not remember many specifics about the trial, though she did recollect that Klingeberg was sentenced to death and that his "public defender," camp commandant Berg, greeted the verdict with the words, *"Ich bin damit einverstanden."* ("I concur"). Another witness called to testify at the *Kriegsgericht* was Dr Van Breda Vriesman. He had a much better memory of the trial than Mrs Hansen. In November 1945 he informed the Political Investigation Service in a letter that Klingeberg "had been sentenced to death several times for blackmailing the wives of Jews into having sexual relations with him."[7] Van Breda Vriesman had already been warned about him at Camp Amersfoort. He wrote to the office of the public prosecutor after the war: "I cannot understand why Klingeberg's sentence was never carried out. Hopefully this mistake will now be rectified."

We know the Germans eventually commuted his sentence to life in prison, the prison in question being the Neuengamme concentration camp. He survived the horrible camp, as well as a naval disaster in the Gulf of Lübeck that cost the lives of thousands of fellow prisoners. After the war he returned to the Netherlands by way of Brussels. He was imprisoned at Camp Vught, which was then being used as a detention centre for collaborators. From there he was sent to the internment camp on Da Costastraat in Amsterdam.

It was not until March 11, 1949 that Klingeberg had his (second) day in court, this time the Fifth Division of the Special Court in Amsterdam. Klingeberg, we read in the subpoena, was aggressive, abusive and violent. The fact that he regularly went out on assignments with Henneicke himself suggested a certain status within the Colonne. The judgment was delayed for six months because the defense successfully lobbied for the defendant to be given a psychological examination. In September the psychiatrist Tammenoms Bakkers concluded that Klingeberg was competent to stand trial, and on September 29, 1949, the judgment was read: Henk Klingeberg was sentenced to death, for the second time in his life. Like the *Kriegsgericht* at Camp Amersfoort, the Special Court in Amsterdam also decided that his life should be brought to an end.

However, the sentence was not carried out, and, for once, the reason was not the clemency policy of the crown, but the Special Court of Appeals, which unearthed an instance in his dossier of an exhausted fellow prisoner who claimed he owed his life to Klingeberg. This demonstrated that even he was not totally devoid of "human emotions," though they were certainly well hidden. This single incident was considered reason enough to spare Klingeberg's life. And thus Henk Klingeberg survived two death sentences, one from each of the warring parties in the Second World War.

Joop den Ouden

The "real" underworld was also represented in the Colonne Henneicke. According to some sources, the boss himself was no stranger to the world of crime, but the best-known criminal was Joop den Ouden. At the time of the bounty hunt, he was thirty-two: a big man, a former auto mechanic, blond hair, blue-gray eyes, six foot three. According to a physical description in his file, he had an "oval face with a generally disgruntled expression."[8] While preparing the case against him, investigators from the PRA discovered that he had four prior convictions: for theft, blackmail, fraud and pandering. Den Ouden himself was decidedly nonchalant about everything; during an interrogation he opined, "[I] did all right, despite the lack of guidance in my youth."

Joop never knew his father. His mother divorced him shortly after Joop's birth and raised her son alone. After primary school he was placed in a special school, which he attended until he was sixteen: "And by then I had only passed three classes." Writing would remain a problem for the rest of his life, judging from the clumsily phrased notes he mailed from prison after the war. In an interrogation he said, "I was told I couldn't keep up, and that was true, because I had problems learning." His mother was not in a position to advise him about future career choices and left him to his own devices. He became a "bicycle boy," and after seeing a bit of the world as a seaman apprentice, he became a "black" taxi driver: "That is to say, I started driving people around without a permit. I took them to the prostitutes on Achterburgwal in Amsterdam."

During that period Den Ouden managed to build up a fairly voluminous police record. Shortly before the war he got into the used automobile racket. In the course of his work he was involved in a serious accident. He spent a year and a half in hospital and came out with a stiff leg. He went back to driving his cab and dealing in used automobiles. He had never meddled in politics, but the Germans took away his livelihood when they impounded his cab. He received a summons to go to work in Germany, but he chose instead to go into hiding in Alkmaar. He subsequently received a tip that the firm Lippmann, Rosenthal & Co. had a job for him: sorting confiscated Jewish property. After a few days he was transferred to the Colonne Henneicke.

It was there that Den Ouden was truly able to develop his talents: he was a hustler, a con man, a deal maker. He arrested people, assaulted people and once a month he collected a pay check for his efforts. Den Ouden was a vicious man with a mouth to match. "You let this Jew make out with your wife right in front of you," he said to a man who had a Jewish man staying with him and his wife. In the course of the arrest he saw that the family had eggs, a rarity in 1943. Den Ouden demanded that the lady of the house, Mrs Duba, fry them up. He even put on a record, for a little atmosphere. He then said to the woman: "If you were a bit younger, I wouldn't mind going to bed with you." Finally, he confiscated fl.1,800; he had the woman count it out with him, up to fl.1,160. The rest he kept for himself. The entire house of this well-to-do, non-Jewish family was cleaned out. A neighbor later saw Den Ouden's girlfriend, known in the red light district as Black Beppie, walking around in Mrs Duba's fur coat.

Eddy Moerberg, Henneicke's bookkeeper, had nothing but bad things to say about Den Ouden. He told of a visit to an address on Nicolaas Witsenstraat, where Joop knew everybody who had anything to do with the sex trade. Moerberg: "Joop den Ouden took us there once in a while, to that street, to show us what went on in the houses there, and he'd just walk right in, since he knew practically all the people on the street."

In August 1945 a survivor from Auschwitz wrote to the Political Investigation Service to say that he had been arrested during the war by Den Ouden, "the well-known blackguard and pimp." Den Ouden, wrote H. de Lange with barely suppressed rage, "robbed me of 9,600 guilders in cash, six shares in Royal Oil, 4 rings with very large stones and a number of small gold articles. He told me that ownership of . . . stocks and diamonds and gold by Jews was a capital offense, and so he appropriated these items, to spare me and enrich himself."[9] It is an explanation of such outrageous depravity that it doesn't appear in any of the other Henneicke dossiers: pocketing money and possessions, ostensibly out of benevolence toward the Jewish owner, and then having the owner deported.

De Lange was sent to Westerbork, and ten days later to Auschwitz-Birkenau. "Of all the people who were arrested with me . . . I was the only one to return. The others were gassed and burned, the same day we arrived in that hell." The others he was referring to were his Hungarian girlfriend, their child and De Lange's sister. "Upon arriving my sister, my wife and our little child were sent straight to the gas chamber," De Lange wrote to investigators. Five days before, De Lange's first wife was arrested as well, also by Den Ouden. She returned from Auschwitz, and his two children from that first marriage survived by going into hiding. In his letter De Lange demanded that he be compensated for his suffering "from the many possessions that fine gentleman so scandalously misappropriated."

It is known that after his time with the Colonne Henneicke, Den Ouden went on doing the same sort of work with the police. He was hired as a detective by the former Bureau of Jewish Affairs, by then part of the *Sicherheitspolizei*, where Abraham Kaper was in charge of the day-to-day operations. After the Colonne was dissolved, this department continued to hunt for Jews. Kaper knew Den Ouden from his days with the vice squad; as a pimp, Den Ouden was a familiar face at the station house. And even though he could barely get a legible sentence on paper, he was hired. Den Ouden had connections, received many tips and was thus productive. After the war his former colleagues from the police department spoke fairly positively about him. In his courtroom testimony, Maarten Kuiper (one of those present for the arrest of Anne Frank and her family) was the only one to dwell on Den Ouden's abusive conduct and his black market activities, particularly trading in stolen jewels.

Dries Riphagen

Den Ouden's partner in crime was Dries Riphagen, who was known in the Amsterdam underworld as Al Capone. Riphagen was born in 1909 and took to crime at a young age. At fifteen he was sent to a juvenile detention center; after that he was convicted a number of times of various minor offenses. In the 1930s he established his fame in the capital; at that time his main occupation was pimping. The colorful Riphagen only worked part-time for the Colonne Henneicke, as a sort of freelancer. In their 1990 book on Riphagen, journalists Bart Middelburg and René ter Steege described his rise as follows: "After Riphagen divorced his first (official) wife in 1936, he came in contact with the then-leaders of the Amsterdam underworld, primarily through the used car trade, which has always had a questionable reputation but which was then dominated almost exclusively by criminals. A group soon formed around him . . . with Riphagen as the undisputed leader. He almost always carried a gun, which was exceptional in those days, even in the underworld. It was also in this period that Riphagen acquired the nickname Al Capone."[10]

The war was a profitable time for Riphagen. Middelburg and Ter Steege write: "From the dossier a picture emerges of a pimp who was driven solely by anti-Semitism and greed, a man who seized his chance when the Germans started deporting Jews to the death camps. As an employee of several official German organizations, Riphagen amassed a fortune from the theft of Jewish property, turning over countless people to the *Sicherheitsdienst*. According to estimates he sent at least two hundred people to their deaths."[11]

Riphagen was the central figure in one of the biggest hauls the Jew hunters ever made, at a raid in the city of Hilversum.[12] It began with a certain Van E., a junk dealer and small-time hustler. Dries Riphagen came to his shop on St Willibrordusstraat to ask if he would be interested in buying a small coal-burning stove from him. They made an appointment for Van W. to come by and take a look at it the following day. But he never showed up, and Riphagen went back to set things right: he didn't appreciate being given the run-around. There was a heated discussion in Van W.'s shop, in which a certain S. also took part. He was an acquaintance of Van W.'s who was being sought by the authorities for dealing in stolen goods. Van W. was letting him hide out at his place as long as the police were after him. The dispute eventually turned to the topic of "Hilversum," and Riphagen, who always had his feelers out for an opportunity to make a little money, asked if there were any Jews living there. S. knew where to find them, and they agreed that S. would go along to point them out. The documents on this operation are absent from Riphagen's file, and they are not to be found anywhere else either, but their intended quarry was evidently a group of no fewer than thirty Jews, who were hiding out at a farm called the White Horse.

Den Ouden and Riphagen went out together on assignments countless times. They had the same informants, and they both operated in the same way: wangling, wheedling, conning, coaxing – whatever it took to catch their prey. Riphagen worked not only for Henneicke, but also for the *Devisenschutzkommando*, a German agency responsible for making sure Dutch citizens were following the rules governing the ownership of money and securities. In practice, they tracked down the contents of safe deposit boxes and other possible storage places for money and gold.[13] Riphagen continued working there after the Colonne Henneicke was disbanded.

Riphagen also had a reputation for being exceptionally abusive and violent. He hunted down a Jewish man, one Simon Bacherach, who had called him a "filthy pimp" years before. Riphagen later said to the owner of a pub which Bacherach was known to frequent: "Now listen, I just punched that dirty kike in the face and I'm warning you again not to let that dirty kike back in here, because I'm from the SD, and if I see him here, he's a dead man." At that point, according to the pub owner, Riphagen drew his gun to show that he meant business.[14]

After the war he and Den Ouden proved to be two of the most difficult cases for Special Justice. Den Ouden told investigators he was actually a resistance fighter, who was involved in a top secret mission to infiltrate the *Sicherheitsdienst*. To bolster his story, he took to sporting a Domestic Forces armband shortly after the liberation. But so many incriminating statements started coming in that the net soon began to close around him. However, Den Ouden lacked the patience and talent for solitary confinement and decided to escape. On October 27, 1945, Joop den Ouden broke out of the House of Detention on Amstelveenseweg. The chief of police's criminal division immediately put his name on the telex.[15]

Den Ouden hid out with a family for whom he had once done a favor: he had got a diamond cutter released from prison after the latter had been picked up by Riphagen in 1944 for having too much money in his house. Out of gratitude the family had said they would be glad to help him in return, and one Saturday morning they found Joop den Ouden standing at the door, asking if they would put him up for a few days. The diamond cutter, who had already generously paid Den Ouden for his help, naturally said yes. Den Ouden stayed there for about three days.

For the next three weeks Den Ouden moved from place to place, always one step ahead of his pursuers, but on November 22 he was arrested, to the great satisfaction of the Bureau of National Security. Obviously Joop den Ouden was not your run-of-the-mill collaborator, and the same could be said for Dries Riphagen. These were men who were part of an extensive criminal network and consequently possessed a great deal of interesting information. As Middelburg and Ter Steege show, after the liberation Riphagen made a deal with the Bureau of National Security, with the consent of chief of operations W. Sanders. In exchange for preferential treatment he would provide them with information about traitors and other ringleaders.[16] The upshot was that he was placed under house arrest at the home of a detective, Frits Kerkhoven, with whom he had become friendly. His pal Joop den Ouden worked out a similar deal for himself. For a short time he moved in with detective Jan Schouw. The reasoning behind such unorthodox living arrangements was that the prisoners would be more inclined to cooperate from this position than from a jail cell.

It is unclear how useful Riphagen was in that respect, though he is known to have facilitated the arrest of the *V-Frau* Betje W., in a convent in Limburg. She was sentenced to life in prison. But when it came time for Riphagen himself to face the music, he bolted, on February 18, 1946, before criminal proceedings could be launched against him. He fled to Spain, where he was arrested in late 1946. But just before he was to be extradited to the Netherlands in 1948, he escaped again, this time to Argentina. There was no reason to doubt that he would be able to support himself there: Riphagen had made a fortune in the war. He invested some of the money in the Netherlands but much of it was stashed away in foreign banks; he had taken full advantage of the freedom of movement he enjoyed as a currency controller. In the 1950s he came to Europe with ex-president Juan Péron, who had become a personal friend, and died of cancer in Switzerland in 1973.[17]

Den Ouden also helped out the authorities, but his cooperation was grudging, to say the least. Den Ouden simply refused to stay in prison, escaping again on July 11, 1946.[18] At that time he was being held in the House of Detention in Maastricht, because the political crimes division in the nearby city of Heerlen wanted time to interrogate him. But the grate on the window of his cell was so loose you could lift it up and climb out, even someone with Joop den Ouden's stocky build. One night he did just that. He left the complex and found himself in a cemetery near the prison, a free man. But Joop den Ouden, an Amsterdammer born and bred, had no idea where to go. In desperation he returned to his cell, through the same loose grate by which he had left it. On the way back to Amsterdam he told the two policemen accompanying him that he knew the names of some witnesses they were looking for. He explained to his chaperones that he had left a paper with the names at the home of his friend Piet de Graaf, a boxing instructor from Amsterdam. He asked them to drive him there. They did so, and they also allowed him to visit the toilet while he was there. And thus Joop was able to escape again. He darted through another door and ran out on to the street. He went to stay with an acquaintance, Abraham Bontenbal, and two days later he was arrested there, at a house on Kromme Waal. A short time later Joop den Ouden wrote from his cell to Inspector Botti, the head of the PRA. The note is still in his criminal record: "Please come see me as soon as you can. Cause I urgently have to talk to you. Joop den Ouden."

Joop wanted to make a deal, that much was clear. He helped the investigators, giving them the names of informants. On August 2 a police officer from District

III C wrote him a note, at his home address at 179 Noorder Amstellaan, thanking him for his cooperation in tracking down three men and testifying against them. Negotiations about giving evidence against two other suspects were apparently still ongoing. "You can count on my discretion in these matters," wrote the policeman.

There are strong indications that Den Ouden was rewarded for his cooperative attitude. Even though he was one of the most serious cases, with a wartime record that can only be called reprehensible, his life was ultimately spared, in May 1950. He was given a mere eight years, and after that he was transferred to a psychiatric institution for continued monitoring. Den Ouden was the only member of the Colonne to receive such a sentence.[19]

The court's sentence is absent from Den Ouden's dossier, as are many other relevant documents, including the psychiatric report, which formed the basis of Den Ouden's commitment. However, we do know the date he was released on parole: October 2, 1951. If this was indeed the case, Den Ouden's psychiatric treatment could not have lasted longer than a year and a half. When he was allowed to return home on probation, he had to abide by all sorts of conditions; this state of affairs lasted until August 1954. Later he moved in with a half-brother in Alkmaar, where he got a job as a valet in a hotel. Following that, he moved to Haarlem.

By then his relationship with the prostitute Black Beppie had been over for some time. She had left him while he was still incarcerated. She was bitter because he had left her in poverty with two children to bring up. He did not want to lose her, judging by the primitive notes he sent. One time he asked her to stand in front of a certain shop on a side street of Amstelveenseweg with her young sons Harrie and Wimpie. He made a hole in his cell, so he could see them at that very spot.

Joop den Ouden was an expert in tracking down and arresting Jews, but he could not bear confinement himself. He was, however, shrewd enough to ensure that his time behind bars would be minimal.

–16–

What Did the Jew Hunters Know?

The summer of 1943: a fifteen-year-old Jewish girl, Lilly van Gelder, who was hiding out with the Witjas family prior to her arrest, was interrogated by a member of the Colonne Henneicke. Mrs Witjas could follow the conversation in the adjoining room word for word. At a certain point she heard Lilly sobbing loudly. She then heard the man who discovered her – it was Henk Saaldijk – ask, "What is it, why are you crying?" And she also overheard the girl's reply, "Because we're being murdered." And finally she was also able to make out Saaldijk's response: "It's not as bad as all that. You're going there to *work*."[1]

Knowing what we know today, it seems an improbable situation: the Jew hunter who denied that his prey would be murdered, and the prey who, at fifteen, was convinced of the contrary. The question of how much everyone, victims and perpetrators alike, knew about the Jews' ultimate fate will probably never be fully answered. Historian Loe de Jong devoted a very lengthy section to the subject in his standard work on the Netherlands during the Second World War.[2] He highlighted the significant difference between the "contemporary perspective" ("How did people see it then?") and the historical perspective ("How do we see it now?"). According to De Jong, to truly understand the events of the time, it is necessary to banish all knowledge of the genocide from one's mind and accept that "to the vast majority of Dutch people living at the time, the idea that millions of people were being eliminated was utterly implausible." In other words, "the notion that masses of people were being murdered with an assembly line-like efficiency was beyond their comprehension." According to De Jong, the same could be said for a substantial number of Jews as well. With the help of many examples he shows that, to a large extent, the victims suppressed the reports and rumors of mass extermination. They refused to believe it, because if they did, they would not be able to go on.

Nevertheless, there were many who did realize what was going on. That must have been the motive for the hundreds of suicides beginning in May 1940. And this realisation must have prompted many others to go into hiding, to flee the country, to pay huge sums of money to reach freedom, or at least a chance at it. But tens of thousands of Dutch Jews deliberately ignored signs that pointed to the grim reality of things: they reported for the *Arbeitseinsatz* in Germany, or they did not resist arrest when their hiding places were discovered. Their motto seemed to be: "Everything will be all right," or "We'll get through it somehow."

Philip Mechanicus, the journalist for the *Algemeen Handelsblad* who kept a diary of the nearly one and a half years he spent at Camp Westerbork, overheard a discussion among three camp inmates about their prospects for the future.[3]

One of them, who had previously been imprisoned at Camp Vught, said, "If I had to choose between Vught and Poland, I'd take Poland. Poland can't be as bad as Vught. [It was] a hell, a hell."

The second inmate: "I'm also optimistic about Poland. Things will be all right. I know people who came back from Buchenwald and Dachau."

The third man, a Jew of Austrian extraction: "Do you think Poland is some sort of pleasure garden? I know for certain that if I'm sent to Poland – and I'm going Tuesday – I won't survive. I can't work anymore, and they're not going to feed good-for-nothings. That doesn't fit their plans."

This must have been an accurate portrayal of the emotional turmoil that Jews were going through in 1943, wavering between hope and fear, belief and disbelief.

In his book Loe de Jong proceeds from the assumption that the leading German Nazis in the Netherlands were aware that Jews were being massacred in Poland. "Numerous Dutch collaborators," he writes, "had learned that Jews were being murdered on a large scale in Eastern Europe, the same Eastern Europe to which the Dutch Jews were being deported." However, he was unable to determine which people knew this and which did not. At first De Jong thought differently about the matter, but over time his views changed. One of the men he interviewed for his book was Hanns Albin Rauter, the highest ranking SS official in the Netherlands. The discussion took place in the latter's prison cell. De Jong was there, along with Jacques Presser and the founder of the National Institute for War Documentation, Professor N.W. Posthumus, and all three of them were impressed by Rauter's "emphatic and very convincing denials" that he had known what awaited the Jews in Poland.[4] In fact, even the Special Court in The Hague believed Rauter to a certain extent, given the following excerpt from their judgment of May 1948: "[A]t the time [he] may not have foreseen that virtually all Jews would be killed in the manner which later proved to be the case." It was not until De Jong actually began to write about the Holocaust in his book, after having read all the relevant documents and examined the facts in their proper context, that he came to the conclusion that Rauter was well aware of all plans.[5]

In the interim De Jong had got his hands on a copy of a speech Rauter gave to his staff in March 1943, the same month the Colonne Henneicke began hunting for

Jews. Rauter reported that 55,000 Jews had already been deported and another 12,000 were being held at the camp. He continued: "We hope that in the near future there will be no more Jews freely walking the streets in the Netherlands. This is not a pretty task; it is a dirty job. But it is a measure that will be of great historical significance."[6] Rauter was referring to Hitler's 1939 proclamation, in which the *Führer* predicted that the Jewish race in Europe would be destroyed, if international Jewry, in Hitler's words, "should succeed in plunging the world into a new crisis." To which Rauter said: "And this will come to pass. There mustn't be a single Jew left in Europe." He knew that some people had protested these actions, saying their conscience would not allow them to take part in such work, but Rauter was not bothered by such reservations. "I will gladly . . . do penance in heaven for my sins against the Jews here [on Earth]," he said, and according to the minutes of the meeting the Dutch SS leadership laughed heartily at this heartfelt admission. Rauter, De Jong concluded, knew everything.

Rauter's right-hand man in the Netherlands, Dr Wilhelm Harster, the head of the *Sicherheitspolizei*-SD, had always denied knowing anything about the fate of the Jews just as stubbornly as his boss. But twenty years after the war, when preparations were being made in Munich for a second trial against him, his interrogators suddenly got a confession out of him. They were discussing Jewish children and the elderly, two groups who could not possibly be expected to work but who were nevertheless deported in conjunction with the *Arbeitseinsatz*. German investigators recorded him as saying: "Rather, it should be obvious that those people who weren't capable of working were being sent to the East to be killed, sooner or later."[7] So Harster knew as well.

And we could go on like this. After the war everybody pleaded ignorance. De Jong: "Seyss-Inquart, Wimmer, Rauter, Harster, Lages, Fischer, Aus der Fünten, Gemmeker and so many others were fighting for their lives." If they confessed, their fate would be sealed, and they would also be putting others' lives in jeopardy. Albert Konrad Gemmeker, the gentleman commandant of Westerbork, was asked dozens of times by detective J. Schoenmaker if he knew what awaited the Jews in the East.[8] His answer was always the same: "As improbable as it may sound to you, I didn't know what was going to happen to the Jews in Auschwitz. I knew nothing of the killing and the way it was done." In the end Gemmeker was given a ten-year prison sentence – far less than the Jew hunters of the *Hausraterfassung*. But it is now clear, according to Johannes Houwink ten Cate, researcher at the Institute for War Documentation, that Gemmeker *did* know what went on at Auschwitz.[9] The men who accompanied the death trains to the camp knew the facts; they had smelled the stench of the crematoria, and they talked about it with anyone who would listen. Thus Gemmeker must also have known the fate of the Jews, just like countless other high-ranking members of the Nazi hierarchy. De Jong tells of a Nazi of the second tier, *Kreisschulungsleiter* (regional educational officer) F.P.

Reible, who gave a speech on September 11, 1942 in Deventer which was heard by dozens of Nazis.[10] The *Deventer Dagblad* reported on it, and the next day thousands of Dutch people could read: "This war is a war of destruction and it is the Jew who must be destroyed, for God's sake, and not us. We will solve the Jewish problem once and for all." According to De Jong, this instructor was given a good dressing down for his candor; in the future such matters were never again spoken about publicly, not by Reible or anyone else.

Then there is the question of whether Henneicke and Briedé's Jew hunters knew what would happen to their victims. A striking number of signals can be found in the testimony of survivors, suggesting that at least some of them were aware of what was going on. Naturally, in their trials all of them denied knowing what was in store for their victims, just as they denied receiving bonuses. But according to Jacobs Rubens, who was arrested by Willem Briedé on August 16, 1943, the top man of the *Hausraterfassung* plainly said, "I'll be straight with you, since you're going to be gassed anyway. You're going right to Germany, and you won't be coming back."[11] There is, of course, a chance that Rubens invented this aside to get revenge on the man who had arrested him and eight others, but Rubens later returned to this exchange during Briedé's trial in absentia. He had asked Briedé who had betrayed him, and Briedé had answered, "You're going to be gassed, and dead men tell no tales. I can tell you it was Mrs X. She works for us." In fact Rubens had already heard what would happen to the Jews, from the woman he had been staying with. She had heard from a German "with whom she was in contact" that the Jews in Poland were being gassed; no wonder Rubens was willing to spend any amount of money to buy his freedom, which he eventually succeeded in doing.

Briedé was at the top of the *Hausraterfassung* hierarchy and had the best sources of information at his disposal. The same can be said of Eddy Moerberg, Henneicke's bookkeeper. During the mass arrest of Jews at a rest home in Oss, he said to nurse Bertha Zilverberg: "Come work for the SD. Otherwise you're going to Poland, and you'll never come back."[12] And there is also testimony from a Jewish barber who had to supply Moerberg with addresses where Jews were hiding: "If you give me the addresses of Jews you can go home, otherwise you're going to Poland too, and you know you won't be coming back."[13]

We also know of similar remarks from the lesser figures in the Colonne Henneicke. The upstairs neighbor of Lambert Schipper, the commercial agent from Limburg, knew her neighbor was rounding up Jews, and one day she asked him how he could do such a thing as the father of three children. He replied, "They're only Jew children, and the entire Jewish race has to be exterminated."[14] Schipper had said something similar when he took little André Ossendrijver away from his foster parents in Zuilen.

During one operation Sjef Sweeger was asked by an arrestee if she could get some clothes to take with her. His response: "Where you're going, you won't need clothes."[15]

Fred Cool, formerly a hotel manager, but in 1943 one of the most dedicated Jew hunters, arrested Elisabeth Ziekenoppasser-Swaab, who was not wearing a Star of David. She denied being Jewish, and Cool barked at her, "You're going to Buchenwald too, you filthy Jew, where your whole family has already been gassed."[16] This is patently untrue, incidentally, since Buchenwald was not an extermination camp, but if Cool said it, it is a sign that he knew the fate of the Jews.

Finally, it should come as no surprise that Tonny Kroon also earned himself a place on this list. This active, crafty Jew hunter, who later would pursue resistance fighters with the same zeal, once visited an NSB family in order to gather information about their Jewish neighbors. The lady of the house had said to Kroon that her heart broke every time she thought about Jewish children being taken away from their mothers. Tonny Kroon had responded "that all Jews should be gassed."[17]

All these statements and official declarations contribute to the impression that certain members of the Colonne Henneicke knew very well what would happen to the Jews. That impression is reinforced by the fact that a significant number (approximately fifty percent) of Henneicke and Briedé's subordinates were members of the NSKK, the *Nationalsozialistische Kraftfahrkorps*, the Nazi lorry drivers' guild. Before going to work for the *Hausraterfassung*, most of them had gained experience on the Eastern Front. The detectives who questioned them after the war were not interested in their exploits there, and thus we have no statements about that period. It is, however, common knowledge that the men in the NSKK knew more than anyone else about the mass executions carried out in Eastern Europe by the *Sonderkommandos*. They witnessed them, and sometimes they even had to help out with them. At the very least they would have heard colleagues talking about them. A number of the reports from Poland and the Soviet Union that filtered back to the Netherlands came from NSKK men who were passing on what they had seen or heard. And thus it was not merely the victims and the perpetrators who were learning about what was taking place thousands of kilometres to the east, but ordinary Dutch people as well. Loe de Jong may rightly contend that many people *couldn't* believe the rumors and reports, but this does not alter the fact that there were also a great many who *did*.

This is quite clear from a study by thirteen students at the University of Amsterdam who pored over seventy diaries kept by ordinary Dutch people during the war.[18] It was not a representative sample, but the study was the first attempt to examine how the average man and woman reacted at the time. The results were striking: of those seventy writers, no fewer than twenty-four were pessimistic about the fate of the Jews. They suspected that a mass murder was taking place and used words like "slaughter," "murder," and "extermination."

A number of them based that pessimism on news they had heard from Radio Oranje or the Dutch news division of the BBC. In June and December 1942, reports from the Polish government concerning the mass murder of Jews were broadcast. And gradually these kinds of reports started turning up in the diaries. In his diary entry for September 29, 1942 a barley husker from Zaandam noted that 2,250 Jews had been tortured to death.[19] On November 15 a student heard from NSB men that the Jewish problem in the Netherlands would be solved by "murdering them in the Polish death-trap." A notary from the east of the country wrote on December 29, 1942 that "people say that [a deportation] means we shall probably never hear anything from them again." On February 20, 1943 he wrote that there were rumors making the rounds about gassings. A Rotterdammer wrote: "Executions of Jews in Poland continue: in one place 6,000 a day; first they strip; then . . . (gas?)." A woman from Heiloo, in late 1942: "There is apparently a plan to kill all the Jews in Poland before the year is out and that's where almost all the Jews are going." An assistant accountant from Rotterdam: "In Poland the mass murder of the Jews continues. It is said that Himmler wants to kill all the Jews before '43."

The study of the diaries shows that much more was known about the true nature of the Holocaust than was generally assumed. If that was the case for "ordinary" people, it must certainly also have been true for the Jew hunters, who had been earning their living by arresting Jews since March 1943. One can also read suspicions of mass murder fairly early on in Anne Frank's diary, for example on October 9, 1942: "If things are this bad in Holland, how will they live in the far-off and barbaric places they're being sent to? We assume most of them are being murdered. The English radio talks of gassing. Maybe that's the quickest way to die."[20] On June 2, 1943, Philip Mechanicus noted in his diary in Westerbork: "The few intellectuals who have been in the camp so far share the conviction that Poland means the end of everything, and that the Jews will not survive this hell if the war goes on much longer."[21] During that period Mechanicus was occasionally in touch with Jewish Council staff member Etty Hillesum, who also kept a diary. As early as July 3, 1942 she wrote: "They seek our downfall and our destruction; one shouldn't harbor any illusions about that anymore. They are out for our total annihilation."[22]

But just as with Mechanicus, in Hillesum's diary you will sometimes read a much more positive observation just a few pages later. In that respect De Jong's basic assumption is certainly correct: even those who did believe the horror stories must have buried that knowledge to some extent. People were apparently capable of suppressing the worst of it, at least temporarily. That must also have been true for the perpetrators, like Chris de Hout. We have already seen how astounded he was when he read in magazines what had happened in the camps. "The things I read horrified me. The insane butchering of the people I had arrested is a heavy burden I will have to bear my whole life long."[23]

These are the words of a man who worked as a lorry driver for the Nazis for several months in 1941 and 1942. While there, he undoubtedly must have seen or heard what was happening to the Jews of that country. Moreover, De Hout was the only member of the Colonne Henneicke who worked at Westerbork for seven months, as part of the team of men who robbed the Jews of their last money and possessions when they arrived, and sometimes shortly before they left for the death camps as well. He too claimed to have known nothing in 1943.

–17–

On Trial

The Netherlands took great pains with the prosecution of the professional Jew hunters. Almost eighty percent of the suspects were tried and convicted. Moreover, the punishments that were handed down by the Special Courts were generally quite severe, with many death sentences among them. All in all it was a highly intensive legal operation. But in a number of instances the post-war prosecutors missed the boat. Three of the fifty-four bounty hunters were already dead before their cases could be adjudicated, and two were not punished for various reasons.[1] Six others succeeded in fleeing the country in time: eleven percent of the suspects were able to elude justice in this way, a remarkably high proportion however you look at it. Among this number was Andries "Al Capone" Riphagen, who had sufficient protection to slip out of the country in time and settle in Argentina, as a friend of Peron's. Another was Willem Briedé who, together with Henneicke (who had been liquidated in 1944), bore the greatest responsibility of all the Jew hunters. Briedé moved to a small village outside Essen and kept a low profile. The Dutch authorities were never able to find any trace of him, and no attempts were ever made to have him extradited.

Essentially the same thing happened to the only German in the Colonne Henneicke, Hugo Berten.[2] At the height of the deportations, this former owner of a lumber company was already in his early fifties. Berten continued working for the *Hausraterfassung* right until the very end. At that point just three former bounty hunters were working there, at the fur department, and one of them was Berten. In 1944 he fled to Germany and disappeared. Prosecutors did not try him in absentia; he was apparently deemed to be too insignificant. Berten functioned as a sort of helper, who was used only occasionally, but he was nonetheless responsible for the arrest of a number of Jews. He was barred from re-entering the Netherlands. Up until 1971, the year in which the statute of limitations on his war crimes lapsed, the authorities were still trying to track down Berten, but without success.

Jaap Rademakers* was another member of the Colonne who never saw the inside of a prison cell.[3] In 1943 this native of Haarlem was thirty-seven. He would later move to Euterpestraat in South Amsterdam, just around the corner from his job. He was a buddy of Harm Jan van den Heuvel's, and they made many arrests together. At the end of the war Rademakers fled to Bregenz in western Austria. He took off again in March 1946, leaving behind "not inconsiderable debts," as the Dutch consul reported to the judicial authorities. Rademakers was probably in France at that time. The police kept a close eye on his wife, who moved back to Haarlem in 1946, in the hope they could catch Rademakers through her. They had statements from numerous witnesses, so a conviction would not be a problem. Success was within their grasp when Rademakers was picked up in Belgium in 1946, but, shortly before he was to be taken back to the Netherlands, he escaped yet again. The trail first led to France, because an intelligence service had discovered that Mrs Rademakers had applied for a job in Paris. But in the end Rademakers went to Germany. In 1956 he was living on Paulusstrasse in Düsseldorf, where he was visited by a process server, who came to inform him on behalf of the Dutch state that he had been sentenced to life in prison seven years before, in April 1949. Rademakers even signed a writ, as proof of receipt. This would seem to clear the way for an extradition procedure, but nothing ever came of it. Rademakers' dossier reeks of a disheartening amateurism. The authorities knew where he was living; he was aware of his punishment and the fact that Dutch prosecutors knew his whereabouts. But still nothing happened. Thirteen years later an alert civil servant asked the consulate in Düsseldorf if Mr Rademakers knew he was a wanted man. The official threateningly added that there was no statue of limitation on this punishment, but in reality Rademakers had nothing to fear. As long as he did not set foot in the Netherlands, the authorities could not touch him. No extradition request had ever been submitted to the German government. This was actually the case for all the fugitive former Jew hunters; there was nobody out hunting for *them*.

The blame for this, however, did not lie exclusively with the Dutch judicial authorities. At the time the Ministry of Justice was enmeshed in an intra-governmental conflict with the Foreign Ministry, which was then striving to normalize relations with Germany and which had little interest in dredging up sensitive wartime issues.[4] In the early 1950s there were a number of highly complex factors that contributed to this tense situation: not only the treatment of German war criminals (like Lages and Aus der Fünten) in Dutch prisons, but also the aftermath of a spectacular jailbreak. On Christmas night of 1952 seven Dutch war criminals escaped from a prison in Breda and fled to Germany. On the border they had to pay a fine of ten marks for crossing the border illegally, but they were not sent back. The legal battle for their extradition or deportation dragged on for years, and in the end the Netherlands emerged the loser. Whenever it looked as if victory was in sight, there was always a German *Oberlandesgericht* (appellate court) to rule in favor of the suspects. In that climate, tracking down unknown Jew hunters was an almost hopeless task; in any case it had the lowest imaginable priority.

And thus Johan Keuling was also able to escape justice. This former carpenter was a leading member of the Colonne Henneicke. During the war he arrested scores of Jews and was also involved in apprehending two-year-old André Ossendrijver in Zuilen.[5] Keuling could expect a severe punishment, especially when one considers that, after his period in Amsterdam, he continued hunting down Jews and resistance fighters as a member of the *Landwacht*. Keuling was arrested quite early on, in 1945, and the authorities worked hard on his case. Gradually it became clear that Keuling had been one of the most productive bounty hunters; the evidence against him just kept mounting. Higher-ups within the PRA decided that he should be subjected to intensive interrogation. But when G. Bakker and H. Sminia, two officials from the office of the public prosecutor, reported to the internment camp Hoogerheide on April 2, 1948 to pick up Keuling and bring him to Amsterdam, they were greeted with the news that he had flown the coop. He had not shown up for roll call that morning. He had to have escaped the night before, immediately after he had been informed that he would have to go to the capital for interrogation the next day. "That was to be expected," wrote the head of the Amsterdam PRA, Inspector J. Haije, in a furious letter to the directors of the camp. "He should have been under close surveillance, all the more so since it was known in the camp for some time that he had plans to escape."[6]

When Keuling's case appeared on the docket a year later, he was high and dry in Germany, in the extreme north of the country, in Drochtersen to be exact, a resort for water sport enthusiasts on the Elbe. His wife, Anna Challa, had gone on ahead of him. In Amsterdam the court sentenced him to death, in absentia. But Keuling had no cause to worry. The Dutch authorities left him in peace. He even had his German lawyer ask the Dutch consulate-general if there were criminal proceedings pending against him. Keuling needed this information "in connection with private affairs in Germany." The Netherlands made no use of this opportunity to contact him or to find out where the condemned man was now living. Keuling's inquiry did however unleash a deluge of paperwork, which was dominated by confusion: prosecutors, police and the consul general spent most of their time sending each other letters requesting confirmation that their previous letter had been received. But in all that time no one ever got around to asking the Federal Republic of Germany for Johan Keuling's extradition. The prosecutors' one success was a 1979 ruling that ensured that Keuling's punishment would not lapse; if he ever set foot on Dutch soil, he would be promptly arrested. But Keuling never made that mistake.

Then there was Engelbert Koops, the former bartender, who, according to his colleagues, could faultlessly pick out Jews who weren't wearing their star on the street.[7] He was the man who beat David Sander for so long that he divulged the addresses where his children, Elbert (4), Marie (8) and Eline (10), were hiding. As we have already seen, Koops then went to Sliedrecht to pick them up himself. Right after his time with the Colonne Henneicke, Engelbert Koops fled to Germany, in the direction of Hannover, as the police learned after the war. For a time it seemed that the trail had gone cold, so that in April 1949 Koops' trial proceeded without a defendant.

In reaching its sentence, the court took into consideration the fact that the defendant "frequently helped the enemy in their repugnant and inhuman ambition to eliminate Dutch Jews from society, condemning these Jews to a terrible fate. He had no scruples about arresting children, including one very young child. His conduct was violent and unwarranted, and he was short-tempered."[8] The court sentenced Koops to death, but at the time it was doubtful whether Koops would ever hear about it. Shortly after the judgment, there were reports that Koops was living just across the border in Meppen. The English Security Police in Germany – the Federal Republic was divided into four sectors, and Koops fell under the British sector – had put together a report on Koops. He had been living on Bahnhofstrasse in Meppen since 1945, and all that time he had been unemployed. He had a bad reputation; it was common knowledge that he was wanted by the Dutch police. He was forever quarreling with his landlord, and he did not pay his rent.

As soon as this news was received, by way of the state police in Groningen, the police in Amsterdam sent a note to the military police in Assen, saying that Koops had been sentenced to death and urgently requesting his extradition. The military police looked into the matter and was eventually informed by the Dutch Military Mission in Germany that there was "no longer any possibility of securing the extradition of E.H. Koops."

That report led to new action. On February 9, 1950, at his home in Meppen, Koops was officially notified that he had been sentenced to death by the Special Court. This made the sentence irrevocable, and it would seem that this move should have opened up new possibilities for extradition. But any hopes of this were soon dashed, when it turned out that Koops had managed to acquire the German nationality. And considering that Germany almost never turned over its citizens to foreign countries, Koops was able to live out the rest of his life as a free man.

But his new life was far from perfect. Even in Germany, Koops found himself embroiled in a major family conflict. He regularly wrote letters to his sister and brother-in-law in Amstelveen, complaining that life in Meppen was harder than he expected.[9] He was living with his girlfriend Tilly in a garret, and they lacked many basic necessities. He asked his family to come to Meppen with coffee, tea, butter, soap, cigarettes and cologne. In 1948 Koops asked his family if the police were looking for him and what he could anticipate. "Feel free to write openly, then I'll know where I stand. Now I'm committed to staying in Meppen, in the hope of receiving good news." But two years later his relationship with his family was badly strained. Koops wanted to hire a lawyer to deal with his relatives. In an angry letter he lashed out at his brother-in-law, who apparently had not taken very good care of the things he had left behind: "You, your wife and your sons wore out [our] clothes . . ., tore out the lining of the drapes for a costume for a fancy dress party, turned the kitchen curtains into a sarong and spent all our savings."

And thus Koops lived out the rest of his exile a tortured man. His troubles would not last much longer. He moved to Elberfeld, a village near Wuppertal, and died there on December 11, 1956, his sixtieth birthday. A year and a half later the Netherlands struck his name from its list of wanted war criminals.

Six Jew hunters fled the country, and not a single one of them was ever tracked down. There is no better illustration of the impotence of the Dutch authorities than this unfortunate statistic.

The Arrests

There seemed to be no common factor in the arrest of the Jew hunters. A few of them were dragged out of their houses at the time of the liberation, amid jeers from onlookers. This was the fate of a number of notorious NSB men, who had incurred the wrath of their neighbors during the war. They included Joop Bouman, found hiding underneath the floorboards beneath a dresser in his bedroom.[10] The men of the Domestic Forces pulled him out, in the same way he himself had rousted so many Jews from their hiding places. But this was the exception to the rule. Most of the men had left Amsterdam and fled to the east of the country or Germany, where they were interned shortly after the liberation. For two years the Amsterdammer Alex Hoogers managed to elude the authorities, who were looking for him in connection with his role in the hunt for Jews.[11] The former appraiser of paintings had taken on a new identity. He had false papers in the name of Willem Elias Jansen, and he wore an imposing moustache which made him unrecognizable. He had also moved to Rotterdam. Eventually he was located and arrested, with the help of a former neighbor, Simon Frank, a photographer. At first Frank was not aware that Hoogers was in the NSB, though he regularly had German visitors, and from time to time he was dropped off at his house by a German lorry. In the neighborhood Hoogers had claimed that he did innocuous work for a German agency. But one day his neighbor Frank had seen his name on a list that had been drawn up by the resistance, a list of suspected Gestapo agents. "On September 29, 1947 I saw Hoogers in Rotterdam, and on the basis of my tip he was then arrested by the Political Investigation Department there," he testified. Frank had reported him to the police before, in September 1945, since he felt that the authorities were doing too little to capture his neighbor. The Rotterdam police brought him to Camp Crailo in Laren and noted in an accompanying letter that he was a "dangerous and cunning fellow," who would soon try to escape. It was an accurate assessment. A year later, in late 1948, Hoogers broke out of the camp not long before his case was scheduled to come before the Special Court. Following his escape, he was tried in absentia. But on the day the sentence was read (Hoogers was given the death penalty) he was spotted at a police checkpoint and arrested. According to reports from the state police he had "informed himself of the sentence" a short time before.[12] It is unclear whether he was actually in the courtroom himself, incognito, or sent someone else in his place and waited outside for news of this sentence.

It was not until 1948 that Richard Kopper was recognized on the street by Abraham Pach, who had seen him at work several times at the Dutch Theater.[13] Pach stopped a policeman and pointed out the former Jew hunter. This came as a huge blow to Kopper. He had already been interned for a year and convicted by a Tribunal, the court which handled most post-war treason cases. It seemed that that would be the extent of his punishment, until Pach recognized him. Kopper was ultimately sentenced to fifteen years, which was later reduced to ten on appeal.

And then there was Sjef Sweeger, one of the most productive members of the Colonne, who tried a very obvious method to escape detection: celebrating the liberation along with everybody else.[14] But this attempt was thwarted by a certain Gerard Pranger, a salesman from Bloemendaal, who knew Sweeger from his school days. During the occupation he had seen Sweeger in his *Weerafdeling* uniform several times, and he once observed him in action in The Hague, escorting a Jewish woman. Pranger knew that Sweeger had worked for the Germans and then made the connection: he must have been arresting the woman he had seen him with. This only served to increase Pranger's outrage when he happened to meet Sweeger on May 9, 1945 at the railroad crossing on Kleverlaan in Bloemendaal. "On his lapel Sweeger was wearing the orange-red-white and blue colors," Pranger later told investigators. It must have been like a scene from a film. The two men passed each other on their bikes at the railroad crossing in Bloemendaal and got into an enormous shouting match. Pranger denounced Sweeger for collaborating with the krauts and arresting Jews. In his defense, Sweeger told his old schoolmate that since early 1945 he "had begun to think differently about the wartime situation." After that Pranger sounded the alarm, and members of the Domestic Forces rushed to the scene, dragging Sweeger off his ladies' bicycle and taking him away for interrogation. It turned out the PRA already had a whole file full of incriminating material against Sweeger, so investigators were able to get right to work. Later it would transpire that Sweeger had at least 200 arrests to his name.

Joop den Ouden, the pimp who continued hunting Jews with the police after his time with the Colonne, tried to escape detection by mixing in with the crowds of patriotic Dutch people who poured into the streets after the war.[15] On May 6 he was sighted in Amsterdam wearing the orange Domestic Forces armband. He was not arrested until later that month, however, and thanks to his connections and his wealth of information, he would get off lightly.

To the Tribunal

For most suspects, arrest marked the start of a long period of uncertainty. Without question, hunting for Jews was regarded by Special Justice as one of the most serious crimes of the war. But the authorities had enormous difficulties gathering evidence: virtually none of the victims had come back, and it seemed as if all traces of the crime had been expertly erased. For that reason it took some time before prosecutors could build solid cases against the Jew hunters. The wheels of justice only began to turn following the discovery of some of the *Zentralstelle*'s records.[16] Until that time the exact role of individuals in the betrayal and arrest of thousands of Jews was extremely hazy. There were also dozens of Jew hunters being held in internment camps, even though the judicial authorities were not aware of exactly what they had done. And various Jew hunters appeared before the Tribunals, even though they actually belonged before the Special Courts, which were able to impose much more severe punishments.

The Tribunals were set up to try the vast majority of collaborators. They were established on the basis of the so-called Tribunal Decree of September 18, 1944, a royal decree which dealt with Dutch citizens who had helped the enemy.[17] The government's original intention was that political delinquents who were suspected of crimes under the pre-war penal code would be tried by Special Courts. All other political delinquents would be sent to the Tribunals. A total of nineteen Tribunals were set up throughout the country, each of which had several criminal divisions. The Tribunals were staffed by non-professionals, and under the chairmanship of a jurist they would adjudicate cases, with the power to sentence defendants to a maximum of ten years' internment, deprive them of certain rights and confiscate their property. The basic operating principle was speed. Following brief trials, the Tribunals could impose ten-year sentences; today we would call this summary justice.

In theory it was also possible for a Tribunal to remand a suspect for up to ten years in anticipation of a trial by a Special Court, but this rarely happened in practice. The Tribunals wanted to function as full-fledged courts, and did so. They did not automatically impose the maximum penalty, but considered the defendant's personal circumstances. Gradually they also began to take over less serious cases from the Special Courts, in order to lighten their caseload.

In total the Tribunals handled approximately 50,000 cases. Things took much longer than had been anticipated, but the Tribunals were hardly a failure. In a retrospective evaluation legal specialists concluded that the members of the Tribunals who had no legal training had functioned very well under the circumstances.[18]

Nine of the civilian Jew hunters would appear before a Tribunal. Later, some of them ended up before a Special Court as well, for one reason or another, while still others had only limited contact with the criminal justice system. Piet Kruyver*, for example, a salesman who was thirty-six in 1943. A photograph shows him as a blond man with an energetic expression, intense eyes, hair combed back, looking smart in a suit.[19] Kruyver had worked for the *Einsatzstab Reichsleiter Rosenberg* for some time. He was something of an exception in that milieu; he had never been a member of the NSB. Unfortunately for him he was listed as an inventory clerk on the payroll well into 1944. His wife wrote a letter to the authorities as early as August 1945 to request his release. She pointed out that her husband never hurt anybody; the problem is that there were letters to that effect about virtually every one of the 150,000 detainees. Kruyver would have to stay behind bars; in April 1946 the courts decided to extend his custody again. Then Kruyver himself petitioned the authorities to be released. He enumerated all the good things he had done for his fellow men, especially Jews, and noted that he had not been a member of the NSB. He speculated that a Tribunal would not sentence him to more than the eleven months he had already served in pre-trial detention. His well-written text might have helped, for on June 26, 1946 Kruyver was released, following his session before the Tribunal. Piet Kruyver was found guilty, but his punishment was limited to time served and loss of the right to vote.

But later, in March 1948, things started looking bleak for Kruyver. His name was found in the records of the *Zentralstelle*, as one of Henneicke's Jew hunters. According to the paperwork, he had assisted in the arrest of various Jews and was also accused of taking part in the big raid of June 1943. Kruyver categorically denied this. An arrest warrant was issued, but his arrest was stopped at the last minute. The judge-advocate would only allow Kruyver to be taken into custody if there was concrete evidence that he had arrested Jews. That came in the form of a *Bericht* discovered in the Colonne's records, showing that Kruyver had made an arrest together with Casteels and Sweeger.[20] Together with Alex Hoogers he also brought a couple and their young daughter to the Theater. But even this was not enough, and Gelinck eventually decided to let the matter rest. On a notepad the judge-advocate wrote: "The new material is worrisome, but it is fairly plausible that the suspect was a hanger-on with no initiative of his own. There is no evidence to the contrary. Therefore no new prosecution, unless more should emerge later."[21] Kruyver got away by the skin of his teeth.

The same could be said for Johan Smid*, the youngest member of Wim Henneicke's team, a traveling salesman who was not yet twenty-three when the hunt for Jews began.[22] When he was arrested in early June 1945, he stated that he had never been a member of the NSB. But this was soon shown to be false; by then, the complete card catalogue of the NSB had been confiscated, so these sorts of lies were easy to expose. During the eighteen months that Smid spent in custody, investigators came to learn a great deal about him – even without the written evidence that would later be found in the records of the *Zentralstelle*. In fact the secretary of the Tribunal, a lawyer who functioned as prosecutor and presented the case, already knew Smid had been a Jew hunter and charged him as such. On November 15, 1945 Smid was sentenced to three and a half years' internment.[23] It was a remarkable sentence. It would appear that the Tribunal seriously underestimated the severity of the case; a Special Court would have issued a much harsher punishment.

There were others surprised at the Tribunal's leniency. In 1948, when the *Berichte* and the transfer receipts surfaced, and it could be shown that Smid's productivity as a Jew hunter was average for a member of the Colonne Henneicke, political investigators advised Gelinck to have Smid retried, this time by a Special Court. The judge-advocate was faced with a difficult dilemma. On the one hand, they now knew that Johan Smid had worked with notorious Jew hunters like Van der Kraal and Bouman. But on the other hand this would mean trying Smid twice for the same crime. And although that would have, strictly speaking, been possible under the rules of Special Justice, Gelinck preferred not to open that particular can of worms.[24]

On March 1, 1949 Gelinck decided to drop the charges against Smid. The motivation for his decision can be found on a slip of paper in the dossier: "I don't think it would be fair to start over again." That said, he was still of the opinion that the Tribunal's sentence was inexplicably lenient, considering that Smid had confessed to arresting forty Jews in the meantime. Gelinck was also perplexed by the fact that this young suspect's case had been adjudicated by a Tribunal in the first place, instead of by a Special Court. Later on, in reviewing the prosecution of the Colonne Henneicke, Gelinck would lament hesitating for so long over this case.[25] Without a doubt, the time of the case, March 1949, also played a role. The war had been over for four years; public opinion had had enough of Special Justice, and the press had lost interest as well. Gelinck was still willing to do his utmost to bring the leaders of the Colonne to justice, but he was evidently not as interested in the lesser figures. Before making his decision, he was able to read a letter from Smid's wife, who had previously written to the Tribunal that her husband had always been driven by only one thing: his desire to support his parents. His father had been a tailor before he was discharged for deafness and forced to go on disability; his mother was sickly and the young Johan had always worked for them. Their poverty was more than he could bear. Gelinck also learned that the young Smid was troubled by his work. When questioned by investigators, his mother said, "My son also had to round up Jews, he told me. There were evenings he would sit at the table crying because he felt so bad for the Jews." Whether it was due to his sensitive nature is impossible to say, but the fact remains that, with his three and a half years, Johan Smid was given one of the lightest sentences of any of the Jew hunters.

We know that in similar cases Gelinck generally referred Smid's colleagues to the Special Court, even if they had already been tried by a Tribunal. Rinus

Schutten unquestionably had fewer arrests on his conscience than Smid, but he was put on trial a second time.[26] He was thirty-nine when the hunt for Jews began, and he regularly worked as a guard at the Dutch Theater. We already know him as the man who would parade through the main auditorium in his WA uniform. On September 24, 1946 it looked as if he would get off lightly when the Tribunal sentenced him to two years' internment, for membership in the NSB and the *Landwacht*. But there was more to come. His name appeared in numerous documents that only turned up after his trial. On April 7, 1948 a warrant was issued for his arrest; his name had been found at the bottom of a letter, as an Official of the Investigative Service of the *Zentralstelle, Gruppe Henneicke*, and thus he could also be charged with membership of the Colonne. He was arrested the very next day. He was known to have made one arrest, a certain Boy Frenk, whom he picked up at work.

Schutten pled not guilty. He had not been a member of the Colonne, he protested, though he did write in a job application of August 1943 that he had worked for the SD and as a guard at the Jewish Theater. He would later say, "I was just bragging." Gelinck decided to have him retried by a Special Court; in the meantime new facts had come to light, of which the Tribunal had not been aware. On March 4, 1949 the prosecution demanded five years, less time served. The court granted the demand and more: seven years, on top of the two the Tribunal had already imposed.[27] There can be no doubt that the court dealt with Rinus Schutten extra harshly due to his role as a guard who allowed no escapes. And this was also what the sentence said: he helped the enemy deport as many Jews as possible.

Frans Takkert was sentenced by the Tribunal to five years in prison.[28] He had been a member of the NSB, but he was also in the *Landwacht* and was the leader of the South Holland division of the National Labour Front; he was thus a higher-up in the Movement, hence the five year sentence. When documents showed in late 1947 that he had been involved in the hunt for Jews, prosecutors began preparing a new case against him. Under interrogation, Takkert used a new variation of the euphemistic language that had always typified the hunt for Jews. He said he had "had to summon" people for a conversation with his boss Briedé. The new trial before the Special Court did not result in a significant increase in his punishment. An additional three years were tacked on to the sentence for his participation in the hunt for Jews. Despite that, on June 24, 1950 he was back on the street, thanks to Queen Juliana, who had granted his petition for clemency.

Mattijs van de Wert's role in the hunt for Jews was already quite clear by the time his case came before the Tribunal.[29] He denied all charges, regardless of who made them, but there was little he could do in the face of damning testimony from colleagues like Elmink and Den Ouden. They stated plainly that Van de Wert participated fully in picking up Jews. Given this, it is remarkable that in 1947 the Tribunal sentenced him to a mere four and a half years for his crimes. His age might have had something to do with it. Van de Wert was sixty-three when he appeared before the Tribunal; by November 1948 he was back at home. But a short time after that, Gelinck wanted to subpoena him again. The PRA had discovered that Van de Wert had more to answer for than the Tribunal had known about. Their investigation had turned up eighteen new arrests; fourteen of these victims never came back. Gelinck wrote a letter to the Ministry of Justice, arguing that a new case should be opened against Van de Wert. "The suspect deserves a considerably harsher punishment than the one imposed by the Tribunal." A new prosecution was also necessary "to maintain equality before the law," according to Marinus Gelinck. Quite unexpectedly, Van de Wert began to confess, that is to say, he admitted that he would sometimes bring in people for interrogation, although he denied ever being in a leadership position. In December, Gelinck demanded five and a half years for Van de Wert. On Christmas Eve the court's sentence was read: Van de West was given five more years. In spite of his age, Van de Wert would be going back behind bars for another few years. In 1951 he was released for good behavior; he would live another sixteen years, dying at the age of eighty-three.

The blow must have been even harder for Richard Kopper, the insurance agent who seemed to be home free after just a year's detention.[30] The Tribunal only charged him with aiding and abetting the enemy, a relatively minor offense which stemmed from his membership in the NSB. Kopper was evidently a dedicated member (although he was forced out of the organization for a time due to lack of funds), as he had talked his wife into joining the Movement as well. The fact that he was given such a light sentence must have been the result of the countless letters the Tribunal received from the defendant's friends and acquaintances. Without exception they described Kopper and his wife as noble, selfless, sober-minded individuals who had to endure a great deal of hardship. A letter from a neighbor was signed by ten others, and a Miss Meijer of Willemsparkweg, who was a frequent guest at Kopper's home, pled for the duo in a well-worded letter: "These are not traitors or subversives; they are two noble, sincere and good people." This is, to put it mildly, a decidedly incomplete characterization, as a closer examination of the facts of the case will reveal. When Kopper was rearrested after being recognized by a former Jewish Council staff member, it was discovered that he was responsible for the arrest of eighty-nine Jews.

At first Kopper pled not guilty. He was just a little man; he had been forced to go along from time to time; he never took any initiative himself. In short, Kopper told the same story as all his colleagues. But one day in December 1948 detective Prasing grilled him about all the evidence that had since been found, and at a certain point Kopper gave up protesting his innocence. He confessed to one crime after the other, including going out with Casteels and Sweeger to arrest Jews. Later, in court, Prasing spoke of the day Kopper had confessed so readily. To the detective's surprise, when Kopper came back from a coffee break with his wife, he appeared to have suffered a sudden bout of amnesia.[31]

The session had to be adjourned for some time, because Kopper's attorney P. Kolff sought to have the summons quashed. His motion was denied, but it did buy them some time. The trial itself took a number of bizarre turns. Judge-advocate Gelinck presented a strong case; he wanted Kopper to be given an additional eight years, but Kolff defended Kopper much more ardently than most of his colleagues had the other members of the Colonne. He contended that Kopper had not arrested anyone and that he had only been present when others (Casteels, Sweeger, etc.) did so. Kopper's task was simply to accompany the Jews to the Theater. He was not a member of the Colonne Henneicke, but had been posted there temporarily. According to Kolff, this was the crucial difference between Kopper and most of the others. Kolff underscored the responsibility of the Employment Office, which had referred so many men, Kopper among them, to this job. "Refusing was not an option. Kopper had two young children and would have been sent to Germany had he said no." Kolff's arguments could not have made much of an impression on the justices, since the court was already aware that his colleague Rietveld, in the same circumstance, *had* chosen to go to Germany rather than continue to hunt Jews.[32] Kolff's most cynical argument was the last one: he found it strange that members of the Jewish Council were not prosecuted for their role in the deportations, even though they "also helped the enemy carry out their policy of *jüdische Auswanderung*."

It may be that the Special Court was irritated by Kolff's passionate defense. How else to explain the court's exceptional decision to impose a sentence that far exceeded the one demanded by the prosecution? The former insurance agent Richard Kopper was given fifteen years, seven more than had been requested, though on March 15, 1950 the Special Court of Appeals reduced the sentence to ten years.[33]

Nico Evertsen, a member of the Colonne who was first tried by the Amsterdam Tribunal, had a similar experience with Special Justice.[34] This Amsterdam truck driver, who was thirty-two years old when the hunt began, was sentenced by the Tribunal to two years. Having registered stolen Jewish goods, he was punished for the umbrella offense of aiding and abetting the enemy. He had only worked there a short time, until March 1943, and for that reason he was considered a minor case. The troubles did not really start for Evertsen until after he had served his sentence. The two detectives who were perhaps most familiar with these cases, Prasing and Tump, had him arrested again and subjected him to a fresh interrogation. In the interim they had found a few *Berichte* with Evertsen's name at the bottom. Together with Cool he apparently picked up one Abraham Sarfatie, on August 10,

1943, on Van Woustraat. And the next day, according to the paperwork, the two men arrested Lore Sara Kahn and dropped her off at the Theater.

The detectives attempted to track down Sarfatie, but to no avail. His name did not appear in any registers; he seemed to have fallen off the face of the earth. They were however able to find Mrs Kahn. She had left for Chicago in 1947. After that the detectives organized a confrontation between Cool and Evertsen. The result: they claimed they had never seen each other before, although Evertsen did say that Cool's face looked vaguely familiar. It would take a thorough investigation before prosecutors would be able to charge Evertsen with anything else. Prasing and Tump pored over the records of Lippmann, Rosenthal & Co. and noticed that Evertsen's resignation did not take effect until August 19 – far later than he had claimed in his testimony before the Tribunal. Next they questioned other members of the Colonne, but with little result. No one knew whether he had actually worked there or not. The detectives then decided to pay another visit to Evertsen, who told them in the course of the interrogation that his wife was now expecting their third child; they already had two daughters, Marie and Louise. Evertsen emphatically denied arresting anyone in August 1943. He had not worked there after March, he insisted. But then the detectives showed him the evidence proving that he was not discharged until August. Evertsen was clearly taken aback and asked the two interrogators if they could come back the next day; he needed to think a few things over.

They returned the next day. Evertsen had thought long and hard about everything, the whole night, and he had decided to come clean. The crucial part of his story was his admission that he had been lent out to the *Einsatzstab Reichsleiter Rosenberg* for some time – for the purpose of clearing Jewish homes of furniture – and that he returned to his old job. In early August the leadership wanted to assign him to the Colonne. He reported sick for a few days but subsequently went back to work. He had been there when Cool made two arrests, although he had not recognized Cool during the recent confrontation. He was there, he confessed, although he did not actively take part. Prasing and Tump's tenacious detective work had paid off.

At the end of the interrogation he said that his heart had stopped when he was arrested for a second time on April 1, 1948, in front of his boss. Lately he had been working hard for his family, so he could afford food and a decent place to live. In the evening he earned a little extra by upholstering chairs; thus he was working day and night. His world fell apart. He thought about the two people who had been arrested all the time, he said. The day before, he had heard from the detectives that the woman was still alive and the man could not be found and might not have been deported at all. That had left him so relieved that he now wanted to unburden himself and tell the truth. Evertsen added that his boss was willing to take him back as soon as he was available again. The question now was: what would the prosecution do?

The decision was made a week after Evertsen's confession. The former taxi driver was released; he could go back to his job. His dossier contains a small sheet of paper on which Gelinck had written: "release pending trial." But the trial never materialized; the prosecution elected not to pursue the matter. There was no evidence and no victim. In his review of the prosecution's strategy, the judge-advocate wrote: "Evertsen was a follower. I could find no grounds for a new prosecution."[35]

The fact that Evertsen's actions had no fatal consequences might have played a role in this. Later the authorities succeeded in tracking down the mysterious victim Sarfatie. It turned out that this was in fact an alias; the arrestee's real name was Rijksman. In a confrontation he only recognized Cool; he did not remember a second man. He had fled the Theater after a day and a half. He was able to keep his name a secret at the time. A week earlier he had already been arrested and even loaded on to a train, but in Zwolle he leapt from the train and returned to Amsterdam. Later Rijksman was picked up again and deported, but he survived Auschwitz. And thus the man who arrested him escaped punishment. Two years' internment, imposed by the Tribunal, and no new trial: Nico Evertsen had no reason to complain about Special Justice.

The opposite happened to Lambert Schipper, who had a number of very serious crimes to his name. In the early days after the war there was no significant evidence connecting him to any wrongdoings.[36] Halfway through 1946 Schipper had already received a summons from the Tribunal for a number of minor offenses, but gradually it became clear that there was more to this suspect than met the eye. Marinus Gelinck then decided to place Schipper's name on the list of "suspected members of the Colonne Henneicke," and his trial was postponed. He did not appear before the Special Court until two years later, at which time he was sentenced to twenty years in prison. It was during that session that the authorities first heard something resembling a confession from Schipper, who was by that time sixty. He would remain in prison until November 9, 1956.

Then there was Gerrit Mijnsma, the man whose experiences in the criminal justice system were more complicated than those of any other member of the Colonne.[37] During his first interrogation in 1945 Mijnsma denied any involvement in the hunt for Jews. He did admit to being present for the big round-ups in the summer of 1943, but, according to him, he did not arrest anyone. Mijnsma wound up before the Tribunal because his case had been prepared by two not very well informed investigators from the Bureau of National Security. They made the mistaken assumption that Mijnsma was telling the truth when he said that he only accompanied the *Grüne Polizei* and did not make any arrests himself. This was good luck for Mijnsma: on September 27, 1946 the Seventh Division of the Amsterdam Tribunal sentenced him to two years' internment.

But this was not the end of it. All rulings by the Tribunals had to be submitted to the so-called High Authority for approval. This was the body that examined all sentences that were handed down, in an attempt to ensure uniformity in the judgments of the nineteen Tribunals, on the basis of the rules governing Special Justice.[38] The High Authority refused to issue a "writ of execution" in Mijnsma's case and referred the case back to another division of the Tribunal.

Mijnsma had to appear before the Eleventh Division of the Amsterdam Tribunal on April 11, 1947. This time around the charges against him were considerably more serious. He was accused not only of being a member of the NSB and *Landwacht* but also of arresting Jews. It is apparent from the sentence in this case that the Tribunal saw the handwriting on the wall: this was a much bigger fish than had initially been assumed. Thus there was a chance that the High Authority would again refuse to issue a "writ of execution" for whatever sentence they decided upon and would refer the case to a court that could impose a more severe punishment. In its judgment the Eleventh Division of the Tribunal spoke of Mijnsma's "abhorrent work," earning "blood money" at the cost of an unknown number of human lives.[39]

Gerrit Mijnsma was given ten years' internment. The president of the Tribunal personally sent the conviction to judge-advocate Gelinck, who had to decide if there was cause to refer the case to the Special Court. He did not have to think long: Mijnsma belonged before the court. Because of all the false starts Mijnsma, along with his regular partner Elmink, did not have his day in court until January 1949. The case was crystal clear, not only for the prosecution but also for the justices of the Special Court. Mijnsma and Elmink were both sentenced to death. The grounds for this verdict were the same as those for most of their colleagues: they turned over their victims to their mortal enemies, and their consciences were apparently so deadened that they went on doing this degrading work for some time.[40] For those reasons, in the view of the court, the ultimate punishment was entirely appropriate. On appeal both sentences were commuted to life imprisonment.

The Prosecution's Strategy

At one time or another all suspected Jew hunters came into contact with Marinus Gelinck, the judge-advocate of the Amsterdam Special Court. This rather young lawyer (he was born in 1911) had a heavy burden to shoulder. Not only did he present all these complex cases to the court, but he also personally decided on the prosecution policy. Few details are known, since Gelinck never wrote down his closing arguments. Like so many magistrates of his time, he spoke from a piece of scrap paper with some notes on it – reading such an important address off a paper was beneath his dignity. It is history's loss. The popular press is not terribly helpful either, since fairly little was written about the trials of the members of the Colonne Henneicke. They took place at a time when public interest in the trials of war criminals had declined substantially. Newspapers were still quite thin due to the paper shortage. And furthermore, crime journalism was not the industry it is today. In general, editors found these sorts of stories somewhat unsavory. In some cases only the prosecution's demand and the eventual sentence were printed. Most cases did not even make the paper, not even when the defendants were sentenced to death.

That said, we do know a few things about Gelinck's considerations. His personal archive contains a letter the judge-advocate wrote to the president of the Special Court of Appeals, H. Haga, on February 16, 1949.[41] In early 1949 a whole series of appeals began pouring in, as a result of the stiff sentences that had been given to the Jew hunters in the spring and summer of 1948. Haga wanted more insight about why the prosecution had dealt so firmly with these particulars defendants, and Gelinck granted that request, setting down his policy on the Colonne Henneicke on paper.

To begin with, Gelinck had worked out that thousands of Jews had been arrested. He did not write down how many thousands, but we can safely assume it was considerably more than the 3,600 catalogued in the records of the *Zentralstelle*. The information was not complete; many more Jews were picked up by the professional Jew hunters, and Gelinck took that into consideration in his treatment of the suspects. "In the trials," he wrote to H. Haga, "I always contended that each member of the Colonne Henneicke bore not only individual responsibility but also responsibility for the actions of the group as a whole. This is the only way one can allow for the large number of Jews who were arrested . . . by persons whose identity is unknown to us." In other words, the Office of the Public Prosecutor regarded the Colonne Henneicke as a kind of criminal organization, the mere membership of which merited severe punishment. This is a remarkable standpoint, given that the concept of a "criminal enterprise" did not enter Dutch jurisprudence until much later, but it dovetailed nicely with the intentions of Special Justice. After all, membership of the NSB was also a criminal offense.

Gelinck wrote that he was not the least bit impressed by the "not guilty" pleas he had to listen to in court. It was exactly what he had expected: "They will plead not guilty and maintain they did nothing wrong in the face of all our evidence, but in most cases this cannot possibly be true." Many defendants told detectives or Gelinck himself that their name "just happened" to be written at the bottom of a transfer receipt, even if they had nothing to do with the arrest in question. But Gelinck did not believe a word of it. It did not escape his attention that in all cases in which both a transfer receipt and a *Bericht* of an arrest had been found, the names of the signatories matched. There was not a single exception. This meant, in Gelinck's view, that the records were accurate and proved that the Jew hunters were trying to weasel out of their just punishment.

Gelinck also did not believe that Henneicke and Briedé's subordinates only acted under duress. In his view the Jew hunters did not need any additional motivation. According to Gelinck, most files contained no indication of any reluctance on the part of the Colonne's members. And those who did have reservations about the work, the judge-advocate soberly concluded, could feign illness. The biggest complainers obviously never attempted that. Those who did were successful: Evertsen, Rietveld, Smid, Van Eiken, Kopper and Dassen managed to get out of making arrests by calling in sick or going to work elsewhere. "At the end of the day, of the two evils, [working for] the Colonne Henneicke or serving in the German army, the latter is the lesser," Gelinck wrote in his letter to the president of the Court of Appeals.[42]

He even went a step further. Most members of the Colonne Henneicke used the argument "*Befehl ist Befehl*": they could not disobey their superiors' orders and for that reason did not see themselves as guilty. Gelinck felt that taking refuge behind orders was indefensible. Checking identity cards on the street and arbitrarily arresting people suggested, he contended, that many Jew hunters were willing to go above and beyond the call of duty. This was also evidenced by their efforts to unearth the addresses of other Jews. As we have already seen, that happened quite often, and, according to Gelinck, the men had never received orders to do this. It was the Colonne members themselves who took the initiative to ask for those addresses, or who went off in search of letters or who promised to release an arrestee if he or she revealed addresses of other Jews in hiding. In Gelinck's view there was no reason to believe that such actions were mandated by orders from above.

Gelinck was convinced that the members of the Colonne Henneicke had received premiums, even though he never attempted to prove that in any trial (excepting that of the three men from the card catalogue). In his letter to H. Haga, the president of the Special Court of Appeals, he ran through all the evidence that had already been discussed: Hintink's full confession, which he later retracted; Cool's frequently quoted remark that he could not pass up fl.15 on a Sunday afternoon and his subsequent arrest of a Jewish-looking woman on the street; the statements of the relatives of Kroon and Bouman.[43] And Gelinck also pointed out the contradictory testimony of Colonne members about their additional income: one claimed he received nothing, the other was given travel expenses, the next one overtime, while still another received a bonus for working as a guard at the Theater. For Gelinck it was clear that they were earning a good living from arresting Jews: "In my view the evidence demonstrates conclusively that – however the money was distributed – the group as a whole had a financial interest in the arrests of Jews, and each individual's responsibility for that whole made it so that the 'permanent' members of the Colonne Henneicke can be held liable for these actions." This shows that the judge-advocate implicitly took the financial factor into account in evaluating the facts and determining the appropriate sentence. It was for reasons of efficiency that he did not try to prove in court that premiums were received: "Apart from that, my standpoint is that the arrests in and of themselves are so reprehensible that details (financial benefit, threats, assault and other aggravating factors) are of relatively little importance." Gelinck undoubtedly feared evidentiary problems if he had to show that every defendant received a bonus for every arrest he had made, given that the traces of the crimes had largely been erased. His position is understandable, but one of its unfortunate consequences was that it was never proved in court that premiums were paid for the arrest of Jews.

In his letter to the Court of Appeals, Gelinck also discussed the issue of whether the Jew hunters knew what would happen to their prey.[44] He pointed out that, even before the war, people knew about the treatment of Jews in Germany. In February 1943 the Roman Catholic Church had spoken of the plight of the Jews and taken a stand "against the murderous persecution of the Jews." And furthermore Gelinck also mentioned the remarks made by Jew hunters to their victims, which we have come across earlier: you'll be gassed anyway, you won't be coming back, etc. He expressed his conclusion as follows: "I presume that the members of the Colonne Henneicke were not aware of the grisly details of the gas chambers, etc., but they should have known that a harsh and terrible fate, with little chance of survival, awaited the Jews they had arrested."

The Lawyers

Marinus Gelinck was a professional; he knew the dossiers of the defendants who would appear before him backward and forward. He was also informed by the best detectives in Amsterdam, but despite that his job was at times a difficult one. The members of the Colonne Henneicke brought in high-powered attorneys who sometimes created fireworks in the courtroom. Although their tactics varied, from the closing statements that have survived it is apparent that their method of choice was to emphasize that their clients were insignificant, inconsequential men, small-time crooks, who happened to be at the wrong place at the wrong time and who were, all things considered, far too unimportant to merit such severe punishments.[45] "The Amsterdam Special Court was too harsh on the Colonne Henneicke," said B.N. Grolleman, in the trial of Gerrit Mijnsma.[46] He was referring to the judgments of other courts in what were, according to him, similar cases. He found the punishments unjustified. He argued: "These were not high-minded people, not leading politicians[. They were] undistinguished men who lacked the self-criticism and the moral consciousness one might expect from the more educated." They were ordinary men, who had been lured into German organizations, which "could use such people as willing instruments to do their dirty work."

In the case of Mijnsma, Grolleman's plea initially had little effect: the defendant was given the death penalty. But this Amsterdam lawyer continued his battle against the views of M. Gelinck and the Fifth Division of the Amsterdam Special Court when another client, Egbert Elmink, appealed his death sentence. He raised questions about the individual guilt of his client: according to Grolleman, Elmink and his cohorts were "unquestionably in the grip of a sort of mass psychosis, which diminishes their individual responsibility."[47] And he added a near-irrefutable argument: "They also had the poor example of a segment of the Dutch police force." This argument is nowhere to be found in the eventual ruling of the Special Court of Appeals; nevertheless, both Mijnsma and Elmink had their sentences commuted to life imprisonment.

J. Viskil, council to Martin Hintink, attempted to save his client by arguing a much more fundamental point in his plea to the Court of Appeals: causality.[48] That is, how important was the role of the Colonne Henneicke in the totality of the Jewish genocide? Viskil took it for granted that his client did not know what fate awaited his victims and posed the question: how direct is the connection between the arrest and the death of a given Jew? To be sure, the arrest was the first link in the chain, but death was not the direct consequence of the arrest, Viskil contended. "The chain is simply too long." His reasoning was rejected by the Special Court of Appeals, who remained convinced that Hintink had sent hundreds of Jews to their deaths by turning them over to their greatest enemy.

G.W. Blom was Henk Hopman's attorney, and he took an entirely different tack. With a 1943 calendar in hand, he attempted to show that Hopman did not have time to hunt Jews in Amsterdam: he was hardly ever *there*.[49] From March to July 1943 Hopman had been manager of the warehouse of Lippmann, Rosenthal & Co. on Vondelstraat. After that he worked in Maastricht as an inventory clerk until the end of August. In the meantime he never received any orders from Henneicke, according to Blom. This argument was belied by a virtually endless list of arrests in which Hopman had been involved. Although he denied everything, the evidence Gelinck produced was overwhelming. In his plea Blom also made much of the defendant's naïveté: Hopman knew absolutely nothing about the world in which he had ended up. "This man never understood and perhaps still does not understand how all these organizations – Lippmann, Rosenthal & Co., *Hausraterfassung, Jüdische Auswanderung, Einsatzstab Rosenberg*, SD, the investigative division and Colonne Henneicke – were linked together. For him the only thing that existed was the façade Lippmann Rosenthal, the venerable old banking firm." But it was all in vain. Gelinck regarded Hopman as one of the most fanatical Jew hunters, and he based his opinion on the conviction of detective Prasing, who had been able to compel Hopman to write out a confession prior to his trial. But Hopman refused to sign it, and in court he again denied any involvement in the arrests, as he had in the past. Shortly before the session began, his attorney submitted a request for Hopman's release; he had been in custody long enough. The request was not honored. Judge-advocate Gelinck noted dryly in pencil in the margin of the petition: "Hopman must have lost his optimism by now, if not, we will make sure that he does so during his trial."

One of Gelinck's fiercest opponents in the courtroom was B. Perridon, who defended various members of the Colonne. In the case against Adolf Smit, Perridon took the court through a curious bit of arithmetic.[50] He contended that "Smit was a substitute; he did not do this work every day, but only one day in May, ten days in June, four days in July and twelve days in August." Hardly a persuasive argument: it still comes to twenty-seven days of Jew hunting. Furthermore, according to his lawyer, Smit helped numerous Jews. Only they were later arrested by others and did not return, so Smit was unable to prove his good deeds. In addition to that, Perridon contended, Smit had the bad luck of always being partnered with the most militant Jew hunters, making him present for many arrests: "Unfortunately most of the time he was assigned to a fanatic as a helper." There were no arguments left untried by the defenders of the members of the Colonne.

But as mentioned above, the most frequently used arguments in the various trials were those that stressed the defendants' unimportance. "He is a man who looks for the good on the wrong path," said J.M. Nieubuur about her client Lambert Schipper. "He let others live his life for him."[51] She admitted that Schipper had regularly shown Nazi sympathies, but that was just a façade. Beneath that was, according to Ms Nieubuur, "a person of flesh and blood, impulsive, good-hearted, fallible and with a big mouth, somewhat rough around the edges, but honest." And she added a more topographically tinted argumentation: "To some extent a divided man: he grew up in easy-going Limburg, near the German border, and then settled in Amsterdam, a sort of Amsterdammer with a Limburg accent."

The lawyers sometimes even showed traces of desperation; most cases were hardly even worth the effort. There was abundant evidence; the investigators had done impeccable work, and the crimes of the Colonne were unquestionably shocking. And thus defense attorney Jelger de Jonge lamented at a certain point during Jan Casteels' appeal: "This man knew little happiness or worldly gain in his life; I ask you not to rob him of the one thing he still has left, his life."[52] And indeed, on appeal Casteels was given life in prison.

In their defense of the Colonne's members, the lawyers could generally count on the unconditional support of the defendant's families. A nearly endless series of letters and notes were mailed to the judicial authorities with requests for clemency, reduction of a sentence or even immediate release. They seem rather naïve, those wives who wanted to have their husbands back home as soon as possible, but their despair is understandable. Everything had been taken away from them, including the men they loved. Even for those who were not in financial trouble, the wife of a political criminal did not have it easy so soon after the war. Mrs Tomson had to support herself and her two children on fl.11 a week in welfare. She claimed to know nothing of her husband's second income, and that might well have been the case, as a number of Jew hunters chose to say little or nothing about their work at home. Out of shame, for reasons of safety, or because they wanted to keep their extra earnings for themselves.[53]

Marie Hogeveen, for example, was kept in the dark about everything. In 1943 she was married to the former distiller Frans Takkert, and she pled ignorance of her husband's crimes. At one stage she wrote a letter, imploring the authorities to release her husband, if only for the sake of their two children, Johannes and Maruschka: "I never knew anything about my husband's activities, otherwise I would have intervened."[54]

Sometimes the heart-rending letters were from women who had to bear the burden of poverty and disgrace alone. Rie van Eiken decided to write to the Queen in 1947 with this *cri de coeur*: "I only have one blanket; sometimes I get very sad because the oldest girl just pines away and everything is in her dead. It is as if she is wasting away. There is nothing I can do to make her happy."[55] Her worried husband, Herman, wrote to his father to say that he feared that things were not going well at home. His wife was malnourished; his little son Arthur had meningitis, and he did not think the boy would pull through. Later it transpired that two of his children had come down with tuberculosis. Herman van Eiken's father discussed the case with Lady Wttewaal van Stoetwegen, MP for the CHU, a Christian-Democratic party which took an interest in the fate of political delinquents and their families. "Seems to be a serious case," reads a note scribbled in the dossier. The family's troubles would thus continue for some time. "Queen," Rie van Eiken wrote to Her Royal Highness Queen Wilhelmina, "I love my children so much, they are all I have."

Christiaan van den Borch's 75-year-old father put in a good word for his son in an exceedingly polite, almost quaint letter to the court: "We are both of an advanced age (75) and therefore I trust Your Honors will not take it amiss if, in view of the very poor health of my wife, who is most distressed over her son's incarceration, and partly for the sake of the children, I request clemency for my son."[56]

Henk Saaldijk's mother, Mrs Saaldijk-Stoutenbeek, stepped into the ring for her son: "I could not live with myself if I did not do everything for him, and for that reason I venture to appeal to you once again."[57] At that time she was looking after Saaldijk's only son, Karl Heinz, who was then seven year old. Saaldijk's wife was German; she lived in Wiesbaden and was not allowed back into the Netherlands to visit her husband. Saaldijk himself had not seen his son in more than three years. His mother begged the authorities to transfer Saaldijk to an internment camp, so his child would be able to visit him from time to time. "It is so very important that my son comes home with his mind intact," she wrote in desperation.

The judicial authorities also received letters from people who owed their lives to a Jew hunter. A Mr De Krey pled for Henk van der Kraal, who allowed him to let the eight Jews he was hiding escape.[58] Afterward De Krey was released by the SD following an interrogation, and that too must have been the work of Van der Kraal. "Quite selflessly," wrote De Krey. "I could see during that time that he was not a bad fellow." A similar letter was sent on behalf of Martin Hintink, from a certain Van Huet of Van Baerlestraat.[59] "I am certain that he is not a bad fellow at heart," he wrote about the man who, according to the records of the *Zentralstelle*, brought in more Jews than anyone else, "and I am also still willing to give him a job in my firm." Hintink's wife stood behind him as well; in a letter to the Ministry of Justice she told of the treatment her husband received at Camp Westerbork, where he was beaten by his former victims: "If he did anything wrong, he has more than paid for it, when the people [there] took the law into their own hands."

And then there were also the medical complaints that the relatives put forward in the hope of bringing the suspects home quickly. It would seem as if more than half of the Colonne's members were at death's door, so insistent were the appeals for a speedy release. Mrs Hopman-Boogers wrote that her husband was not getting enough oxygen in his cell, that his feet were swollen and that his condition was visibly deteriorating.[60] She also alleged that he had been badly beaten by a detective interrogating him. There is no way of determining the veracity of that claim; there is no record of any complaint against the police in his file. One petition for clemency after another came in for Adolf Smit, mostly on the grounds of ill health, either his or his wife's.[61] In time this evidently began to annoy the authorities, because at a certain point a justice of the High Court of Appeals made a note in the margins: "The health of Smit and his wife is still better than that of his Jewish victims."

Smit died a full fifteen years after his release, at the age of eighty-two.

The Sentences

The Fifth Criminal Division of the Amsterdam Special Court of Justice had a fixed line up of justices. E.H.F.W. van Schaeck Mathon was the president; on occasion he was replaced by justice H. Houthoff. Although dozens of Jew hunters passed through their courtroom, they plainly did not take such cases lightly. This is clear from the language they used in sentencing the offenders; it was here that the gravity of each defendant's crimes was expressed, even though the various sentences might only differ from one another by the addition of a phrase or two. In most cases against members of the Colonne Henneicke the standard judgment read as follows: "Found guilty of aiding and abetting the enemy, subjecting people to persecution and depriving them of their liberty, actions which, it could reasonably be concluded, resulted in their demise." In most cases this judgment was good for the death penalty. Only in cases where defendants clearly helped Jews, by saving individuals, did the court deviate from this punishment. This happened in the case of Joop Bouman, for example, who was able to prove that he helped many Jews escape during his period with the Colonne. He was sentenced to twelve years.

In instances of exceptionally harsh or cruel conduct the phrasing of the judgment was altered slightly. The court ruled that Elmink and Mijnsma "turned their victims over to their mortal enemies, and [their consciences] were evidently so deadened . . . that they continued doing this degrading work for some time."[62] In the case of Eggink and Hoogers another clause was tacked on to the verdict. In the view of the judges, they "turned over countless Jewish people to their mortal enemy despite repeatedly seeing their victims' suffering and terror at what awaited them with their own eyes."[63] It is no surprise that these words were followed by the conclusion: death. The Special Court justices were evidently so upset by the crimes they had to pass judgment on that they sometimes added an adjective or two to the standard formulation. The judgment against the fugitive Engelbert Koops read that the defendant "frequently helped the enemy in their repugnant and inhuman ambition to eliminate Dutch Jews from society, condemning these Jews to a terrible fate."[64]

In the case of the fervent Jew hunter Klingeberg, the judges took an additional element into account in reaching their decision: "He did not even shrink from turning over a young Jewish child to its mortal enemy."[65] This is a reference to the fact that Klingeberg once arrested a mother with small children. There are other members of the Colonne with such add-ons in their sentences. In two cases the issue of bonuses was mentioned outright: the brothers-in-law, Jan Rudolfs and Martin Hintink, the man who confessed, in Westerbork and afterward as well, to receiving premiums. The court tacked on the following sentence to their judgment: "The defendants generally committed the crimes with which they are charged on their own initiative, in return for pecuniary compensation, in the form of either overtime or premiums."[66] This is the only time any mention was made of the bonuses, apart from in the sentences given to the men from the card catalogue.

In contrast to the aforementioned was the sentence given to Cornelis Rietveld, the man who refused to go on hunting Jews and chose to go to work in Germany instead. In their judgment the court considered it "highly mitigating that he voluntarily and at great personal risk ended his duties for the *Zentralstelle*, and by conducting himself as befits a good Dutchman, he has largely rehabilitated himself."[67] Nevertheless, he was sentenced to four years for what he *had* done.

All things considered, one cannot help but conclude that the Special Court showed little mercy to the Colonne Henneicke. In 1954, when attorney general G.E. Langemeijer was asked to give his advice about a petition for clemency (in this case from Anton Veldhuisen, a guard at the Theater), he wrote: "It has always been my impression as well that the members of the Henneicke group received relatively harsh punishments."[68] The numbers speak for themselves: in total, twenty-five of the civilian Jew hunters were sentenced to death; that is no fewer than forty-six percent of all cases. In fact, all core members of the Colonne were given the death sentence, including two of the three men from the card catalogue. Five were sentenced to life in prison, almost ten percent of the total. Seventeen were given shorter prison sentences, varying from twenty years to twelve months. The average prison term was 10.4 years. Seven of the fifty-four bounty hunters were not punished, either because they were already dead or for some other reason.

However, these statistics changed somewhat on appeal. Although it would be unfair to say that the Special Court of Appeals made short work of the sentences handed down by the Fifth Criminal Division, there was nevertheless a clear pattern of "adjustment." No fewer than nine death sentences were overturned, and in doing so the Court of Appeals gave the unmistakable signal that the Fifth Criminal Division had been a bit too free in imposing the ultimate punishment.[69] In the judges' commentary on their decisions, there is usually a remark to the effect that, in the absence of any evidence of serious mistreatment or cruelty, a life sentence would suffice. Jan Casteels, Sjef Sweeger, Egbert Elmink, Henk Klingeberg, Gerrit Mijnsma, Adolf Smit and Anton Veldhuijsen all saw their death sentences commuted to life in prison. Herman van Eiken had his life sentence reduced to twenty years; Frans van Tol's punishment was lowered from twenty to fifteen years and that of Richard Kooper from fifteen to ten. That led to the following end result after appeal: seven Jew hunters were already dead or could not be prosecuted; sixteen death sentences were upheld; eleven members of the Colonne were given life in prison, and the average punishment of the remaining nineteen convicts was ten years.

Clemency

As we have seen earlier, of the sixteen death sentences that remained after appeal, only two were actually carried out. The two men from the card catalogue who had been sentenced to die, Herman Bertinga and Frans Meiloo, were shot by a firing squad in March 1947. It would not be an exaggeration to say that they were not among the most serious offenders; with the benefit of hindsight, we can say that they had the misfortune of being tried close to the end of the war. The trials of the members of the Colonne Henneicke did not begin until much later, so that the other death sentences were handed down well after that time: in late 1948, or some time in 1949 or even 1950. At that moment a policy of clemency was in place which significantly reduced the chance that the death sentences would actually be carried out. In 1949 ten condemned Jew hunters from the Colonne were pardoned, as was another in 1950. There were just three irrevocable death sentences left, those of the three men who were high and dry in Germany: Briedé, Koops and Keuling. Even the most serious cases, like Eddy Moerberg and Tonny Kroon, saw their sentences commuted to life in prison. Why was this?

The most obvious reason was the new head of state. In 1948 Wilhelmina, who was herself a hard-liner, abdicated in favor of her daughter Juliana, who proved to be an opponent of capital punishment. But it was not quite as simple as that. In his study of Special Justice, Professor A.D. Belinfante points out the difference between the two monarchs was not as great as has often been supposed. During Wilhelmina's reign, almost fifty pardons were granted to men who had been sentenced to die. And under Juliana, eighteen executions were carried out (out of a total of forty). Thus the queens' influence could not have been that great.[70] According to Belinfante it was the successive ministers of justice who sought to keep the number of victims of Special Justice limited to "a few dozen" for moral reasons. This was done on the basis of a memorandum drawn up by Minister Kolfschoten of the Catholic People's Party, which had been approved by the government as a foundation for the clemency policy. Because 140 death sentences had been imposed, this memorandum led to mass pardons; about 100 were issued in total. The eleven most serious offenders in the Colonne Henneicke were able to profit from this. Belinfante himself is critical of this policy. He concludes that the Special Courts and the Special Court of Appeals did not impose death sentences lightly and assessed each case on its merits. The various ministers of justice showed little confidence in the judiciary, operating instead on the basis of a secret system of guidelines. "One hundred and forty executions would have caused fewer moral qualms than the unpredictable outcomes of a clemency procedure that was hammered out behind closed doors," writes Belinfante.[71] It is logical that this sense of injustice and arbitrariness also applies to the trials of the members of the Colonne Henneicke. Sixteen death sentences, only two of which were carried out, and the men who *were* executed were certainly not the most serious offenders – this is hardly in keeping with a sense of justice.

We have already seen how eleven death sentences were commuted to life in prison. For those concerned, it was uncertain for some time how long a "life sentence" would actually last. In the early 1950s the authorities were bombarded with petitions for clemency. They were submitted by the condemned men themselves, by their parents, cousins, nieces, nephews and anyone else you could think of. During that period, only the Colonne members with relatively short sentences had their requests for clemency honored; many of them were even released at that point. But until the late 1950s the core members were in the dark about how long their incarceration would last. It was only in 1958 and 1959 that they were given any certainty. Following their petitions for clemency, their life sentences were reduced to around twenty years: Moerberg was given twenty-three years, Saaldijk twenty-two, Hintink twenty-one years and five months, Elmink twenty-one years and three months, Casteels, Veldhuijsen and Kroon twenty-one years. This did not mean, however, that they remained in prison until well into the 1960s. As a rule, even the worst offenders were granted parole after serving two-thirds of their sentence. And that meant that by 1960 virtually all members of the Colonne were free men. The exceptions were Henk Hopman and Henk van der Kraal – these two leading Jew hunters did not survive their imprisonment, dying in 1954 and 1955, respectively.

Among the last to be released was the former hotel manager and fanatical anti-Semite Fred Cool, who arrested hundreds of Jews and was initially sentenced to die. In 1949 he was the only one who refused to apply for clemency. He wanted to die. His lawyer: "Conversations with Cool and a long letter give me great doubts as to whether he is entirely normal. He wants to be executed, preferably as soon as possible."[72] Cool has the idea that "as a nature lover [and] dreamer, with an artistic bent," he would be better off dying than spending the rest of his days in prison. It was decided that Cool should be given a psychiatric examination, but no mental defects were found: Cool was in full possession of his faculties. Right after that, Cool's sister wrote to the Queen, requesting clemency. Contrary to the wishes of her eighteen year younger (!) brother, she hoped that he would be spared the death penalty. In doing so, she saved the state from a thorny dilemma, since without such a request the sentence would have had to be carried out, in contravention of the policies of the Ministry of Justice. Cool's sister wrote to the Queen that her brother was totally confused: "Therefore in her despair his sister turns to your majesty in the hope that it might please your majesty to spare her brother's life."[73] The sister's wish, which was entirely in keeping with the existing policy, was granted. On April 4, 1950, Cool's sentence was commuted to life in prison.

–18–

Group Portrait

In the spring and summer of 1943, fifty-four grown men arrested their Jewish countrymen and turned them over to their mortal enemies, spurred on by the possibility of bonuses. All fifty-four of them did this more than once and, by the end of the year, most of the men had numerous arrests under their belts. What kind of people were they, what drove them, why did they do it? These are difficult questions to answer. In evaluating a group, generalizations are almost unavoidable. Nevertheless there are certain obvious shared characteristics, which make it possible – with the usual reservations – to sketch a group portrait of the civilian Jew hunters in and around the Colonne Henneicke.

To begin with, there is no reason whatsoever to characterize the group's crimes as youthful indiscretions. In fact there were hardly any young people involved. On March 1, 1943, the start of operations, the average age was thirty-nine years and eleven months. Thus, when the Colonne was disbanded six months later, the average age was over forty. One man, Herman Bertinga, was over sixty. The youngest was Johan Smid, whose mother claimed he sometimes cried at the table "because he felt so sorry for the Jews." Smid was twenty-three. It is a fact that some of the most fanatical Jew hunters were in their twenties. Bob Verlugt was twenty-six, as was Tonny Kroon, and Martin Hintink was twenty-nine. All three of them were remarkable for their ambitiousness. Henneicke himself was thirty-four and Briedé nearly forty when the bounty hunt began.

Henneicke's men could not be called well-educated by any standards. Among the incidental personnel, there was just one with a post-secondary education, Jacob R. He normally worked for the *Sicherheitspolizei* and was very active in tracking down Jews. His name appears in the Colonne's records because he would occasionally go out on a job with members of that group. In addition, a handful of men made it through high school, but most of them were hardly star pupils. And their occupations were certainly not representative of 1940s Holland. There was a notable lack of factory and construction workers: there were only six of them, which is to say less than eleven percent. Most of the men who ended up in this line of work came from the service sector. More than twenty percent of the Colonne consisted of (traveling) salesmen, and fifteen percent worked in the automobile industry – the textbook example of an unregulated business – as drivers or mechanics. Furthermore, over twenty percent of the men had previously been office clerks; this was more or less consistent with the norms of the time. Eight percent could be considered small businessmen. That said, we should not take these reported occupations too seriously, since for many of the men "occupation" was a decidedly relative concept. The most striking thing in this context was the fact that many members of the Colonne had worked a whole series of highly diverse jobs before they came under the wing of Henneicke and Briedé. A substantial portion of the group could politely be called jacks-of-all-trades. Alex Hoogers, for example, who would eventually find a good job as an art appraiser, said that he had a hard time keeping up in school and was placed in special classes. According to Hoogers himself, he initially had trouble finding his place in society. School was also an ordeal for Joop den Ouden: he had learning disabilities and was repeatedly left behind. In the end, it turned out that the profession most suitable for him was that of pimp.

Most of the future Jew hunters were hard hit by the economic crisis that gripped the Netherlands in the 1930s. Henk Hopman spent "a large part of his life trying to find work through the Municipal Employment Office," according to his lawyer G. Blom.[1] The attorney described his client thus: "He is one of the victims of the mass unemployment that so ravaged the country before the war." Earlier we saw how Frans Meiloo, who would later be executed, was registered as unemployed for sixteen years before being hired to work at the card catalogue of the *Zentralstelle*. Inactivity was truly a way of life for him. There were others like him among the future members of the Colonne, including Wim Henneicke himself, but no one was quite as committed to unemployment as Meiloo. The Depression also hurt small businessmen like Gerrit Mijnsma. At first he earned a decent living as a decorator, but after suffering a number of setbacks, he too had to go on welfare at the start of the war.

There were also a few downright absurd reasons for employment. Christiaan van den Borch, for example, an insurance broker by profession, was hired at a certain point by Nautic, a shipyard in Haarlem. He was discharged after a month because he proved incapable of operating an adding machine. Even more curious is the reason for Jan Rudolfs' less than glittering career in the food service industry. A bartender by trade, he was offered a job as buffet chef at the Café National in Venlo in 1941. He was let go after just one week, when it turned out that he was unable to pour a proper beer. Rudolfs evidently did not make good use of his time out of work. Some time after that he was hired by Café Ter Merwe in Dordrecht, but he was fired after three months for the exact same reason. The detectives who questioned Rudolfs after the war noted all this with dry eyes.

During the occupation the economic crisis continued unabated in certain sectors; indeed, in some cases it was the Germans themselves who precipitated the crisis. Henk Klingeberg started out as an office clerk, but in the late 1930s he had a well-paying job in the gasoline industry. When the war broke out, the gasoline trade ground to an immediate halt, and Klingeberg was out of work for eight months. The same thing happened to Paul Rooskens. He had worked for eight years as a foreign exchange broker, but the occupation virtually shut down business, and Rooskens soon found himself out of a job. Egbert Elmink probably never thought his flourishing radio shops would succumb to the economic downturn. Before the war he had been a dedicated member of the NSB, a fervent adherent of the Nazi ideology, yet it was these very doctrines that put an end to the sale of radios in the Netherlands. For a time he tried to compensate for this by repairing radios for the *Wehrmacht*, but in the end his business went up the flue. Klingeberg, Rooskens and Elmink were robbed of their livelihoods by the economic policies of the occupying authority, and yet all of them would become fanatical members of the Colonne Henneicke.

Gradually we begin to get an idea of the sort of people who joined the Colonne: schlemiels, social failures, life's losers. This was not true for everyone, but it was the dominant image of the civilian Jew hunters. And this was no coincidence. Time and again, in the dossiers of the Jew hunters, we find instances of out-of-work men being referred to the *Hausraterfassung* by the Municipal Employment Office. This happened so often that it was clearly official policy. The expression did not exist at the time, but if it had, this state of affairs would surely have been described as a "win-win situation." The *Hausraterfassung* was benefitted with employees who were prepared to help deport Jews, and the Employment Office could report that a high percentage of applicants had found new work. The result was that, starting in the summer of 1942, unemployed members of the NSB were more or less automatically sent to Briedé, the head of personnel at the *Hausraterfassung*. With this knowledge it is not surprising that no less than eighty-five percent of the men who can be counted as civilian Jew hunters were members of the NSB, and one or two belonged to the even more anti-Semitic splinter group, the NSNAP. From the fact that some forty percent of the civilian Jew hunters had already joined the NSB by 1935, we may infer that, for many, the decision to join the Movement was not motivated (solely) by opportunism but by genuine convictions. The Amsterdam detective Tump attempted to find out if the Employment Office was required to refer members of the NSB to the *Hausraterfassung*, but he was unable to discover any evidence of that.[2] No written agreement was ever found, and an interrogation of G. Rövecamp, an official with the Employment Office who made most of the referrals, did not confirm the detective's theory. He stated that he was not obliged to pass any names on. But the fact remains that the majority of the personnel of the Colonne Henneicke, core members as well as those who were only posted there temporarily, were unemployed NSB members who had been advised by the Employment Office to apply for a position with the *Hausraterfassung*, where they could sign a lucrative contract with the *roofbank* Lippmann, Rosenthal & Co.

It goes without saying that the Jew hunters were no less responsible for their actions and decisions than anybody else. But there are also indications that some of them were under intense pressure from their home environment to get a job, so they could start providing for their families again. That must have boosted their willingness to hunt down Jews. Take Joop Bouman, for example. During this period he got his girlfriend Riki pregnant. They were forced to get married. The bills started mounting up, and Bouman soon needed a source of income. He chose to become a bounty hunter. According to friends, Christiaan van den Borch was a henpecked husband, whose wife forced him to join the NSB, to the shock of the friends in question. Martin Hintink was pressured by his father to become more active in the Movement; "my father talked me into [joining] the NSB," he would later say himself. Sjef Sweeger had married a Finnish woman from a wealthy family and lived there for a time in comfort, with a good job, a flat and a child.[3] When the situation in Finland deteriorated, he sent his wife to the Netherlands. He followed her a short time later, into a life of poverty. Sweeger went into the flower bulb business, commuting back and forth between Germany and the Netherlands, but after May 10, 1940 the bottom fell out of the market. Sweeger's wife became increasingly sombre and morose, demanding that her husband bring in more money. And thus Sweeger signed a contract with the *Hausraterfassung* for fl.230 a month.

And then there was also the inevitable figure of the domineering mother-in-law. We can read about this in a letter written by Henk Saaldijk's mother to the judge-advocate: "Then the baby came, and it is my understanding that his mother-in-law often reproached him for not providing better for her daughter. And indeed, they were badly off, I know it. That must have been the reason for his lapse."[4]

This kind of pressure may have played a role in the actions of some members of the Colonne Henneicke, but it is far from the definitive explanation for their crimes. There were more important factors, like the anti-Semitism that was undoubtedly rife within the Colonne. If the employees were not already anti-Semites when they joined, they surely would have become so during their tenure there. Henneicke and Briedé were described by everyone as rabid anti-Semites, and there is no reason to believe that they made any secret of their convictions. The few times that anyone called them to account for their activities, they justified themselves in overtly anti-Semitic language. "It's still a baby Jew yet," said Lambert Schipper when he took two-year-old André Ossendrijver away from his foster parents in Zuilen, "but a baby Jew turns into a Jew boy and then a full-grown Jew."[5] The same Schipper said something similar to his upstairs neighbor, Wilmke

Braak. She knew he was in the NSB and that he arrested Jews; he had told her as much and had even spoken about Jewish children. She asked him how he could do such a thing as the father of three, and he retorted: "They're just Jew children, and the whole Jewish race has to be exterminated." When he was later questioned by investigators about the motives for his anti-Semitism, the former acolyte responded with the expected cliché: "I never hated the Jews personally, but that was what the church had always taught us."

After the war Frans van Tol was a great deal more honest. "I admit to being an anti-Semite during the occupation," he said to the detective who questioned him.[6] A Holocaust survivor from Soest, who had been arrested by Van Tol along with her husband, was told: "The game's up, you dirty, stinking Jews. We're in charge now." Van Tol's anti-Semitism did not develop in the Colonne or during the time he worked for the *Einsatzstab Reichsleiter Rosenberg*. As early as 1941 he wrote a letter to a bailiff, in which he said that he would not "be put off by the threats of a Jew like you" and that "we were now getting even with your kind."

In the Colonne Henneicke anti-Jewish sentiment can be found in all shapes and sizes. For example, Egbert Elmink said during an interrogation: "In principle I was anti-Semitic, but some of my best friends were Jews."[7] Joop Bouman combined his hatred of Jews with a personal veneration of Adolf Hitler.[8] When his wife demanded that he take down the portrait of the *Führer* in their living room, he solemnly replied, "Hitler is my comrade." During post-war interrogations he said that he agreed with the Germans that "the Jewish question had to be solved." He had not initially thought of eliminating them; he would have preferred to give them their own country. Former commercial agent Jaap Gist, one of Briedé's lackeys, said after the war: "I became a member of the NSB out of idealism and not because I was an anti-Semite. After that I gradually became anti-Jewish."[9]

The Colonne's bookkeeper, Eddy Moerberg, whose family couldn't imagine that such a nice boy could have sunk so low, once pressured a Jewish woman to reveal the addresses of other Jews in hiding, shouting, "I'll find those Jews, whatever it takes. I hate the Jews, and I'll exterminate every last one of them."[10]

Joop den Ouden and Christiaan van den Borch had been consumed with feelings of hatred toward Jews for much longer. Once they went out together in search of a member of the underground, J. Nieuwenhuizen, and when it turned out he was not at home, they waited for him, in the company of Mrs Nieuwenhuizen, who testified after the war: "Both Van den Borch and Den Ouden were convinced that the Jews did not belong in our society and that their main purpose was to track down Jews in hiding. Van den Borch, in particular, offered a passionate defense of National Socialism."[11] Mrs Hermes, who sheltered a number of Jews during the war, had the same experience when she was visited by the duo Eggink-Hoogers.[12]

"It was clear from the remarks the two men made that they were virulently anti-Semitic." Hoogers had also intimated that he did not feel particularly confident about the future. "Now you are the ones being rounded up," he had said to a Jewish woman, "but if the tables turn later on, they'll come for us. We've got children too, and that won't matter to them either."

After the war Henk Klingeberg claimed he had cancelled his brief membership of the NSB "because he did not agree with the persecution of Jews." That sounds more noble than it was, since he added: "It galled me that the poor Jews were being taken away but not the rich ones." In practice there was little evidence of any reluctance on Klingeberg's part. "So are you a Jew-lover too?" he said to an acquaintance he found in a house to which he had come to arrest some Jews. And to one of the arrestees: "In Poland we'll teach you all to work." We know of no anti-Semitic comments from his colleague Van der Kraal, but a former employee of the Jewish Council, who was occasionally sent to the offices of the *Zentralstelle* as a courier, remembered that "the defendant brought the poor wretches in with a sneering laugh."[13]

And naturally we mustn't forget to mention Martin Hintink, who made more arrests than anyone else, together with his brother-in-law Rudolfs. He picked up two Jewish women at the home of the 72-year-old Mrs H. Westman. At one point Hintink made a face at the beds his victims had just climbed out of and said to his partner, "Look, that's where those Jews were sleeping."[14] Hintink made no secret of his anti-Semitism. One of his victims who survived the war, Isaac de Winter, said to the court: "It was also this defendant who said he was a great anti-Semite and that he had personally arrested an old school chum who was a Jew."

All in all, it is a veritable litany of anti-Semitism. The hatred of Jews was undoubtedly one of the crucial factors behind the effectiveness of the Colonne Henneicke. But there were other examples of abusive behavior on the part of the Jew hunters in addition to those mentioned above. We have already seen that the use of violence to compel Jews into revealing addresses where other Jews were hiding was commonplace. It is also clear that various members of the Colonne carried guns. That was officially *verboten*, and the German authorities who were asked about it, like Lages and Aus der Fünten, vehemently denied ever allowing it. Not a single member of the Colonne admitted carrying a revolver, but there were dozens of witnesses who testified to the contrary. The bounty hunters were plainly scared of receiving longer sentences if they were also charged with illegal possession of a firearm. "If you say another word, you dirty Jew, I'll fill you full of lead," Willem Briedé said when he arrested the businessman Jacob Rubens.[15] And Henk Saaldijk was also known to have made a similar threat. Saaldijk, who according to his neighbors kept to himself and never said a word to anyone, said to a Mr J. Belder during a raid: "Don't try to escape, or you're going to get shot."[16] Wilhelm Lesegeld, a teacher who was originally from Poland, remembered all too well how

Egbert Elmink held a pistol up to his temple at the Colonne's headquarters on Noorder Amstellaan.[17] If he didn't confess to being Jewish at once, Elmink would pull the trigger.

Another story concerns Anton Veldhuijsen, one of the guards at the Theater, who regularly went into town to arrest Jews. In June 1943 he entered the workshop of the Frank Company on Nieuwe Achtergracht, where a group of seamstresses witnessed him storm up to a Jewish man, Maurits Viskooper, and demand to see his identity card. Viskooper saw he was in danger, took off, kicked out a window and squeezed through the hole. It was then that he saw how far up he was. He clung desperately to the window sill, while Veldhuijsen picked up his truncheon and struck him on his head and hands with all his might. Viskooper was forced to let go and fell about five meters. He broke his wrist. There are two identical statements from workers who witnessed the incident.[18] Viskooper fled despite his injury, but a short time later he was picked up by movers from the Puls firm who happened to be in the neighborhood, clearing out a Jewish home. He was taken to the Theater, from which he also escaped. He was later rearrested and ultimately perished in a concentration camp.

In court, the man who struck him on the hands with a truncheon, Anton Veldhuijsen, swore up and down that the incident never happened. The way he told it, he had wanted to let Viskooper get away and staged "a sham fight" with him: "I was afraid the Jews who were standing around me would betray me for deliberately letting Viskooper get away." The Special Court did not believe him and Viskooper's death would weigh heavily in their eventual judgment and sentence.[19]

We have already seen enough examples of the verbal abusiveness of the Jew hunters. Perhaps the coarsest of all was Klingeberg.[20] He once got into an altercation with his neighbor, Mrs M. Tulfer, because her daughter had rung his doorbell and run away. He insinuated that Mrs Tulfer was raising her children to be anti-NSB. She denied this, but Klingeberg felt she was being impertinent and said, "You should shut you mouth." After that he began swearing in German and said, "*Ich bin von der Nationalsozialistische Sicherheitspolizei, ohne weiteres*." When she said she preferred to use her own language, Klingeberg barked, "If you don't shut your mouth, I'll have you taken away tonight."

Another person to testify against Klingeberg was Maurits M., a Jew who was arrested by Klingeberg ("Get out of bed, you!") in March 1943 on IJsselstraat, even though he was in a mixed marriage and his wife was pregnant. Klingeberg had sensitively remarked: "It might still be a miscarriage. In fact, in Westerbork you'll be forced to get a divorce."

Yet the overall picture of the Colonne is rather more subtle than the above might suggest. In the face of all this brutality there were also examples of the opposite. Even the most notorious Jew hunters were known to have saved someone from time to time. Bob Verlugt once succeeded in getting an acquaintance of his father's released by swiping a folder with information; that one action saved him from the death penalty on appeal. Henk van den Heuvel helped Jews escape from the Dutch Theater (twenty-four by his own count); he even brought a Jewish woman to a safe-house on the back of his bicycle. After his time with the Colonne, Joop Bouman also helped Jews find places to hide and supplied them with false papers. Even Frans van Tol, who blackmailed and arrested Jews on a large scale, helped someone: his own mother-in-law. Mrs A. Koopman-Engelbert was arrested for harboring Jews at her home. After the war she stated that she was released through the efforts of her son-in-law, to her surprise, since the two had never had any contact prior to that time.[21]

A flicker of humanity among the Jew hunters; it is surprising but true. Among their number were quite a few family men, who were genuinely missed by their wives and children. One such man was Jaap Gist, who lived together with his girlfriend and their son Paul. A relative of his girlfriend's wrote to prosecutors after the war: "I hope Gist can soon return to his family. It would do his little son good; he misses him ever so much and talks about him constantly."[22]

Veronika Krenn wrote from Austria to the president of the court with the request that her husband, Henk van den Heuvel, be granted a speedy release. "As a mother and wife who has gone through more than one could possibly write down, I beg you to temper justice with mercy and give my husband the opportunity to take care of his family as a good father in the near future."[23] After his conviction Aaldert Dassen requested a conversation with attorney general Langemeijer to explain his personal circumstances.[24] His wife, he wrote, had had a nervous breakdown, due to the fact that he had been punished much more severely than had been expected. He was afraid she might never recover, if the sentence was upheld. They had a five-year-old daughter, who would be left without a mother. The marriage was still good, but Dassen feared that that could change.

Anna van den Borch-De Vries tried to make clear to judge-advocate Gelinck that she could not go on without her Christiaan: "I have three children, nine, seven and six. For more than four years I've had to look after them on my own, but at this point I can barely do it anymore. My nerves are so shattered that the children are often the ones who suffer. The youngest dreams of his father, and the eldest needs a strict upbringing. Our marriage was extremely happy; I miss my husband terribly."[25] Van den Borch's sister also saw that the family was in dire straits, as was her brother, whose incarceration had left him a broken man: "We all feel so very sorry for the children; it was such a nice, happy family. Let us forgive and try to put this family back together again."

All these appeals for clemency went unheeded. Personal circumstances played little or no part in the sentencing process or the granting of pardons. This is understandable, for any comparison with the fate of their victims instantly reduced the perpetrators' problems to minor complaints, and at the time the Special Court was not particularly receptive to such pleas. But in spite of that, it remains puzzling, the contrast between the Colonne members as Jew hunters and as private individuals. Even a wise and experienced man like G.E. Langemeijer, attorney general at the Supreme Court, could not figure it out. In an explanatory note on a petition for clemency from Chris de Hout, he lamented: "Time and again I have already had occasion to explain . . . why this fairly large group of convicts presents a particular problem for me. To be brief, this is due to the psychological mystery that certain crimes, which seem to attest to the most utter depravity, have been committed on a large scale by individuals whom the facts show to be otherwise perfectly normal people and who not infrequently make a favorable impression in the way they have submitted to their punishment, a characterization which also applies to De Hout."[26]

Meanwhile, in the internment camps and prisons, significant numbers of former Jew hunters were beginning to repent their past misdeeds as they slowly began to realize what had taken place in the extermination camps. It is hard to say whether they truly felt remorse or whether they were simply giving socially acceptable answers to the questions posed by investigators, with a view to their upcoming trials and their eventual futures. In general, they tried to distance themselves from their past, in language that varied from one suspect to another. "My misconduct during the occupation was such that I can find no words to apologize. I don't understand how I ever could have come to that," Sjef Sweeger said candidly.[27] Christiaan van den Borch maintained that he never knew what would happen to the Jews: "If that had been the case I would never have assisted in carrying out the [anti-]Jewish directives. I profoundly regret [what I have done]."[28] Henk Hopman, by contrast, continued to sit on the fence. He had always denied actively participating in any arrests, despite persuasive evidence to the contrary; he claimed he had only been there as a witness. In a note following his conviction, he wrote that he was even sorry "for witnessing arrests."[29] He was somewhat more frank about his contract with Lippmann, Rosenthal & Co. He now felt that it had been a mistake to sign it and deeply regretted it. He had also come to understand the "appalling suffering" experienced by Jewish men, women and children.

Van der Kraal, the brutal ex-policeman, explained to investigators: "If I'd known the Jewish people I picked up would be killed, I would have refused."[30] Rudolfs, the dim-witted assistant of his brother-in-law Hintink, came to a deeper understanding of things: "After the war I saw trainloads of Jewish people coming back from the German concentrations camps. Then I was ashamed of myself for helping to deport those people. Only now do I realize that there is Jewish blood on my hands."[31] There are similar statements from Paul Rooskens and even from Frans van Tol, the junk dealer from Vondelstraat, who said he felt "deep remorse." The children of Anton Veldhuijsen, the heavy-handed guard at the Dutch Theater, wrote in a well-worded petition for clemency: "In the many quiet hours of his detention, father has seen the error of his ways."[32]

Aaldert Dassen had a mental collapse when he heard, at Camp De Harskamp, what happened to the Jews.[33] "For about a fortnight I had to cope with a severe mental breakdown, but I was able to recover from this breakdown thanks to my reborn faith in Jesus," he wrote at the camp in a personal history. "If I had known the fate of the Jews at the time," he added, "a bullet would be too good for me now." He was only with the Colonne Henneicke for a short time. He enlisted in the *Landwacht*, and his unit was later incorporated into the SS, where he swore the oath to Hitler. He had no reason to expect a short prison term. After the war Dassen felt that he had been betrayed, that his idealism had been misused. The former KLM steward looked back on his life and concluded that his choice to follow his ideals had been the wrong one. If he had opted for money instead, he wrote in his personal history, he could have worked in hotels during the war and earned a little extra under the table, and after the liberation he could have flown with KLM again, as a good citizen with a happy family. But he chose his ideals and now saw himself as a traitor with a broken family and a lifetime of prison ahead of him.

Another Colonne member who returned to his faith in prison was Lambert Schipper.[34] His spiritual counsellor, chaplain Molenaar, attested to this, from the Hendrik Mining Camp in Brunssum, where Schipper was being held. "How could he commit such acts? He impresses me as an honest, plain-spoken man, and I have heard him speak about his mistakes, which he now recognizes, though at the time he did not see the ramifications and consequences of his actions, because he gradually slipped into [that life]." According to the chaplain, Schipper did not have a clear understanding, or often even an inkling, of what was happening to the Jews. Molenaar continued: "He is now in very poor health, yet he has a very strong will and has served his sentence in the spirit of true penance, something that certainly cannot be said of every inmate. I know of an act of true heroism from his personal life, which I am not at liberty to reveal, but which I respect as a priest."

After reading the rest of the dossier, it becomes a bit clearer what the chaplain was being so secretive about. For twenty years Schipper "lived in sin," as was then said, with an American woman. This was a source of much grief for his children, and he eventually decided to end the relationship and return to his wife, whom he had left many years before. He wrote to the attorney general to ask permission to accompany his girlfriend to the boat that would take her back to her homeland. If Schipper had hoped this would hasten his release, he was mistaken. Two petitions for clemency were rejected in rapid succession. But in 1956 – Schipper was then sixty-seven and, according to a report, in failing health – he was allowed to return to his wife, who had requested his release herself. The Supreme Court was somewhat surprised at this, as Schipper had been accused of seriously assaulting her twenty years earlier, but time had evidently healed that wound, and on November 9, 1956, Schipper was allowed to spend the rest of his days at home.

Not only Schipper and Dassen found comfort in faith. After being unmasked as a Jew hunter, Herman van Eiken also turned to religion. In the internment camp he was allowed to assist the minister. His wife begged the Queen to set him free; he wanted so much to become a productive member of society again. Van Eiken himself composed a well-written letter to his attorney in which he spoke openly about his new-found faith: "I hope with all my heart that God will deign to empower me to work for his Kingdom among the Dutch people, like a Saul transformed into a Paul, for without Christ, one cannot be a Christian, and I can testify from experience, now that I am left with the broken pieces of my own life, that without Christ all things are doomed to failure."[35]

The group portrait is slowly beginning to take shape: these were middle-aged men, social failures, almost all of them members of the NSB, most of them profoundly anti-Semitic. They are not utterly devoid of humanity, but were nevertheless prepared to go quite far in following orders. Yet there were still a number of key factors necessary to make them into the merciless Jew hunters they would eventually become. Undoubtedly the personalities and style of the leaders was one such factor. Wim Henneicke was the authoritarian, hard-driving, fearsome boss, who forced his men to extremes with his divide-and-conquer strategy. He worked hard, set himself up as an example to others, threatened reprisals and hounded his personnel mercilessly. In the last few months Briedé played a similar role for the group that stayed behind on Adama van Scheltemaplein after Henneicke and his core staff had left. Henneicke's organizational model must also have played a major role. By sending his people off in pairs, he prevented them from cutting corners. He put the teams together in such a way that the men drove each other to higher "production." In that way he introduced the element of peer pressure, which unquestionably also influenced the collective. The men shared a secret; they earned the hatred of countless countrymen and the Dutch underground, and that reinforced group ties and thus their fanaticism. Colonne member Jaap Gits said in an interrogation that at a certain point the men of the *Hausraterfassung* started receiving a card at home on their birthdays, which read: "Happy birthday, it may be your last." The card was signed "The Resistance" or "The Underground."[36] An investigation revealed that a large number of pay sheets, containing names, addresses and birth dates, had been stolen from the *Hausraterfassung* some time before. There were other threats as well. Anton Veldhuijsen reported to the police that someone had smashed a plate-glass window at his house on New Year's Eve, 1943.[37] There are indications that he was hated in the neighborhood for his aggressive behavior. "*Sicherheitsdienst* Inventory Clerk Reports Crime," reads the heading of the police report, dated January 2.

Finally, the most important motivating factor for the civilian Jew hunters was, of course, the money. Their basic salaries alone were certainly nothing to sneeze at and must have kept many of them from resigning. All things considered, the bonuses and other fringe benefits were critical for the effectiveness of the organization. Because of their backgrounds, most of the men in the Colonne were obsessed with money; they yearned for a life without poverty, for themselves and their families. The astronomical amounts that Tonny Kroon took home – testified to by his sisters-in-law – were probably not within everyone's reach, but thanks to this job virtually everybody could escape from the misery of the Depression and the gray existence of the early years of the war. The premiums were the fuse in the powder keg; they turned the frustrated anti-Semites of the *Recherchegruppe Henneicke* into an explosive mixture, which was fatal to thousands of Jews.

The Colonne Henneicke was a unique phenomenon. I am not aware of any studies of similar groups of professional Jew hunters outside the Netherlands. In Belgium it was largely volunteer SS men who did the dirty work of deporting Jews. Twenty of them stepped forward in September 1942 when the Antwerp NSB *Stormbanleider* (major) August Schollen asked for volunteers to track down Jews. They were between twenty and forty-five years old. Special bonuses were apparently not necessary.[38]

In France, the Germans had only a very small occupying force. The job of organizing the deportations fell to the French police, but they faithfully followed all orders and, with a few exceptions, they proved to be fanatical Jew hunters, particularly in Paris. The enormous raid of July 16 and July 17, 1942, in which 13,000 Jews were rounded up and taken to the Vélodrome d'Hiver and the transit camp Drancy, was conducted by 9,000 Parisian police officers. Germans never entered the picture. Later special anti-Jewish police units were established, the SEC (*Sections d'Enquête et Controle*), the French counterpart to the Dutch Bureau of Jewish Affairs.[39] French studies make no mention of bounty hunters, though the police often availed themselves of the services of informants and snitches. "Thousands of Jews fell victim to informants, who thought they were serving the French cause since their leaders had said the Jews were the enemy," writes Susan Zuccotti in her book about the deportations of the Jews in France.[40]

In some respects there is another comparison we can make, a comparison with another group of ordinary men who proved capable of serious crimes: the men of the *Reserve Polizeibataillon 101*. This was a division of the German *Ordnungspolizei*, which was sent to Poland in June 1942 to assist in murdering the many thousands of Jews in German-occupied territory. The men of *Reserve Polizeibataillon 101* led their victims to deserted spots outside their village and shot them, one by one. Their task was somewhat different from that of the Colonne Henneicke, considerably more gruesome, but there are nonetheless striking similarities between the two groups. In the first place there is the fact that a few hundred members of the battalion were questioned about their actions after the war. On the basis of 125 of these interrogations, the American historian Christopher Browning wrote the horrifying book *Ordinary Men*.[41]

The vast majority of the men of *Reserve Polizeibataillon 101* came from the area around Hamburg. Their average age was thirty-nine, as was the case for the Colonne Henneicke. Most of the men were deemed too old for the army, but after September 1939 they were recruited in large numbers for the reserve police. Approximately sixty-three percent came from a working-class background, but only a small number were skilled workers. Most of them had typical Hamburg jobs: dock workers and lorry drivers were the two most common, but there were also many warehousemen and construction workers, lathe operators, seamen and waiters. About thirty-five percent could be classified as lower middle class, almost all of them from the white collar sector. Three-quarters of this group were salesmen or shop assistants. The number of self-employed artisans or small businessmen was very small.[42]

The background of the members of the Colonne Henneicke is murky; in half the cases, no mention was made of such personal details in their files. However, what we do know roughly corresponds with the data from the group from Hamburg, though there is one significant difference when we come to the subject of previous occupations: there was not a single dockworker in the Colonne. In Holland that group tended to be left wing and felt little sympathy for the ideas of the NSB.

Approximately twenty-five percent of *Reserve Polizeibataillon 101* were party members in 1942. Six were even *Alte Kämpfer*: they were already Nazis before Hitler came to power in 1933. Twenty-five percent was a remarkably high figure for German troops, and Browning sees this as a reason for the troops' willingness to follow the grisly orders they were given. The fact that eighty-five percent of the men in the Colonne were in the NSB was virtually unprecedented by Dutch standards, but the effect was the same. That percentage guaranteed a high level of motivation for the ultimate goal.

From conversations with the German police troops, we know the men initially had great difficulty with the work, for which they had neither been trained nor properly prepared. The first massacre, near Józefów, led to great shock. But by the time of the second massacre, a few days later, near the village of Lomazy, some men were already settling in to their new task, writes Browning. "Habituation played a role as well. Having killed once already, the men did not experience such a traumatic shock the second time. Like much else, killing was something one could get used to."[43] The same picture is painted by the members of the Colonne Henneicke. The first time one of the men participated in arresting Jews, he was shocked and wanted to quit, but with the passage of time that feeling gradually wore off.

One clear difference between the two groups was their eventual punishment, or lack thereof. We have already seen that by and large the Colonne Henneicke was dealt with quite severely. The policemen from Hamburg received far more lenient treatment. It was not until quite late, between 1962 and 1967, that the 210 former members of *Reserve Polizeibataillon 101* were interrogated, some of them more than once. Fourteen of them – five regular policemen and nine officers – were served with subpoenas. The trial lasted six months, beginning in October 1967. Three of the men were given eight year prison sentences; one was given six years and another five. Six men, among them the five non-officers, were found guilty but not punished, and three were discharged from prosecution for reasons of ill health. The sentences were later reduced significantly or even completely remitted, and the other members of *Reserve Polizeibataillon 101* were never prosecuted because of insufficient evidence. Yet the battalion was one of the very few police organizations that was ever the subject of an investigation, and so in that sense the operation was a rare success for German prosecutors.[44]

In evaluating the men who participated in the massacres in Poland, Browning found that it was possible to get out of the work. Those who tried to do so, by feigning illness or by requesting a transfer, were usually successful. This did, however, earn them the contempt of their colleagues, who felt they had been let down. But the objectors got away without any serious consequences. In fact the same was true for members of the Colonne Henneicke. As prosecutor Gelinck wrote: those who shirked duty by reporting sick or by some other method experienced no adverse effects.

In his study of the German police troop Browning makes frequent reference to the famous experiments of the American psychologist Stanley Milgram, who demonstrated that, for most test subjects, obedience to legal authorities was apparently limitless. They were prepared to hurt and torture others to the very limit if ordered to do so. Milgram was himself so shocked by his own findings that he ended his book on the experiments, *Obedience to Authority*, with the sombre observation that modern civilization offered no protection whatsoever against the perpetration of atrocities, if people were ordered to commit them.[45] If this was true of randomly chosen test subjects in peace time, one can only imagine what the results would be for the highly motivated men who voluntarily joined organizations like the *Reserve Polizeibataillon 101* of the *Ordnungspolizei* or the *Hausraterfassungsstelle* of the *Zentralstelle für jüdische Auswanderung* during the Second World War.

Browning concludes his study by highlighting the difficulties of rendering a final judgment on such a group so long after the fact. In the end every individual bears his own responsibility; one man goes on following orders, while another stops. It is impossible to give a complete picture. But, according to Browning, if you consider them as a group and establish that under these circumstances this group was capable of killing thousands of innocent people – which group would not be?[46]

In a Dutch study that examined the mental state of collaborators and political criminals from the period 1940–45, psychiatrist J. Hofman also concludes that it is virtually impossible to identify common characteristics that would be determinant factors for this group's misconduct.[47] The Depression certainly played a role, and a striking number of the criminals were emotionally immature and unstable. But in the end it is Hofman's contention that the causes were to be found in Nazism and the organization of the Third Reich rather than in specific characteristics of the wrongdoers themselves.

One can say much the same for the Colonne Henneicke. Henneicke's team was also made up of "ordinary men," with ordinary backgrounds and very ordinary occupations. As a consequence of the economic misery of the Depression, they lost their way in life and became susceptible to the ideals of the NSB and fit to carry out the Nazis' chief objective after 1942: the deportation of the Dutch Jews. When a tightly regimented organization was established for this purpose and the work was made extra attractive with the introduction of an extremely profitable bonus system, there was nothing to stand in the way of the Colonne's success.

–19–

The End of the Leaders

On October 1, 1943 the Colonne Henneicke ended operations. The reason is obvious: there was simply no more work left to do. The number of Jews found was steadily decreasing, and the infrastructure of the deportations was being dismantled. The Dutch Theater was closed, as was the nursery across the street; the Jewish Council was shut down, and the leadership was shipped to Westerbork at the end of September. Yet there are strong indications that there was an additional reason for Willi Lages to disband the Colonne Henneicke: fraud. "The colonne [sic] Henneicke was dissolved by SD chief Lages in connection with various cases of misappropriation," Abraham Kaper stated in a deposition he gave to detectives Prasing and Verduin.[1] Kaper was the station sergeant in charge of the Bureau of Jewish Affairs, the Colonne Henneicke's main competitor, and was thus in a position to know about such things. There is also a passage in a letter written by judge-advocate Gelinck suggesting the same thing. Looking back on the prosecution of the Colonne Henneicke, he wrote that the Klingeberg affair was one of the reasons Lages eventually pulled the plug on the group.[2] Klingeberg was arrested in September because he could not keep his hands off his female arrestees, and for Lages that may very well have been the last straw.

But whatever the cause, the Colonne was now history. Eighteen core members were discharged. A report the *Zentralstelle* sent to the Provincial Employment Office contained the following names: Hopman, Lam, Rademakers, Van de Wert, Harm Jan van den Heuvel, Van den Borch, De Hout, Kroon, Elmink, Hintink, Hoogers, Cool, Mijnsma, Den Ouden, Rooskens, Schipper, Rudolfs and Sweeger.[3] The big shots were allowed to stay on: Henneicke himself – who remained on the payroll of Lippmann, Rosenthal & Co. as a sort of one-man column – and Briedé and Moerberg. After the staff reduction, Willem Briedé was put in charge of the fur department, the only section of the *Hausraterfassung* to remain open, as a subdivision of the *Sicherheitsdienst*. He retained a handful of faithful followers: Moerberg stayed on, as did Van Amersfoort, Casteels, Eggink and the German Berten, in addition to a few old acquaintances from the *Hausraterfassung*. The only thing we know about the fur department is that the employees tracked down hidden fur, which had belonged to Jews. In Briedé's file there is a police report, which reads: "This service was created after the vast majority of Jewish property had been carted away. Briedé was in charge of this service and worked with approximately ten people [and together they would] visit fur auctions and fur businesses. More or less arbitrarily, they would impound large quantities of fur whenever the Germans needed it for the Eastern Front."[4] If these fur hunters ran into Jews in the course of their work, they were no longer permitted to arrest them. They were supposed to notify the police, or better yet the *Sicherheitspolizei*, which had since incorporated the former Bureau of Jewish Affairs. That must have happened increasingly often, since a number of former members of the Colonne Henneicke went to work there. Initially there were three of them: Henk van der Kraal, who was returning to his old profession (he had previously been a police officer in Zaandam), Joop den Ouden and Henk Saaldijk. Later Eddy Moerberg would also join this division of the Amsterdam police. In reality these men were simply continuing the work they had been doing before, under a similar incentive scheme.

Then several Colonne members were offered another possibility; they were approached by Kaper to work for the police "on commission" as Jew hunters. Tonny was one of the men to receive such an offer. He told the detectives who interrogated him: "When the personnel were discharged in October, due to a drop in work, I was asked – I believe by Kaper – to stay on with six others and supply him with the addresses of Jews in hiding. I declined the offer."[5] It is likely they all refused: the decline in income would have been too dramatic.

So where did they go? In most cases we actually know the answer. As should be obvious by this point, the majority ended up in organizations that were firmly on the German side during the last eighteen months of the war. A quarter of the men continued their careers in the *Landstorm* or the *Landwacht*, with some of them receiving training at the police academy in Schalkhaar, where the Germans molded new police officers. No fewer than twenty-six percent wound up in leadership positions within the NSB, the Labour Front or other similar organizations that aided the occupier. Eleven percent went to work in Germany after the Colonne Henneicke was dissolved. This percentage increased significantly after Mad Tuesday, when countless NSB men fled across the eastern border for fear of reprisals. Finally, two members of the Colonne were confined to their homes due to ill health; three were languishing in German prisons for various reasons, and three others were able to find "normal" jobs in the private sector.

What remained of the fur department and the Jew patrol departed for the eastern part of the country around Mad Tuesday. Briedé and his men were stationed with the *Sicherheitsdienst* in Velp for a time, but the club broke up soon afterward, as everyone sought safety elsewhere, particularly in Germany. The day after Mad

Tuesday two former Colonne members suffered serious personal losses. A train with National Socialist refugees was bombed near Diemen. Among the passengers were the wives of Jan Casteels and Gerrit Mijnsma. Both of them, Jansje Waanders and Geetrui Jernberg, were killed. Mijnsma also lost his fourteen-year-old daughter Gerda, who was killed instantly.

After September 5, 1944, Willem Hendrik Benjamin Briedé was never heard from again. With his German wife, Maria Johann, and his nine-year-old daughter, he left Velp for Germany, most likely in November, since he officially started working for the *Sicherheitsdienst* on November 11, 1944. Briedé had already left his home on Zacharias Jansestraat in East Amsterdam on September 5, Mad Tuesday. From that moment on, according to an anonymous letter, his upstairs neighbors paid his rent in his name. "Those people were living high on the hog. The house was filled with expensive furniture. And nothing is being done about it. That's not right," complained a jealous neighbor.[6] It is unlikely Briedé was bothered by any of this. He disappeared without a trace and settled in Germany. He was tried in absentia in 1949; his case came before the court on April 29.[7] Once again, the prosecutor was Marinus Gelinck. The witnesses called included Isaac Rubens, who was threatened and arrested by Briedé but managed to get away by bribing his captors; Mrs Dirkje Kamperman-De Vries from Schipbeekstraat in Utrecht, who had been looking after Flipje Plas and others; her daughter Marie Susanna, and Reverend Hugenholtz from Ammerstol, who had been sheltering a number of Jews until they were picked up by Henneicke and Briedé. The elder Mrs Kamperman could not come because of heart problems, her husband wrote. Hugenholtz was in Geneva and thus he too was unable to testify. Because the whereabouts of the defendant himself were unknown, the subpoena was posted on the wall of the courthouse at 466 Herengracht. During the trial the court would also look into a financial crime, a question of fl.100,000 in missing securities which Briedé had confiscated from a notary. It remains unclear whether Briedé turned this Jewish property over to the *Sicherheitsdienst* or kept it himself, but the whole affair smacks of embezzlement. There is little hard evidence, however, and we have no way of telling if Briedé succeeded in stealing enough to live off the interest following his relocation to Germany.

On May 13, 1949 the court found Briedé guilty on all counts. In their sentence the judges added that Briedé actively helped carry out criminal measures, which had as their goal the deportation and extermination of the Jews. Furthermore, he "did not even shrink from personally turning over young Jewish children to their mortal enemy, and did so on a number of occasions."[8]

The court decided that he should be executed, but the sentence never reached Briedé. The only thing we know is that he was able to look back on his career as a Jew hunter for seventeen years, in complete freedom. The man who hunted down so many people had apparently vanished into thin air. His last known address was

Lintorf, a village belonging to the municipality of Ratingen, not far from Essen, in the Ruhr Valley. His address was 5 Am Speckamp. It is a roomy, terraced house on a side street of the main road. Today it is somewhat dilapidated, with flower pots in front of the windows. He died on New Year's Day 1962, at 6:30 in the evening, fifty-eight years old, a completely unknown figure. It is a true mystery how Willem Briedé, a man who led the hunt for thousands of innocent people, somehow managed to get off scot-free.

His partner in crime, Wim Henneicke, was not so lucky. He stayed in Amsterdam, keeping a low profile from late 1943 until September 1944. Little is known about his activities during this time. He was no longer working at the office on Noorder Amstellaan, which had been the home of Colonne member Frans Takkert since mid-October. The building on Adama van Scheltemaplein gradually emptied out as well. The archive was still located there, as was the cafeteria for the members of the SD who worked across the street at the school on Euterpestraat. Today there is nothing left of the building, as it was hit in a bombardment carried out by twenty-four Typhoons. The planes had taken off in Deurne, in the province of Brabant, which had already been liberated.[9] It was intended to be a precision operation, which would deal a fatal blow to the *Sicherheitsdienst*, the scourge of the Dutch resistance. But the mission was a failure. According to unofficial figures, a sum total of four SD men were killed. The bombs fell after most of the staff had just left the dining hall. As the two buildings were now unusable, the SD moved its office to a hotel. The bombardments had disastrous consequences for the neighborhood: contrary to instructions, bombs were also dropped on private homes, killing an estimated fifty civilians and wounding dozens.

By that time Wim Henneicke had already moved into a new line of work. From Mad Tuesday on, Henneicke began to focus on his future. That evening Henneicke went to see A.N.J. den Hollander of Watteaustraat in Amsterdam. Henneicke knew this man because he had once searched his home; he also knew that Den Hollander had ties to the resistance. The former head Jew hunter explained that he wanted to defect to the other side and demonstrated his good will by providing Den Hollander with a great deal of information about the organization of the *Sicherheitsdienst* and its informants. Den Hollander later wrote up a report on the visit. From this we know that that evening Henneicke ratted out his own men to the resistance: Joop den Ouden, for example, and Dries Riphagen, the two underworld figures in his own network. But he also betrayed his pal Briedé, as well as his former neighbor Van Eiken and his co-worker and fellow Colonne leader Docter. He gave the names of people who had infiltrated the Dutch underground and betrayed resistance fighters.[10]

To all appearances, Henneicke's openness was greatly appreciated by certain segments of the resistance, particular the LO, or *Landelijke Organizatie* (National Organization), which regarded him as a useful source. But it is also true that other groups found it inconceivable that they were doing business with a man like Henneicke. The so-called KP "bureau of investigation" had information on Henneicke and saw him as an infiltrator who sought to sabotage the resistance movement.[11]

It is quite likely that Henneicke was attempting to work both sides of the street. Facing the prospect of an uncertain future, he forged ties with the underground, from which he could profit after the war. On the other hand, in this way he could also infiltrate the resistance and thereby be of use to the *Sicherheitsdienst*, if the Allies failed to liberate the northern Netherlands. But Henneicke overplayed his hand, a fact that became abundantly clear on December 8, 1944. Around nine o'clock he left his ground floor flat at 79 Linnaeusparkweg, as he did every morning. He bicycled down the street toward Hogeweg. Fifty meters beyond the intersection an unknown man stepped out of the doorway of number 25. He had been able to conceal himself in a small recess. He shot Henneicke from close range: two shots to the head, one to the right arm, one to the left leg, and one through the right leg to the abdomen, coroner Dr L. Snoek later determined, after Henneicke had been taken to hospital.[12] A five-year-old boy witnessed the attack. After sixty years he is still convinced there was a second gunman, on a bicycle, a short distance behind Henneicke, who shouted out to his comrade, "This is the man!"[13]

Mrs Van Zoest, who lives around the corner on Hogeweg, the same place she was living at the time, remembers hearing the shots, but she didn't dare to venture outside.[14] She later heard that the victim was "that man with that black jacket," whom she had frequently seen cycling down the street. The neighborhood was immediately cordoned off and every house was searched, but the assailants were never found. One can gather from the chronicle of the armed resistance, *Het Grote Gebod*, that the men must have been active in the Amsterdam KP, which subsequently called the assassination "justified and necessary."[15]

After the war Amsterdam prosecutors received a letter from someone wanting to know who shot Henneicke. "Worked for the SD since July 1942. He very likely contacted the underground resistance during the last months of his life. Can't imagine this movement would have associated with people like that at that time."[16] The author of the note was a certain B. Rust, of Amsterdam. And he had another shocking piece of news for the authorities: Henneicke's widow was receiving fl.50 in benefits from the underground. Evidently Henneicke was seen by some as a resistance fighter, whose widow had a right to financial support.

The office of the public prosecutor decided to investigate the matter. The chief prosecutor himself was told by the police that it was impossible to answer the question of who committed the murder. The police heard from the resistance that Henneicke had actually provided useful information. "Yet no one sees his death as a great loss for the better Holland that will come one day," the police added.[17]

Following that was a confirmation that Maria Cornelia Henneicke-Trilling was indeed receiving fl.200 a month from the former resistance, as if she were the widow of a hero.

Wim Henneicke was buried on December 9 at the New Eastern Cemetery. He wound up with a first class location, section 79, row 10. The headstone was removed in 1983, but his remains are still there. In the spring a Japanese cherry tree blooms over his bones. It is one of the most beautiful trees in the whole cemetery.

Notes

Preface

Translator's Note

a. For the benefit of those inclined to look up the addresses mentioned in this book on a map of Amsterdam or perhaps even visit them in person, I have left all street names in the original Dutch. Thus, Amstelveenseweg and not Amstelveen Road. In the interest of clarity, however, here are translations of the most frequently used words in Dutch addresses: *straat* (street), *weg* (road), *plein* (square), *laan* (avenue), *gracht* (canal), *singel* (canal), *kade* (quay), *dijk* (dike), *wal* (embankment) and *dreef* (lane).

Notes to Chapter 1

1. Most of the information in this chapter comes from the file on Willem Hendrik Benjamin Briedé at the Central Archive for Special Justice (*Centraal Archief Bijzondere Rechtspleging*, henceforth CABR), inventory number 64373, original number BG Amsterdam 221/49. Today the CABR can be consulted at the National Archive (NA) in The Hague.
2. The information about Willem Christiaan Heinrich Henneicke comes from files on him at the CABR (as well as other sources), though he was never tried for his crimes, since he died before the liberation on December 8, 1944. The inventory number in the CABR is 107967; the original numbers are PRA Amsterdam 25135 and PF Amsterdam 13460 G.
3. See Bert Jan Flim, *Omdat hun hart sprak: Geschiedenis van de georganiseerde hulp aan Joodse kinderen in Nederland, 1942–1945* (Because their heart spoke: history of organized aid to Jewish children in the Netherlands, 1942–1945), Kampen, 1996. Starting on p. 71 of this superbly well-documented book, one can read about the role of the residents of the Utrecht River District in hiding Jewish children.

4. See the police interview of Mrs Kamperman-De Vries. On October 26, 1948 she was questioned by detective W. Prasing, the man who was most familiar with the Henneicke case. He went to see her in Utrecht, and that same day he went to Schipluiden, where he questioned Kamperman's daughter Suze. The transcripts of the interviews are in Briedé's CABR file.
5. Maria Susanna Kamperman, wife of L.J. de Bruijn, testified about the events of that day at Briedé's trial, which was held before the Fifth Criminal Division of the Special Court in Amsterdam on April 29, 1949. Briedé himself was at large and was thus tried in absentia. See the transcript of the session in Briedé's CABR file.
6. Interview with Mrs Suze De Bruijn-Kamperman by the author, August 2002.
7. Transfer receipt from the records of the Colonne Henneicke, added to the CABR files of various members of the Colonne, including Briedé.
8. Hundreds of *Berichte* have been found in the records of the Colonne Henneicke. Prior to being entered as evidence in the case against the bounty hunters, they were typed up (and initialled for verification) and added to the files. This particular *Bericht* comes from Briedé's file. Most original *Berichte* can be found in the archives of the Netherlands Institute for War Documentation (*Nederlands Instituut voor Oorlogsdocumentatie*, NIOD). Documents HSSpf 167/262 through 265.
9. Investigators from the Amsterdam Division of the Political Investigation Department (*Politieke Recherche Afdeling*, PRA) would often jot down the information they received from the Red Cross about the fate of deported Jews in pencil on the relevant *Berichte*. This was true in this case: the *Berichte* were marked "NT" for *Niet Teruggekeerd* (Did Not Return). If the date of death was known, it was also noted . The dates given here are taken from these notes.
10. See Mrs Kamperman-De Vries's statement to the Amsterdam PRA and the statement given by her daughter Maria Susanna to the Amsterdam PRA and her testimony in the trial of Willem Briedé on April 29, 1948. Transcripts in Briedé's CABR file. For ways in which one could escape from the nursery, see Bert Jan Flim, *Omdat hun hart sprak*, pp. 142–4.
11. See Bert Jan Flim, *Omdat hun hart sprak*, p. 150 and p. 404. Flipje Plas was one of the very few cases where a Jewish child was under the care of two different organizations: first the Utrecht Children's Committee and later the Loyalty Group.
12. This information was gratefully borrowed from the database kept by Bert Jan Flim.
13. Interview with Philip Plas by the author, June 2002.
14. See chapters 6 and 19 in particular.

Notes to Chapter 2

1. L. de Jong, *Het Koninkrijk der Nederlanden in de Tweede Wereldoorlog* (The Kingdom of the Netherlands in the Second World War), vol. 4, first half, p. 14. Those affected were told by management that the reason for their dismissal was "company policy."
2. J. Presser, *Ondergang* (available in English, in abbreviated form, as *Ashes in the Wind*), p. 18.
3. L. de Jong, *De Bezetting na 50 jaar* (The Occupation, 50 years on), vol. 1, The Hague, 1990, p. 69.
4. J. Presser, *Ondergang*, p. 30.
5. J. Presser, *Ondergang*, p. 31 *et seq.*, where Presser also discusses the general lack of protests against the Aryan Declaration.
6. G. Aalders, *Roof: De ontvreemding van joods bezit tijdens de Tweede Wereldoorlog* (available in English as *Nazi Looting: The Plunder of Dutch Jewry during the Second World War*), The Hague, 1999, p. 127 *et seq.*
7. J. Presser, *Ondergang*, p. 58 *et seq.*
8. L. de Jong, *De Bezetting na 50 jaar*, vol. 1, p. 83.
9. Friso Roest, Jos Scheren, *Oorlog in de stad: Amsterdam 1939–1942* (War in the city: Amsterdam 1939–1942), Amsterdam, 1998. In chapter 13, pp. 335–62, Roest and Scheren describe the preparations for a ghetto in Amsterdam as well as the process that led to this decision.
10. B.A. Sijes, *De Februaristaking* (The February strike), Amsterdam, 1978 (and most of the other books on the Holocaust listed in the bibliography).
11. L. de Jong, *De Bezetting na 50 jaar*, vol. 1, p. 104.
12. See also Bob Moore, *Slachtoffers en overlevenden: De nazi-vervolging van de joden in Nederland* (originally published in English as *Victims and Survivors: The Nazi Persecution of the Jews in the Netherlands, 1940–1945*), Amsterdam, 1998, p. 100 *et seq.*, which describes the isolation of the Dutch Jews.
13. G. Aalders, *Roof*. In chapters 6, 7 and 8 (pp. 149–211), the establishment of the bank and the two decrees on which the theft of Jewish property was based are described in detail.
14. G. Aalders, *Roof*, p. 149.
15. G. Aalders, *Roof*, p. 151.
16. Erik Somers: *Vrijgegeven door de Duitsche censuur: Fotograaf in dienst van de bezetter* (Passed by the German censor: photographer in the service of the occupier), Amsterdam, 1986. The photographs in question can be found on pages 97 and 98. They were taken by the *Stapf Bilderdienst*, a German photo press agency in Amsterdam. The negatives were not returned to the Netherlands until 1981. After the war they were taken by a Canadian soldier,

and after his death they narrowly escaped the trash heap. They were ultimately donated to the Institute for War Documentation.
17. L. de Jong, *De Bezetting na 50 jaar*, vol. 2, p. 204.
18. J. Presser, *Ondergang*, for an exhaustive description of the Jewish labor camps, pp. 175–202.
19. G. Meershoek, *Dienaren van het gezag: De Amsterdamse politie tijdens de bezetting* (Servants to authority: the Amsterdam police during the occupation), Amsterdam, 1999, pp. 216–17.
20. G. Meershoek, *Dienaren van het gezag*, p. 228.
21. J. Presser, *Ondergang*, for an in-depth description of the introduction of the Star of David, pp. 218–31.
22. J. Presser, *Ondergang*, p. 247.
23. Philip Mechanicus, *In depot: Dagboek uit Westerbork* (In depot: diary from Westerbork), Amsterdam, 1964. Journalist Philip Mechanicus described his time in Camp Westerbork in a chronicle. His story is not only extraordinarily moving but also one of the best sources about what went on there. Mechanicus was deported in one of the final transports.
24. Bob Moore, *Slachtoffers en overlevenden*, p. 145 *et seq.*
25. L. de Jong, *De Bezetting na 50 jaar*, vol. 2, p. 197.
26. For a further discussion of the Jewish Council, see also W. Lindwer, *Het fatale dilemma* (The fatal dilemma), The Hague, 1995, and H. Knoop, *De Joodse Raad: Het drama van Abraham Asscher en David Cohen* (The Jewish Council: the drama of Abraham Asscher and David Cohen), Amsterdam, 1983.
27. G. Meershoek, *Dienaren van het gezag*, p. 218.
28. G. Meershoek, *Dienaren van het gezag*. The activities of the Jewish Council are described in detail, starting on page 220 of this excellent book. In his research Meershoek relied mainly on the archives of the Amsterdam police and was in fact the first scholar to be given access to them.
29. L. de Jong, *De Bezetting na 50 jaar*, vol. 2, p. 194.
30. J. Presser, *Ondergang*. Starting on page 280 Rauter's letter to Himmler is printed in its entirety, including Himmler's handwritten comment.
31. As yet the historiography of the Netherlands lacks a biography of Albert Gemmeker. For more information, see J. Presser, *Ondergang*, pp. 326–32, and L. de Jong, *Het Koninkrijk . . .*, vol. 8, second half, p. 698 *et seq.*, and Ad van Liempt (ed.), *Andere Tijden* (Different times), Amsterdam, 2000, pp. 53–8.
32. Philip Mechanicus, *In depot*, p. 92.
33. J. Presser, *Ondergang*, pp. 221–33, for a detailed and dramatic description of this event.
34. L. de Jong, *De Bezetting na 50 jaar*, p. 203.
35. Jules Schelvis, *Vernietigingskamp Sobibor* (Death camp Sobibor),

Amsterdam, 1997. Schelvis was one of the nineteen survivors of the camp and would make history his life's work. The book, which he worked on for many years and for the purpose of which he attended every Sobibor trial, gives a complete picture of the most radical annihilation machine of the Third Reich. Many victims of the Colonne Henneicke ended up in Sobibor.

36. For various estimates of the number of Jews who went into hiding and what happened to them, see Bob Moore, *Slachtoffers en overlevenden*, p. 178 *et seq*.
37. Gitta Sereny, *Albert Speer, verstrikt in de waarheid* (originally published in English as *Albert Speer: His Battle with Truth*), New York/Amsterdam, 1995. On pages 472–4 there is a lengthy excerpt from the speech Himmler gave in Poznan to the *Gauleiter* and other leading figures of the Third Reich.
38. L. de Jong, *Het Koninkrijk* . . ., vol. 6, first half, p. 347.

Notes to Chapter 3

1. For a description of the *Einsatzstab Reichsleiter Rosenberg*, see Gerard Aalders, *Roof*, chapter 2, pp. 66–77.
2. L. de Jong, *Het Koninkrijk* . . ., vol. 6, p. 322 *et seq*.
3. G. Aalders, *Roof*, chapter 10, p. 229 *et seq*.
4. G. Aalders, *Roof*, chapter 10, p. 231 *et seq*. In addition, there is also a great deal of information about the methods of the *Hausraterfassungsstelle* in the CABR files on the members of the Colonne Henneicke, including Briedé (CABR inventory number 64373).
5. This information is taken in part from the interrogation of Willi Lages by detectives Prasing and Verduin, on March 3, 1948, included in Henneicke's CABR file, original number PRA Amsterdam 25135, CABR inventory number 107967.
6. G. Aalders, *Roof*, chapter 10, p. 231.
7. Of the fifty-four men who were counted as members of the Colonne Henneicke for the purposes of this study, only six were not members of the NSB.
8. L. de Jong, *Het Koninkrijk* . . ., vol. 6, p. 323.
9. CABR file on Aaldert *Dassen* (names in italics are pseudonyms), original number Special Court of Appeals 92/49, CABR inventory number 75087. This file contains a personal history written by Dassen during his detention, which mentions this speech by Lages.
10. The story of Harmans' fraud can be found in the CABR file on Gerrit de Groot, original number BG Amsterdam 1099B/48, CABR inventory number 456. Inside is the original of detective Posthuma's exhaustive report.
11. From Henneicke's file, CABR inventory number 107967, original numbers PRA Amsterdam 25135 and PF Amsterdam 13460 G.

12. G. Meershoek, *Dienaren van het gezag*, p. 228.
13. File on Hylke Wierda, CABR inventory number 105670, dossier numbers PRA Amsterdam 6225 and PF Amsterdam T 20137.
14. In virtually all the CABR files on the members of the Colonne Henneicke (and the other employees of the *Hausraterfassung*), a copy is enclosed of their employment contract with Lippmann, Rosenthal & Co., Sarphatistraat.
15. According to the Dutch Central Statistics Bureau, in February 2002 the guilder of 1943 was worth approximately eleven times as much as the guilder of December 31, 2001. This factor was used consistently in converting the guilder of 1943 to the euro of 2002. (*Translator's note*: all amounts in euros have been converted to US Dollars for the English edition. This was done based on values obtained from the Universal Currency Converter, http://www.xe.com/ucc, in February 2004.) All converted values are approximate.
16. Interrogation of Bernard Marinus Christiaan *Eggink*, not in his own file, but in that of Alex *Hoogers*, CABR inventory number 64195, dossier number Amsterdam Special Court 270/49 and 1048/48.
17. See Gerard Aalders, *Roof*, chapter 10, p. 231.
18. See the CABR file on Willem Briedé, CABR inventory number 64373, original number BG Amsterdam 221/49.
19. Otto Kempin, *Kriminalsekretär* for the SD and from 1943 on, the head of the Bureau of Jewish Affairs of the Amsterdam police, told detectives Prasing and Verduin in an interrogation on March 15, 1948 that Lages made this announcement, in the form of an official order, during a general meeting of the *Sicherheitspolizei*. This interrogation is quoted in the two investigators' report on the Colonne Henneicke, mimeographs of which are included in virtually all the CABR files on the members of the Colonne.
20. Interrogation of Lages by detectives Prasing and Verduin on March 3, 1948, incorporated into their report on the Colonne Henneicke.
21. File on Hugo Heinrich Berten, CABR inventory number 107766, dossier numbers PRA Amsterdam 61016 and PF Amsterdam 12496.
22. Transcript of the trial of Bruno Barend *Verlugt* on October 8, 1948, before the Fifth Division of the Special Court, Amsterdam. The transcript can be found in *Verlugt*'s CABR file, CABR inventory number 712, dossier number BRC 798/48.
23. A copy of this list, which contains not only many names but also many spelling errors, can be found in various CABR files on Colonne members, including that of *Van der Kraal*, CABR inventory number 548, dossier numbers BRC 861/48 and PRA Alkmaar 4073.
24. The standard work on the subject of Special Justice is A.D. Belinfante, *In plaats van Bijltjesdag* (The history of Special Justice after the Second World War), Assen, 1978.

25. See chapters 7 and 8.
26. See "Onderzoek naar de werkwijze van de Colonne Henneicke van de Zentralstrelle für jüdische Auswanderung" (A study of the methods of the Colonne Henneicke of the *Zentralstelle für jüdische Auswanderung*), Prasing and Verduin's report, which was deposited in nearly all the CABR files on members of the Colonne.
27. *Het Vrije Volk*, "SD-archief bewijst schuld Joden-jagers" (SD archive proves Jew hunters' guilt), April 21, 1948.
28. For example, Richard *Kopper*, a former insurance agent who was sentenced to one year's detention by a Tribunal and released in September 1946. In 1948 he was picked up again on suspicion of being involved in the hunt for Jews and given a fifteen-year prison sentence by the Special Court. The Court of Appeals eventually reduced this to ten years.
29. Quote is taken from "Onderzoek naar de werkwijze van de Colonne Henneicke" by detectives Prasing and Verduin.
30. L. de Jong, *Het Koninkrijk* . . ., vol. 6, first half, p. 349.
31. Found in Henneicke's file, CABR inventory number 107967, original number PRA Amsterdam 25135.
32. Interrogation of *Moerberg*, in his file, CABR inventory number 554, dossier number Special Court of Appeals 860/48.
33. Special Court transcript, in the file on *Saaldijk*. CABR inventory number 134, dossier number BRC 402/49.
34. The person in question is one Jacob Polak, born in 1921, of 45 Retiefstraat, No. 3. When called to testify in *Van Amersfoort*'s trial, he claimed to have been arrested four times by a member of the Colonne and to have escaped as many times. All the same, in the end he was sent to Auschwitz, which he survived, returning home a broken man. See the file on *Van Amersfoort*, CABR inventory number 64163, dossier number BG Amsterdam 1014/48.
35. From *Sweeger*'s file, CABR inventory number 507, dossier number BRC 96/49.
36. From *Dassen*'s file, CABR number 75087, dossier number BRC 92/49. This statement is taken from the personal history written by Dassen.
37. From *Rudolfs*' file, CABR number 711, dossier number BRC 776/48.
38. The statements by Pach and Allegro were taken from the aforementioned report by Prasing and Verduin.
39. *Het Parool*, October 8, 1946. It is an appeal for anyone with information about him to report to the West Precinct at 327 Nassaukade. The text continues: "A photo of H. is available at the above address. H. was a salesman by profession but in 1943 he began working for the SD and among his duties was arresting Jews. He is suspected of having made approximately 200 arrests." This was no everyday advertisement. The police would often request that

newspapers, like *Het Parool*, include these sorts of appeals on their editorial page.
40. From *Hintink*'s file, CABR inventory number 710 I and II, dossier number BRC 776/48. The quote is taken from a letter that Jannetje *Hintink-Rudolfs* wrote to the Political Investigation Department.
41. From *Rudolfs*' file, CABR inventory number 711, dossier number BRC 776/48.
42. From *Casteels*' file, CABR inventory number 501 I and II, dossier number BRC 96B/49. Quote is from a PRA interrogation of *Casteels* in Amsterdam.
43. From *Sweeger*'s file, CABR inventory number 507, dossier number BRC 96/49. The letter *Sweeger* wrote to the Labour Front in an effort to leave the *Zentralstelle* can be found in this file.
44. From *Van den Heuvel*'s file, CABR inventory number 429, dossier number 166/49. The quote is from a lengthy defense *Van den Heuvel* wrote for the appeal of his verdict. In it he portrayed himself as the savior of countless Jews, a man who did his best to help everyone. On appeal, his twenty-year sentence (the prosecution had demanded life in prison) was upheld. In 1957 he was pardoned and released.
45. From *Hoogers*' file, CABR inventory numbers 64195 and 64196, dossier numbers BG Amsterdam 270/49 and BG Amsterdam 1048/48. The quote is from a PRA interrogation. Incidentally, the detective who questioned *Hoogers* considered him "abnormal," in part because the suspect had accused the detective's colleagues of having arrested Jews themselves. It is worth noting that this accusation was not necessarily untrue.
46. From *Evertsen*'s file, CABR number 20554, dossier number Trib. Amsterdam 3084. In 1948 the PRA discovered that *Evertsen* did have at least one arrest to his name. He eventually admitted this but was never subpoenaed by the Special Court.
47. Information from his file, CABR inventory number 500, dossier number BG Amsterdam 1079/48.
48. From the court transcript, in *Hintink*'s file, CABR inventory number 710 I and II, dossier number BRC 776/48.
49. From *Elmink*'s file, CABR inventory number 451, dossier number BRC 139/49, which includes a statement from the neighbor in question, Mrs Danker.
50. This story is based on the testimony of various witnesses and on the transcript of this session of the Fifth Division of the Special Court, Amsterdam, October 15, 1948. See *Cool*'s dossier, CABR number 590 I and II, dossier number BRC 824/48.
51. Official statements about this incident in the files on *De Hout* (CABR inventory number 676 I, II and III, dossier number BRC 798/48) and *Saaldijk* (CABR inventory number 134, dossier number BRC 402/49).

52. From *Saaldijk*'s file, CABR inventory number 134, dossier number BRC 402/29. Detective Wijnand Prasing conducted a special investigation into the way *Saaldijk* arrested sick Jews, and the report on his findings is, like all his work, a model of clarity and thoroughness.
53. This can also be found in *Saaldijk*'s file.
54. In *Schipper*'s file, CABR number 642, dossier number BRC 11/49, one can read the reconstruction of this entire affair, in which both *Schipper* and *Keuling* played a role. *Keuling* eluded justice by escaping shortly before his trial and fleeing to Germany.
55. Details in the files on *Elmink* (CABR inventory number 451, dossier number BRC 139/49) and *Van der Kraal* (CABR inventory number 548, dossier number 270/49).
56. From *Gist*'s file, CABR inventory number 64347, dossier number BG Amsterdam 123/49 and PRA Amsterdam 63451.
57. J. Presser, *Ondergang*, p. 368. The pictures in *Storm* were accompanied by a sneering article which concluded with, "It wasn't hard to say goodbye."
58. Statement in the report on the methods of the Colonne Henneicke, by detectives Prasing and Verduin.
59. J. Presser, *Ondergang*, p. 373.
60. Statement by officer Karel C.B. Weeling, to his colleagues Verduin and Prasing, included in their report on the methods of the Colonne Henneicke.
61. Today this street is known as Gerrit van der Veenstraat, because "Euterpestraat" had acquired such a negative connotation for many Amsterdammers.
62. Interrogation of *Hintink*, in his file, CABR inventory number 710 I and II, dossier number BRC 776/48.
63. Report by the SS officer Otto Bene, cited in J. Presser, *Ondergang*, p. 379.

Translator's Notes
a. A kind of social club for German soldiers
b. The PRAs were the successors to the PODs, the *Politieke Opsporingsdiensten* (Political Investigative Services), which were established shortly after the liberation. The PODs were controlled by the military authority and were often staffed by people with no background in police work. The PODs were replaced in March 1946 by the PRAs, which were staffed by professionals and operated under the authority of the Ministry of Justice. That said, their basic task was the same: tracking down and interrogating Dutch collaborators. (From www.nationaalarchief.nl, the website of the Dutch National Archive.)
c. An umbrella trade union under direct control of the occupying forces, the Germans having disbanded all legitimate unions in 1942.

Notes to Chapter 4

1. From *Elmink*'s file, CABR inventory number 451, dossier number BRC 139/49.
2. This story can be found in a *Bericht* in Henneicke's file, CABR inventory number 107967, dossier number PRA Amsterdam 25135. It was almost certainly written by a co-worker, as Henneicke was not very handy with a pen and left the writing of reports to others.
3. One time such a file was stolen from Henneicke's drawer. The guilty party was one of the members of the Colonne, but Henneicke never found out who it was. When he discovered the theft, he was furious and fumed that he had lost information on 400 Jewish families. See also chapter 14.
4. In 1943 the Amsterdam police had a special Documentation Service, which specialized in gathering intelligence in Jewish circles and was not above using brute force. See Guus Meershoek, *Dienaren van het gezag*, p. 277 et seq.
5. This story was told by Colonne member Mattijs *van de Wert* during an interrogation and is included in *Elmink*'s file, CABR inventory number 451, dossier number BRS 139/49.
6. *Klingeberg*'s file (CABR inventory number 64458, dossier number BG Amsterdam 344/39) contains official statements on this incident and some correspondence.
7. Van Tol's file, CABR inventory number 344, dossier number BRC 239/49. See also the report of the special court session against Van Tol, February 25 and March 25, 1949.
8. This episode was described by *Sweeger* in his interrogation by the Amsterdam PRA, which can be found in his file, CABR inventory number 507, dossier number BRC 96/49.
9. Ibid.
10. Information about this episode can be found in the PRA interrogations, in *Cool*'s file, CABR inventory number 590 I and II, dossier number BRC 824/48, as well as in a lengthy letter from Elfriede Heinemann, written from New York. In addition I have also drawn from P.'s police record, which formed the basis for his trial before the Amsterdam Special Court, Third Criminal Division on December 16, 1948.
11. The Ans van Dijk affair is described in detail by Koos Groen, in *Als slachtoffers daders worden: De zaak van de joodse verraadster Ans van Dijk* (When victims become perpetrators: the case of the Jewish informant Ans van Dijk), Baarn, 1994.
12. L. de Jong, *Het Koninkrijk . . .*, vol. 12, p. 568.
13. Quote from *Van den Heuvel*'s detailed defense, written for the appeal of his case in December 1949. From *Van den Heuvel*'s file, CABR inventory number 429, dossier number BRC 166/49.

14. From *Van der Kraal*'s file, CABR inventory number 548, dossier number BRC 861/48. Incidentally, after the war *Van der Kraal* was arrested after a tip from the deeply disillusioned Mrs D.
15. Quote from the closing speech delivered by prosecutor Bakhoven before the Court of Appeals in the trial of *Van der Kraal*, April 1949. It can be found in the same file.
16. Statement by Poul Kaiser, in *Hintink*'s file, CABR inventory number 710 I and II, dossier number BRC 776/48.
17. From *Smit*'s file, CABR inventory number 640, dossier number BRC 32/49.
18. Cited from a PRA interrogation of Gerrit *Mijnsma*, in *Koops*' file, CABR number 64407, dossier number BG Amsterdam 220/49.
19. Hollebrands' report, from which most of this information has been taken, can be found in *Koops*' file. Part of it is also in *Schipper*'s file, CABR number 642, dossier number BRC 11/49.

Notes to Chapter 5

1. From *Mijnsma*'s CABR file, original number BRC 139/49, inventory number CABR 450 I, II and III. *Mijnsma* had previously attempted to find work as a Price Inspector, but that did not work out and he eventually ended up with the Labour Front.
2. From *Hopman*'s CABR file, original number BRC 824/48, inventory number CABR 590 I and II.
3. From *Van den Borch*'s CABR file, original number BG Amsterdam 154A/49; PRA Amsterdam 23722; inventory number CABR 64326. After his period with the Colonne Henneicke, *Van den Borch* went on to earn even more, holding various leadership positions in the NSB at a salary of fl.300 a month.
4. Letter from Mrs Van Lith, dated August 2, 1948, in the CABR file on Jacob *Gist*, original number BG Amsterdam 123/49; PRA Amsterdam 63451; CABR inventory number 64347.
5. From *Van Amersfoort*'s CABR file, original number BG Amsterdam 1014/48; CABR inventory number 64163. It was common practice for the PRA to canvas a suspect's neighborhood to find out what acquaintances knew about the person's conduct during the occupation.
6. This remark is included in the "Onderzoek naar de werkwijze van de Colonne Henneicke," Prasing and Verduin's report, which was deposited in nearly all the CABR dossiers on the members of the Colonne.
7. A number of these issues are clarified in a letter from M.H. Gelinck to the president of the Special Court of Appeals, dated February 16, 1949. The letter is in Gelinck's personal archive, which can be found at the National Archive, Gelinck Collection, no. 605, Colonne Henneicke file.

8. Described at length in chapter 7.
9. *De Volkskrant*, March 5, 1946: "Een gulden voor een jood" (A guilder for a Jew); *Trouw*, March 5, 1946: "Beroep gemaakt van joden verraad" (Betraying Jews was their profession).
10. In the file on the Colonne Henneicke, NIOD, Amsterdam, Doc. II, 317, file B.
11. Memorandum of defense counsel B. Perridon's address to the court in the trial of Bob *Verlugt* on October 8, 1948. It can be found in *Verlugt*'s CABR file, original number BRC 798/48, CABR number 712.
12. The first death sentence was handed down on October 8, 1948, in the case against the two brothers-in-law *Hintink* and *Rudolfs*. For more on this, see the records of the trial and the court's sentence in the combined CABR file on both men, original number BRC 776/48, CABR inventory number 710 I and II and 711. In October 1948 more death sentences would follow, for *De Hout*, *Hopman*, *Cool* and *Van der Kraal*, among others.
13. This statement and those immediately following it are included in detectives Prasing and Verduin's report "Onderzoek naar de werkwijze van de Colonne Henneicke."
14. Statement included in the transcript of the trial of the brothers-in-law *Hintink* and *Rudolfs*, original number BRC 776/48, CABR inventory number 710 I and II and 711.
15. This witness's testimony is also included in the records of the same session.
16. Statement included in the report by Prasing and Verduin, see notes 6 and 13.
17. Statement included in the police interrogation of Joop *Bouman*. It can be found in his CABR file, original number BG Amsterdam 863/46, CABR inventory number 61761.
18. Statement contained in the transcript of *Bouman*'s trial, in the aforementioned CABR file.
19. From police interrogations, in the aforementioned CABR file.
20. Evidence given in the trial of the brothers-in-law *Hintink* and *Rudolfs*.
21. Deposition to the Special Court, included in the aforementioned, combined CABR file (see note 12).
22. Testimony of L. Benninga, included in the combined CABR file on *Hintink* and *Rudolfs*.
23. Official statement, in English, also included in this combined CABR file.
24. Personal history of Martin *Hintink*, included in his CABR file.
25. Interrogation of *Hintink* by the Salland PRA, included in the same file.
26. Interrogation of *Hintink* by the Amsterdam PRA.
27. From the transcript of the trial of *Hintink* and *Rudolfs*, also in the same file.
28. Statement by Jannetje *Hintink-Rudolfs*, in the same file.
29. From the transcript of the session of the Special Court of Appeals in the matter of Ben *Eggink*, included in his CABR file, original number BRC

89/50, CABR inventory number 35.
30. Statement by Jan *Rudolf* to investigators, included in the same file.
31. Statement by Henk *Hopman* in a police interrogation, included in his CABR file, original number BRC 824/48, CABR inventory number 590 I and II.
32. Statement by Anna *Kroon*-Van der Meer to detectives, in the case against her brother-in-law, Tonny *Kroon*. It can be found in his CABR file, original number BRC 191/49, CABR inventory number 386.
33. Statement by Christiaan *van den Borch* during a police interrogation, included in his CABR file, original number BG Amsterdam 154A/49, PRA Amsterdam 23722, CABR inventory number 64326.
34. Testimony of J. Barend in the trial of H. *van den Heuvel*, taken from the transcript, which is included in *Van den Heuvel*'s CABR dossier, original number BRC 166/49, CABR inventory number 429.
35. See *Hopman*'s statement to detectives, in his CABR file, original number BRC 824/48, CABR inventory number 590 I and II.
36. Transcript of Van Tol's trial, in his CABR file, original number BRC 239/49, CABR inventory number 344.
37. Statement made during police questioning in the case against Van Tol, in the same CABR file.
38. Statement made to police in the case against Gerrit *Mijnsma*, in his CABR file, original number BRC 139/49, CABR inventory number 450 I and II.
39. This "transaction" can be reconstructed on the basis of *Berichte* in the aforementioned CABR file.
40. Statement made during police questioning in the case against Lambertus *Schipper*, in his CABR file, original number BRC 11/49, CABR inventory number 642.
41. From the police interrogation of Mattijs *van de Wert*, in his CABR file, original number BG Amsterdam 1099/48, CABR inventory number 64219.
42. Statement by Henk *Saaldijk* during police interrogation and the letter in question, both of which are in *Saaldijk*'s CABR file, original number BRC 402/49, CABR inventory number 134.
43. Statements by the parties involved, made during police interviews, in the case against Christiaan *van den Borch*, in his CABR file, original number BG Amsterdam 154A/49, PRA Amsterdam 23722, CABR inventory number 64326.
44. This episode was discussed by Henk *van der Kraal* during police interrogations. It is included in his CABR file, original number BRC 861/48, CABR inventory number 548.

Notes to Chapter 6

1. Alien identification card and family card in the name of Henneicke, Willem Christiaan Heinrich, at the Amsterdam Municipal Archive.
2. From Henneicke's file with Amsterdam Social Services Archive, access number 5256, inventory number 5287, dossier 104/919.
3. Details about Henneicke's employment history are taken from a "Report on the Conduct, Lifestyle, Occupations, Etc. of the Applicant and Members of His Family," written in response to Henneicke's welfare application of January 6, 1940.
4. The letter in question is included not only in Henneicke's file at Social Services, but also his dossier at the Ministry of Justice, original number PRA Amsterdam 25135, PF Amsterdam 13460 G, CABR inventory number 107967. One can also read about the repercussions of the letter in his CABR dossier.
5. Statement made by Eduard Gijsbertus *Moerberg* during a police interrogation, in his CABR file, original number BRC 860/48, CABR inventory number 554.
6. Taken from a police interview with witness Klaas Westerhoff, in the case against Christiaan *van den Borch*. It can be found in the latter's CABR file, original number BG Amsterdam 154A/49, PRA Amsterdam 23722, CABR inventory number 64326.
7. From a police interview with Mrs Steenman. It can be found in Henneicke's CABR file, original number PRA Amsterdam 25135, PF Amsterdam 13460 G, CABR inventory number 107967.
8. *Bericht* in the collection *Höhere SS- und Polizeiführer*, 262e, NIOD, Amsterdam.
9. Memorandum of Perridon's plea before the Court of Appeals in the matter of Bob *Verlugt*, in his CABR file, original number BRC 798/48, CABR inventory number 712.
10. In his CABR file, original number PRA Amsterdam 25135, PF Amsterdam 13460 G, CABR inventory number 107967.
11. Briedé's registration form can be found in his CABR file, original number BG Amsterdam 221/49, CABR inventory number 64373.
12. Statement made during police questioning, in the case against Egbertus *Elmink*, in his CABR file, original number BRV 139/49, CABR inventory number 64373.
13. Report by detective W. Prasing, in Briedé's CABR file, original number BG Amsterdam 221/49, CABR inventory number 64373.
14. This arrest was investigated by the Amsterdam PRA and described in a report in Briedé's CABR dossier, original number BG Amsterdam 221/49, CABR inventory number 64373.

15. Ibid.
16. See the relevant *Bericht* in Briedé's CABR file.
17. The complaint was filed on June 21, 1945. For more about the way it was handled, see the transcript of the trial (*in absentia*) of Willem Briedé, in his CABR file.
18. See the transcript of the trial of Eduard *Moerberg*, in which Leyden van Amstel testified against Moerberg and Henneicke. The document is included in *Moerberg*'s CABR file, original number BRC 860/48, CABR inventory number 554.
19. The attorney in question, Mr Nieuwboer, said in the trial of Lambertus *Schipper*: "In the evenings Henneicke would pay one hundred guilders or more for good tips." See the trial transcript, in *Schipper*'s CABR dossier, original number BRC 11/49, CABR inventory number 134.
20. The *Bericht* on this incident is in his CABR file, original number PRA Amsterdam 25135, PF Amsterdam 13460 G, CABR inventory number 107967.
21. Ibid.
22. Ibid.
23. Cited from a police interrogation of Herman *van Eiken*, in his CABR file, original number BRC 56/49, CABR inventory number 594.
24. Transcript of the trial of Herman *van Eiken*, in his CABR file; see previous note.
25. Personal history, written by Herman *van Eiken*, which can be found in his CABR file.

Notes to Chapter 7

1. The course of events can be pieced together from the testimony of the employees of the card catalogue: *Bertinga*, *Meiloo* and *Tomson*.
2. Interrogation of *Meiloo* by the Amsterdam POD, included in his CABR file, original number BRC 184/46, CABR inventory number 74600.
3. Police interviews with neighbors, included in *Meiloo*'s CABR file; see previous note.
4. All the members of the Colonne Henneicke the police were able to interrogate were asked how they came to work for the *Hausraterfassung*. From their answers we know that more than half, about thirty, were referred to the *Zentralstelle* by the Labour Front.
5. *Meiloo*'s contract is, like that of his colleagues, included in his CABR file. Apparently, copies of the contracts were found in the archives of Lippmann, Rosenthal & Co. and turned over to investigators.
6. Quoted from a police interrogation of *Meiloo*, included in his CABR file.

7. Quoted from a police interrogation of *Meiloo*, by detective Henk van den Broek, also included in his CABR file.
8. Transcript of the trial of Fred *Meiloo*, included in his CABR file.
9. *De Volkskrant*, March 5, 1946, NIOD, KB I 4838.
10. Excerpt from the Special Court's sentence, included in *Meiloo*'s CABR file.
11. *Tomson*'s story is taken from his CABR file, original number BRC 186/46, CABR inventory number 74605.
12. *Tomson*'s letter to the Amsterdam POD, included in his CABR file; see previous note.
13. Interrogation of *Tomson* by detective Henk van den Broek, included in his CABR file.
14. Letter from Mrs *Tomson*-Kleiman to Amsterdam POD, included in the CABR file.
15. See transcript of *Tomson*'s trial, included in his CABR file.
16. Letter by Reverend Verhoekx to the Amsterdam Special Court, included in *Tomson*'s CABR file.
17. Letter from Mrs *Tomson*-Kleiman to the Amsterdam Special Court, included in *Tomson*'s CABR file.
18. Judgment of the Court of Appeals, included in *Tomson*'s CABR file.
19. Judgment of the Court of Appeals, included in *Meiloo*'s CABR file.
20. The information about Huisman comes from the brief file on him in the National Archive; the original number is PF Amsterdam A-65428–T, CABR inventory number 107331.
21. Interrogation of *Bertinga* by the Amsterdam POD, in *Bertinga*'s CABR file, original number BRC 185/46, CABR inventory number 74603.
22. Interview of Mrs Noteboom by the Amsterdam POD, included in *Huisman*'s CABR file.

Notes to Chapter 8

1. *Het Nationale Dagblad*, June 15, 1942, p. 6, classified ads, NIOD Archive.
2. CABR file on Hermanus P.M. *Bertinga*, original number BRC 185/46, CABR inventory number 74603.
3. A copy of the contract with Lippmann, Rosenthal & Co. is in the aforementioned CABR file.
4. NSB correspondence regarding *Bertinga* in his CABR file.
5. NSB conduct report on *Bertinga*, also in his CABR file.
6. Interrogation by detective Henk van den Broek in *Bertinga*'s CABR file.
7. *Bertinga*'s letter to the Bureau of National Security in the aforementioned CABR file.
8. Transcript of *Bertinga*'s trial, in his CABR file.

9. Sentence of the Special Court, Fifth Criminal Division, in *Bertinga*'s CABR file.
10. Memorandum of defense attorney Dunselman's address to the Court of Appeals, also in *Bertinga*'s CABR file.
11. Verdict of the Court of Appeals, in *Bertinga*'s CABR file.
12. *De Maasbode*, March 6, 1946, NIOD Archive.

Notes to Chapter 9

1. This transfer receipt is one of those found in the records of the *Zentralstelle*. The investigators placed copies of a number of these receipts, including this one, in the CABR files on the members of the Colonne Henneicke, as evidence of the recordkeeping system used by the Colonne. The originals are now at the NIOD.
2. Said by Hendrik *van den Heuvel* during an interrogation, included in his CABR file, BRC 166/49, CABR inventory number 429.
3. This and other details about the Dutch Theater are from the unpublished report "Alfons Zündler and the guarding of the prison camp on 24 Plantage Middenlaan, Amsterdam," by J. Houwink ten Cate, researcher at the NIOD. He studied the role of this German guard following the outcry over the decision to honor him for helping Jewish inmates. The report is available for perusal at the NIOD. It appeared in January 1995.
4. J. Presser, *Ondergang*, p. 287.
5. Santcroos's account was enclosed with Houwink ten Cate's report on Zündler. It is part of the NIOD collection, Documents on the Deportation of Jews, II 361.
6. L. de Jong, *Het Koninkrijk . . .*, vol. 6, p. 246.
7. B. Stokvis, *Advocaat in bezettingstijd* (Lawyer during the occupation), Amsterdam, 1968, p. 9.
8. J. Houwink ten Cate, "Zündler report," p. 23.
9. J. Houwink ten Cate, "Zündler report," p. 24, cited from R. Roegholt, *Driehonderd jaar Plantage* (Three hundred years of the Plantage), Amsterdam, 1983.
10. J. Houwink ten Cate, "Zündler report," p. 25, cited from a report by S.I. Troostwijk, "Report on the Treatment of Jews during the German Occupation of the Netherlands," NIOD, Doc. II 363.
11. E. Werkman in the foreword to J. van der Kar, *Joods verzet: Terugblik op de periode rond de Tweede Wereldoorlog* (Jewish resistance: a review of the period around the Second World War), Amsterdam, 1981.
12. J. Houwink ten Cate, "Zündler report," p. 48. Cited from testimony given in the trial of a guard at the Dutch Theater.

13. Statement made during a police interview in the case against Rinus *Schutten*, in his CABR file, BG Amsterdam 142/49, CABR inventory number 64358.
14. The details about Anton *Veldhuijsen* are taken from his CABR file, original number PRA 17467 and BG 105/49, CABR inventory number 480.
15. J. Houwink ten Cate, "Zündler report," p. 48. Taken from testimony given in the trial of a guard at the Dutch Theater.
16. For background on this issue, see Elma Verhey, "Was Alfons Zündler een goede SS-bewaker in de Hollandsche Schouwburg?" (Was Alfons Zündler a good SS guard at the Dutch Theater?), an article which appeared in the magazine *Vrij Nederland*, March 20, 1983.
17. J. Presser, *Ondergang*, vol. II, p. 11; L. de Jong: *Het Koninkrijk . . .*, vol. 6, p. 258.
18. J. Houwink ten Cate, "Zündler report," chapter 8, Conclusions, p. 75.
19. The transcript of the trial is in the CABR file on Hendrik *van den Heuvel*, BRC 166/49, CABR inventory number 429.
20. Sentence of the Special Court, in the CABR file on Hendrik *van den Heuvel*, BRC 166/49, CABR inventory number 429.
21. Most of the facts about the nursery are from B.J. Flim, *Omdat hun hart sprak: Geschiedenis van de georganizeerde hulp aan Joodse kinderen in Nederland*, Kampen, 1996.
22. B.J. Flim, *Omdat hun hart sprak*, pp. 126–33.
23. B.J. Flim, *Omdat hun hart sprak*, p. 134, testimony of Semmy Woortman-Glasoog, who employed this method on several occasions.
24. B.J. Flim, *Omdat hun hart sprak*, p. 136.
25. B.J. Flim, *Omdat hun hart sprak*, p. 139.
26. B.J. Flim, *Omdat hun hart sprak*, p. 144.
27. B.J. Flim, *Omdat hun hart sprak*, p. 147.
28. B.J. Flim, *Omdat hun hart sprak*, p. 150.
29. B.J. Flim, *Omdat hun hart sprak*, p. 163.

Notes for Chapter 10

1. Statement made during a police interview, included in the CABR file on Harm Jan *van den Heuvel,* original number BG Amsterdam 159/39, CABR inventory number 64333.
2. Taken from a police report included in the aforementioned CABR file.
3. The matter was the subject of an extensive investigation, which can be reconstructed on the basis of police interrogations in the aforementioned CABR file, which also contains copies of the interrogations of Johan *Keuling* and Lambertus *Schipper*.
4. The testimony of Gobets, Koopman, Van der Kar, Barend and Wijnschenk can

be found in both police interviews and the transcript of the trial of Harm Jan *van den Heuvel*.
5. Testimony of Judith Hofman and Mrs Roet-Scheffer, which is included in the CABR file on Harm Jan *van den Heuvel*.
6. Tammenoms Bakker's report was added to Harm Jan *van den Heuvel*'s CABR file.
7. A copy of *Van den Heuvel*'s employment contract with Lippmann, Rosenthal & Co. was added to his CABR file.
8. From the transcript of the trial, which can be found in the aforementioned CABR file.
9. Sentence of the Special Court, in the CABR file.
10. Letter from G. van der Heide to the Special Court, also in *Van den Heuvel*'s CABR file.

Notes to Chapter 11

1. From an interrogation of Joseph Nicolaas *Sweeger*, included in his CABR file, original number BRC 96/49, CABR inventory number 507.
2. Remark made by Mattijs *van de Wert* during an interrogation, included in his CABR file, original number BG Amsterdam 1099/48, CABR inventory 64219.
3. Statement made by Henk *Hopman* during an interrogation, included in his CABR file, original number BRC 824/48, CABR inventory number 590 I and II.
4. Memorandum of the address given by defense counsel B. Perridon to the Court of Appeals, included in the CABR file on Bruno Barend *Verlugt*, original number BRS 798/48, CABR inventory number 712.
5. Transcript of the police interrogation of Egbertus *Elmink*, included in his CABR file, original number BRC 139/49, CABR inventory number 451.
6. Transcript of an interrogation in the case against Egbertus *Elmink*, also included in his CABR file.
7. The transfer receipt of the arrest described here was added to most of the CABR dossiers, as an example of the Column's recordkeeping practices. The information on Jan *Casteels* is taken from transcripts of interrogations, which are included in his CABR file, original number BRC 86B/49, CABR inventory number 501 I and II.
8. Interrogation of Richard *Kopper*, by detective W. Prasing, included in his CABR file, original number BRC 237/49, CABR inventory number 348.
9. This arrest is described in the police's interrogations of Gerrit *Mijnsma*, included in CABR file BRC 138/49, CABR inventory number 450 I through III.

10. The same source cited in note 9 was also used for details about this attempted arrest.
11. This arrest was discussed by Adolf *Smit* during police interrogations, included in his CABR file BRC 32/49, CABR inventory number 640.
12. From the defense attorney's plea to the Court of Appeals in the case of Adolf *Smit*. The memorandum of Perridon's plea can be found in *Smit*'s CABR file, see note 11.
13. The attempted arrest of Robby Aak was discussed by Pieter *van Amersfoort* during interrogations by the police. The transcripts are included in his CABR file BG Amsterdam 1014/48, CABR inventory number 64163.
14. This film was shown in a documentary produced by Balbo TV and broadcast by the VARA on April 28, 1985. Fragments of this film were also used in the remake of *De Bezetting* (The Occupation) by L. de Jong, in the episode broadcast on February 15, 1990.
15. The arrest of the Jews hiding above the Alcazar is mentioned in interrogations conducted in the case against Henk *Saaldijk*, included in his CABR file BRC 401/49, CABR inventory number 134.
16. The fateful arrest of A. Smit was described by Aaldert *Dassen* in a police interrogation, included in the latter's CABR file BRC 92/49, CABR inventory number 75087.
17. Statement made during the trial of Aaldert *Dassen*, from the transcript in his CABR file. For location of the file, see note 16.
18. The arrests described here were discussed by Christiaan *van den Borch* during interrogation by the police. The transcripts are included in his CABR file BG Amsterdam 154A/49, PRA Amsterdam 23722, CABR inventory number 64326.
19. This arrest, which was carried out by the two brothers-in-law *Hintink* and *Rudolfs*, was mentioned in the course of their interrogations by the police, included in the combined CABR file on both men, BRC 776/48, CABR inventory number 710 and 711.
20. Henk *Hopman* spoke to police about this arrest during interrogation; transcripts are included in his CABR file BRC 824/48, CABR inventory number 590 I and II.
21. With thanks to the present occupant of the house on Rafaelplein, Ms Joustra.
22. Information on Henk *van der Kraal* and a copy of Wörlein's letter of reference can be found in *Van der Kraal*'s CABR file, BRC 861/48, PRA Alkmaar 4073, CABR inventory number 548 and 4321.

Notes to Chapter 12

1. Letter from a relative to the judge-advocate, in the CABR file on Eduard Gijsbertus *Moerberg*, original number BRC 860/48, CABR inventory number 554.
2. Letter from H. de Gans, Hoofdweg, Amsterdam, in the same CABR file.
3. Notes by N. Bakhoven for use during the appeals case, located in the same file.
4. Report on *Moerberg* by the Bureau of National Security, in his CABR file.
5. Explanatory note written on the NSB application form, in *Moerberg*'s CABR file.
6. The details of these arrests are in W. Henneicke's CABR file, original number PRA Amsterdam 25135 and PF Amsterdam 13460 G, CABR inventory number 107967.
7. Interrogation of *Moerberg* by W. Prasing, located in *Moerberg*'s CABR file.
8. Statements made by Krikke, Kaper and Kempin during questioning by W. Prasing, in *Moerberg*'s CABR file.
9. Information taken from an interrogation of Elize van der H., who was herself the subject of criminal proceedings after the war; the interrogation can be found in the CABR file on Eddy *Moerberg*.
10. The mass arrest in Huizen is described in detail in a special report, which can be found in *Moerberg*'s file.
11. The investigation of the mass arrests in Oss is discussed in a separate report, also located in *Moerberg*'s file.
12. Levie Kool's letter of July 15, 1942, and the enclosed list of items, are in *Moerberg*'s CABR file.
13. Information contained in a letter from the director of the House of Detention II in Amsterdam. It can be found in *Moerberg*'s CABR file.
14. Transcript of *Moerberg*'s trial, November 5, 1948, included in his CABR file.
15. Notes by N. Bakhoven for use during the appeal of *Moerberg*'s sentence, also included in his CABR file.
16. Transcript of the appeal, included in *Moerberg*'s CABR file.
17. Letter written by Edna *Moerberg*-Mohan, in *Moerberg*'s CABR file.

Translator's Note

a. A portmanteau word coined during the occupation. It consists of the Dutch words *bewaren* (to keep) and *ariër* (Aryan). It referred to Aryans who accepted Jewish property for safekeeping and had a distinctly pejorative connotation, as it was often used to describe those who refused to return the property after the war was over.

Notes to Chapter 13

1. NSB report on Christoffel *de Hout*, located in his CABR file, original number BRC 798/48, CABR inventory number 676 I through III.
2. Correspondence between *De Hout* and the NSB in *De Hout*'s CABR file.
3. Gerard Aalders, *Roof*, p. 153.
4. See *De Hout*'s employment contract with LiRo, in his CABR dossier.
5. Letter from *De Hout*, dated December 5, 1944, to his parents, in his CABR file.
6. See remarks on this subject by J. Houwink ten Cate in Ad van Liempt (ed.), "Albert Konrad Gemmeker," in *Andere Tijden*, Amsterdam, 2000.
7. Transcript of the trial of Chris *de Hout*, October 8, 1948, in his CABR file.
8. Details about these arrests are taken from interrogations of *de Hout* and the testimony of investigators from the Amsterdam PRA.
9. See the transcript of the trial of Chris *de Hout*, October 8, 1948, in his CABR file.
10. The story of the Citroen family can also be found in this transcript, as well as in the records of the PRA.
11. The trials and tribulations of the Horn family can be found in both *De Hout*'s CABR file and, in part, that of Henk *van der Kraal*, original number BRC 861/48 and PRA Alkmaar 4073, CABR inventory number 548 and 4321.
12. Leo Horn has told the story in a number of interviews, including one given to the *Rotterdams Dagblad*, April 9, 1994; see also Matty Verkamman, "Het andere leven van Leo Horn" (The other life of Leo Horn) in the September 19, 1995 issue of *Trouw*.
13. See the statement given by V.S. Ohmstede to detectives and his testimony before the Special Court, in *De Hout*'s CABR file.
14. From correspondence in *De Hout*'s CABR file.
15. See the sentence of the Special Court, October 22, 1948, included in his CABR file.
16. Letter from *De Hout*'s wife, in his CABR file.
17. Letter from Christoffel *de Hout* to the president of the Court of Appeals, in his CABR file.

Notes to Chapter 14

1. Taken from an attachment to a letter written by M.H. Gelinck to H. Haga, the President of the Special Court of Appeals. Located in the National Archive, Gelinck Collection, number 605, file on the Colonne Henneicke.
2. Memorandum of the defense counsel's plea before the Court of Appeals, included in the CABR file on Tonny *Kroon*, original number BRC 191/49, inventory number 386.

3. Among the documents from the appeals case is a personal history written by *Kroon* in 1949, comprising four closely typed pages, from which this and other information is taken.
4. NSB registration form in the aforementioned CABR file.
5. Taken from the personal history mentioned above.
6. Statement by Mrs Sterman to a PRA detective, included in *Kroon*'s CABR file.
7. Statement by Mrs Liscaljet to a PRA detective, included in *Kroon*'s CABR file.
8. Statement by Mrs Teunisse to a PRA detective, included in *Kroon*'s CABR file.
9. Statement by Mrs Van Ekeren-Schneijer to PRA detective Voordenhout, included in *Kroon*'s CABR file.
10. Statement by K. ter Horst to PRA detective Voordenhout, included in *Kroon*'s CABR file.
11. Statement by D. Blom to PRA detectives, included in *Kroon*'s CABR dossier.
12. See *Het Parool*, May 14, 1947, and *Het Vrije Volk*, May 17, 1947.
13. Statements made by family members during interrogation, in the report by detective Voordenhout, included in *Kroon*'s CABR file.
14. *Kroon*'s activities in the eastern part of the Netherlands were dealt with at some length in his trial, on February 18, 1949, as well as in a report by detective Voordenhout. The latter also wrote a supplemental report on the subject, also included in the CABR file, expressing his displeasure that the Bakker group never appeared before the Special Court for its actions in Almelo. Captain Bakker himself was dead, and the other members of the group were convicted of various crimes, but hunting people was not one of them.
15. Letter from Tonny *Kroon* to his wife Jenny, in his CABR file.
16. Trial transcripts from January 21 and February 18, 1949, in his CABR file.
17. Transcript of Court of Appeals session, in *Kroon*'s CABR file.

Translator's Note
a. Many people in the Netherlands, Dutch and Germans alike, believed that this date – Tuesday, September 5, 1944 – would mark the Allied liberation of the Netherlands. Nazis and collaborators fled the country as ordinary Dutch people prepared to greet their liberators. But the invasion stalled, and the country would not be fully liberated for another eight months.

Notes to Chapter 15

1. This episode is described in a police report, written April 29, 1946 by G. Clement, who was then with the POD, but in 1943 he was still working for the

National Bureau of Investigation. This lengthy document is included in the file on Hendrik *van den Heuvel*, original number BRC 166/49, CBR inventory number 429.
2. The incidents involving Hendricus *Klingeberg* have been reconstructed on the basis of documents in his CABR file, original number BG Amsterdam 344/49, the CABR inventory number 64458.
3. Transcript of *Klingeberg*'s trial, March 11, 1949, included in his CABR file.
4. See *Het Parool*, June 7, 1946.
5. Transcript of *Klingeberg*'s trial, March 11, 1949, included in his CABR file.
6. This can also be found in the aforementioned transcript.
7. Deposition by Van Breda Vriesman, also in *Klingeberg*'s CABR file.
8. Details from the CABR file on Johannes Wilhelmus *den Ouden*, original number BG Amsterdam 21/50, CABR inventory number 64572.
9. Letter from H. de Lange, dated August 28, 1945, to the Amsterdam POD, included in *Den Ouden*'s police dossier.
10. Bart Middelburg and René ter Steege, *Riphagen*, Amsterdam, 1990, p. 18.
11. Middelburg and Ter Steege, *Riphagen*, p. 9.
12. This story is included in an official report, which is in the police record of Eddy *Moerberg*, the Colonne Henneicke's bookkeeper. The original number is BRC 860/48, and the CABR inventory number is 554.
13. More information on the *Devisenschutzkommando* can be found in Gerard Aalders, *Roof*, The Hague, 1999, p. 55 *et seq.*
14. Interrogation of pub owner Groen, in the CABR file on Bernardus Andres Riphagen, inventory number 107787.
15. *Den Ouden*'s various escapes are described in police reports in his (very incomplete) criminal record.
16. Middelburg and Ter Steege, *Riphagen*, pp. 92–105. Riphagen's CABR file, which Middelburg and Ter Steege were apparently unable to consult, also contains indications of these deals. There is a strong possibility that W. Sanders of the Bureau of National Security employed "special investigative methods." He wanted to keep the arrest of *Den Ouden* and Riphagen secret by putting them up with detectives, and in so doing extract additional information from the suspects. The police reports in Riphagen's CABR file present a complicated picture of deals and double-deals, which lie outside the scope of the present book.
17. Facts are taken from Middelburg and Ter Steege, *Riphagen*, pp. 92–105.
18. This escape is described in an interrogation of July 15, 1946, included in *Den Ouden*'s CABR file.
19. The trial transcript is missing from *Den Ouden*'s CABR file; these facts are taken from an agreement regarding his release, which *is* in his dossier.

Notes to Chapter 16

1. This incident is described in a police report in the CABR file on Hendricus Christiaan *Saaldijk*. Original number BRC 402/49, CABR inventory number 134.
2. It is in vol. 7, chapter 2, the section "Wat wist men van Auschwitz en Sobibor?" (What did people know about Auschwitz and Sobibor?), starting on p. 308.
3. Philip Mechanicus, *In depot*, Amsterdam, 1964, p. 88.
4. L. de Jong, *Het Koninkrijk . . .,* vol. 7, p. 324, footnote.
5. L. de Jong, *Het Koninkrijk . . .,* vol. 7, p. 320.
6. L. de Jong, *Het Koninkrijk . . .,* vol. 7, p. 319.
7. L. de Jong, *Het Koninkrijk . . .,* vol. 7, p. 325.
8. A copy of the transcripts of these interrogations is available in the library of the Westerbork Memorial Centre in Hooghalen.
9. See Ad van Liempt (ed.), "Albert Konrad Gemmeker," in *Andere Tijden*, Amsterdam, 2000, p. 57.
10. L. de Jong, *Het Koninkrijk . . .,* vol. 7, p. 318.
11. See the PRA's interview of Rubens and the transcript of the trial (in absentia) of W. Briedé, both included in Briedé's CABR file, original number BG Amsterdam 221/49, CABR inventory number 64373.
12. Transcript of the trial of Eddy *Moerberg*, included in his CABR file, original number BRC 860/48, CABR inventory number 554.
13. Ibid.
14. Said by Wilmke Braak during questioning by the Amsterdam PRA, included in the CABR file on Lambertus *Schipper*, original number BRC 11/49, CABR inventory number 642.
15. Transcript of the trial of Sjef *Sweeger*, November 19, 1948, in his CABR file, original number BRC 96/49, CABR inventory number 507.
16. Statement made by Mrs Ziekenoppasser-Swaab during an interview by the Amsterdam PRA, included in the CABR file on Frederik Willem *Cool*, original number BRC 824/48, CABR inventory number 590 I and II.
17. Said by Mrs T. during questioning by the Amsterdam PRA, included in the CABR file on Tonny *Kroon*, original number BRC 191/49, CABR inventory number 386.
18. Anna Voolstra and Eefje Blankevoort (eds.), *Oorlogsdagboeken over de jodenvervolging* (Wartime diaries on the persecution of Jews), Amsterdam, 2001.
19. This and the following quotes are from *Oorlogsdagboeken*, pp. 114 and 115.
20. Anne Frank, *Het Achterhuis*, Amsterdam, 1947.
21. Philip Mechanicus, *In depot*, Amsterdam, 1964, p. 24.
22. Etty Hillesum, *Het verstoorde leven: Dagboeken van Etty Hillesum, 1941–1943* (available in English as *An Interrupted Life: The Diaries, 1941–1943,*

and Letters from Westerbork), Haarlem, 1981, p. 108.
23. Letter written by Christoffel *de Hout*, in his CABR file, original number BRC 798/48, CABR inventory number 676 I through III.

Notes to Chapter 17

1. The one was not prosecuted because, according to his physician, he *could* not be prosecuted: he had suffered a serious brain injury as a result of a fall and had lost a good deal of his memory. The other (a "minor case" with only a few arrests to his name) was acquitted because a serious mistake had been made in his subpoena. He was not prosecuted a second time.
2. Information about Hugo Berten can be found in his very limited CABR file, original numbers PRA Amsterdam 61016 and PF Amsterdam 12496, CABR inventory number 107766.
3. Information about *Rademakers* in his CABR file, original number BG Amsterdam 176/49, CABR inventory number 64342.
4. For a detailed examination of this issue, as well as the problems surrounding extradition and deportation, see Friso Wielinga, *West-Duitsland, partner uit noodzaak: Nederland en de Bondsrepubliek, 1949–1955* (West Germany, partner out of necessity: the Netherlands and the Federal Republic, 1949–1955), Utrecht, 1989.
5. The details about *Keuling* are from his CABR file, original number BG Amsterdam 178/49, CABR inventory number 64354.
6. Letter from Inspector J. Haije, head of the Amsterdam PRA, dated April 7, 1948, included in *Keuling*'s CABR file.
7. Information on Engelbert Hendrik *Koops* is from his CABR file, original number BG Amsterdam 220/49, CABR inventory number 64407.
8. Quoted from the sentence of the Special Court in the *Koops* case, pronounced on May 13, 1949, included in his CABR file.
9. A significant part of the correspondence has survived and is included in his CABR file.
10. This is mentioned in the police report on the arrest of Joop *Bouman*, included in his CABR file, original number BG Amsterdam 863/46, CABR inventory number 61761.
11. Details about the arrest of Alex *Hoogers* are contained in the relevant police report, included in his CABR file, original number BG Amsterdam 270/49 and BG 1048/48, CABR inventory numbers 64195 and 64196.
12. *De Volkskrant*, December 11, 1948: "Gevlucht, berecht, gegrepen" (Escaped, tried, caught).
13. See the CABR file on Richard *Kopper*, original number BRC 237/39, CABR inventory number 348.

14. The police report on *Sweeger*'s arrest, along with the accompanying interrogations, are in his CABR file, original number BRC 96/49, CABR inventory number 507.
15. Details on *Den Ouden*'s arrest are in his CABR file, original number BG Amsterdam 21/50, CABR inventory number 64572.
16. See chapter 3 for a description of this discovery.
17. For the basic principles of Special Justice, see the two most important books on the subject: A.D. Belinfante, *In plaats van Bijltjesdag: De geschiedenis van de Bijzondere Rechtspleging na de Tweede Wereldoorlog*, Assen, 1978, and Peter Romijn, *Snel, streng en rechtvaardig: De afrekening met de "foute" Nederlanders* (Swift, harsh and fair: settling the score with Dutch collaborators), Amsterdam, 1989/2002.
18. Belinfante, *In plaats van Bijltjesdag*, p. 105.
19. Details on Petrus Johannes *Kruyver* are from his CABR file, original number Tribunal Amsterdam 1034, CABR inventory number 18669.
20. A copy of the relevant *Bericht* is included in *Kruyver*'s CABR file.
21. Also found in *Kruyver*'s CABR file.
22. Information on Johannes Arnoldus Antonius *Smid* is from his CABR file, original number Tribunal Amsterdam 2802, CABR dossier number 20231.
23. A copy of the verdict of the Tribunal in the *Smid* case is included in his CABR file.
24. In the complicated relationship between the Tribunals and the Special Courts, the legal principle "*ne bis in idem*" (or double jeopardy) did not apply, according to Professor S. Faber, in a letter to the author, August 23, 2002, although it evidently played a role in the judge-advocate's assessment of such cases.
25. He mentioned the case in an attachment to a letter to the President of the Court of Appeals, H. Haga, in which he set forth his prosecution policy. This letter of February 16, 1949, which will be discussed at some length later on in this chapter, can be found in Gelinck's personal archive, which is in the holdings of the NA, Gelinck Collection, no. 605, Colonne Hennecke file.
26. Details on Marinus *Schutten* are taken from his CABR file, original number BG Amsterdam 124/49, CABR inventory number 64358.
27. Sentence of the Special Court included in *Schutten*'s CABR file.
28. Details taken from the CABR file on Franciscus *Takkert*, original number BG Amsterdam 1099/48, CABR inventory number 64219.
29. Information taken from the CABR file on Mattijs *van de Wert*, original number BG Amsterdam 1099/48, CABR inventory number 64219.
30. See the CABR file on Richard *Kopper*, original number BRC 237/49, CABR inventory number 348.
31. Details taken from the transcript of *Kopper*'s Special Court trial, March 4 and

April 1, 1949, included in his CABR file.
32. For more on Rietveld, see Chapter 3.
33. The sentence of the court, along with all the considerations that motivated it, are included in *Kopper*'s CABR dossier.
34. Details taken from the CABR file on Nicolaas Johannes *Evertsen*, original number Tribunal Amsterdam 3084, CABR inventory number 20554.
35. Remark contained in an attachment to the aforementioned letter from Gelinck to Haga (note 25).
36. Information taken from the CABR file on Lambertus Hubert Joseph *Schipper*, original number BRC 11/49, CABR inventory number 642.
37. Information taken from the CABR file on Gerrit Hendrik *Mijnsma*, original number BRC 139/49, CABR inventory number 450 I through III.
38. Belinfante, *In plaats van Bijltjesdag*, p. 90 *et seq*.
39. The sentence of the Tribunal is included in *Mijnsma*'s CABR file.
40. The sentence of the Special Court, also included in *Mijnsma*'s CABR file.
41. See the aforementioned letter from Gelinck to Haga (note 25).
42. Gelinck makes a strong point here, but he creates a somewhat distorted impression of things, since it was unlikely that members of the Colonne Henneicke who refused to arrest Jews would be drafted into the *Wehrmacht*. At most they would be sent to Germany to work in heavy industry, as happened to *Rietveld*.
43. See Chapter 5.
44. See also Chapter 18.
45. The forceful language of the lawyers must be seen in the context of the time. Beginning in 1948, the image of Special Justice was becoming increasingly negative. The criticism from the Dutch public grew more vocal, and there were more and more stories about unjust verdicts. Everyone felt that the trials were taking too long, and the general consensus was that Special Justice was starting to outlive its usefulness. The attorneys' tone was in keeping with the general feeling in Holland about this issue.
46. Memorandum of the address to the court given by defense counsel B. Grolleman, in the CABR file on Gerrit *Mijnsma*, see note 37.
47. Memorandum of the address given by defense counsel B. Grolleman, in the CABR file on Egbert *Elmink*, original number BRC 139/49, CABR inventory number 451.
48. Memoranda of the address given by defense counsel Viskil, in the CABR file on Martin *Hintink*, original number BRC 776/48, CABR inventory number 710 I and II.
49. Memoranda of the address given by defense counsel Blom, in the CABR file on Hendrik *Hopman*, original number BRC 824/48, CABR inventory number 590 I and II.

50. Memoranda of the address given by defense counsel Perridon, in the CABR file on Adolf *Smit*, original number BRC 32/49, CABR inventory number 640.
51. Memoranda of the address given by defense counsel Nieubuur, in the CABR file on Lambert *Schipper*, see note 36.
52. Memoranda of the address given by defense counsel Jelger de Jonge, in the CABR file on Jan *Casteels*, original number BRC 96B/49, CABR inventory number 501 I and II.
53. Letters from Mrs *Tomson*, in her husband's CABR file, original number RBC 186/46, CABR inventory number 74605.
54. Letters from Mrs *Takkert*, in her husband's CABR dossier, see note 28.
55. Correspondence between Mr and Mrs *Van Eiken* in the CABR file on Hermanus *van Eiken*, original number BRC 56/49, CABR inventory number 594.
56. Letter from father *Van den Borch* in his son's CABR file, original number BG Amsterdam 154A/49 and PRA Amsterdam 23722, CABR inventory number 64326.
57. Letter from the mother of Henk *Saaldijk* in her son's CABR file, original number BRC 402/49, CABR inventory number 134.
58. Letter in the CABR file on Hendrik *van der Kraal*, original number BRC 861/48 and PRA Alkmaar 4073, CABR inventory number 548 and 4321.
59. Letter in the CABR file on Martin *Hintink*.
60. Letter in the CABR file on Henk *Hopman*.
61. Letter in the CABR file on Adolf *Smit*.
62. Sentence in the CABR files on *Elmink* and *Mijnsma*.
63. Sentence in the CABR files on *Eggink* and *Hoogers*. The original number of *Eggink*'s file is BRC 89/50, CABR inventory number 35.
64. Sentence in *Koops*' CABR file.
65. Sentence in *Klingeberg*'s CABR file, original number BG Amsterdam 344/39, CABR inventory number 64458.
66. Sentence in the CABR files on *Rudolfs* and *Hintink*. The original number of *Rudolfs*' file is BRC 776/48, CABR inventory number 711.
67. Sentence in the CABR file on Cornelis *Rietveld*, original number BG Amsterdam 1079/48, CABR inventory number 5000.
68. Note by G.E. Landemeijer in the CABR file on Anton *Veldhuijsen*, original number PRA 17467 and BG 105/49, CABR inventory number 480.
69. It is obvious that the Special Court of Appeals knew that many of the death sentences would never be carried out. In a letter to the author (August 27, 2002), Peter Romijn wrote: "After all, the SC of A was aware of the essence of the clemency policy, if not the exact guidelines underlying it, and apparently it did not want to impose any death sentences that were certain to be commuted to life imprisonment."

70. In his book *Snel, streng en rechtvaardig*, Peter Romijn also comes to the conclusion that the pardons were based on government policy and not on the principles of the sovereign.
71. *In plaats van Bijltjesdag*, p. 559. The clemency policy could hardly have come as a surprise for Belinfante. As a high-ranking official in the Ministry of Justice, he was party to the decision-making process that led up to it.
72. Memorandum of the address given by defense counsel Blom in the CABR file on Frederik *Cool*, original number BRC 824/48, CABR inventory number 590 I and II.
73. Letter from *Cool*'s sister and from her attorney, La Croix, in *Cool*'s CABR file.

Notes to Chapter 18

1. Memorandum of the address given by defense counsel Blom, in the CABR file on Hendrik Wouter *Hopman*, original number BRC 824/48, CABR inventory number 590 I and II.
2. Tump looked into this question in the course his investigation of Hendricus *Klingeberg*, according to information in the latter's CABR file, original number BG Amsterdam 344/49, CABR inventory number 64458.
3. Details about Sjef *Sweeger*'s background are taken from the memorandum of the address that his attorney, P. Smink, gave to the court. It can be found in *Sweeger*'s CABR file, original number BRC 96/49, CABR inventory number 35.
4. Letter from Mrs *Saaldijk*-Stoutenbeek, dated March 31, 1948, to the attorney general's office, included in the CABR file on Henk *Saaldijk*, original number BRC 402/49, CABR inventory number 134.
5. Quoted from the official report on the arrests in Zuilen, included in the CABR file on Lambert *Schipper*, original number BRC 11/49, CABR inventory number 642.
6. Remark made by Franciscus van Tol during a PRA interrogation, included in his CABR file, original number BRC 2339/49, CABR inventory number 344.
7. Remark made by Egbert *Elmink* during a PRA interrogation, included in his CABR file, original number BRC 139/49, CABR inventory number 451.
8. Quoted from a PRA interrogation of Johannes Bernardus *Bouman*, included in his CABR file, original number BG Amsterdam 863/46, CABR inventory number 61761.
9. Remark made by Jacobus Adrianus *Gist* during a PRA interrogation, included in his CABR file, original number BG Amsterdam 123/49 and PRA Amsterdam 63451, CABR inventory number 64347.
10. Quoted from a PRA interview with Frouwina S., who was one of *Moerberg*'s

victims after his period with the Colonne Henneicke. At that time, he was working for the Amsterdam police. Interview included in *Moerberg*'s CABR file, original number BRC 860/48, CABR number 554.
11. Statement taken from a PRA interrogation of Christiaan Cornelis *van den Borch*, included in his CABR file, original number BG Amsterdam 154A/49 and PRA Amsterdam 23722, CABR inventory number 64326.
12. Statements taken from an official report on Alexander Dirk *Hoogers*, included in his CABR file, original number BG Amsterdam 270/49 and BG Amsterdam 1048/48, CABR inventory number 64195/6.
13. Statement taken from an official report on Hendrik *van der Kraal*, included in his CABR file, original number BRC 861/48 and PRA Alkmaar 4073, CABR inventory number 548 and 4321.
14. Remark taken from an official report on Martinus *Hintink*, included in his CABR file, original number BRC 776/48, CABR inventory number 710 I and II.
15. Remark can be found in Briedé's CABR file, original number BG Amsterdam 221/49, CABR inventory 64373.
16. See CABR file on Henk *Saaldijk*.
17. See CABR file on Egbert *Elmink*.
18. Testimony from Maria Jostmeijer (and others) in the CABR file on Anton *Veldhuijsen*, original number PRA 17467 and BG 105/49, CABR inventory number 480.
19. Refer to the sentence given to *Veldhuijsen*, in his police record.
20. See the CABR file on Henk *Klingeberg*.
21. See the CABR file on Frans van Tol.
22. See the CABR file on Jaap *Gist*.
23. Letter included in the CABR file on Henk *van den Heuvel*, original number BRC 166/49, CABR inventory number 429.
24. Letter from Aaldert *Dassen* to Attorney General Langemeijer, included in his CABR file, original number BRC 798/48, CABR number 676 I through III.
25. See the CABR file on Christiaan *van den Borch*.
26. See a note by G.E. Langemeijer in the CABR file on Chris *de Hout*, original number BRC 798/48, CABR number 676 I through III.
27. See the CABR file on Sjef *Sweeger*.
28. See the CABR file on Christiaan *van den Borch*.
29. See the CABR file on Henk *Hopman*.
30. See the CABR file on Henk *van der Kraal*.
31. Statement can be found in the CABR file on Jan *Rudolfs*, original number BRC 776/48, CABR inventory number 711.
32. See the CABR file on Anton *Veldhuijsen*, original number PRA 17467 and BG 105/49, CABR number 480.

33. See the CABR file on Aaldert *Dassen*.
34. See the CABR file on Lambert *Schipper*.
35. Letter written by Herman *van Eiken*, included in his CABR file, original number BRC 56/49, CABR inventory number 594.
36. Quoted from an interrogation of Jaap *Gist*, see his CABR file.
37. Police report in *Veldhuijsen*'s CABR file, original number PRA 17467 and BG 105/49, CABR number 480.
38. See Lieven Saerens, *Vreemdelingen in een wereldstad: Een geschiedenis van Antwerpen en zijn joodse bevolking* (Strangers in a metropolis: a history of Antwerp and its Jewish population), Antwerp, 2000.
39. Michael R. Marrus and Robert O. Paxton, *Vichy et les Juifs* (available in English as *Vichy France and the Jews*), Paris, 1981.
40. Susan Zuccotti, *The Holocaust, the French and the Jews*, New York, 1993.
41. Christopher R. Browning, *Ordinary Men: Reserve Police Battalion 101 and the Final Solution in Poland*, New York, 1993.
42. *Ordinary Men*, p. 47.
43. *Ordinary Men*, p. 85.
44. *Ordinary Men*, p. 145.
45. Stanley Milgram, *Obedience to Authority*, New York, 1974.
46. *Ordinary Men*, p. 185.
47. J. Hofman, *De Collaborateur*, Meppel, 1981. For this book the author studied fifty-two patients who had been subjected to psychiatric examinations, all of whom had been given lengthy prison sentences by the Special Courts. Between 1949 and 1964 they were under observation at a psychiatric clinic in Utrecht.

Notes to Chapter 19

1. Quoted from "Onderzoek naar de werkwijze van de Colonne Henneicke," the report by PRA detectives Prasing and Verduin, which was deposited in the police records of virtually all the members of the Colonne.
2. Letter from Gelinck to the president of the Court of Appeals, H. Haga, in which he sets forth his prosecution policy. This letter of February 16, 1949 can be found in Gelinck's personal archive, which is in the holdings of the National Archive, Gelinck Collection, no. 605, file on the Colonne Henneicke.
3. This list of discharged personnel can be found in the CABR files of most of those concerned, including Henneicke, original number PRA Amsterdam 25135, CABR inventory number 107967.
4. Report from the PRA in the CABR file on Willem Briedé, original number BG Amsterdam 221/49, CABR inventory number 64373.

5. Quoted from a PRA interrogation of Tonny *Kroon*, included in his CABR file, original number BRC 191/49, CABR inventory number 386.
6. Note in Briedé's CABR file.
7. Information taken from the transcript of the relevant Special Court session, in Briedé's CABR file.
8. Sentence in Briedé's trial, in his CABR file.
9. This is described in Frank van Kolfschooten, *De Koningin van Plan Zuid: Geschiedenissen uit de Beethovenstraat* (The queen of Plan Zuid: stories from Beethovenstraat), Amsterdam, 1997, pp. 82 *et seq*.
10. Information taken from Henneicke's CABR file, original number PRA Amsterdam 25135 and PF Amsterdam 13460 G, CABR inventory number 107967. It contains a list of names which Henneicke had allegedly given to the resistance.
11. See also K. Norel in *Het Grote Gebod: Gedenkboek van het verzet in LO en LKP* (The great commandment: chronicle of the resistance in the LO and LKP), vol. 1, Bilthoven, 1951, pp. 540–42.
12. Facts on Henneicke's assassination from: Linnaeusstraat Precinct Crime Reports, Municipal Police Archive, archive 5225, inventory number 6283.
13. Conversation with the author, January 2003.
14. Conversation with the author, March 2002.
15. K. Norel in *Het Grote Gebod*, vol. 1, pp. 540–42.
16. Note in Henneicke's CABR file.
17. Correspondence in Henneicke's CABR file.

Bibliography

Aalders, Gerard. *Roof: De ontvreemding van joods bezit tijdens de Tweede Wereldoorlog.* The Hague: Sdu, 1999. Published in English as *Nazi Looting: The Plunder of Dutch Jewry during the Second World War.* Oxford: Berg Publishers, 2004.

Aalders, Gerard, and Coen Hilbrink. *De affaire-Sanders, spionage en intriges in herrijzend Nederland.* The Hague: Sdu, 1996.

Arendt, Hannah. *Eichmann in Jerusalem: A Report on the Banality of Evil.* New York: Viking Press, 1963.

Asscher-Pinkhof, Clara. *Sterrekinderen.* The Hague: Leopold, 1946.

Belinfante, A.D. *In plaats van Bijltjesdag: De geschiedenis van de Bijzondere Rechtspleging na de Tweede Wereldoorlog.* Assen: Van Gorcum, 1978.

Berkley, K. *Overzicht van het ontstaan, de werkzaamheden en het streven van de Joodse Raad voor Amsterdam.* Amsterdam: Plastica, 1945.

Blom, J.C.H. *Crisis, bezetting en herstel: Tien studies over Nederland 1930–1950.* The Hague: Universitaire Pers Rotterdam, 1989.

Boas, J. *Boulevard des Misères: Het verhaal van doorgangskamp Westerbork.* Amsterdam, 1985.

Browning, Christopher R. *Ordinary Men: Reserve Police Battalion 101 and the Final Solution in Poland.* New York: HarperCollins, 1993.

———. *The Path to Genocide.* Cambridge: Cambridge University Press, 1995.

———. *Nazi Policy, Jewish Labor, German Killers.* Cambridge: Cambridge University Press, 2000.

Bullock, A. *Hitler: A Study in Tyranny.* New York: Harper & Row, 1964.

Charité, J., ed. *Biografisch woordenboek van Nederland.* 5 vols. Amsterdam: Nijhoff, 1985–2002.

De Haan, Ido. *Na de ondergang: De herinnering aan de Jodenvervolging in Nederland, 1945–1995.* The Hague: Sdu, 1997.

De Jong, L. *Het Koninkrijk der Nederlanden in de Tweede Wereldoorlog.* 24 Vols. The Hague: Sdu, 1969–91.

———. *De Bezetting na 50 jaar*. 3 vols. The Hague: Sdu, 1990.
Faber, Sjoerd, and Gretha Donker. *Bijzonder gewoon: Het Centraal Archief Bijzondere Rechtspleging en de "lichte gevallen."* Haarlem: More, 2000.
Fest, Joachim C. *Hitler, eine Biographie*. Berlin: Ullstein, 1973.
Fishman, Joël. "De Joodse oorlogswezen, interview met Gesina van der Molen." In *Zevende Jaarboek van het Rijksinstituut voor Oorlogsdocumentatie*. Zutphen: Walburg Press, 1996.
Flim, Bert Jan. *Omdat hun hart sprak: Geschiedenis van de georganiseerde hulp aan Joodse kinderen in Nederland, 1942–1945*. Kampen: Kok, 1996.
Frank, Anne. *Het Achterhuis*. Amsterdam: Bert Bakker, 1947.
Friedlander, S. *Nazi Germany and the Jews: The Years of Persecution*. London: Weidenfeld & Nicholson, 1997.
Goldhagen, D. *Hitler's Willing Executioners: Ordinary Germans and the Holocaust*. New York: Knopf, 1996.
Groen, Koos. *Als slachtoffers daders worden: De zaak van de joodse verraadster Ans van Dijk*. Baarn, 1994.
Haffner, S. *Kanttekeningen bij Hitler*. Amsterdam: Roularta, 1978.
Herzberg, Abel. *Amor fati: Zeven opstellen over Bergen-Belsen*. Amsterdam: Moussault, 1946.
———. "Kroniek der jodenvervolging 1940–1945." In *Onderdrukking en verzet: Nederland in oorlogstijd*. Amsterdam: Moussault, 1950.
———. *Tweestromenland: Dagboek uit Bergen-Belsen*. Amsterdam: Arnhem, 1950.
———. *Eichmann in Jeruzalem*. The Hague: Bert Bakker/Daanen, 1962.
Hilberg, R. *The Destruction of the European Jews*. New York: Holmes & Meier, 1985.
———. *Perpetrators, Victims, Bystanders*. New York: HarperCollins, 1992.
Hillesum, Etty. *Het verstoorde leven: Dagboeken van Etty Hillesum, 1941–1943*. Haarlem: Amerigo, 1981.
Hirschfeld, G. *Nazi Rule and Dutch Collaboration*. Oxford: Berg Publishers, 1988.
Hofman, J. *De Collaborateur: Een sociaal-psychologisch onderzoek naar misdadig gedrag in dienst van de Duitse bezetter*. Meppel: Boom, 1981.
Houwink ten Cate, J.Th.M. "Het jongere deel: Demografische en sociale kenmerken van het jodendom in Nederland tijdens de vervolging." In *Jaarboek van het Rijksinstituut voor Oorlogsdocumentatie 1989*. Zutphen: Walburg Press, 1989.
Houwink ten Cate, J.Th.M., and N.K.C.A. in 't Veld. *FOUT: Getuigenissen van NSB-ers*. The Hague: Sdu, 1992.
Huizing, Bert, and Koen Aartsma. *De Zwarte Politie, 1940–1945*. Weesp: De Haan, 1986.
In 't Veld, N.K.C.A. *De SS en Nederland*. The Hague: Sijthoff, 1987.
Jackel, E., and J. Rohwer eds *Der Mord an den Juden im Zweiten Weltkrieg*. Frankfurt: Fischer, 1987.

Kershaw, Ian. *Hitler, 1889–1936: Hubris*. London: Allen Lane, 1998.
———. *Hitler, 1936–1945: Nemesis*. London: Allen Lane, 2000.
Klein, P.W. *Kaddisj voor Isaäc Roet (1891–1944)*. Amsterdam: Contact, 2001.
Klemperer, Victor. *Tot het bittere einde: Dagboek 1933–1945*. Amsterdam: Atlas, 1997.
Knoop, H. *De Joodse Raad: Het drama van Abraham Asscher en David Cohen*. Amsterdam: Elsevier, 1983.
Knopp, Guido. *Hitler: eine Bilanz*. Berlin: Goldmann, 1995.
Koker, David. *Dagboek geschreven in Vught*. Amsterdam: VanOorschot, 1977.
Kooy, G.A. *Het echec van een "volkse" beweging: Nazificatie en denazificatie in Nederland, 1931–1945*. Utrecht: Hes, 1982.
Kristel, Conny. *Geschiedschrijving als opdracht: Abel Herzberg, Jacob Presser en Loe de Jong over de jodenvervolging*. Amsterdam: Meulenhoff, 1998.
Kuiper, Arie. *Een wijze ging voorbij: Het leven van Abel J. Herzberg*. Amsterdam: Querido, 1997.
Lindwer, W. *Het fatale dilemma*. The Hague: Sdu, 1995.
Manasse, Peter. *Verdwenen archieven en bibliotheken: De verrichtingen van de Einsatzstab Rosenberg gedurende de Tweede Wereldoorlog*. The Hague: NLBC, 1995.
Marrus, Michael R., and Robert O. Paxton. *Vichy et les Juifs*. Paris: Librairie générale française, 1981.
Mechanicus, Philip. *In depot: Dagboek uit Westerbork*. Amsterdam: Polak & Van Gennep, 1964.
Meershoek, Guus. *Dienaren van het Gezag: De Amsterdamse politie tijdens de bezetting*. Amsterdam: Van Gennep, 1999.
Michman, J. *Met voorbedachten rade*. Amsterdam: Meulenhoff, 1987.
Middelburg, Bart, and René ter Steege. *Riphagen*. Amsterdam: Arbeiderspers, 1990.
Milgram, Stanley. *Obedience to Authority*. New York: HarperCollins, 1974.
Moore, Bob. *Victims and Survivors: The Nazi Persecution of the Jews in the Netherlands, 1940–1945*. London: Arnold, 1997.
Mulisch, Harry. *De zaak 40/61: Een reportage*. Amsterdam: De Bezige Bij, 1962.
Norel, K., et al. *Het Grote Gebod: Gedenkboek van het verzet in LO en LKP*. Vol. 1. Bilthoven, 1951.
Presser, J. *De Nacht der Girondijnen*. Amsterdam: Vereniging ter bevordering van de belangen des boekhandels, 1957.
———. *Ondergang: De vervolging en verdelging van het Nederlandse jodendom 1940–1945*. 2 vols. The Hague: Staatsuitgeverij, 1965.
Roegholt, R. *Amsterdam na 1900*. The Hague: Sdu, 1993.
Roest, F., and J. Scheren. *Oorlog in de stad: Amsterdam 1939–1942*. Amsterdam: Van Gennep, 1998.
Romijn, Peter. *Snel, streng en rechtvaardig: De afrekening met de "foute" Nederlanders*. Amsterdam: Olympus, 2002.

Roseman, Mark. *De Villa, Het Meer, De Conferentie: Wannsee, 20 januari 1942*. Amsterdam: Balans, 2002.

Saerens, Lieven. *Vreemdelingen in een wereldstad: Een geschiedenis van Antwerpen en zijn joodse bevolking*. Tielt: Lannoo, 2000.

Schelvis, Jules. *Vernietigingskamp Sobibor*. Amsterdam: De Bataafsche Leeuw, 1997.

Schrijvers, Piet. *Rome, Athene, Jeruzalem: Leven en werk van prof. dr. David Cohen*. Amsterdam, 2000.

Sereny, Gitta. *Albert Speer, verstrikt in de waarheid*. Amsterdam: Contact, 1995.

Sijes, B.A. *Studies over jodenvervolging*. Assen: Van Gorcum, 1974.

——. *De Februaristaking*, Amsterdam: Becht, 1978.

Sluiser, Meyer. *Er groeit gras in de Weesperstraat*. Amsterdam: Parool, 1947.

Somers, Erik. *Vrijgegeven door de Duitsche censuur: Fotograaf in dienst van de bezetter*. Amsterdam: Sijthoff, 1986.

Stokvis, Benno. *Advocaat in bezettingstijd*. Amsterdam: Polak & Van Gennep, 1968.

Van Beek, Flory A. *Flory*. Amsterdam: Arena, 2000.

Van Bockxmeer, J.M.L., et al. *Onderzoekgids Archieven Joodse Oorlogsgetroffenen*. The Hague: Nijgh & Van Ditmar, 1998.

Van Dam, C. *Jodenvervolging in de stad Utrecht*. Zutphen: Walburg Press, 1985.

Van der Heijden, Chris. *Grijs verleden: Nederland en de Tweede Wereldoorlog*. Amsterdam: Olympus, 2001.

Van der Zee, Nanda. *Om erger te voorkomen: De voorbereiding en uitvoering van de vernietiging van het Nederlandse jodendom tijdens de Tweede Wereldoorlog*. Amsterdam: Meulenhoff, 1997.

Van Gelder, Henk. *De Spookschrijver: Het raadsel Jacques van Tol, tekstschrijver*. Amsterdam: Amber, 1992.

Van Kolfschooten, Frank. *De Koningin van Plan Zuid: Geschiedenissen uit de Beethovenstraat*. Amsterdam: Veen, 1997.

Van Liempt, Ad, ed. "Albert Konrad Gemmeker." In *Andere Tijden*. Amsterdam: Veen, 2000.

Verhey, Elma. *Om het joodse kind*. Amsterdam: Nijgh & Van Ditmar, 1991.

Voolstra, Anna, and Eefje Blankevoort, eds. *Oorlogsdagboeken (. . .) over de jodenvervolging*. Amsterdam: Contact, 2001.

Voordewind, H. *De Commissaris vertelt*. The Hague: Daamen, 1949.

——. *De Commissaris vertelt verder*. The Hague: Daamen, 1950.

Wielek, H. *De oorlog die Hitler won*. Amsterdam: Boek en Courantmij, 1947.

Wielinga, Friso. *West-Duitsland, partner uit noodzaak: Nederland en de Bondsrepubliek 1949–1955*. Utrecht: Het Spectrum, 1989.

Zuccotti, Susan. *The Holocaust, the French and the Jews*. New York: Basic Books, 1993.

Zwaan, J., ed. *De Zwarte Kameraden*. Weesp: Van Holkema & Warendorf, 1994.

Index

Note: The following abbreviations/ codes are used in the index

CH   = Colonne Henneicke
DT   = Dutch Theater
J/a = Jewish adult († indicates death, name of camp is given where known)
J/c = Jewish child († indicates death, name of camp is given where known)
JC   = Jewish Council
SC   = Special Court
SP   = *Sicherheitpolitzei*
ZCC = *Zentralstelle* card catalogue department

Aak, Robby (J/c) 118–19
Aalders, Gerard (historian) 20, 27, 137
Algemeen Handelsblad (newspaper) 167
Alkmaar 160, 165
Allegro, Maurits (JC employee) 35, 59
Allied bombardments 17, 19, 217
Amersfoort concentration camp 13, 158–9
Ammerstol 5, 81
Amstelveenseweg Prison 92
Amsterdam
  Amstel Station 2–3
  Central Station 14, 100, 114
  Communist instigated strikes 10
  ghetto preparations 8–9, 12
  Main Synagogue, Tulpstraat 30–4, 60
  municipal police force 15, 28, 52
  Special Courthouse 59
Amsterdam Health Authority 39
Amsterdam Police Battalion 15, 44
Amsterdam Social Services 75
Andriesse-Keyl, Mrs (J/a †, Auschwitz) 148
anti-Semitism
  German 6
  within Colonne Henneicke 130, 162, 202–5, 209, 210
Apeldoornse Bos psychiatric center: deportation of patients 16–17
Arbeitseinsatz (forced labor) 44, 167
  call up of Jewish Council staff 43–4
  deportation of children and elderly 15, 40, 168
  introduction of *kopgeld* (premiums) 28
  measures 13–14
  sham postal service (Great Lie) 17
  summonses and deportations 14, 15
  see also bounty hunters
Arbeitskontrolldienst (Labor Supervisory Agency) 151
Arnhem 25, 26, 151
arrests 114–25

257

1941: February round-ups 9–10
1942: July/October raids 13–16, 210
1943: intensification 37–45
1943: June raid 110, 180
1944: July/August raids 130–4
of children and elderly 15, 39–42
Floortje Citroen hunt 140–1
handicapped and sick 15, 35, 39–40, 71–2
hunts and tracking down 44, 46–7, 62, 95, 128, 134, 138
and Jewish Council role 13–15
penal cases 18, 38, 51, 57, 62, 69, 105, 122
"street cases/patrols" 38, 54
use of violence 10, 54–5, 103, 108–9
Zentralstelle lists and records 32–3
see also betrayals; deportation(s)
Asman-Del Valle, Mrs (J/a †) 123–4
Asscher, Abraham (JC co-chairman) 10, 13
sent to Westerbok 44
Auschwitz death camp 16, 101, 108, 110
De Lange family 161
Ferares family 116–17
first deportees 14–15
Heinemann family 51
Hes-Parfumeurs family 133
murder of Apeldoornse Bos patients 16–17
survivors 132, 140, 148, 161, 184–5
Van Dien, Rubens, Koopman families 117
Aus der Fünten, Ferdinand (*SS-Hauptsturmführer*) 13–14, 60, 106, 168, 204
and bounty hunting 85, 86
and deportations 15, 16–17, 100, 102

postwar justice 174
AVRO (Dutch broadcasting company) 6

Bacherach, Simon (J/a) 163
Bakhoven, N. (attorney general) 54, 127, 135
Bakker, Captain 151–2
Bakker, G. (PRA investigator) 175
Barend, Jacob (DT employee: witness) 69, 110
Barneveld group 78
BBC Dutch news division 171
Beekvliet hostage camp 16
Belder, J. (J/a) 204
Belgium
  deportations 17, 210
  house clearances 19
Belinfante, Professor A.D. 197
Benninga, L. (J/a) 65
Benninga Nopol, Catharina (J/a †) 65
Beppie (*V-Frau*) 129–30, 165
Berg, Commandant Karl Peter (Camp Amersfoort) 158
Berichte (arrest reports) 99, 103, 108, 180, 181, 188
  Colonne Heinnecke archives 31, 35, 49, 52–3
  for confiscated goods 78
  in Henneicke's name 83
  Mrs V.'s betrayals 46, 47
  Utrecht arrests (June 1943) 1–4
Berten, Hugo Heinrich (German/CH) 29, 75, 109, 173, 214
Bertinga*, Hermanus Petrus Maria (ZCC) 85, 86, 87, 88, 89, 91, 92, 199
  arrest and interrogation 95–6
  early life and career 93–5
  embezzlement/imprisonment 95
  NSB membership 93, 94–5

trial, sentence, execution 96–8, 196
Zentralstelle application and employment 93–4
betrayals 40, 46–57
 among Jews 52–3
 and CH records 46, 49
 film record of hiding place 119–20
 Houthakker family 48
 "Jew traps" 50–7
 see also V-Frauen
Beugeltas, Bernard (J/a) 117–18
Blanken, Günter (informant) 132
Blom*, Daniel (J/a: survivor) 148
Blom, G.W. (attorney) 135, 191, 200
Boersma, H. 82
Böhmcker, H. (Amsterdam CC commissioner) 8, 9
 and blackmail of Jewish Council 10–11
Bonenkamp, Inspector H. (Amsterdam police) 156
Bontenbal, Abraham 164
bonus payments 18, 28–9, 38, 46, 58–74, 85, 189–90, 199, 210
 Bertinga's disclosures 95–6
 and betrayals 47
 and closure of Jewish Council 43–4
 and lifestyle of CH members 59–60
 and postwar trials 61, 62, 195
 receipts/proof of payments 31, 60–4, 189–90, 195
Botti, Inspector (PRA investigator) 164
Bouman*, Joop (CH) 63–4, 177, 181, 189, 195, 202, 203, 206
Bouman, Riki 63–4
bounty hunters 114–15
 arrests and internment 177–8
 contracts 26–7
 final justice 195–6
 tribunals 179–87

see also bonus payments; Colonne Henneicke; postwar investigations/trials
Brandes, Lea (J/c) 130–1
Brand, Jacob (JC employee) 61
Breda jailbreak (1952) 174
Bremen 87–8
bribery 69–70, 73
Briedé, Willem (CH) 33, 43, 79–82, 199
 anti-Semitism 202, 204
 as bounty hunter 1–5, 47, 114, 124
 as Colonne leader 80–3
 disappearance into Germany and death 216–17
 early life and career 27, 79
 as head of fur department 214–15
 knowledge of Jews' fate 169
 and subordinates 36–7, 61, 115, 209
 trial and sentence in absentia 75, 173, 197, 216–17
Brillenslijper, Jacob (J/a †) 130–1
Broeksma, C.J. (paramedic) 39
Brouwer family: and racial laws 47–8
Browing, Christopher (author) 211–13
Büchenbacher, Sofie (J/a) 99
Buchenwald concentration camp 170
Buchholz, R. Dahmen von (Nazi) 15, 28
Bureau of Jewish Affairs 15, 129, 146, 161, 215
 and arrest premiums/bonuses 18, 28, 62–3
 arrests and informants 47, 52–3, 120
Bureau of National Security 113, 127, 133, 163, 186
Busnach, Maria (shelterer) 117–18

Camp De Harskamp 208
Camp Duinoord, Scheveningen 89

card catalogue department 21, 30, 59, 105
  Jews' identity cards and deportees records 85
  postwar investigations/trials 86, 87–92, 189, 195–6
  staff 85–92, 94, 95, 200
Casteels*, Jan 36, 116, 180, 184, 214
  trial sentence and appeal 192, 196, 198
Central Bureau for Jewish Emigration, see Zentralstelle für jüdische Auswanderung
Central Synagogue, Amsterdam 30–4, 60
Chefsitzung 6–7, 9
Citroen, Florence Rosette (Floortje), (J/c †, Sobibor) 140–1, 144
Citroen, Marcus (J/a) 140
Citroen-Sluys, Louise (J/a: †, Sobibor) 140
Clement, G. (Amsterdam police) 155
Cohen, Abraham (J/a †, Vught) 73, 74
Cohen-Godhelp, Mrs (J/a) 116
Cohen, Professor David (JC co-chairman) 10, 13
  sent to Westerbork 44
Cohen, Virrie (childcare worker) 106
Colijn, C.J. (lawyer) 145
collaborators
  postwar imprisonment/prosecutions 30, 159, 179
  study of mental states 213
Colonne Docter 21
Colonne Harmans 21, 22–5
Colonne Henneicke 25, 209
  anti-Semitism 102, 115, 202–5, 209, 210
  arrest documents and totals 32–3, 44
  Ausweis (identification cards) 29
  bookkeeping and records 128–9
  bribery, fraud and corruption 69–74, 214
  brutality and gun toting 29, 36, 82, 140, 151, 158, 162, 163, 204–5
  closure of organization 44, 199, 214–19
  funding of organization 47
  genocide role 191
  goods/people-tracking transition 114–15
  group knowledge of Jews' fate 166–72
  informants 27, 47
  intensification of hunts 37–45
  and Jewish Council 43
  lifestyles of personnel 59, 84, 210
  and NSB membership 34, 115, 201–2, 211
  personnel backgrounds and characters 199–215
  postwar repentance and religion 207–9
  and Public Prosecutor 188–9
  refusals to work 36–7
  salaries and allowances 26–7, 58, 67–74
  see also bonus payments; postwar investigations/trials
Colonne Ragut 21
Colonne Stork 21
Cool*, Frederik (CH) 38, 50–2, 70, 170, 184–5, 189, 214
  death sentence and appeal 198
curfew imposition 13

Dachau concentration camp 167
Da Costastraat, Amsterdam internment camp 159
Dassen*, Aaldert (CH) 34, 46–7, 120–1, 189, 208

trial and sentence 121, 206
Davids, Emanuel (J/a) 109
death camps 16
De Boer, Eelkje (J/a: survivor/witness) 122–3
decrees and sanctions
   First LiRo Decree (August 1941) 11, 49
   Second LiRO Decree (May 1942) 11–12, 21, 27, 49
Defense Division (*Weerafdeling*, WA) 9
De Graaf, Piet 164
De Haan-Moscou, Bertje (J/a †, Auschwitz) 108–9
De Haan, Simon (J/a †) 108
De Hoop, Lena (J/a †) 110
De Hoop, Mr and Mrs (J/a †) 109–10
De Hout*, Christofel (Chris) (CH) 38–9, 44, 137–44, 171–2, 214
   Camp Westerbork (LiRo) appointment 137, 139
   CH activities 137–8
   confiscation of money/valuables 139, 142
   as *Landwacht* commandant 138, 139–40
   Nazi sympathies 138–9
   NSB membership 137, 138
   NSKK driver 137, 139
   trial and sentence 140, 143, 207
   witnesses' testimonies 142–3
De Jong, Loe (author/historian) 8, 15, 30, 53
   and bounty payments 28
   on deportations 103
   and fire at Dutch Theater 100
   and totals of arrests 32
   on transportation of furniture 20, 21
   and wartime knowledge of Holocaust 167, 170, 171

De Jonge, Jelger (defense attorney) 192
De Lange, H. (J/a: Auschwitz survivor/witness) 161
Delden-Hofman, Judith (J/a) 110
Delden, S. (J/a †, Auschwitz) 110
De Leeuw-Cardozo, Judith (J/a: survivor/witness) 122
De Leeuw-Cardozo, Liena (J/a †, Auschwitz) 122
De Leeuw, Rosetta (J/a) 71
Del Valle family (J/a) 123–4
Demmink-Oostinga, Mrs (shelterer) 140
Den Bosch 26
Den Hartoch*, Celine (J/a) 73–4
Den Hollander, A.N.J. 217
Den Ouden*, Joop (CH) 68, 72–3, 121–2, 159–61, 178, 183, 203, 214, 215, 217
   arrest and sentence 163–5
   early life and police record 159–60, 200
   fraud and property misappropriation 160–1
   as postwar informant 164–5
   sex trade/black market connections 161
Department for Tracking Jewish Goods 42–3
deportation(s) 4
   administrative machinery 21
   Apeldoornse Bos patients 16–17
   assembly points 99–100
   on closure of Jewish Council (1943) 43–4
   deportee lists 85
   Eichmann's quotas 9–10, 13, 44
   exemptions (*sperren*) 14–15, 101–2
   of families 40
   financing of 11, 12

German policy 12
and "missing" Jews 18
organizational structure 12–13
sperren (exemptions) 14–15, 34, 38, 101, 102, 142, 147
transfer receipts (*Wachezettel*) 4, 32, 116, 181, 188
transportation 100
"voluntary emigration" 12
the Depression (1930s) 200, 201, 210, 213
Deutsche Zeitung in den Niederlanden 8
Deventer Dagblad 169
Devisenschutzkommando (German agency for Jewish money/securities) 163
De Volkskrant 60
De Vos, Maria (witness) 157
De Winter, Isaac (J/a: survivor) 204
De Wit, Mr (resistance) 140–1
Dienaren van hetgezag (Servants to Authority) (Meerhoek) 28
Dienststelle Westen (ERR Administrative Office for the West) 19
Docter, Piet (Colonne head) 23–4, 26, 27, 34, 78, 79, 217
Domestic Forces (resistance organization) 142, 163, 177
and postwar justice for bounty hunters 177, 178
Drenthe deportation depot 14, 15
Drijf, Mrs J. (J/a) 130–1
Dukker, Mr and Mrs (J/a †) 81
Dunselman, A. (attorney) 97
Dutch Communist Party, strikes and demonstrations 10
Dutch Jews
commando groups 9–10

confiscation of property/valuables 11
extent of knowledge of ultimate fate 166–72
extermination strategy 11, 166, 167, 171, 216
German occupation restrictions and purging 6–13
registration/identity cards 6–9, 10–11, 38–9, 85
sexual assaults 113, 157–8
suicides 6, 166–7
see also arrests; deportation(s); escapes
Dutch Military Mission in Germany 176
Dutch National Socialist Movement, *see* NSB (*Nationaal-Socialistische Beweging der Niederlande*)
Dutch Press Agency 7
Dutch Reformed Teacher Training College 105–6
Dutch Theater (Amsterdam) deportation depot 4, 15, 31, 39, 99–107, 117
atmosphere and numbers held 101
and CH personnel 99, 102–3, 108–10, 112, 182, 189
closure 44, 214
deportee records 4, 32, 105
escapes 34, 57, 69, 81, 82, 101–5, 109, 205, 206
German guards 99, 101, 102, 103–4, 105, 106
and Jewish Council 99, 100, 101, 102
as a memorial 106–7
security guards/bribery 34, 81, 99, 102, 103, 104, 106
Dutch Volunteer Legion 116

Eastern Front Medal (*Ost Medaille*) 116
Egger family (J/a †, Auschwitz) 141
Egger, Selma (J/c: †, Auschwitz) 141
Eggink*, Ben (CH) 27, 195, 203, 214
Eichmann, Adolf: deportations policy 13, 14, 16, 17
Eindhoven 140
Einsatzstab Reichsleiter Rosenberg (ERR) 19, 20, 180, 185, 203
  Hauptarbeitsgruppe Niederlände (Main Task Force for the Netherlands) 19
  Sonderkonto HR II account 27
Elias, J. (police officer) 26, 29
Elmink, Egbert (CH) 38, 42, 46, 79, 80, 83, 115–17, 201, 203, 205, 214
  trial and sentence 183, 191, 195, 196, 198
Emmanuel, Markus, Martha and 8 children (J/a/c) 83
Emmerik, Vogeltje (J/a †, Auschwitz) 42
Endlösung der Judenfrage philosophy 18
English Security Police in Germany 176
ERR, *see Einsatzstab Reichsleiter Rosenberg*
escapes 50–1, 52–3, 118, 131
  donning of SS uniforms 105
  Eberhard Rebling 131
  from Dutch Theater 34, 57, 69, 81, 82, 101–5, 109, 205, 206
  from nursery 105–6
  organization of hiding places 105–6
  postwar CH personnel 163, 164–5, 174–5, 177–8
  Robby Aak (child) 118–19
Evangelical Lutheran Church 75

Evertsen*, Nico (CH) 37, 58–9, 184–6, 189
  interrogation and confession 185–6
executions
  Ans van Dijk (*V-Frau*) 53
  mass 170–1
  strikers (Feb 1941) 10
  of war criminals 197
  Zentralstelle staff 59, 91, 98, 196
Expositur (subdivision of Jewish Council) 101
extradition procedures
  failures 174, 176, 177
  impotence of Dutch authorities 177

Federation of Playground Associations 48
Ferares, Salomon and Frieda and 4 children (J/a/c †, Auschwitz) 116–17
Flim, Bert Jan (author) 105, 106
forced labor
  and international law 13–14
  see also Arbeitseinsatz
France
  deportation quotas 13, 17, 210
  house clearances 19
Frank family
  Anne's diary 171
  arrest 131, 133, 161
  company 205
  hiding place 123
Frank, Simon (photographer) 177
Franken, J. (acting Amsterdam city manager) 8
Friesland 5
furniture clearance 185
  fraud and corruption 22–5, 62, 69, 71, 82, 149–50, 216
  postwar claims for return 89–90

registration and inventory system 1, 20–1, 34
transportation 19, 20, 21, 27
furs
  appropriation 152, 160, 215
  Hausraterfassungsstelle department 44, 129, 173, 214, 215

Gallasch, Max (J/a: witness) 90
Gelinck, Marinus H. (Judge-Advocate) 31–2, 113, 212
  on CH brutality and corruption 108, 214
  CH personnel trials 136, 145, 180–4, 186, 187, 189, 216–17
  and CH premiums 189–90
  and dismissed cases 180, 181–2
  passing of death sentences 59–60, 88, 104, 113, 153, 187
  and Special Court lawyers 190–4
  strategy as judge-advocate 187–90
Gemmeker, Albert Konrad (Westerbork commandant) 16, 168
  War Crimes Tribunal/sentence 16
genocide policy 18
Germans/Germany
  anti-Semitism 6
  and ex-Colonne Henneicke personnel 215
  racial laws 48
Gestapo agents 29–30
Gist*, Jacob (CH) 42–3, 51, 58–9, 82, 203, 206
Gits, Jaap (CH) 209
Glauberg, Dr (Auschwitz experimental doctor) 122
Gobets, Machiel (JC employee) 38, 62, 109, 110
Gompertz, Kaatje (J/a) 50
Gompertz, Lodewijk (J/c) 49–50

Greek Jews 17
Groenman, Hartog (J/a) 99
Groenman-Polak, Hester (J/a) 99
Grolleman, B.N. (SC lawyer) 190–1
Groningen 26, 112, 153
Groot, Gerrit de (inventory clerk) 25
Gulf of Lübuck naval disaster 159

Haarlem 10, 58, 165, 173
Haga, H. (president, Special Court of Appeals) 189
The Hague 13, 18
Haije, Inspector J. (PRA head) 175
Halverstad, Felix (JC employee) 105
Hansen, Mrs (witness) 158–9
Harmans (Colonne head) fraud incident 22–5, 69, 82
Harster, Dr Wilhelm (SP commander) 13, 18, 168
Hassel, Untersturmführer E. 46
Hausraterfassungsstelle (Office for the Registration of Household Effects) 1, 20, 26, 56, 114, 170
  branch offices 26–7
  Colonnes (subdivisions) 1, 2, 21
  Department for Tracking Jewish Goods 42–3
  fur department 44, 129, 173, 214, 215
  inventory system/staff 20–1, 111–12, 128, 146, 180
  and Municipal Employment Office 201, 202
  NSB membership 21
  records 60
  see also card catalogue department
Haye, Chief Inspector (PRA) 31
Heinemann, Elfriede (J/a) 50–1
Heinemann family (J/a †, Auschwitz) 51
Hendrik Mining Camp, Brunssum 208

Henneicke-Trilling, Maria 218–19
Henneicke, Wim (CH) 46, 70, 82, 86, 124, 127, 155, 214
  anti-Semitism 202
  appearance and character 78–9, 84, 199, 209
  assassination and burial 61, 75, 154, 173, 218–19
  betrayal of colleagues 217–18
  career/employment 76–8
  CH finances and bonus payments 62–3, 69, 82–3
  Colonne appointment and leadership 25–6, 79, 80
  day-to-day working system 34–7
  documents and records 32–3, 60, 83, 128
  dossier 79, 83
  early life, marriages, children 75–6
  ideological background 34–5
  informants and funding 47
  NSB membership 77
  post-Colonne organization 217–18
  and subordinates 36, 115, 209
  threats and extortion 72
  Utrecht arrests 1–5
Herbschleb-Hooyer, Christina (shelterer: witness) 118
Hermes, Mrs (shelterer) 203–4
Hes-Parfumeurs family (J/a/c †, Auschwitz) 133
Het Parool (newspaper) 149, 158
Het Vrije Volk (newspaper) 30, 31, 148
Hidde ter Horst, Klaas (J/a) 147–8
hiding places 33, 51, 54, 123–5, 167
  Alcazar film record 119–20
  Frank family 123
  for Jewish children 2, 5, 105–6
  Rebling house 130–1
Hillesum, Etty (JC employee) 171

Hilversum 10
  raid 162–3
Himmler, Heinrich 9, 16, 18, 171
Hintink*, Martin (CH) 35, 36, 44, 50, 115, 122–3, 199, 202, 204, 207, 214
  confessions and statements 66–7, 189, 195
  trial and sentence 62–3, 64, 67, 198
  witness support 194
Hintink-Rudolfs, Jannetje 35–6, 67
Hitler, Adolf 19, 168, 203
Hofman, J. (psychiatrist) 213
Hollebrands, John (police detective) 55–7
Hollebrands, Mrs (witness) 55–7
the Holocaust 16, 94, 167
  Dutch Theater memorial 106
  wartime knowledge of 167, 171
Hoogerheide internment camp 175
Hoogers*, Alex (CH) 36–7, 177–8, 180, 200, 203, 214
  Gestapo agent and alias 177
  trial in absentia/death sentence 178, 195
Hooghalen train station 14
Hopman*, Henk (CH) 58, 68, 69, 70, 114, 117, 124, 207, 214
  trial and sentence 191–2, 198, 200
Hopman-Boogers, Mrs 194
Horn, Leo (J/a: resistance/survivor) 141–2
house clearances 17, 19–20, 185
  and housing for CH members 71–2
  inventory lists and system 20–1, 69–70
  transportation 20, 21–2
Houthoff, Justice H. (Special Court) 194
Houwink ten Cate, Johannes 103–4, 168

Hovestad-Iprenburg, Mrs (shelterer) 139
Hugenholtz, Rev. B.T. (Jew shelterer) 81, 216
Huisman*, Pieter (ZCC) 6, 85, 90, 92, 95
Huisman-Noteboom, Francisco 92
Huizen (town) 130
"hunger winter" (1944) 112

identification
 cards 8–9, 10–11, 85
 HR numbers and cards 21
 yellow star/Star of David 13, 170, 175
IJmuiden (port) 6, 58
informants 52–4, 163–4
 Beppie (*V-Frau*) 129–30
 Betje W. (*V-Frau*) 164
 as CH income source 70–1
 network 2
 premiums/rewards 18, 44
 V-Frauen (*Vertrauensfrauen*) 47, 52–3
 V-Männer (*Vertrauensmänner*) 132
inventory system 21, 69–70
IVB4 (*Sicherheitspolizei* bureau) 13, 14

Jacobs, Alexander (DT employee: witness) 43
Jacobs, Mozes (JC employee) 62
 at Westerbork 64
Jäger, G. (J/a: survivor) 130–1
Jäger-Teixeira de Mattos, Mrs G. (J/a: survivor) 130–1
Jessurun de Mesquita, Samuel (J/a) 150
Jew hunters, *see* bounty hunters
Jewish children
 arrests 39–42

 deportations/deaths 40, 42
 education 10–11
 in hiding/safe houses 2, 5, 105
 "orphans"/orphanages 15, 105
 see also Jewish nursery
Jewish Community 10, 12, 14, 15, 30, 106
Jewish Council
 blackmail by Germans 10
 chairmen 10, 13, 44
 closure and staff deportation (1943) 43–4, 214
 and Dutch Theater 99, 100, 101, 102
 employees 59, 204
 establishment 10
 and forced labor measures 13–14
 and the Great Lie 17
 and Jewish nursery 104
 and labor camps for men and boys 12
 moral conduct debate 15
Jewish nursery 4, 5, 40, 44
 childcare training 104
 closure 106, 214
 escapes and their organization 104–6
 rescue of children 105–6
Jews, *see* Dutch Jews; non-Dutch Jews
jodenbegunstiging (favoritism toward Jews) 89, 90, 92, 103
Joodsch Weekblad (Jewish Council newspaper) 10, 14
Joods Verzet (Jewish resistance) (Van der Kar) 102
Joseph, Bernard (SD: *V-Mann*) 132
Juliana, Queen
 and clemency appeals 136, 143, 154, 182, 198, 209
 opposition to capital punishment 197

Kaay (police investigator) 24
Kamperman-De Vries, Dirkje (shelterer) 2, 3, 216
  freeing of Appie de Leeuwe 5
Kamperman, Suze (shelterer) 2, 3, 4
Kampman, Herman 152
Kaper, Abraham (Bureau of Jewish Affairs) 62–3, 129, 134, 161, 214, 215
Keizer, Philip (J/a) 109
Keizer, Poul (J/a: witness) 54
Kempin, Otto (German Chief Inspector) 28, 62, 120, 129, 130
  Oss rest home arrest 131–2
Kerkhoven, Detective Frits 164
Keuling*, Johan (CH) 40–1, 56, 109
  trial and death sentence in absentia 175, 197
Keuling-Challa, Anna 175
Kisch, Professor I. (J/a) 48
Klijn, Henk (*Einsatzstab Rosenberg* employee) 62
Klingeberg*, Henk (CH) 48, 70, 157–9, 201, 204, 214
  Camp Amersfoort trial and sentence 158–9
  death sentences 159
  imprisonment at Neuengamme, Vught and Da Costaraat camps 159
  postwar trial and sentence 157–9, 196
  psychological examination and report 159
  violence and sexual assault charges 157–9, 205
Kolff, P. (attorney) 184
Kolfschoten, Minister (Catholic People's Party) 197
Konzentrationslager Herzogenbusch (Vught) 17

Kool, Levie (J/a †) 133–4
Koopman, Emanuel (J/a †, Auschwitz) 117
Koopman-Hijman, Alida (J/a †, Auschwitz) 117
Koopman, Joseph (J/a: Auschwitz survivor) 139–40
Koopman, Samson (J/a †, Auschwitz) 117
Koopman, Samson (JC employee) 61, 103, 109
Koops*, Engelbert (CH) 54–6, 175–7
  exile and death 176–7
  trial and death sentence in absentia 176, 195, 197
Koot, H. (WA) 9
Kopper*, Richard (CH) 116–17, 189
  postwar trial and sentence 178, 183–4, 196
Koster-Horn, Sophie (J/a: survivor) 141
Kraan, Willem (Dutch Communist) 10
Kreefel S.J. (J/a †) 130–1
Krikke, Police Officer 129, 132, 133
Kristallnacht 6
Kroon*, Tonny (CH) 44, 68, 145–54, 170, 189, 199, 210, 214
  brutality and abusiveness 145–8, 152–3
  early days/family life 145–6
  family testimony 149
  Hausraterfassung staff member 146
  hunting-down resistance fighters 145
  Nijverdal affair 151–2
  post-CH activities 151–2
  seizure of Jewish property 150
  trial and sentence 152–4, 197, 198
  witnesses' testimony 148–53
Kroonenburg, Theresia (J/c †, Auschwitz) 117

Kroon-Klumper, Jenny 148, 150–1, 153
Kroon-Van der Meer, Anna 68, 149, 150
Kroon-Wolfrat, Mrs C.S. 149
Kruyver*, Piet (CH) 179–80
Kuiper, Maarten (SD) 161
Kulle, J.H. (German witness) 151

labor camps 12, 16
Lages, Willi (SP chief) 13, 18, 21–2, 23, 25, 168, 204
  and CH involvement 28–9, 156, 214
  deposition on Colonne Henneicke 214
  introduction of *Arbeitseinsatz* 28
  June 1943 raid 43–4
  postwar 174
Lam (CH) 214
Landelijke Organizatie (LO: National Organization) 217
Landstorm (Dutch Waffen-SS unit) 215
Landwacht (NSB militia) 44, 121, 138, 175, 182, 187, 208, 215
Langemeijer, G.A. (SC prosecutor) 97
Langemeijer, G.E. (attorney general) 97, 195–6, 206, 207
Leeuwe, Appie de (J/c) 3, 4
Leiden student protests 7
Leijden van Amstel, Jozeph (J/a) 82
Lentink-De Boer, Mrs (shelterer) 83
Lesegeld, Wilhelm (J/a) 204–5
Levantkade camp, Amsterdam 142
Lippmann, Rosenthal & Co. (LiRo)
  organizational links 191
  records 185
  roofbank 11, 19, 20
  Westerbork branch 137
  Zentralstelle employment contracts 26, 44, 58, 79, 87, 92, 94, 111, 202

Liscaljet, Mrs (J/a: shelterer/witness) 146
Lodeizen, Willem (resistance member: J/a †, Auschwitz) 121–2
Loeb, Norbert (J/a: witness) 90
Low German Reformed Church 57
Loyalty Group 5, 106

Maastricht 26
  House of Detention 164
Mad Tuesday 215–16, 217
Mauthausen concentration camp 10, 13, 14
Mechanicus, Philip (J/a: journalist) 14, 167
  Westerbork diary 167, 171
Meerhoek, Guus (author) 28
Meiloo, Anna 86–7
Meiloo*, Fred/Frans (CH) 85, 92, 95
  life history 86–8, 200
  trial/execution 88–9, 91, 97, 98, 196
Mensink, Evert Jan (police sergeant) 66
Metzelaar, Marianne (grandmother: J/a †, Sobibor 4
Metzelaar, Victor, Bertha and 2 children (J/a/c †, Sobibor) 2, 4–5
Middelburg, Bart (journalist) 162, 163
Mijnsma*, Gerrit (CH) 58, 71, 116, 117–18, 190, 200, 214
  trial and death sentence 186–7, 191, 195, 196
Milgram, Stanley (psychologist) 212
Moerberg*, Eduard Gijsbertus (Eddy) (CH) 33, 78, 82, 161, 169, 203, 214, 215
  arrests/raids 127–8
  early life and marriage 126–7, 128
  interrogation and trial 128–9, 132–3
  NSB membership 127
  sentence and appeal 134–6, 197

Moerberg-Mohan, Edna 127, 134, 135–6
Mogendorf, Simone (J/a †) 81
Molenaar, Revd (chaplain) 208
Moorland Reclamation Society 77
Mozer family (J/a †, Auschwitz) 148
Muiderpoort train station 43
Municipal Bureau of Public Records 8
Municipal Employment Office 200, 201
Municipal Welfare Bureau (later Amsterdam Social Services) 75, 77
Mussert, Anton (NSB head) 79, 137, 138

Nagel, G. (SS-*Oberscharführer*) 89
Nak, Piet (Dutch Communist) 10
National Bureau of Investigation 155
Nationale Jeugdstorm (Dutch Nazi youth group) 87
National Institute for War Documentation (RIOD) 30, 103, 167, 168
  Zentralstelle archive discovery 31–4
National Labour Front 58, 182
National Socialists/Socialism 38, 137, 138, 216
National-Sozialistische KraftfahrerKorps (*Brigade Luftwaffe*) 95
Nazis/Nazism
  and causes of political criminality 213
  deceptions and lies 17
  Poznan meeting (October 1943) 18
  Reserve Polizeibataillon 101 members 211
the Netherlands
  1930s/'40s economic crisis 200, 201, 210
  anti-German mood (1943) 105

anti-Jewish laws 6–7
anti-pogrom strikes (Feb 1941) 10
Declaration of Aryan Origin 7–8
definition of Jewishness 7–8
Eichmann visit/quotas 13
German decrees and sanctions 7–9, 11–12, 21, 27, 49
German invasion (May 1940) 6
judenrein plan 17
protests against anti-Semitic measures 13
registration of businesses 7–8
Neuengamme concentration camp 92, 159
New Israelite Hospital 5, 83
Nieubuur, J.M. (attorney) 192
Nieuwenhuizen, J. (resistance) 203
non-Dutch Jews: deportations 12, 13
non-Jews: protests against anti-Semitic measures 13
Noorder Amstellaan 127
Nouwen-Van Hommert, Beppie 64, 70
NSB (*Nationaal-Socialistische Beweging der Niederlande*) 9, 15, 103, 201
  ATL (*Algemeen Toezicht Leden*) network 137
  and ex-Colonne Henniecke personnel 215
  and *Hausraterfassung* staffing 21
  membership 180, 182, 187, 188, 209
  postwar justice 177
  and *Zentralstelle* staffing 87, 93, 201
NSKK (Nazi transportation organization) 94, 137, 170
NSNAP (Dutch Nazi Party) 112–13, 201
nursery, *see* Jewish nursery

Obedience to Authority (Milgram) 212
Oberlandesgerichte (German appellate courts) 174
Office of the Public Prosecutor 30
Office of Public Records 8, 13
Ohmstede, V.S. (resistance/witness) 142–3
Omdat hunhart sprak (Because Their Heart Spoke) (Film) 105, 106
Omnia Treuhand organization 95
Ondergang/Doom (Presser) 8, 16
Ordinary Men (Browning) 211
Ordnungspolizei (Order Police, ORPO) 10
Ossendrijver, André (J/c †) 40–2, 169, 175, 202
Ost Medaille mit Verwundetenabzeichen (Eastern Front Medal with wound badge) 116
Ottenstein, Hans Simon (RIOD) 30
Oudinga*, (CH) 82

Pach, Abraham (JC employee: witness) 35, 178
Peeper-De Swarte, Estella (J/a †, Sobibor) 4
Peeper, Eliazar (J/a †, Sobibor) 4
Péron, Juan (Argentinian president) 164
Perridon, B. (attorney) 60–1, 78, 118, 192
Pijtak, Pieter (witness) 70
Pimentel, Henriëtte (nursery director) 104
Plas, Flipje (J/c) xi, 2–3, 4, 5, 216
Polak, Raphael (DT employee: witness) 102, 103, 110
Polak, Sara (J/a) 99
Poland 34, 42, 167, 169
  deportations to 13, 48, 78, 109, 130, 132, 133, 135
  massacres of Jews at Józefów and Lomazy 211, 212
  occupation and genocide 171, 210–11
Polderweg train station 43
Political Investigation Department (PRA) 30, 149, 175
Political Investigation Service (POD) 72, 73, 86, 92, 161
Polizei Freiwilligen Battalion Niederlände (Dutch Volunteer Police Battalion) 151
Portuguese-Israelite Synagogue, Amsterdam 100
Posthuma, Inspector J. 23–5
Postumus, Professor N.W. (RIOD founder) 167
postwar investigations/trials 30, 59–60
  bonuses issue 195
  CH archives 29–31, 60
  dossiers 4, 30, 32, 38, 48, 67, 73, 87, 108
  Dutch/German war criminals 174
  extraditions and German courts 174
  families' support 192–4, 206
  lawyers participating 190–4
  lists of arrested Jews 32
  pardons 125, 136, 154, 196–7, 206
  prosecutions and public opinion 173, 181
  prosecutor's office
    bonuses issue 61
    report 31–2, 61
  survivors' testimonies 48, 50–1
  witnesses' testimonies 32, 61–74
  see also Special Courts; tribunals
Pouw-Van der Horst, Betje (J/a: witness) 158
Pranger, Gerard (witness) 178

PRA (*Politieke Recherche Afdelingen*), see Political Investigation Department
Prasing, Wijnand (PRA investigator) 30, 31, 59, 114, 183–4, 214
  on Briedé 79–80
  interrogations 128–9, 191
  investigation into arrests of sick and disabled 39
  report on Colonne Henneicke's records 32, 33
  statement on bonus payments 67
Presser, Jacques (historian) 8, 28, 34, 100, 103, 167
Presser, Yte and Joke (J/c †, Sobibor) 40, 42
Preusz (Theater guard) 4
Prins-Goel, Suze (J/a) 49–50
Prins, Nico (J/a) 49–50
property/possessions
  acquisition by CH members 150
  looting and thefts 20, 39, 73, 138, 152, 162, 172
  recovery postwar 73–4, 140
  registration 1, 20–1, 34, 114
  seizure by Germans 11–12, 17
  and Stewardship Institute 133, 134
  transportation to Ruhr Valley 20
  see also furniture clearance; furs; valuables
Provincial Employment Office 87
Puls, A. (removal company) 20, 21
pulsen ("to rob") 20

Rademakers*, Jaap (CH) 173–4, 214
  trial and sentence in absentia 174
Radio Oranje 171
Ragut, (*Haus.*) 114
Rassenschande (sexual relations with Jewish women) 104, 109

Rauter, Hans Albin (SS official) 9, 10
  attack and hostage shootings 152
  and deportation numbers 16, 168
  and extermination of Jews 167–8
Ravensbrück concentration camp 122
Rebling-Brillenslijper, Rebecca (J/a) 130–1
Rebling, Eberhard (German anti-Nazi: shelterer) 130–1
Rebling, Kathinka (J/c) 130–1
Recherchegruppe Henneicke 103
Red Cross records 57, 116, 117, 123
Reformed Apostolic Church, Amsterdam 92
Reformed Teacher Training College, Utrecht 5
Reible, *Kreisschulungsleiter* F.P. 169–70
Reich Commissariat, and plunder of Jewish property 11
Reichsleiter Rosenberg 19
Reinig (card catalogue department head) 85
Reserve Polizeibataillon 101 (German *Ordnungspolizei* division) 210–12
  postwar trials and sentences 212
resistance organization 44, 91, 170, 217
  abduction/rescue of Flipje Plas 5
  arrest of Willem Lodeizen 121
  arson attempt of Dutch Theater 100
  betrayals 130, 139, 151–2, 217
  contacts/informers 26, 29, 151
  and Den Ouden 121, 163
  Henneicke's betrayal and assassination 61, 75, 217–19
  hunting down by CH members 44, 139, 145, 151, 153, 170, 175
  KP "bureau of investigation" 218
  list of Gestapo agents 177
  members 139–40, 142, 203

nursery rescues 106
threats to CH personnel 209
see also Domestic Forces
Rietveld*, Cornelis (CH) 37, 184, 189, 195
Rijksinstituut voor Oorlogsdocumentatie, see National Institute for War Documentation (RIOD)
Rijksman (aka Abraham Sarfatie) (J/a: Auschwitz survivor) 184–5, 186
Riphagen, Dries (CH) 162–5, 217
  as criminal and pimp 162
  escape to Argentina via Spain/Péron friendship 164–5, 173
Roe, Barend (J/a †) 117–18
Roet, M. (J/a †, Auschwitz) 110
Roet-Scheffer, Mrs (J/a: witness) 110–11
Roman Catholic Church 190
roofbank ("plunder bank") 11, 19, 44, 80, 137, 202
  functions 26
  informant funds 27
  inventory lists 20
Roos family (J/a/c) arrest 60
Rooskens*, Paul (CH) 155, 201, 207, 214
Rosenberg, Alfred 19, 20
Rövecamp, G. (Municipal Employment Office) 201
Royal Concertgebouw Orchestra 78
Rubens-Aap, Elisabeth (J/a †, Auschwitz) 117
Rubens, Abraham (J/a †, Auschwitz) 117
Rubens, Jacob (J/a: survivor/witness) 80–1, 169, 204, 216
Rudolfs*, Jan (CH) 35, 36, 50, 123, 200–1, 204, 207, 214

and bonus payments 67–8, 195
trial 62–3

Saaldijk*, Henk (CH) 40, 71–2, 80, 115, 120, 166, 202, 204, 215
trial and sentence 33, 38–9, 197–8
Saaldijk-Stoutenbeek, Mrs (HS's mother) 193–4, 202
Sachs, Mr and Mrs (J/a †, Auschwitz) 115–16
Salomon, Werner (J/a) 115
Sanders, David (J/a †) 54–7, 175
Sanders, Eline, Marie and Elbert (J/c †) 55–7, 175
Sanders-Keizer, Clara (J/a †) 54–7
Santcroos, S. (journalist) 100, 101
Sarfatie, Abraham (J/a: Auschwitz survivor) 184–5, 186
Schaaberg, Dr 131
Schaap, Police Officer 129
Schalkhaar Police Academy 138, 151, 215
Scharlach family (J/a/c †, Sobibor) 115–16
Scheveningen 89
Schipper*, Lambert (CH) 40–1, 56, 71, 109, 169, 208–9, 214
  anti-Semitism 202–3
  trial and sentence 186, 192
Schmidt, General Commissioner F. 6
Schmidt-Stähler, A. (ERR head) 20
Schoonderwoerd-Alkelijen, Nel 40–2
Schouten, Detective (POD) 66
Schouw, Detective Jan 164
Schrijver, Roosje (J/a) 65
Schröder, Mr and Mrs (shelterers) 128
Schulenklapper, Heinz (J/a) 50
Schutten*, Rinus (CH) 102, 181–2
  trial and sentence 182
Schutzstaffel (SS) 43
Schuyt, Sietske (J/a) 55–6

SD, *see Sicherheitsdienst*
Sealtiel, Rafael (J/c) 54
Security Police, *see Sicherheitspolizei* (SP)
Seyss-Inquart, Reich Commissioner Arthur 6, 7, 8, 9, 168
  and deportation structure 12–13
  Eichmann's quotas 13
  furniture removal 19–20
Sicherheitsdienst (Security Service: SD) 26, 44, 64, 77, 92, 120, 147, 162, 214
Sicherheitspolizei (Security Police: SP) 13, 129, 161, 199, 215
Sicherungskonto (security account) 12
Sijdzes, F. (Bureau of Public Records head) 8–9
Sipsma, Clazina (shelterer) 121–2
Slob, Willem (police detective) 44, 51–2
Smid*, Johan (CH) 180–1, 189, 199
Sminia, H. (PRA investigator) 175
Smit*, Adolf (CH) 54, 118, 192, 194, 196
Smit, Mr and Mrs A. (J/a †) 120
Snoek, Dr L. (coroner) 218
Sobibor death camp 4, 17, 40
  victims 47, 116, 123, 141
Soep, Mr (J/a) 110
Sonderkommandos 170
South Holland Labour Front 44
SP, *see Sicherheitspolizei*
Special Court of Appeals 67, 91, 97, 145, 184
  and clemency 97–8, 143–4, 182, 187, 195–8, 206–7
  and Fifth Criminal Division sentences 196
  and Gelinck's opinions 188–90
  Klingeberg case 159
  Kroon case 154

Moerberg case 134–6
Special Court in The Hague 167
Special Courts 30, 36, 58, 60, 108, 157, 173, 179
  Amsterdam Fifth Criminal Division 86, 159, 190, 191, 194
  and Colonne Henneicke 126–7, 190–1, 194–6
  death sentences 59–60, 61, 88, 103, 104, 113, 125, 134, 154, 173, 175, 187, 195, 196–7
  executions 59, 98, 196
  and psychiatric reports 111
  sentences 37, 113, 195–6
  see also Warcrimes Tribunals
Special Justice 145, 184, 186
  and bounty hunters 179
  Central Archive (CABR) 20n1
  and concept of "criminal enterprise" 188
  criticism 247n45
  difficult cases 163
  High Authority 187
  insanity defense 111
  life sentences 197–8
  Office of the Public Prosecutor 188
  rules of retrial 181
  studies 197, 225n4, 246n17
Special Justice Act 30
sperren (deportation exemptions) 14–15, 34, 38, 101, 102, 142, 147
Spier, Rosa (J/a) 78
Sterman, Mrs (shelterer) 146
Stewardship Institute 133, 134
Stokvis, Benno (lawyer) 100–1
Storm (SS weekly publication) 43
strikes
  April/May 1943 10, 105
  Communist instigated (Feb 1941) 10

studies
    on mental state of collaborators and political criminals (1940–45) (Hofman) 213
    Obedience to Authority (Milgram) 212
    Ordinary Men (Browning) 211–13
    "A study of the methods of the Colonne Henneicke of the *Zentralstelle für jüdische Auswanderung*" 31–2, 61
Sukale, P. (SS officer) 116
Suskind, Walter (JC employee) 102, 104, 105, 106
Sweeger*, Sjef (CH) 34, 36, 49–50, 69, 170, 180, 184, 202, 214
    number of arrests 114, 115, 178
    postwar justice 178, 196, 207

Takkert*, Frans (Jan) (CH) 44–5, 119, 182, 217
Takkert-Hogeveen, Marie 193
Tammenoms Bakker, Dr S. (psychiatrist) 111, 112
Teixeira de Mattos, A. (J/a †) 130–1
Teixeira de Mattos-Comperz, Mrs L. (J/a †) 130–1
Ter Steege, René (journalist) 162, 163
Theresienstadt concentration camp 48
Tijhuis, Frans (dentist: witness) 120
Tomson*, Hubert (ZCC) 85, 88, 92, 95
    Gestapo agent 91
    trial, witnesses, sentence 88–91, 97
Tomson-Kleiman, Wilhelmina 90, 91
transportation
    for deportations 100
    for furniture removal 20, 21
Tribunal Decree (1944) 179
tribunals, *see* Warcrimes Tribunals
Troostwijk, Koosje (J/c) 4

Trouw (newspaper) 60
Tump, Detective 143, 184, 185, 201

Umschlagplatz (transit center) 108
    see also Dutch Theater
underground, *see* resistance organization
University of Amsterdam study 170–1
Utrecht
    arrests 1–2, 81
    Communist instigated strikes (Feb 1941) 10
    River District 1, 2, 4
Utrecht Children's Committee 2

valuables
    and bribery 81
    confiscation 11–12, 70, 137, 139, 147
    gold fraud incident 22–3
    gold and jewelry 73, 158, 160–1
    misappropriation 25
    recovery postwar 73–4, 134
    in safekeeping 21, 133, 163
    tracking down 21
Van Amerongen, Alida (J/a) 46
Van Amerongen-Polak, Esther (J/a †, Auschwitz) 118
Van Amersfoort*, Pieter 118–19, 214
Van Bergen, Meijer and Rebecca (J/c †) 41, 42
Van Blankenzees family (shelterers) 118–19
Van Breda Vriesman, Dr (witness) 159
Van den Berg, Dr 131
Van den Berg family (J/a/c) betrayal 48–9
Van den Berg-Walvis, Paulina (J/a: survivor) 130–1

Van den Borch*, Christiaan (CH) 58, 72–3, 121–2, 200, 202, 203, 207, 214
    trial 68–9, 193
Van den Borch-De Vries, Anna 206
Van den Brink, Tiny (J/a) 110
Van den Broek, Henk (POD detective) 88, 89–90, 91, 95
Van den Heuvel, Harm Jan 108–13, 174, 214
    arrest report 108–9
    dossier 112–13
    early life/psychiatrist's report 111–13
    NSB membership 112–13
    trial and sentence 108–13
    use of violence 108–10
    witness testimonies 108–11
Van den Heuvel*, Henk (CH) 36, 53, 69, 71, 99, 155–7, 206
    dismissal from Colonne Henneicke 155–7
    sentence 104
Van den Heuvel-Krenn, Veronika 206
Van den Oort (ZCC) 85
Van der Haaf, Marie (J/a: witness) 90
Van der Hal, Dr Jozef (J/a) 71
Van der Heide, Gerard (J/a: witness) 113
Van der Heul, Commissioner M. (Amsterdam police) 156
Van der Kar, Hijman 102, 103
Van der Kar, Jacques (JC employee) 62, 102–3
Van der Kar, Louis (J/a: witness) 109–10
Van der Kraal, Christina 73–4
Van der Kraal*, Henk (CH) 42, 46, 53–4, 73, 124–5, 141, 181, 204, 207, 215

sentence and death in prison 125, 198
    witness support 194
Van der Maas, Simon and Josina (fraud case) 22, 69
Van der Meulen family 42
Van der Molen, Gesina (teachers' college) 106
Van de Wert*, Mattijs (CH) 71, 114, 182–3, 214
Van de Wieken, Jacob (J/a) 139
Van de Wieken-Wijnschenk, Grietje (J/a) 139
Van de Ziels family (J/a †, Auschwitz) 141
Van Dien, Gerrit (J/a †, Auschwitz) 117
Van Dien-Kokernoot, Gerrit (J/a †, Auschwitz) 117
Van Dijk, Ans (J/a: *V-Frau*): betrayals and execution 52–3
Van Eiken*, Herman (CH) 83–4, 189, 193, 196, 209, 217
Van Eiken, Rie 193
Van Ekeren, Mr (J/a) 147
Van Ekeren-Schneijer, Geertruida (J/a: witness) 147
Van Gelder, Lilly (J/c) 166
Van Gelder, Mr (J/a) 117–18
Van het Lam (ZCC) 85
Van Hulst, Johan W. (college director) 105
Van Leer-Keyl, Mr and Mrs (J/a †, Auschwitz) 148
Van Leeuwen, Arie (*Sonderkommando*) 151, 152
Van Lennep, Hester (shelterer) 5
Van Lier, S.J. (former Amsterdam city manager) 28
Van Ouden*, Jan (CH) 68
Van Schaeck Mathon, E.H.F.W. (SC president) 59, 88, 96, 194

Van Thijn, Salomon (JC employee) 61
Van Tol*, Frans (CH) 48–9, 70, 196, 203, 206, 207
Van Weezep, Betsie 151–2, 153–4
Van Zoelen, A.J. 116
Van Zoelen, Mrs (witness) 116
Van Zoest, Mrs (witness to Henneicke's death) 218
Van Zon, Jan (nurse/witness) 39
Vastmaar (CH): and Harmans fraud 24–5
Vaz Dias, Mozes (journalist) 38–9
Veldhuijsen*, Anton (CH/DT guard) 61, 102–3, 205, 207–8, 209
  trial and sentence 103, 196, 198
Velp (town) 87
Verduin, C.J. (PRA investigator) 30, 31, 59, 214
Verhoeckx, Father (priest: witness) 91
Verlugt*, Bob (CH) 29, 53, 78, 140, 205–6
  trial and sentence 60–1, 115, 143
Vermeulen, Gerrit (J/a: witness) 90
V-Frauen (*Vertrauensfrauen*: female informants) 47, 52–3, 130, 164
Vieyra, Herman (nurse/witness) 39–40
Viskil, J. (lawyer) 191
Viskoop, Charrel (J/c) 146–7
Viskooper, Maurits (J/a †) 205
V-Männer (*Vertrauensmänner*: male informants) 132
V. Mrs (J/a †, Sobibor) 46–7
Vogel, Max (J/c) 42
Von Buchholz, Dahmen (Nazi) 15, 28
Voordenhout, Detective 149, 150, 152
Vos, Saliena (J/a) 49–50
Vreeswijk, Dirk (shelterer) 119–20
Vught concentration camp 17, 89, 92, 99, 123, 159, 167

Wachezettel (detainee transfer slips) 4, 32, 116, 181, 188
Waffenschein (weapons permits) 29
Waffen SS 10, 149
Wagener, Mrs (J/a †, Auschwitz) 118
Wageningen arrests 139
Warcrimes Tribunals 30, 179–87
  and bounty hunters 179–80
  powers 179
  prosecutor's strategy 187–90
  trial of collaborators 179
  see also Special Courts
Wassenaar 114
Wassenberg, H.A. (prosecutor) 22–5
WA (*Weerafdeling*) 102, 182
  see also Defense Division
Weeling, Karel (*Zentralstelle* plant) 63
Wegloop family (J/a/c): betrayal 49
Wehrmacht 37, 92, 101, 130, 132, 201
werkverruiming 77
Westerbork transit camp 4, 12, 14, 99, 100, 172
  commandants 16
  deportations 49, 108, 116, 117, 123, 161
  Dienstleiter 16
  and Jewish Council 214
  liberation 64–5
  Mechanicus diary 167, 171
  postwar internments 64–7, 194
  quota celebration (1942) 16
  shipment of children 104
Westerhoff, Klaas (fur dealer) 72–3
Wierda, Hylke (police) 26
Wijnschenk, Belia (J/a) 139
Wijnschenk, Harry (J/a: witness) 108, 110
Wijsmuller-Meijer, Truus 6
Wilhelmina, Queen 193, 197
Wimmer, General Commissioner F. 7, 168

winkler, J.H. (Ammerstol mayor) 81
Witjas, Mrs (shelterer: witness) 166
Witmond-Visser, Mrs (shelterer) 140
Wörlein, K. (SP) 13, 79
Wttewaal van Stoetwegen, Lady (MP) 193

Yad Vashem medal 103–4

Zaandam 10
Zaccotti, Susan 210
Zandvoort, J. (J/a) 153
Zandvoort (place) 114
Zentralstelle für jüdische Auswanderung (Central Bureau for Jewish Emigration)
   archive discovery 30–4
   and bounty hunting premiums 18, 85
   deportation system 15–16, 85
   house content inventories 20, 87
   LiRo contracts 87, 92
   and NSB membership 87, 182
   records of arrests 188
   Roxy Theater outing 43–4
   staff employment contracts/records 26, 180
   see also card catalogue department
Ziekenoppasser-Swaab, Elisabeth (J/a) 170
Zilverberg, Bertha (J/a: survivor) 132, 169
Zilver (CH staff) 24
Zöpf, Willi (IVB4) 18
Zuilin 40–1
Zündler, Alfons (German guard) 103–4

Printed in Great Britain
by Amazon